W9-AYD-393

INTRODUCTION TO

Psychology

nextext

Table of Contents

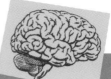

Chapter 21
THERAPIES FOR MENTAL HEALTH

PSYCHOLOGY FEATURES

The World of Psychology

In this chapter, you will learn about:

- **what psychology is and what psychologists do**
- **how the field of psychology developed**
- **different approaches to understanding behavior**

Do violent video games encourage violent behavior? What are the best colors to use in a fast-food restaurant? Why do some people worry more than others? Why do people in a crowd behave differently from when they are alone? These are questions that people in the field of psychology try to answer.

From earliest recorded history, people have developed explanations for why and how they behave as they do. The first experimental psychology laboratory was founded in 1879, and the modern field of psychology began. Wilhelm Wundt and others studied the conscious mind. Sigmund Freud offered explanations about the unconscious.

The definition of psychology has changed over the years with research findings, cultural variations, and the refinement of scientific methodology. Today, it is defined as the study of mind and behavior. A variety of perspectives influences the way today's psychologists approach their work.

What Is Psychology?

Is there anything you've done today that made you wonder, "Why'd I do that?" Have you ever heard people in school or on the news say, "How could anyone do something like that?" Psychology tries to answer such questions.

Psychology is the study of the mind and behavior. The word comes from two Greek words: *psyche,* meaning "life" or "self," and *logos,* referring to reasoning and logic. The term **behavior** includes every measurable internal and external activity a living thing does. Some behaviors can be observed. Others—such as the actions of the mind, ideas, and strategies—cannot. Emotional states, attitudes, stress, the way we interact with our environment, physical reactions such as "butterflies in the stomach"—all these are included in behavior.

What Psychologists Do

Many people think of psychologists as people who help others solve their problems, but that is only a small part of what they do. The American Psychological Association lists **five** major areas in which psychologists work.

1. **Psychologists Conduct Research.** Many psychologists conduct research, both in the laboratory and in natural settings. They study animal behavior, individual behavior, and the behavior of complex social organizations, such as companies or prison populations.

Psychologists study infants, students, the elderly, emotionally disturbed people, computer workers, truck drivers, or families. They research how the environment affects human behavior, how art or music affects mental states, and how advertising can be made more effective. Just about any area of human behavior is a potential topic for research.

2. **Psychologists Promote Physical and Mental Health.** Psychologists work to help people change unhealthy behaviors that cause problems in their lives. Phobias, compulsions, anxieties, and eating disorders are just a few of the issues that psychologists address. Psychologists may work with people individually or in groups.

Many psychologists are members of health care teams where the physical, emotional, and psychological factors of illness are all acknowledged and treated together.

3. **Psychologists Help People Learn.** Psychologists use tools from research to help people learn. They can help students with motivation. They can provide effective strategies for taking in new information, organizing it, and remembering it. They can provide relief for test anxiety and help with other learning-related issues.

School psychologists provide counseling services and may help students with learning disabilities or with behavior that disrupts their own learning and that of others.

4. **Psychologists Work in the Community.** Psychologists work with organizations such as Boys' and Girls' Clubs, community centers, religious organizations, and other service organizations. They work with correctional facilities and with juvenile offenders to help people in trouble cope with their problems and become productive members of society.

5. **Psychologists Contribute to the Work Environment.** Psychologists are involved in designing comfortable and less stressful work environments, in recommending organizational changes to reduce employee stress, and in helping to design "user-friendly" products. Company psychologists run employee assistance programs that help employees with drug or alcohol addiction, depression, and other problems.

Sidebar

Psychologists at Work

Dr. Rodney Hammond is a health psychologist who works with boys ages 11–14, who are growing up in environments where violence is a common behavior. Dr. Hammond teaches the boys to recognize situations that could lead to violence and develop skills for responding to conflict. With early intervention, these young men are less likely to use violence or become victims of it.

Dr. Barbara Brauer was born deaf. She is one of about 25 deaf psychologists in the country and is the first deaf woman to become a psychologist. Dr. Brauer worked in a unit for deaf people, doing individual, group, and family therapy. She has translated paper-and-pencil types of psychological tests into sign language in videotape format so that deaf people can take the tests on computers.

The Main Types of Psychology

Work in psychology may be divided into two types: basic research and applied psychology. Basic researchers try, among other things, to find out how and why people behave as they do. They compare the effectiveness of different treatments. Applied psychologists use the knowledge gained from research to help people function more efficiently or in a healthier manner.

EXAMPLE: Basic researchers found that adolescents need more sleep than younger children, especially in the morning hours. Some school districts in Minnesota applied this information by changing their high school starting times to a later hour. Their applied psychology resulted in higher grades, fewer discipline problems, and a better-rested student body.

Basic Research

Psychology is a behavioral science. Research psychologists use the scientific method to study people and their behaviors. They conduct experiments and make measurements to discover relationships. Among other things, research psychologists try to determine the influence of the brain on behavior, identify the factors that cause behaviors, and discover the effects of those behaviors. Research is the basis for what we know.

Because human behavior is affected by so many different things, it is impossible to design a perfect research study. Good research acknowledges that there may be explanations of observed behaviors other than those being reported.

Internet Addiction?

Is it possible to be addicted to the Internet? Research topics often come from issues that concern the general population. People on TV and radio talk shows have expressed concern about the amount of time some people spend on the Internet. Their activity has often been described as an addiction. Can this be true? Only well-designed research can determine that.

Several studies have been done using on-line surveys to gather data from people using the Internet. Although there are many possibilities for error in such experimental design, a significant number of those who responded reported:

* They couldn't stop using the Internet.
* Friends and family told them that they spent too much time on-line.
* Other areas of their lives suffered.

All of these are signs consistent with addiction. Because research on this topic is in its infancy, it is too soon to draw a conclusion. Better experiments must be designed before Internet addiction can be verified.

The Main Types of Psychology

Areas of Study	Basic Research	Applied Psychology
Biological Psychology	Studies the neural, hormonal, and other physical factors that affect behavior.	Helps with addictions, eating disorders, health issues, effects of environmental pollutants or weather on mood, understanding the role of emotions, and anger management.
Cognitive Psychology	Studies how perception, thought, and interpretation affect behaviors and interactions with others.	Provides counseling, therapy, clinical and health psychology, psychotherapy, hypnosis, improved personal growth, and change.
Developmental Psychology	Studies the mental and behavioral changes that occur over the life span of an individual.	Helps parents, teachers, and doctors guide, teach, and heal; designs care for mental retardation and developmental disabilities; helps manage the effects of aging.
Learning and Memory	Studies how new associations are made and how information is stored.	Yields improved curriculum design, effective teaching methods, memory strategies, and school counseling.
Perception	Studies the use of the senses to gain information about the world and give it meaning.	Guides advertising, media design, user-friendly products, interior design for specific effects, and acoustics systems.
Personality	Studies the factors that determine similarities and differences among individuals.	Promotes self-esteem and self-concept, creates appropriate environments for different styles, and works in human resources and personal growth.
Social Psychology	Studies the ways in which human behavior is linked to culture and society.	Works with groups of people—families, ethnic groups, people with alternate lifestyles, religious or community groups, and race relations.

Applied Psychology

Psychology can help us understand every aspect of our lives. From comfort in childbirth to grief and death, from a child's first steps to an adult's recovering from the effects of a stroke, from eating and exercising to shopping and working—in all these activities, psychological research has insights to offer. Applied psychologists have used research about learning to create more effective teaching materials. They have used research about attention to design appealing product labels. They have used research about motivation to help swimmers and runners stay with their training programs.

Careers in Psychology

Might you be interested in a career in psychology? The many different occupations involving psychology all require some training or certification beyond a college bachelor's degree.

You might choose to study the development of infants and children. Sports psychology, advertising psychology, working in industry or with organizations, even the psychology of humor—these are just a few of the specialties.

Some occupations, such as clinical psychology or counseling, require certification by a state or other government agency. In other fields of specialization, you can get your advanced training through hands-on experience.

Psychology in Your Life

You don't have to be a trained psychologist to use psychological principles to improve your life. Psychology can help you:

* Understand and change what is happening in your social relationships.
* Understand how you are influenced by your peers or the media.
* Identify the causes of test anxiety or stress before they create problems for you.
* Understand that you always have choices, that there are people who know how to help you and who want to help you. Knowing that every situation offers choices gives you powerful tools for dealing with life.

Psychology in the Past

Why Study the History of Psychology?

* Many of today's approaches to psychology are built on a foundation of ideas from the past.
* Knowing what worked and what didn't helps save time and energy while exploring new ideas.
* Sometimes, ideas—good ideas—arise at a time when they either don't fit the thinking of the time or there is no easy way to explore them. The concepts of evolution and unconscious motivation are two such examples. When people revisit them later, old ideas may prove very useful.

Key Figures

Modern psychology finds its roots in the thinking of the ancient Greek philosophers. Plato and Aristotle developed theories about learning. Later thinkers through the Renaissance and Enlightenment were interested in the mind and the body. With the rise of science and a methodical approach to the study of nature, scholars began using the scientific method to study the mind and behavior.

Psychology began in 1879 in Leipzig, Germany, when Wilhelm Wundt started the first laboratory for studying human thought. Wundt stated that he wanted to "mark out a new domain of science." He succeeded and is sometimes called the "father of psychology."

1. Wilhelm Wundt (1832–1920)

IDEAS: Wundt proposed that humans use their free will to focus their attention on particular aspects of a situation. He stated that attention and behavior have a purpose related to some kind of internal motivation. He used a method called introspection and conducted experiments on reaction time and attention. Introspection means looking inside oneself and describing what is going on. This approach is still used today, especially in clinical psychology.

After questioning many people about their sensations, perception, thoughts, and emotions, Wundt found very little agreement in what people experienced. He concluded that experiments could be used to study such things as perception and sensation but would not be as useful for studying higher processes.

▲
Wilhelm Wundt believed people could use introspection to learn about themselves.

NAME OF APPROACH: Voluntarism. It emphasized free will, choice, and purpose.

MAJOR CONTRIBUTION: He demonstrated the idea that the mind and behavior can be studied scientifically. Many of Wundt's students came to the United States and began their own laboratories using introspection, a forerunner to what we now call the scientific method.

2. William James (1842–1910)

IDEAS: James, along with John Dewey, was influential in founding American psychology. James wanted to understand how the mind functioned to help people adapt to the environment rather than just describe it. James was very aware of the differences among individuals and was interested in what made them different rather than similar.

NAME OF APPROACH: Functionalism. It focused on how the mind functions rather than on what the mind is. Later, he developed **pragmatism**—the idea that if an idea works, it is valid or useful.

MAJOR CONTRIBUTION: James is best known for his emphasis on studying all aspects of an individual's experience, including behavior and individual differences.

▲
William James believed psychology should focus on the conscious mind of each individual.

Sigmund Freud believed early experiences were important for understanding behavior.
▼

3. **Sigmund Freud (1856–1939)**

IDEAS: Unlike Wundt and James, who concentrated their efforts on the conscious mind, Sigmund Freud focused on how the unconscious mind affects the development of one's personality. Freud suggested that many of the things that occur in childhood shape our personality and account for later behaviors. He devised a way of treating patients with the method of free association, encouraging them to say whatever came into their minds. Freud also believed that dream analysis was an important psychological tool.

NAME OF APPROACH: **Psychoanalysis.** This method of treating mental illness analyzes information contained in the unconscious mind.

MAJOR CONTRIBUTION: Freud emphasized the importance of unconscious processes and the role of early experiences.

John B. Watson believed behavior, not the mind, should be the focus of psychology.
▼

4. **John B. Watson (1878–1958)**

IDEAS: Watson believed that behavior was caused by some association that had previously been created in the brain. He didn't think that mental processes were appropriate subjects for psychology and believed that only behavior could be objectively and scientifically observed and measured. Watson focused on how we learn and how experience produces associations in the brain.

NAME OF APPROACH: Behaviorism. This approach focused on the study of behavior rather than the mind and had the prediction and control of behavior as its goal.

MAJOR CONTRIBUTION: Watson developed learning theories that are still in use today.

Sidebar

Physiology and Behavior

Who were the first people to realize that physiology might be useful in explaining behavior? You may be surprised to know they were actually astronomers. In 1795, two astronomers were using star observations to set the clocks on a ship. When a particular star crossed a hairline on the telescope, they would set the clock. One astronomer noticed that his assistant's observations were always about a half second slower than his own. He warned the assistant of the "error," but instead of improving, the assistant's observations were even farther off. Twenty years later, the astronomer Friedrich Bessel suggested that, rather than an error, there was actually a difference in the way two individuals made observations. In comparing his observations with those of others, Bessel did the first study on reaction time.

CRITICAL THINKING

Is Psychology a Science?

Science began as an attempt to understand nature. Many objects in nature behave in the same way under similar circumstances, but people often don't. Is psychology a science?

THE ISSUES

In the history of psychology, some important people, such as Galileo and Kant, have suggested that psychology can never be a science because it is concerned with subjective experience—that is, experience of the world as seen by a particular individual. Science, on the other hand, has prided itself on objective observations—that is, observations removed from any human interpretation or beliefs. In fact, science developed as a way of explaining nature without the use of religious belief, philosophical arguments, or superstition.

Scientists believe that by using the rules of logical and rational thought on **empirical** (based on experience) observations, they can draw conclusions about how nature behaves and make predictions about how it will behave in the future.

Those who argue against psychology as a science say that, first, psychology doesn't have a single theory under which it operates. Instead, psychology has many different approaches. In response to this charge, psychologists argue that scientists use both Newton's Laws and quantum theory to understand motion; psychology also has different ways to view a single topic.

Next, non-science proponents claim that psychology can't generate laws that apply to everyone as science does because individuals do not always respond in the same way to the same stimulus. Yet, psychologists—particularly those studying the role of the brain and body in behavior—have developed many theories and predictions about factors that can affect behavior.

Do you think that psychology is a science?

THE PROCESS

1. **Restate the issues.** In your own words, state the nature of the disagreement.
2. **Provide evidence.** From your own experience and from the information above, list the evidence *for* psychology's being called a science.
3. **Give opposing arguments.** From your own experience and from the information above, list the evidence *against* psychology's being called a science.
4. **Look for more information.** Make a list of questions you may have. Then search an encyclopedia, the Internet, the library, or psychology books for answers.
5. **Evaluate the information.** Make a chart with two columns:

Psychology as a Science	
For	Against

Record the arguments in each column and rank each column of arguments in importance from 1–5, with 1 as the most important.
6. **Draw conclusions.** Write a paragraph supporting your answer to the question "Is psychology a science?"

Approaches to Psychology Today

Because the mind is so complex, there are many different approaches for studying it—different ways of interpreting and thinking about behavior. Here are **seven** of the major approaches to understanding the mind and behavior.

❶ The Neurobiological Approach

The neurobiological approach studies the ways in which the brain, nervous system, and other body systems are involved in behavior. When a person exhibits a certain behavior, whether it's a change in breathing rate or a feeling of depression, neurobiologists want to know what changes are occurring in the body.

How is the body's chemistry changing, and how does that affect behavior? Where, in the body, are changes occurring? What do molecules have to do with emotion? Where is memory located in the brain?

Neurobiologists don't deny that other factors are important. They are simply most interested in how the physical systems affect behavior, thought, and feelings. For example, some medications for physical symptoms can also affect a person's mood or emotions.

❷ The Behavioral Approach

Continuing in the tradition of Watson, the behavioral approach was carried forward by B. F. Skinner. Skinner claimed that studying anything other than observable behavior made psychology less of a science.

Skinner and other behaviorists insisted that we are the products of all of the different experiences to which we have been exposed in our lives. When we are rewarded or punished for a given behavior, we associate the behavior with the reward or punishment. This determines how we will use that behavior in the future. If the rewards we get from a behavior outweigh the punishment we may receive, we may choose to continue that behavior. Environment plays a key role.

Some people argue that behaviorist theory denies the idea of free will and, in a sense, makes us the "victims" of our environment. Many behaviorists have shifted their studies to focus more on how we learn and create associations.

❸ The Psychodynamic Approach

Freud's psychoanalysis emphasized the sexual and aggressive impulses that we experience in childhood and looked for ways in which they shaped the unconscious mind. The unconscious was then seen to influence behavior later in life.

The psychodynamic approach continues to focus on the inner forces, conflicts, or instincts of the unconscious that may affect

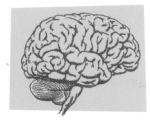

NEUROBIOLOGICAL APPROACH

Studies physical effects in the body and brain related to actions, feelings, and thoughts.

BEHAVIORAL APPROACH

Studies the behaviors of people, the effects of the environment on those behaviors, and learning.

SOCIOCULTURAL APPROACH

Studies the social and cultural influences on behavior.

APPROACHES TO PSYCHOLOGY

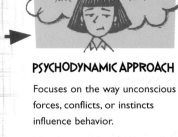

PSYCHODYNAMIC APPROACH

Focuses on the way unconscious forces, conflicts, or instincts influence behavior.

HUMANISTIC APPROACH

Emphasizes personal growth and the achievement of human potential.

EVOLUTIONARY APPROACH

Interested in the way the modules within the brain developed through adaptation to the environment.

COGNITIVE APPROACH

Studies mental processes of perception, memory, language, problem solving, and thinking.

behavior. But it no longer sees sexual and aggressive forces as the only influences on the unconscious.

Carl Jung, a friend of Freud, suggested that the unconscious is influenced by beliefs that we inherit—ideas that are part of every civilization. He called these beliefs the "collective unconscious."

Karen Horney and Alfred Adler are two others who began in the Freudian school but resisted the heavy emphasis on biological and sexual needs. Horney proposed that social forces, such as the need for love, influence the unconscious. Adler emphasized the unconscious need of the individual to feel worthwhile and important.

❹ The Cognitive Approach

Cognitive psychologists study "higher processes"—such as thinking, intelligence, problem solving, reasoning, and creativity. The cognitive approach is concerned with how these thinking processes can be used to deal with problems or to develop a healthy personality. For example, the idea of "positive affirmation"—telling yourself that you are a success or that you can do something—is a cognitive psychology technique.

Cognitive psychology has been criticized because its focus does not include emotion. Recent research strongly indicates that a person who has lost the ability to express emotion no longer exhibits what we call "rational" thought. Emotion seems to be necessary to set values on possible outcomes.

❺ The Evolutionary Approach

The evolutionary approach to psychology is a combination of cognitive psychology and evolutionary biology. As Steven Pinker says in his book, *How the Mind Works,* "Cognitive science helps us to understand how a mind is possible and what kind of mind we have. Evolutionary biology helps us understand *why* we have the kind of mind we have."

The major idea of evolutionary psychology is that the many modules of the mind are evolutionary adaptations arising through natural selection. In simple terms, if a particular behavior increased the chances of an organism's survival, that organism tended to produce more offspring, and thus, more individuals with the same behavior. The ability to think, to reason, and to make logical choices was a useful set of behaviors, so they tended to be passed down.

Evolutionary psychologists don't claim that all of our behaviors are necessarily adaptive, but they have identified many that they can explain in those terms.

❻ The Humanistic Approach

The humanistic approach asserts that we all have within us the potential to become fulfilled and effective people. Just as an acorn contains everything it needs to become a giant oak tree, so we have within us the resources to become fully human.

Of course, the environment plays a role in the development of both the tree and the individual. But unlike the behaviorists, humanists believe that consciousness, self-awareness, and free will allow us to shape our lives as we see fit. Personal experience is an important focus of humanistic study.

Carl Rogers is one of the best known humanistic psychologists. He helped develop what is known as client-centered therapy. It encourages people to identify the resources within themselves that can help them solve their problems.

⑦ The Sociocultural Approach

All of the approaches mentioned so far have tended to study how individuals function. The sociocultural approach is concerned with how individual behavior is influenced by the social groups we belong to or by the culture in which we live.

For example, the expectations of a person born and raised in a rural area may be different from those of a child raised in a large city. In addition, both may be affected by the culture of the country in which they live and the religion of their families.

Sociocultural psychologists study families, ethnic groups, religious groups, and unique populations, such as prisoners, migrants, or people with alternative lifestyles. The experiences, motivations, and emotions of groups such as feminists, gays and lesbians, and homeless people are other examples of studies that a sociocultural psychologist might undertake.

Psychology Across Cultures

Developmental Psychology

1. How are children raised and by whom?
2. At what age is one considered a working member of the culture?
3. What is the role of women in the culture?
4. What is the role of the elderly in the culture?
5. How do languages differ?

Beliefs

1. What do people believe about their relationship to nature?
2. How do beliefs affect the sense of right and wrong?
3. How do beliefs affect the political system of a culture?
4. What role do religious beliefs play in everyday life?
5. Is there a class structure related to beliefs?

Personality

1. How do people of different cultures express emotion?
2. What is the attitude about work and responsibility?
3. Are people generally extroverted or introverted?
4. How does the culture express creativity?
5. How much "personal space" does a person require?

USA

How Does Culture Affect Behavior?

Education/Learning

1. What expectations do people have about education?
2. Are standardized tests culturally biased?
3. How do learning styles differ among cultures?
4. Do people of different cultures exhibit different cognitive processes?
5. What are the effects of being bilingual on learning?

Applied Psychology

1. How can people of different cultures work together in business?
2. Does the same advertising work with different cultures?
3. Is a given behavior considered normal in one culture and abnormal in another?
4. How can a person be integrated into a new culture?
5. Can psychologists work in the same way with people of different cultures?

What About the Future?

Approaches to psychology are limited only by the questions one can think to ask about how the mind works and why we behave as we do. As society changes, the questions change with them, so it is unlikely that we'll soon have a full picture of what humans are about.

Even the definition of *mind* is open to question. Before psychology was recognized as a science, philosopher René Descartes proposed that the mind and the body were separate and played different roles in behavior. Today, that division is much less clear. Although scientists and psychologists don't all agree on what the mind is, many now say that the mind is what the brain does. Newer scientific approaches realize that we must consider the interactions among the entire system of brain, mind, body, and environment in order to understand some of the more complex human behaviors.

It's interesting that the father of modern experimental psychology, Wilhelm Wundt, realized much the same thing after studying the experiences of many different people. Wundt concluded in 1896 that the actual character of a specific mental process depends, for the most part, not on the nature of the parts as much as on the way they combine. Now, more than 100 years later, psychology is, to some extent, returning to its foundations.

Chapter 1 Wrap-up
THE WORLD OF PSYCHOLOGY

Psychology is the study of the mind and behavior. Psychologists conduct research, promote physical and mental health, help people learn, work in the community, and contribute to the work environment. The two main types of psychology are research and applied psychology.

Psychology was first recognized as a science when, in 1879, Wilhelm Wundt started the first laboratory using the scientific method to study humans. Other nineteenth-century figures who contributed to the development of psychology were William James, John Watson, and Sigmund Freud.

Modern approaches to psychology include the neurobiological, behavioral, psychodynamic, cognitive, evolutionary, humanistic, and sociocultural approaches. Each explores some aspect of the mind and behavior, but from a different perspective.

Psychology — WORDS TO KNOW

behavior—every measurable internal and external activity a living thing does. *p. 2*

empirical—relating to facts or experiences in general. *p. 10*

functionalism—psychological approach that focuses on what the mind does rather than what it is. *p. 7*

introspection—research method in which individuals look inside themselves and report on their conscious mental processes. *p. 7*

pragmatism—approach based on the assumption that if an idea works, it is valid. *p. 8*

psychoanalysis—theory of personality and method of treating mental illness that emphasizes unconscious motives and conflicts. *p. 8*

psychology—study of mental processes and behavior and how they are affected by a person's physical states, mental states, and the external environment. *p. 2*

CHAPTER 2

Research in Psychology

In this chapter, you will learn about:

- **the scientific method in psychology**
- **conducting research**
- **ethical issues**

Swiss psychologist Jean Piaget's pioneering work on the development of children's thinking and reasoning began with his observations of his own children. However, his observations were different from those of other parents. When he started to notice things that were different from what he had been taught, he made notes. He observed other children. He developed a theory. He tested it. He published it and invited other psychologists to repeat his experiments and add their own observations. In other words, he used the "scientific method."

In designing research, psychologists choose from a number of methods—such as naturalistic observation, case studies, surveys, and experiments. They gather data using various methods. They process it to make comparisons and draw conclusions.

Psychologists must also consider the ethical aspects of their research. Is it okay for psychologists to deceive people to gather information? Is it wrong to use animals in experiments? Ethical guidelines help psychologists address these and other similar issues.

The Scientific Method

Science is an approach to gaining knowledge—a method of inquiry using certain rules and procedures to answer questions about nature. In science, any statement made about nature must be supported by experimental evidence. The behavioral science of psychology focuses its questions on human mental processes and behavior.

Scientists develop their theories based on objective observations and by conducting research to determine if those theories are true. A **theory** is a statement of underlying principles about some aspect of nature, such as the theory of universal gravitation—the idea that all objects attract one another.

Scientific knowledge is valid and believable only to the extent that the observations are objective and the rules and principles of the scientific method have been followed.

What Are Paradigms?

Scientists work within a given paradigm. A **paradigm** is a particular way of looking at the world. For example, some scientists work from the belief that understanding how each part of the brain works will lead to an understanding of the mind.

Others work from the belief that interaction among the parts of the brain is an important factor in how thought and behavior arise.

Where Do Theories Come From?

Theories are generated by looking at a large set of observations and finding common principles among them. This process is called **inductive thinking**—reasoning from particular instances to general principles.

Theories can rarely, if ever, be *proven* true because one can't reasonably test every possible situation. Even a simple statement such as "crows are black" can't be proven to be true unless one looks at every crow that ever lived and ever will live.

While you can't prove a theory true, you can prove it false by finding observations that don't fit the theory or that contradict it. Karl Popper, a philosopher of science, says that a theory must be able to be tested against observations that could prove it false in order to be a good theory. In the cartoon shown here, Lucy demonstrates why.

What's wrong with Lucy's theory?

How Are Theories Used?

Once scientists have a theory about how the world operates, they can apply those principles to individual people, objects, or circumstances. For example, if a theory says that phobias are caused by earlier traumas, a psychologist could attempt to identify the trauma that produced a client's fear of snakes. This is called deductive thinking—thinking from the general to the particular.

Imagine a psychological theory that says gender—whether an individual is male or female—affects behavior. Although the theory is too broad to be tested, it contains many smaller aspects about which questions can be asked, such as how gender affects shopping behavior, math ability, or job preferences.

Scientific Attitudes and Values

Most scientists share certain attitudes about their work. These include:

* Relying on careful observation.
* Quantifying results wherever possible.
* Relying on verification or duplication of results by other scientists.
* Recognizing that results are tentative and based on probability.
* Being skeptical about conclusions— that is, looking for other possible reasons to explain the observations.

Scientists value observation, questioning, logic, and simple explanations over more complex ones. Because people, including scientists, both perceive and process information in different ways,

scientists rely on the careful steps required by the scientific method and on the duplication of their experiments by others to increase the objectivity of their results. When many scientists are able to repeat an experiment and get similar data, they are satisfied that the experiment is as objective as possible.

Bias in Research

At a party, you notice that a mother of four children, a famous concert violinist, a flashy blond in a sequined dress, and a millionaire are all in attendance. Which of those people would you most want to talk to? Which would you least want to talk to? What if all four descriptions applied to the same person?

Most of us have certain expectations or beliefs about people based on such things as the way they dress, the groups they belong to, or whether they are male or female. Depending on those biases, researchers might, without even realizing it, interpret the same behavior of two experiment participants in different ways. Bias is generally defined as any condition or set of conditions that distorts data from what pure chance would have produced. Several types of bias can affect research results in different ways.

Intentional Bias

Some studies focus on a single factor in behavior, such as the effect of birth order. This bias emphasizes some aspects of a situation while paying less attention to others. As long as an experimenter is open about his or her intent, people recognize that the conclusions drawn are meant to address only one aspect of a situation.

Experimenter Bias

The experimenter may hold a conscious or unconscious bias in terms of gender, ethnic, or socioeconomic groups, or other personal traits. This can lead to error in the selection of participants, creation of tests, interpretation of observations, or in reaching conclusions. An experimenter's tone of voice or facial expression may be affected by bias, thus affecting a participant's own perceptions.

Participant Bias

If people know that they are part of an experiment, they may behave as they think they are expected to behave or may change their behavior so that the experimenter won't know how they really act. In medical experiments, participants may expect a medication to make them better and so they get better, even when they receive a pill with no active ingredients.

Ways researchers avoid bias include:

* Becoming as aware as possible of their own biases.
* Having other people review their work.
* Selecting methods that disguise the identities of the participants.
* Recognizing that subject bias might be affecting behavior.

The Scientific Approach to Research

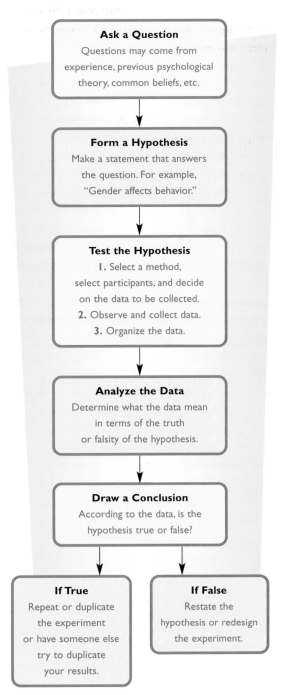

Ask a Question
Questions may come from experience, previous psychological theory, common beliefs, etc.

Form a Hypothesis
Make a statement that answers the question. For example, "Gender affects behavior."

Test the Hypothesis
1. Select a method, select participants, and decide on the data to be collected.
2. Observe and collect data.
3. Organize the data.

Analyze the Data
Determine what the data mean in terms of the truth or falsity of the hypothesis.

Draw a Conclusion
According to the data, is the hypothesis true or false?

If True
Repeat or duplicate the experiment or have someone else try to duplicate your results.

If False
Restate the hypothesis or redesign the experiment.

Designing Research

Psychological research is not always done in labs. Nevertheless, it uses much of the same scientific method that other sciences employ in the laboratory. Let's define a few terms.

What Is a Hypothesis?

As Kelly moves through the halls between classes, she notices that most of the boys carry their books in one hand at about hip level. In contrast, girls seem to wrap both arms around their books and carry them against their chests or stomachs.

Kelly has taken the first step in scientific research. She has noticed a correlation—a relationship between two different things. Kelly says, "Boys carry their books in a different way from girls." Kelly has stated a hypothesis—a statement of something she believes to be true. A more formal hypothesis might be "There is a relationship between gender and book-carrying style."

Here are a few other hypotheses:

* Males are more aggressive than females.
* Practice improves performance on video games.
* People raised on a farm are less likely to engage in criminal behavior than those raised in a city.

Hypotheses are merely statements that can be tested by designing an experiment that may show them to be true or false. Once you have a hypothesis, the next step is to decide who or what you want to observe and under what conditions. Since Kelly can't observe all males and females, she will probably limit her experiment (and her hypothesis) to students at her high school.

Selecting Participants

When Kelly decides which students she will observe, she is selecting participants for her experiment. Here are **three** things to consider when choosing participants:

1. If Kelly wants to make a general statement about all students, then she must select participants that represent all students—students of the different ages, ethnic groups, and various physical characteristics that represent a cross-section of her school's population. Remember that conclusions can only apply to the population observed.

2. The greater the number of participants, the more meaningful the results are likely to be. By choosing a large number of students, Kelly may reduce the possibility that her observations occurred by chance.

3. Participants should be chosen in a way that avoids any bias. Kelly should randomly select students in the various groups to avoid errors such as selecting students she'd already seen who confirmed her hypothesis.

Variables

One of the key parts of designing any experiment is analyzing the variables. A variable is anything that can take on different values or qualities.

In Kelly's experiment, in addition to gender and book-carrying style, variables might include:

* How many books the person had to carry.
* How big or heavy the books were.
* Whether anything else was carried.
* Whether or not students walked alone.
* How crowded the halls were.

Dependent and Independent Variables

In an experiment, the behavior that you are observing is called the dependent variable. In Kelly's case, this is the book-carrying style of the student. Kelly's hypothesis says that this behavior *depends* on something else—the gender of the student.

The factor being studied—and upon which the dependent variable depends—is the independent variable. In Kelly's case, it is gender. Gender is independent of book-carrying style. A boy is a boy no matter how he carries his books.

Controlling Variables

If Kelly wanted to be sure that no other independent variable affected the way people carried their books, she'd have to make certain that every other variable mentioned above stayed the same at all times. That is called *controlling the variables.*

To carry that to extremes, Kelly would have to observe students only when students were walking alone and carrying the same number and weight of books, and when the halls had a certain density of students. Obviously that isn't reasonable. Since these variables may introduce some error into Kelly's data, she should acknowledge them when she draws her conclusions.

It's important for scientists to agree on the variables being measured and those being ignored to understand the conclusions a research study may reach. Many studies list the variables in the conclusion so that those reading the results will understand under what circumstances they apply. For example, results on children under 12 may not apply to adults.

Which Kind of Study?

Researchers may select from a number of different types of studies, including the following **five:**

1. **Longitudinal Studies.** When researchers want to know the long-term effects of some variable, they may do periodic tests on participants over a number of years. These longitudinal studies are particularly useful in studies of child development.

2. **Cross-sectional Studies.** Participants are chosen from a representative sample of the population—including people from a variety of ethnic, occupational, socioeconomic, and other groups. Researchers then form conclusions that may be applicable to the entire population.

3. **Case Studies.** Case studies are in-depth studies of one individual with the goal of finding out as much as possible about what factors have influenced his or her development and personality. Case studies are often used when working with a client's individual problems or to compare and understand individual differences.

4. **Blind/Double-Blind Studies.** To counter effects of experimenter and participant expectations and biases, some studies are done without the participants knowing the purpose of the study. That is called a blind study. Because the researcher's behavior may affect results, other studies are done with neither the participant nor the person administering the test knowing the purpose of the study. This is a double-blind study.

5. **AB/ABA Studies.** Before you can decide if a particular treatment changes behavior, you must know the normal behavior of a person. For example, if you're trying to reduce the number of tantrums a child throws, you need to know how many he or she normally throws in a period of time. That is condition A. After the treatment, the number of tantrums is condition B. If B is less than A, one might conclude that the treatment was effective. To make doubly sure, the researcher will go back to the original conditions, without the treatment, and see if the person reverts to condition A. This is called an ABA study.

Gathering Data

Consider these research topics:

* A sociocultural psychologist wants to know the opinions of various ethnic groups on effective ways of child rearing.
* A behavioral psychologist is curious about how babies respond to different sounds.
* A neurobiologist is concerned with which parts of the brain are most active during sleep.

Depending on the question being asked in psychological research, many different kinds of research methods might be used to gather data. The first of our examples might use a questionnaire, the second might manipulate sounds and observe and record a baby's behavior, and the third might make physiological measurements of brain activity. Each is gathering data, but in very different ways.

Self-Reporting Methods

In one form of data collection, the researcher simply asks the participants about their behaviors or experiences using surveys or interviews.

Surveys. Participants answer questions about the variable being tested. These questions may require simple yes-no answers, a ranking, or a more open-ended response. Often, surveys are sent to people to be filled out at their convenience. Surveys can gather information from many people on a wide variety of topics, such as opinions, behaviors, feelings, or beliefs. If the participants take the survey seriously, it can generate very accurate responses.

However, some people will not take the time to fill out and return surveys, so the sample size is reduced. Because the researcher doesn't speak directly to the participants, there is no way of knowing how the responder understood the questions. That could lead to misinterpretation of answers.

Interviews. Researchers may use the same questions they would in a survey but pose them to participants face to face. Interviews allow much more detailed answers to be obtained with respect to the variables being tested. Interviewers can be certain that participants interpret and understand the questions in the way they were written.

Interviews, however, are very time consuming, so some people aren't willing to participate. Interviewers may influence the participants' answers by their own behaviors or biases, or they may allow themselves to stray from the questions.

Behavioral Methods

Some research questions require that the actual physical behavior or thought processes of a person be observed. This can occur either in a laboratory situation or in a more natural setting.

Naturalistic Observation. Often, particularly in the early phases of research, psychologists simply observe the behavior of participants in their natural environments and record their behaviors. This method, called naturalistic observation, is particularly useful with children or others who may act differently because they are being observed. When they are unaware of being watched, participants act naturally. Naturalistic observation also allows researchers to observe a variety of behaviors to decide what relationships may exist.

However, observers may misinterpret the reasons for certain behaviors. Because researchers are more interested in "what goes with what" than simply "what happens," naturalistic observation is often limited in its results.

Laboratory Experiment. Participants may be brought into a laboratory setting and observed as they are exposed to different stimuli or engage in various tests. In the lab, the number of variables can be limited and controlled. Opportunities to interact with participants can clarify misunderstandings and assist in interpretation of data.

But participants' behavior in a laboratory setting may not reflect their behavior in a more natural setting. And because participants know that they are being observed, their behavior may change.

Field Study. Researchers may move their laboratory to a more naturalistic setting to improve the chances that participants will behave "normally."

Physiological Measurement

For some research, the physiological responses of participants must be measured. Many tools are now available to help psychologists understand body, mind, and behavior interactions well beyond the familiar factors of heart rate and blood pressure.

Galvanic Skin Response (GSR). With measuring devices attached to various parts of the skin, researchers can monitor very small changes in the electrical characteristics of the skin because of perspiration. This is interpreted as having some correlation to emotional arousal or anxiety.

Electromyograph (EMG). This records muscle tension related to psychological tension or stress.

Electroencephalograph (EEG). This records certain electrical characteristics of brain activity. It has, for example, been used in the study of dreams.

Positron Emission Tomography (PET). This brain imaging technique allows researchers to see what parts of the brain are active as a person is speaking, listening, or engaged in other mental activities. The device measures the amount of glucose present in various parts of the brain. More glucose is present in areas of higher brain activity.

Functional Magnetic Resonance Imaging (FMRI). This also measures the activity in the brain but uses strong magnetic fields to determine which parts of the brain contain the highest blood oxygen—a sign of activity.

Because it's assumed that when a person lies, several of his or her physiological measurements will change, a lie detector includes GSR, EEG, and EMG devices.

Naturalistic Research

Jane Goodall conducted the longest field study of any animal species in its natural surroundings in her work with chimpanzees. In 1960, when she began her work in Kenya, it was unheard of for a single female to work in such rugged surroundings. Within a few years, Goodall became intimately familiar with the lives of the chimpanzees, spending her days trailing them through the forest and recording their habits.

Many of her techniques were considered "unscientific." She gave the chimps names, such as Fifi and Passion. In her first scientific article, all of her references to *he* or *she* were crossed out by the editors and replaced with *it* or *which*. She rebelled and won the battle in her insistence that chimpanzees were highly individualistic; that they not only reasoned but also felt emotion; and that they lived in highly complex societies. It came as a shock when Goodall discovered that chimpanzees use tools, because at the time it was assumed that only humans had the intelligence to do so.

Jane Goodall and one of the chimpanzees she studied. ▶

Processing Data

Data gathered in a psychological study may be processed and analyzed in several ways.

The Correlational Approach

Gathering information through surveys and interviews, by observation, and through physiological measurements yields interesting insights into human behavior and mental processes. Psychologists often find it interesting to study how two variables— different behaviors or processes—are correlated or related to one another. What, for example, is the relationship between school grades and the number of hours a student works outside of school?

Correlation Coefficient

The degree of relationship or correlation between two variables is expressed in a value called a correlation coefficient. The values of most correlation coefficients vary between –1 and +1. A positive value means that as one variable increases, the other increases also. The closer the coefficient is to +1, the higher the correlation. A negative correlation means that as the incidence of one variable goes up, the other goes down.

Would you expect a correlation study of students' grades and how much they worked at jobs to show a positive or negative correlation? Why?

Correlation Doesn't Imply Causation

Suppose a study showed a much higher positive correlation between being a patient in a hospital and death rate than between being at home and death rate. In other words, more people die in hospitals than die at home. Does this mean that being in a hospital is likely to *cause* your death?

Think about it. Wouldn't someone who was seriously ill or who required surgery be more likely to be in a hospital than at home? The fact that two things are highly correlated doesn't automatically mean that one causes the other. It simply means that as one changes, the other changes. It could mean that A causes B, B causes A, or some other factor causes both A and B.

In the 1950s and '60s, researchers looked for a correlation between the two variables of cigarette smoking and the incidence of lung cancer. They found a high positive correlation between smoking and lung cancer.

Using this data, the government required the cigarette industry to put warning labels on cigarette packages.

Naturally, the industry fought against this, pointing out that correlation did not prove causality—and correctly so. In fact, several scientists did studies indicating that some other psychological factor (such as anxiety) may cause some personality types both to smoke and to develop cancer.

Later medical studies have demonstrated that many of the chemicals in cigarettes do cause cancer in lab animals, so there is quite probably a causal effect. But the correlational study did not prove that. The requirement of warning labels may have been correct—but it was sought for the wrong reason.

Coincidence

Correlation coefficients can be calculated between any two variables, so one must be careful to look at the theory underlying the study. While it may be possible to show a high positive correlation between, say, the number of people entering the army in a given year and the number of bananas eaten by chimps in the nation's zoos, it would take a pretty strange theory to suggest any way that one causes the other. Such results would be simply a coincidence.

Predictions Based on Correlation

Recently, there have been many claims that the increased violence on television, in movies, and in video games is responsible for increased aggression in young people. If a correlational study does show that there is some positive relationship between a person's aggression and the amount of media violence to which he or she has been exposed, what does it mean?

Correlational studies can demonstrate a relationship but cannot prove the direction of that relationship. Are people more aggressive because they watch media violence, or are they more attracted to violent media because they are more aggressive? While it's possible to answer that question, it requires more than one study to do it.

People in the media, in politics, and in advertising often use correlational data to make claims or predictions. The next time you hear a claim based on a correlation, first ask yourself if the claim is justified.

Graphs and Statistical Analysis

Correlation coefficients are only one way to "crunch numbers" in psychological research. Depending on the method used to collect data, different types of values are generated. A few typical values include measurements of a physical characteristic such as pulse rate, test scores, the time it took someone to complete a task, or the number of times a certain behavior occurred in a given period.

Depending on the hypothesis or question, these numbers would be manipulated in different ways.

Descriptive Statistics

Suppose you are interested in the effect of marijuana on the time it takes a person to recite the Pledge of Allegiance. Your experimental design includes 15 people who have not smoked marijuana (the control group) and 15 who have smoked marijuana within the half-hour prior to the test

(the experimental group). Participants are timed on how long it takes them to say the Pledge. For the sake of simplicity, let's say the test is done only once.

Now, you have 30 numbers—length of time for each of the 30 people in the study. What do you do with the numbers? One thing you could do is generate a graph like the ones shown below. These help you see any obvious tendencies in the data.

Results: Control Group

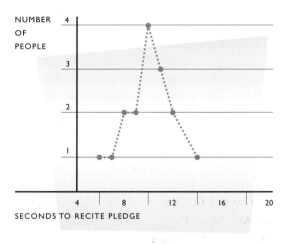

SECONDS TO RECITE PLEDGE

Results: Experimental Group

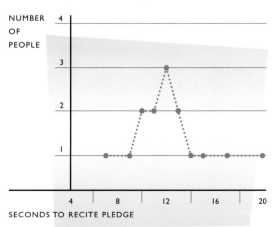

SECONDS TO RECITE PLEDGE

Measures of Central Tendency

The chart opposite shows the distribution of scores in the Pledge of Allegiance study. The tendency of more scores to occur around the middle of a set of numbers is typical of data in many types of studies and is called a central tendency. We might say that central tendency measures the typical score within a range of numbers. (Range is the numerical distance between the highest and lowest score.) This central tendency is measured in several ways. Let's first define them and then demonstrate how they're found.

* *Mean.* The mean is what you might normally call the average. Mean is calculated by adding up all the scores and dividing by the number of scores. The mean is perhaps the most useful and most often used measure of central tendency.
* *Median.* The median is the midpoint of the distribution of numbers. First, you arrange the scores in order. If there is an odd number of scores, such as 15, the median is the eighth score. There are seven scores above and seven below it. The median isn't as affected by extreme scores, such as might occur if one of the experimental group forgot where he or she was in the Pledge and started over.
* *Mode.* The mode is the most frequent score. If more people took 12 seconds to say the Pledge than any other time, that would be the mode.

Measures of Variation

Within any population there is a normal variation in the way people behave. In a perfectly normal population, the mean, median, and mode of a set of scores will be the same. The scores for this population, when plotted on a graph, produce the familiar bell curve. Notice that the graph of the control group (page 29) takes this form.

A measure of how far a set of test scores strays from normal distribution is called standard deviation. Researchers are really asking, "Could this set of data have occurred by chance?" Standard deviation gives one indication of that probability. If it is unlikely that the scores of the experimental group occurred by chance, then the independent variable may have affected them. What are the dependent and independent variables in the marijuana/Pledge of Allegiance study?

Ethical Issues

To help students understand the effects of prejudice, teachers in some schools have had their students participate in an experiment. For one day, all of the students who happen to be wearing a certain color are to be considered "inferior." Other students are encouraged to ignore them or to treat them in ways that express a prejudice against them. While many students agree that this experiment really helped them understand how damaging prejudice can be, possible problems with such an experiment include:

* Students who are not normally prejudiced becoming upset by having to act that way.
* Students who are treated badly suffering lasting effects, even though it was "pretend."

Pledge of Allegiance Study
Scores (In seconds)
Control group 7, 10, 8, 12, 9, 10, 8, 10, 11, 14, 6, 9, 10, 12, 11   **Experimental group** 13, 9, 12, 14, 10, 13, 20, 11, 12, 7, 10, 12, 11, 17, 15
Mean
Sum of control group scores = 147   Sum of experimental group scores = 186   The mean for the control group is 147/15 = 9.8.   The experimental group mean is 186/15 = 12.4.
Median
Control group scores in order: 6, 7, 8, 8, 9, 9, 10, 10, 10, 10, 11, 11, 12, 12, 14   The median, middle (eighth), score of this range = 10.   Experimental group scores in order: 7, 9, 10, 10, 11, 11, 12, 12, 12, 13, 13, 14, 15, 17, 20   The eighth score in this range (the median) = 12.
Mode
The most common score (mode) in the control group = 10.   The most common score in the experimental group = 12.
Observations
1. The mean, median, and mode for the control group are about the same (9.8, 10, 10).   The same is true for the experimental group, but the values are higher.   2. Notice that a score of 30 instead of 20 in the experimental group would have changed the mean to 13, but would not have changed the median and mode.

Risk/Benefit Assessment

Some psychological experiments encourage people to behave in ways that are not comfortable for them, or that subject them to conditions that may affect their emotions. Researchers argue that such experiments are necessary to learn more about behavior. Others say that the risks are too great for the benefits they produce. Who is correct?

Here, the value of increased knowledge conflicts with the value of protecting individual rights. If the knowledge might lead to something that would save or improve many lives, it might be worth the risk. But if a study is done merely to advance the career of a particular scientist, it is doubtful that the risk is justified. This comparison is known as risk/benefit assessment. It's important to assess the value of any experiment involving humans or animals.

What other ethical concerns do psychologists face when designing experiments?

Ethical Concerns

The American Psychological Association (APA) has developed an extensive policy statement related to ethics in research. Here are a few of the issues in that statement:

* *Moral and Ethical Responsibility.* It is the responsibility of the researcher to weigh the potential benefits of the study against the fair and humane treatment of the participants. The APA states that *the participants' welfare is of greater importance than society's gain.*

* **Harm Avoidance.** Harm may refer to physical harm as well as to psychological or emotional harm. For example, studies on perception of pain or on the effect of drugs must be done with the full, informed consent of the participants. Participants should be debriefed after the study to reduce any stress and to determine if there are any lasting psychological or emotional effects. Any such effects must be treated.

* **Fairness and Deception.** Suppose that a person is promised a fee for participating in a study. After the study is completed, the person is told that actually the fee was promised to influence his or her motivation in the study. In another study, people are rewarded for correct answers and punished for incorrect answers. But they were not told that to be "correct" they must use the words *I* or *we*. These are examples of deception.

* **Confidentiality.** If the results of a study are published, researchers should take great care to disguise the identities of participants. If data are entered into a computer or other record that may be seen by outsiders, participants' names should be changed or coded. This prevents private information from becoming public. Double-blind studies help to avoid breaches of confidentiality.

* **Animal Research.** This is a very controversial topic in ethics. Are researchers justified in performing experiments on animals to advance knowledge?

CRITICAL THINKING

Should Animals Be Used in Research?

Many medical and psychological studies have been done using animals. Scientists argue that the benefits gained from animal research far outweigh the rights of animals. Opponents argue that animals have rights that cannot be traded away for the benefit of people. What do you think?

THE ISSUES

Animal research has been a major contributor to our knowledge of basic learning processes; of motivational systems such as hunger, thirst, and reproduction; of modes of adaptation to change; and of the characteristics of disease. Scientists argue that alternatives such as computer simulations and experimentation on tissue cultures cannot give them the kind of information they get from experiments with living animals. The American Psychological Association has a policy for the care and use of animals in research, encouraging humane treatment and the use of animals only when no other alternative is available.

Groups such as People for the Ethical Treatment of Animals (PETA) argue that there is a difference between animal welfare addressed by APA and animal rights. They claim that animals are not ours to use. PETA lists a number of alternatives that it insists can be used in place of animal experimentation, such as computer simulation and human tissue cultures. They claim that because animals are not the same species as humans, tests on human tissue cultures yield more accurate predictions. Acknowledging that animal rights are limited, PETA does say that each case should be decided on an individual basis "wisely and mercifully."

Do you think that animals should be used in research?

THE PROCESS

1. **Restate the issues.** In your own words, state the nature of the disagreement.

2. **Provide evidence.** From your own experience and from the information above, list the evidence *for* animals being used in research.

3. **Give opposing arguments.** From your own experience and from the information above, list the evidence *against* animals being used in research.

4. **Look for more information.** What else would you like to know before you decide? Make a list of your questions. Research issues of *animal research* on the Internet, in the psychology section of the library, or in

the index of psychology books. Check out the APA and PETA web sites.

5. **Evaluate the information.** Make a chart with two columns:

Animals Used in Research	
For	Against

Record the arguments in each column and rank each column of arguments in importance from 1 to 5, with 1 as the most important.

6. **Draw conclusions.** Write one paragraph supporting your answer to the question "Should animals be used in research?" Be sure to state reasons, not just an opinion.

How to Evaluate Research

Locate the report of a psychological study on behavior on the Internet, in the popular press, or in a psychology book. Evaluate the study by asking the following questions. You may find that you have to conduct additional research to complete this checklist.

Hypothesis
✓ Is the hypothesis clearly worded?

✓ Is the question worth the time and effort to study?

Selection of Participants
✓ Do participants represent the population being studied?

✓ Was the test population selected randomly?

✓ Is the sample size large enough to rule out chance?

Identification and Control of Variables
✓ Have all potential variables been identified?

✓ Have variables other than the dependent and independent variable been controlled or accounted for in the conclusion?

Methodology
✓ Has an appropriate method been chosen to test the hypothesis?

✓ Have the rules and principles of scientific research been applied to the experimental design?

Observations and Data Collection
✓ Has every effort been made to keep observations objective?

✓ Have the data been organized and processed in an appropriate manner?

Analysis of Bias
✓ Have potential areas of bias on the part of the experimenters and participants been identified and accounted for?

✓ Have the researchers avoided bias in reporting, processing, and presenting their data?

Ethical Concerns
✓ Have researchers followed the code of ethical conduct in terms of research design, confidentiality, deception, and appropriate concerns for test participants?

Conclusions
✓ Have conclusions been limited to the population studied?

✓ Have other researchers duplicated the experiment?

✓ Have alternative explanations been explored?

Psychologists use the scientific method when designing ways to study human behavior. Researchers generate a question or hypothesis, select participants, identify variables, decide on dependent and independent variables while controlling others, and design their experiments using the rules and procedures of the scientific method. They collect data from the experiments and draw conclusions from the results.

Scientists are concerned with how people are alike, how people are different, and how individual differences affect behavior. They may choose to use surveys, interviews, naturalistic observation, laboratory experiments, field studies, or other methods to explore their questions. Once gathered, data are processed using statistics, and a conclusion is reached regarding the hypothesis.

Psychological researchers are sensitive to the need for ethical standards in their research. They make sure that they assess the risks and benefits of research, avoid harm to participants, avoid deception, and maintain confidentiality. Research on animals follows similar guidelines.

Psychology

bias—any condition or set of conditions that distorts data from what pure chance would have produced. *p. 20*

correlation—relationship between two variables. *p. 22*

deductive thinking—reasoning from a general principle to particular instances. *p. 20*

hypothesis—statement of something a researcher believes to be true—an "educated guess." *p. 22*

inductive thinking—reasoning from particular instances to a general principle. *p. 19*

mean—measure of central tendency calculated by dividing the sum of the scores by the number of scores. *p. 30*

median—middle value in a set of data that have been listed in order. *p. 30*

mode—most common value among a set of data. *p. 30*

paradigm—worldview or set of beliefs about the world in which a scientist works. *p. 19*

standard deviation—measure of how far from normal distribution a set of data falls. *p. 30*

theory—statement of underlying principles used to explain and predict some aspect of nature. *p. 19*

variable—anything that can take on different values or qualities. *p. 22*

Psychology and the Brain

In this chapter, you will learn about:

- **the nervous and endocrine systems**
- **brain cells and how they communicate**
- **structures and functions of the brain**

Picture yourself at a rock concert. The music is loud, and you're surrounded by thousands of other teenagers. You are moving to the beat, applauding or screaming when your favorite songs are played. Your brain is masterminding your every move and processing everything you see and hear, your memory of the songs, and your appreciation of them.

The brain is the command center of the body: planning, coordinating, and guiding actions to avoid trouble and ensure survival. It is the seat of what is uniquely human: language, creativity, logic, and thought.

Through the past decades, researchers have deciphered many of its secrets, but the brain is still considered one of the last frontiers of the human body. To understand why we behave as we do, we must first understand what is going on inside the brain.

Overview of the Nervous System

The brain is the most important part of the nervous system, which—along with the endocrine system—coordinates and controls all actions of the body. The nervous system processes thousands of bits of information from the body's other organs and the outside environment. The nervous system makes sense of them and determines the response the body will make. The endocrine system, which we will discuss later in this chapter, houses the production factories for hormones, which control growth, sexual development, and other processes that keep us alive.

We can begin to get a sense of the elaborate information exchange that goes on in our bodies day and night by dividing the nervous system by its functions.

The nervous system is a massive information highway from the brain down the spinal cord and through a network of nerves that branch throughout the body. The prick of a pin is information. The degree your arm bends to hold this book is information. The facts you read, the intensity of light around you, anything that has to do with your body or its immediate vicinity is information. The primary function of the brain is to send information from one point to another in the nervous system so it can be used.

Nervous System Diagram

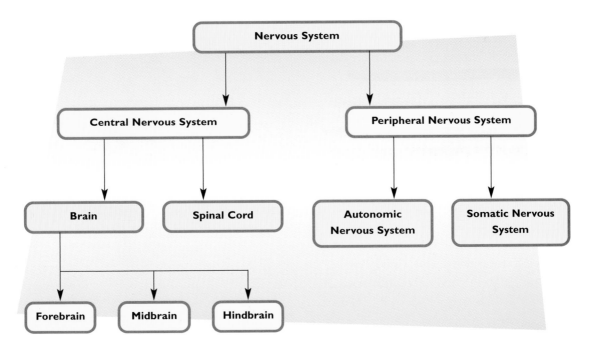

Nerve Cells

The brain is probably the most complex structure known in the universe. It is a mass of tissue composed of about 100 billion nerve cells, more than the number of stars in the Milky Way. These cells, the powerhouse of the whole nervous system, are particularly concentrated in the brain. Because of them, the computing power of your brain is far greater than the most sophisticated computer in existence.

The nervous system is composed of two types of cells, glia and neurons, many of which are smaller than the period at the end of this sentence. There are 10 to 50 times more glial cells than neurons in the brain, but they play more of a supporting role. They participate in the movement of nerve impulses and in the neurons' response to injury. Glia produce myelin, a protective coating along the nerve cells. Just like the coating of a wire, the myelin prevents "crosstalk," such as might happen if telephone wires get crossed. Myelin also speeds up the rate of nerve impulses. The most common forms of brain tumors affect the glia.

Neurons have a *nucleus*, or center, that contains genes, as other cells of the body do, but neurons are vastly different from other cells. There are dozens of different classes of neurons, and each has a particular function (such as motion or senses). Neurons have specialized projections called dendrites and axons: dendrites carry information to the cell body, and axons take information away.

The Neuron

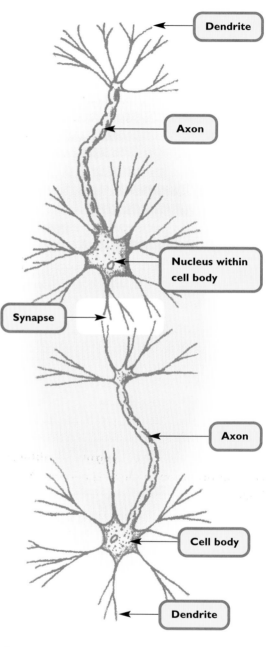

Information enters neurons through the dendrites. The cell body decides to pass along the information, and the axon transmits the message to the nerve endings.

How Nerve Cells Communicate

When your teacher writes a question on the blackboard and turns to you for the answer, your nervous system swings into action. Information from your eyes, ears, and other senses is relayed simultaneously through the nervous system's extremely complicated networks of neurons to the brain. There the information is integrated. That's where you hope some memory of the correct response is stored! Through an equally complicated process, that response is conveyed back and spoken.

Although much is yet to be learned about this seemingly miraculous process, we do know how neurons communicate with one another at a very basic level. A neuron sends a message by first firing electrical impulses (at speeds up to 200 miles per hour) down the axon. When the impulse reaches the synapse, the contact point between two neurons, it triggers the release of chemicals from the vesicles, "storage tanks" at the end of the axons. These chemicals, called neurotransmitters, carry information to the next neuron in line, instructing it either to fire another electrical signal, called an action potential, or to remain silent.

Neurons communicate with each other in a complex network of connections: each neuron may make 1,000 to 10,000 synapses on its target neuron. The timing and rhythm of the electrical impulses are important ways that neurons determine which are the important messages. Neurons that have the same rhythm at the same time connect with each other more easily, like two people who dance well together.

The Importance of Neurotransmitters

Most major psychiatric disorders (schizophrenia, major depression, manic-depression) are now believed to result, in large part, from some form of abnormal chemical transmission in the brain. Scientists in the past several decades have learned an enormous amount about mental illnesses and their possible treatment by focusing on neurotransmitters and their receptors, the sites where they are received by the next neuron.

There are now more than 50 known neurotransmitters. Each plays some role in most behaviors, but in many cases scientists have associated a behavior particular to one neurotransmitter (see chart on the next page). Certain neurotransmitters, like glutamate, serve an excitatory function, causing the firing of nerve impulses; others, like GABA, are inhibitory, stopping an action. Signs of diseases can occur when there is too much or too little of one or more of these neurotransmitters.

The large variety of neurotransmitter receptors increases considerably the different kinds of information that can be sent to the receiving neuron. Hundreds of neurotransmitter receptor genes have been discovered, which combine in various ways to produce receptors.

Major Neurotransmitters		
Neurotransmitter	Function	Associated Disorder
acetylcholine	transmits between nerves and muscle: involuntary body movement; memory	Alzheimer's disease
norephinephrine	sleep; blood pressure; mood	depression
serotonin	mood; appetite; aggression	depression; migraines
dopamine	involuntary body movement	Parkinson's disease; possibly schizophrenia and addictions
GABA (gamma-aminobutyric acid)	major inhibitory transmitter in the brain; keeps seizures from happening	Huntington's disease; epilepsy; schizophrenia
glutamate	major excitatory transmitter in the brain (probably present in all the nervous system)	neuron loss after stroke; seizures
endorphin	modulates sensory system, including relief of pain and feeling of well being; pain relief	addictions

The Peripheral Nervous System

The peripheral nervous system carries information between the organs of the body and the central nervous system. The peripheral nervous system is divided even further into the autonomic nervous system and the somatic nervous system.

Autonomic Nervous System

The autonomic nervous system controls the muscles of the stomach, intestines, and bodily functions including:

* Breathing.
* Heart rate.
* Tears and saliva.
* Urination and defecation.
* The levels of oxygen and carbon dioxide in the bloodstream.
* The "fight or flight" response, which in emergencies diverts blood from our stomach to our muscles, increasing heart and breathing rates, and dilating (opening wide) our pupils.

Somatic Nervous System

The somatic nervous system is generally associated with all of the body's movements. Its nerve network includes:

* All the sensory neurons, which bring information about the environment to the brain to be sorted and processed.
* All the motor neurons, which lead back from the brain to the muscles, telling them what to do.
* Reflexes, such as immediately pulling your hand away from a hot pan, or reactions that don't wait for the brain to dictate action.

The Central Nervous System

The central nervous system consists of the spinal cord and the brain. Information from the peripheral nervous system is conveyed here, where it is coordinated, processed, and relayed back through the peripheral nervous system with a response. In the example of the teacher asking you a question, a response might be a spoken answer. If your brain is not quickly finding an answer, the response might be stress: you start sweating, your heart beats faster, or you flee the room.

Spinal Cord

The main pathway for information between the brain and the peripheral nervous system is the spinal cord. The cord itself, composed of neurons, is housed in a protective spine of bones called *vertebrae.*

The Nervous System

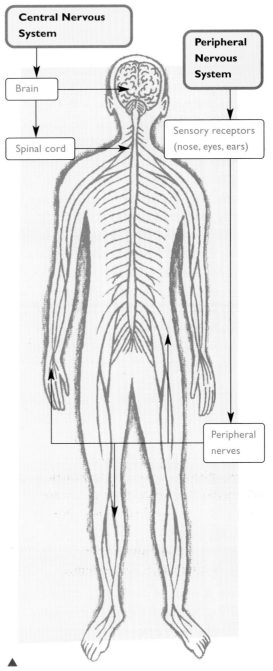

Central Nervous System

Brain

Spinal cord

Peripheral Nervous System

Sensory receptors (nose, eyes, ears)

Peripheral nerves

▲
Your nervous system is made up of your brain, spinal cord, and a network of nerves.

The Lessons of Phineas Gage

Science has often benefited from the misfortunes of humankind. For example, much was learned about the function of the frontal lobe in the brain from the famous case of Phineas Gage. In 1848, an explosion at a railway where Gage was working drove a large metal rod through his head. Remarkably, he recovered with his memory and intelligence intact. But his behavior changed dramatically. Before the accident he was friendly, kind, and conscientious, but afterward he lied, broke his promises, and swore constantly. Scientists have been able to conclude from this case and others that the frontal area of the brain affects the ability to make decisions and to process emotions.

The brain is commonly divided into three areas: hindbrain, midbrain, and forebrain. Although all these parts of the brain work in harmony, they are different structurally, and they affect different aspects of human behavior.

Up and down the spinal cord, 30 pairs of nerve bundles track outward to various parts of the body and brain.

The Brain: Command Central

The brain is far more than the sum of its three pounds of parts. People have compared the texture of the brain to gelatin, but actually it is composed of structures with very different consistencies. These different structures have different functions. Through the centuries, scientists have learned a great deal about which areas of the brain process language, feelings, memory, sexual attraction, musical and artistic ability, and so on. Scientists have made their discoveries by:

* Dissecting brains after death.
* Using imaging technology to observe which areas of the brain are chemically highlighted when a person performs a task such as memorizing a list.
* Observing behavioral changes that result from injury or diseases that affect certain areas of the brain.

How the Brain Thinks

The cerebral cortex is responsible for many higher functions of the brain, such as language and information processing. It is here and in the cerebrum that the "magic" that makes us human takes place.

We are curious creatures, capable of believing in Santa Claus, storing a lifetime of memories, or creating lovely symphonies that make people weep. The human brain has evolved over several million years, growing ever larger and more complex. Our brainpower gives us the unique ability to explore the mystery of how the mass of neurons and structures in the brain makes possible thought, language, reasoning, creativity, and perception.

The Brain

Side View

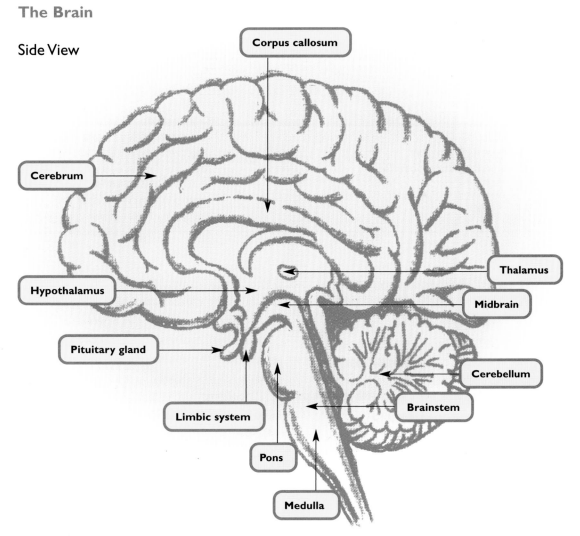

Parts of the Brain

Hindbrain	Midbrain	Forebrain
Brain Stem: evolutionarily the oldest part of the brain and the center of involuntary actions: balance, breathing, heartbeat **Medulla:** switching station to and from the spinal cord; monitors the body's response to injury, blood pressure, and reflexes such as sneezing and laughing **Reticular Activating System:** watchdog for danger; involved in sleeping and wakefulness **Pons:** relay station between cerebellum and cerebral cortex **Cerebellum:** responsible for movement, balance, posture	**Top Inch of Brain Stem:** connecting station for nerve signals; where pathways cross so one half of the brain controls the other half of the body	**Limbic System:** controls emotional response; includes the amygdala and hippocampus (both important for memory and learning) **Hypothalamus:** the size of a pea, it controls body temperature and regulates the pituitary **Thalamus:** relays information from the body to the cerebral cortex; gets back information that it sends to other parts of the brain and spinal cord **Cerebrum:** makes up about two-thirds of brain; is divided into two hemispheres, each with four lobes covered by cerebral cortex, the outermost "bark" of the brain (where most of the brain's neurons reside)

Two Hemispheres

In some ways we actually have two brains, since the cerebrum (and its outermost layer, the cerebral cortex) is divided into two halves, or hemispheres. These hemispheres are connected by a bundle of nerve fibers called the corpus callosum. Communication between the two hemispheres occurs across the corpus callosum, a fact made clear by the Nobel Prize–winning studies of Roger Sperry on "split-brain" patients, whose corpus callosum was cut by accident or in the treatment of disease.

The right hemisphere controls the left side of the body, and the left hemisphere controls the right side. Each hemisphere has some specialized tasks, but for the most important functions, such as memory, they work in harmony by communicating across the corpus callosum. As a result, while victims of stroke (loss of brain function caused by blockage or bursting of the blood vessels in the brain) may not lose much memory, movement may be impaired on the side of the body opposite the affected hemisphere.

In most people—all of us who are right-handed and at least half of us who are left-handed—the left hemisphere domi-nates, and that is where language and speech functions are performed. For other left-handers, the right hemisphere domi-nates. For them, language and speech are centered in the right hemisphere. (Some

lefties even have dominance on both sides!) Though much discussion focuses on the difference between right- and left-hemisphere activities, not all theories are fully proven.

In general, the left hemisphere:

* Controls right side of body.
* Controls language, speech, and reading.
* Plans the day; keeps us on time.

The right hemisphere:

* Controls left side of body.
* Identifies patterns; gets us back after a walk around the block.
* Controls artistic tendencies, holistic thinking abilities, and imagination.

Sidebar

Hemispheres and Handedness

Time yourself and write down how long you can balance a ruler on its end first in your left hand, then in your right hand. Then time yourself while balancing the ruler on its end in each hand while talking at the same time. Compare the results.

Most right-handed people find that talking interferes with the performance of their right hand, but not their left. That is because language is processed in the left hemisphere, as is movement on the right side of their bodies.

Left-handed people can also have lan-guage dominance in the left hemisphere and would also be better with the left hand while talking. But some lefties have lan-guage dominance in the right or in both hemispheres. A lefty with language on both sides will be able to control the ruler equally well in both hands while talking; a lefty with right-side language dominance would be better with the right hand.

Four Functional Lobes

Grooves on the very wrinkled cerebral cortex provide another natural device for dividing the brain and pinpointing where its myriad functions occur. Four lobes have been identified: frontal, parietal, occipital, and temporal. The diagram shows some of what we know takes place within these areas of the brain.

The Parts and Functions of the Brain

Surface View

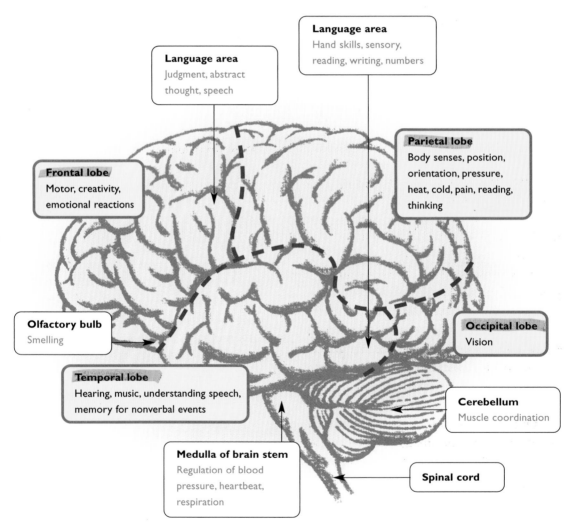

Language area
Hand skills, sensory, reading, writing, numbers

Language area
Judgment, abstract thought, speech

Parietal lobe
Body senses, position, orientation, pressure, heat, cold, pain, reading, thinking

Frontal lobe
Motor, creativity, emotional reactions

Olfactory bulb
Smelling

Occipital lobe
Vision

Temporal lobe
Hearing, music, understanding speech, memory for nonverbal events

Cerebellum
Muscle coordination

Medulla of brain stem
Regulation of blood pressure, heartbeat, respiration

Spinal cord

Relief from Depression

Whether there is an initial trigger (death in the family, the end of a relationship, the loss of a job) or a biochemical deficiency, the final path to depression involves biochemical changes in the brain. These changes are largely what separates clinical depression from the blues we all feel occasionally.

Serotonin is a neurotransmitter that affects mood. Normally when your brain cells release serotonin, they call it back. Selective serotonin reuptake inhibitors (SSRIs), such as Prozac, block that process, allowing more serotonin to be available. This process relieves the symptoms associated with depression. SSRIs seem to be about as effective as other drugs prescribed for depression (helping 60 to 80 percent of those who take them), but with fewer side effects.

The Endocrine System

The endocrine system is the nervous system's partner in controlling and coordinating the body's functions. Usually the nervous system controls immediate responses, whereas the endocrine system can direct functions that the body must perform over days or weeks. The endocrine system's counterparts to neurotransmitters are chemical messengers called **hormones**, which are sent into the bloodstream and are responsible for maintaining normal growth, sexual development, and metabolism— the processes necessary for maintaining life. Organs and tissues scattered throughout the body that produce hormones are called glands.

The nervous and endocrine systems are not entirely separate, however. Some endocrine glands, specifically the pituitary gland, respond to nervous system messages.

* **Pituitary Gland.** The hypothalamus of the brain controls the pituitary, which in turn controls the production of many different critical hormones. The pituitary is called the "master gland" because its hormones influence many of the other endocrine glands. Hormones it manufactures include growth hormone, thyroid-stimulating hormone, and oxytocin, a hormone that causes a woman's uterus to contract.

Similarly, the other endocrine glands regulate various functions:

* **Thyroid Gland.** Produces energy the body can use from nutrients. If it is overactive, you will feel nervous and jittery or warm when others are comfortable. If it is underactive, you will feel slow or drowsy and depressed, and you will likely gain weight.

* **Parathyroid Glands.** Control the level of calcium in the blood, which is important for bones and teeth, and also for nerve function, muscle contraction, and blood clotting.
* **Pineal Body.** Produces the hormone melatonin, which promotes the tanning of skin and recently has been shown to affect the sleep-wake cycle.
* **Thymus Gland.** Plays a role in the body's immune system, which is responsible for recognizing and destroying invaders such as viruses and bacteria.
* **Adrenal Glands.** Influences metabolism and physical characteristics, such as body shape and hairiness; takes instruction from the nervous system, producing epinephrine (also known as adrenaline), in response to stress, fear, and anger.

* **Pancreas.** Makes insulin, which controls the levels of sugars in the bloodstream. (Little or no insulin results in diabetes.)
* **Ovaries.** Produce female sex hormones: estrogen and progesterone. Ovaries also house the 60,000 eggs with which all girls are born. Only about 400 will ripen in a woman's lifetime, one per month during the fertile years.
* **Testicles.** Produce androgens, the hormones responsible for male characteristics, and as many as 12 trillion sperm in a man's lifetime. Testicles lie inside the scrotum, which has a built-in thermostat for keeping the sperm at the correct temperature.

The Endocrine System

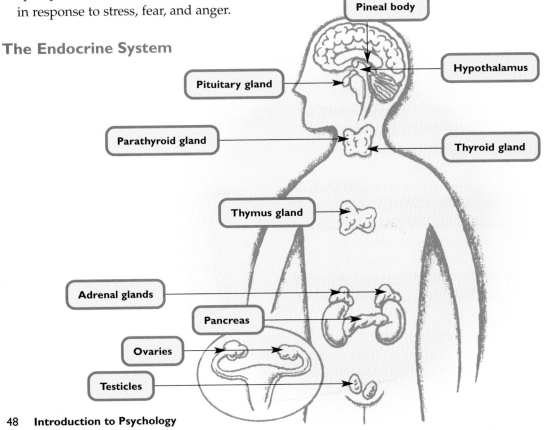

Pineal body

Hypothalamus

Pituitary gland

Parathyroid gland

Thyroid gland

Thymus gland

Adrenal glands

Pancreas

Ovaries

Testicles

CRITICAL THINKING

Who's Winning the Nature vs. Nurture Debate?

A debate has raged for centuries over what influence on behavior is greater: nature, the personality and genes we're born with, or nurture, the environment and experiences in our lives. Do you have an opinion? Check it out.

THE ISSUES

Historically, this debate has been framed in terms of nature vs. nurture. The discoveries of genes and neurotransmitters are modern, but since the time of the Greek physician Hippocrates (c. 460–377 B.C.), people have understood that we are born with a certain nature. At the turn of the twentieth century, Sigmund Freud introduced his theories on the importance of early child-rearing experiences. Those voices who argued that nurture determined our behavior then dominated.

Research over the past several decades, however, has made it clear that genes specify the way many of our behaviors are generated. It also has been suggested that genes make someone's personality more likely to respond to its environment in certain ways. Yet the way you are brought up by your parents, the education you receive, and your life experiences also affect the person you are.

Where do you stand on the nature and nurture debate?

THE PROCESS

❶ **Restate the argument.** In your own words, state the main idea behind the nature vs. nurture conflict.

❷ **Provide evidence.** Use information from this chapter to *support one side* of the issue.

❸ **Give opposing arguments.** Use information from this chapter to *support another view* of the issue.

❹ **Look for more information.** Research *nature vs. nurture* in the library or on the Internet; look up Thomas Buchard's work and that of others who studied twins (look up *twin studies*).

❺ **Evaluate the information.** Make a chart with two columns:

Nature	Nurture

In each column, list ideas supporting that concept. Put a check mark next to the strongest ideas.

❻ **Draw conclusions.** Write two paragraphs describing your ideas on the nature vs. nurture debate. Support your views with evidence from various sources.

The nervous system and endocrine systems control and coordinate all human behavior. Much of our behavior is processed in more than one area of the brain, but some behavior—such as speech and sight—can be linked to specific areas. Nerve cells communicate with each other to speed messages up to the brain and back using neurotransmitters. In the endocrine system, hormones are the chemicals used to carry messages through the body's bloodstream.

Discoveries about these systems have allowed scientists to describe human behavior to a greater degree and to develop drugs that can target diseases that short-circuit normal functions. New technologies enable scientists to study cells, understand and control brain circuits, and change the ways genes are expressed. But there is much more to discover about the brain and its higher functions—memory, intelligence, thoughts, feelings—the processes that make us human.

Psychology

autonomic nervous system—part of the peripheral nervous system that controls the muscles in the stomach, intestines, and other organs. *p. 40*

central nervous system—system consisting of the spinal column and the brain. *p. 41*

endocrine system—glands that regulate the body's growth, metabolism, and sexual development and function. *p. 37*

hormones—chemicals used by the endocrine system that control growth, emotional responses, and physical changes. *p. 47*

nervous system—system made up of the brain, spinal cord, and network of nerves throughout the body. *p. 37*

neuron—nerve cell, the basic unit of the nervous system. A neuron is made up of a cell body, an axon, and one or more dendrites. *p. 38*

neurotransmitters—chemicals that carry information from one neuron to another. *p. 39*

somatic nervous system—part of the peripheral nervous system associated with all of the body's movements. *p. 40*

Sensation

In this chapter, you will learn about:

- how we convert light into images
- how the ear responds to sound waves
- the senses of taste and smell
- the somatic sensory system

English physicist Sir Isaac Newton, in an experiment, observed that a ray of sunlight, or white light, was broken up into the brilliant colors of the spectrum when it passed through a glass prism. He then noticed that the ray recombined into white light when it was beamed back through another prism. It occurred to Newton that since light rays are not colored, color must not be an actual physical quality in the world. He concluded that color must exist only in the mind and not in nature.

If color does not actually exist in the world around us, then where do colors come from? To answer this question, we will need to understand how our visual sensory system translates different wavelengths of light into neural impulses so that our brain can interpret the information it receives as the sensation of color. The other types of sensation we experience—such as sound, smell, taste, touch, and pain—are also products of the brain's response to various kinds of sensory stimuli.

Sensory Systems

It is through our sensory systems—vision, hearing, taste, smell, and touch—that we experience and interact with the environment outside our bodies. Our sensory organs—eyes, ears, nose, tongue, skin—contain **receptors** that allow us to physically process the information we are constantly receiving from the world around us. Highly specialized sensory receptors pick up various specific forms of information. The following table lists the main receptors and the kinds of stimuli to which they respond.

Receptors and Stimuli	
In the eye	Wavelengths of light
In the ear	Vibrations of air molecules
In the nose	Gaseous molecules in the air
On the tongue	Chemicals in food
In the skin	Pressure, temperature

Absolute Thresholds

For a sensation to occur, a minimum amount of stimulation is necessary. Scientists have explored the psychological aspects of physical stimuli and determined the **absolute thresholds,** or the minimum stimuli that can be detected by our main sensory systems. The following table illustrates the incredible sensitivity of the human sensory systems.

Absolute Threshold for Each Sensory System
Vision: A candle flame seen 30 miles away on a clear, dark night (equals 3 photons of light, a photon being the smallest unit of light)
Hearing: The tick of a watch under quiet conditions at 20 feet
Taste: I teaspoon of sugar in 2 gallons of water
Smell: I drop of perfume diffused into the entire volume of a three-room apartment
Touch: The wing of a bee falling on your cheek from a distance of I centimeter

How We Perceive

Sensory organs take in information from the environment by means of receptors and then convey the information to the brain in the form of neural, or nerve, impulses, a language the brain can understand. The brain then uses the information to create impressions. The brain interprets the neural impulses as particular sensations. In a process known as **perception,** the brain organizes the sensory information to make it meaningful. Although we do not yet know how all of this happens, scientists have proposed various theories to explain the process. So, although it may be difficult to grasp, all of our sensations and impressions about the world around us—everything we experience—is really constructed inside our brain. Sensations are based on stimuli from outside. "Seeing" does not take place in the eye but in the brain. And that, as we shall see, is why color exists only in the mind of the beholder.

Each sensory system in the body—the eyes, ears, nose, tongue, and skin—uses a complex form of **sensory coding** to send a message to the brain. Sensory codes are essential parts of a process that enables the brain to understand what it is we are experiencing.

When a sensory receptor receives a stimulus that continues at the same intensity over a period of time, the sensory receptor's response is stronger at first and then usually becomes weaker, as the receptor adapts to the stimulus. This process is called **sensory adaptation.** The manner and rate of adaptation vary, depending on the specific sensory organ and the particular stimulus. For example, adaptation to pain occurs very slowly, if at all, while adaptation to repetitive sounds may occur relatively quickly. While you may never stop noticing pain until the cause of the pain is removed, a sound that is repetitive, such as the ticking of a clock, tends to eventually become background noise.

Vision and Light

For sighted people, vision is the most important sense. About 70 percent of the information reaching their brains comes from vision. To begin to understand the workings of our visual sensory system, and the role of the brain in sight, we first must understand the nature of light.

What Is Light?

Electromagnetic radiation is all around us, in the form of light, gamma rays, ultraviolet rays, infrared rays, and radio waves. Light makes up just a narrow band of the electromagnetic spectrum, but light is the only form of electromagnetic radiation that we can see. Indeed, without light, we would see nothing. Ultraviolet rays move too slowly for us to see, and infrared rays are too fast for us to see. Visible light—white light from the sun or from a light bulb—is broken into different frequencies or wavelengths when it hits objects and bounces back at us. We interpret the different wavelengths as different colors. The visible spectrum of colors ranges from violet, the shortest wavelength at 400 nanometers (a nanometer is one-billionth of a meter), to red, with a wavelength of 700 nanometers. In between are the colors indigo, blue, green, yellow, and orange.

How the Eye Responds to Light

You have probably heard the eyes referred to as a "window into the soul." Indeed, the eyes are an amazingly vulnerable and sensitive sensory organ designed to catch light and convert it to neural impulses that the brain can interpret and understand. It is important to understand the purposes and functions of the main structures in the eye in order to appreciate the process by which we see.

* When light reaches the eye, it enters the cornea. This transparent, curved "window" bends light toward the eye's center.

* The cornea cannot change shape to adjust for distance, so additional focusing is done by the lens, which is behind the cornea.

* Light must pass through the pupil, the dark area in the center of the iris, to reach the lens. The pupil in the iris dilates (enlarges) in dim light to allow more light to enter, and contracts in bright light to limit the amount of light that can enter.

* The lens has often been compared to the lens of a camera. It focuses the incoming image on the **retina** in the interior of the eye by bending the light rays in a process known as *accommodation*. A series of muscles in the lens allows it to control the degree of bending.

The Human Eye

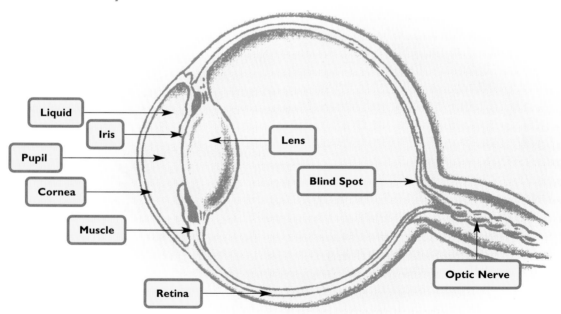

* After passing through the lens, the light reaches the retina, the light-sensitive element of the eye. The retina consists of neurons, and the neurons that are sensitive to light are called **photoreceptors.**
* In the photoreceptor layer, light is converted into electrical activity—the language of the brain. There are two types of photoreceptors—rods and cones.
* There are about 100 million rods in each eye. They function in dim light and at night and send gray, hazy images to the brain.
* Compared to rods, cones are a thousand times less sensitive to light. There are about 6.5 million cones in each eye. The cones function in bright light to produce color sensations and to pick up fine details.
* Each eye has an area where the optic nerve leaves the eye. There are no photoreceptors in this area, so when light hits there, the eye registers nothing. This area is called the blind spot.
* The photoreceptor cells send electrical, or neural, impulses to the optic nerve, which sends them on to the **visual cortex,** the part of the brain that interprets visual images.

How Do We See Color?

We do not have to learn how to see color. We are born with that capability, because that is the way the human visual sensory system and brain are designed. We see color because our eyes have different receptors for different wavelengths of light.

The physical properties of a specific wavelength determine the nature and qualities of the color we will see:

* The *hue*, or name, of a color—such as red—corresponds to a particular wavelength. Black is not a color because no wavelength predominates.
* *Saturation* refers to the purity, richness, or intensity of a color. Colors produced by a very narrow band of wavelengths, such as red, are highly saturated, as compared to pink, which is a mixture of white and red.
* *Brightness* corresponds to the amplitude, or height, of a light wave and to the amount of light energy reaching the retina.

The process by which the human brain interprets various wavelengths of light as different colors is not completely understood. Yet, unless we are partially or totally color-blind, it seems obvious that the world around us is filled with color—an incredible variety of the most beautiful and subtle colors. Just think about the more spectacular sunsets or displays of fall foliage you've seen. What seems strange is the scientific fact that the world is not actually filled with color. An apple appears "red" to us because the apple reflects red light, not because the apple is red. A blue sky on a beautiful sunny day is really not blue. It just appears to be "blue" because the short blue wavelengths of light are scattered more effectively by the atmosphere than are the longer wavelengths of light.

How We See Color	
Trichromatic Theory of Color Vision	**Opponent-Process Theory of Color Vision**
According to the trichromatic, or three-color, theory, there are three types of cones in the retina—red, green, and blue cones.	According to the opponent-process theory, there are three types of receptors, each capable of responding to either red-green, yellow-blue, or black-white, but not to all.
Different photosensitive pigments enable each cone to absorb light mainly in the red, green, or blue portion of the spectrum.	The colors of each pair oppose each other; they cannot be blended. But the four primary colors can be mixed with colors from the other pairs, thereby creating all the colors of the visible spectrum.
All other colors result from a combination of these three primary colors.	

Scientists have proposed several theories—including the trichromatic and the opponent-process—in an attempt to explain how we see color.

Color Blindness

The most common type of color blindness is a partial color blindness known as *color weakness.* This condition affects about 8 percent of the male population and less than 1 percent of the female population. It is usually inherited from the maternal grandfather. People who are partially color-blind are red-green blind. They cannot distinguish between red and green, both of which appear to them as yellowish brown. But they have normal color vision for yellow and blue. Total color blindness is much rarer. An individual with this condition sees the world in shades of gray.

Hearing and Sound

A gigantic, old redwood tree stood in the middle of a deep forest. Recently struck by lightning and partially burned, it was vulnerable to strong winds. One day a strong gust of wind roared through the forest, and a huge section of the redwood tree crashed to the forest floor. Had you been standing nearby, you would probably have covered your ears with your hands because of the loud noise. But what would it have sounded like if neither you nor anyone else was near enough to hear the tree crash? To answer this question, we need to understand the nature of sound.

What Is Sound?

Just as the sights we see are created in our brain in response to light waves activating receptors in our visual sensory system, so too are the sounds we hear created in our brain in response to external stimuli.

* An object generates sound waves when its vibrations cause vibrations in the surrounding air molecules.
* The patterns of vibrations in the air, known as *sound waves,* travel outward in all directions.
* Sound waves travel much more slowly than light waves. Sound waves can also travel through water, although at a slower rate than through air, and they can travel through solid matter, at a still slower speed.
* The sound waves are picked up by our auditory sensory system when the pattern of vibrating air molecules exerts pressure on our eardrum.
* This causes vibrations within the ear that are converted to neural impulses.
* When these impulses reach the brain, we interpret the pattern of impulses as sound.

Now let's go back to that tree in the forest. When the tree hit the ground, it caused sound waves. Patterns of vibrating air molecules traveled outward. But sound waves do not become "sound" until they are picked up by an auditory sensory system and interpreted as "sound" by the brain. So, strange as it may seem, there would not have been any sound at all if nobody had been around to hear it.

Characteristics of Sound

Sound has certain physical characteristics that are always present but that vary greatly. Think about sounds that you have enjoyed—favorite pieces of music, the surf at an ocean beach, or a kitten's purr. Now think of sounds that you may have heard and hope never to hear again—the loud crash of a car accident, or perhaps fingernails scratching the surface of a chalkboard. All of these sounds, pleasant or unpleasant, have the following **three** characteristics: pitch, timbre, and intensity.

1. **Pitch** refers to how high or low a sound is, and it is determined by the frequency of the sound waves.
2. **Timbre** refers to the quality or complexity of a sound.
3. **Intensity** refers to the loudness of a sound, and it is measured in decibels. A sound of zero decibels is the absolute threshold of sound, the softest possible sound humans are capable of hearing. Normal conversation is 60 decibels. Any sound above 130 decibels, the threshold of pain, can be harmful.

How Sound Waves Are Converted in the Ear

Any object set in motion, such as the string of a musical instrument, a tuning fork, or human vocal cords, will produce sound waves as it vibrates. The sound waves travel through the air in all directions. The process of hearing begins when the sound waves—a particular pattern of physical pressure waves of air molecules—are picked up by receptors in the ear and are transformed into neural impulses.

The human ear has **three** main parts:

1. **External Ear.** In the external ear, air conducts sound waves. The visible external part of the ear is shaped to help us capture sound waves. We turn our heads with our ear facing the direction of sound waves in order to pick up faint sounds.

2. **Middle Ear.** Here, bone conducts sound waves. The shape of the ear is designed to funnel sound waves into the ear, where they strike the eardrum in the middle ear. The thin membrane of the eardrum is stretched tightly like a drumhead in the ear canal, covering the entrance to the rest of the middle ear. When a sound wave hits the eardrum, it moves with each vibration of the sound wave, setting in motion three small bones called the *hammer,* the *anvil,* and the *stirrup.* Vibrations of these bones transmit sound to the inner ear.

3. **Inner Ear.** Fluid conducts sound waves in the inner ear. Sound is transmitted to the **cochlea,** a tubular snail-shaped structure filled with fluids and 20,000 tiny hair cells called *cilia.* The sound causes waves in the cochlea's fluid and sets the cilia in motion. As the cilia move, they trigger electrical impulses in the nerve cells to which they are attached. These, in turn, send neural impulses to the brain by way of the **auditory nerve.**

The auditory nerve conveys neural impulses to the hearing areas of the cerebral cortex, where they are interpreted as specific sounds. The brain can determine where a sound is coming from by contrasting the difference in the sound wave's arrival time, however slight, at each ear. The brain can also detect minute differences in the strength of the stimuli reaching the receptors in each ear.

The Human Ear

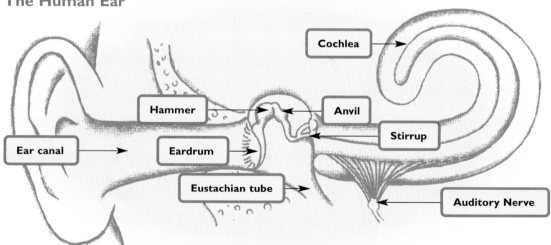

What Happens in Deafness?

Some people are born deaf. Others become partially or totally deaf through illness or injury. The following are the **three** main types of deafness:

1. **Conduction Deafness.** If the eardrums or middle ear bones are immobilized by disease or injury, sound waves are partially or completely prevented from entering the inner ear. This condition is called conduction deafness. Hearing aids, by amplifying sound waves so that they can reach the inner ear, can often alleviate the condition of conduction deafness.

2. **Nerve Deafness.** Nerve deafness is caused by damage to the auditory nerve. Auditory messages cannot reach the brain, no matter how loud the sound, so hearing aids are of no help.

3. **Stimulation Deafness.** Permanent hearing loss can occur when the cochlea is damaged by prolonged exposure to very loud noise. This condition is called stimulation deafness. Loud noise can also cause a persistent ringing in the ears.

Smell and Taste

The senses of smell are known as the *chemical senses.* Receptors for smell in the nose respond to gaseous molecules in the air, and receptors for taste on the tongue and elsewhere in the mouth respond to the chemical composition of foods. Most people would agree that the quality of our lives is greatly enhanced by our senses of smell and taste. One of life's greatest pleasures— eating—would become a dreadfully boring activity if we could not taste anything. And imagine how much duller life would be if we could never experience such things as the intoxicating aroma of a wild rose. Even so, most people would also agree that the senses of smell and taste are not nearly as important to us as the senses of vision and hearing. It is different for some of the other creatures who inhabit this world. Many wild animals depend on their keen sense of smell to avoid deadly predators as well as to hunt prey. At one time in the distant past, humans may have relied on their sense of smell for similar reasons. And, just as with other animals, the sense of taste probably helped early people learn which foods could be safely eaten. Even today this ability can help us avoid harmful substances, which usually have a bitter taste.

How Do We Taste Food?

Most of our taste receptors, or taste buds, are located on the surface of the tongue, but they are also in other parts of the mouth, such as the palate (roof of the mouth). Specific taste buds are especially sensitive to chemicals associated with one of the four primary taste qualities—bitter, sour, salty, or sweet. The brain interprets the pattern of neural impulses from the taste buds as one of four primary tastes or any combination of the four.

People's sense of taste varies. You may remember that as a child you disliked certain foods. You probably refused to eat vegetables and many other items that you now enjoy. Young children like salty food,

The Taste Buds

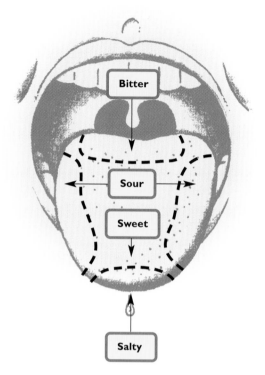

but turn away from spicy, sour, or bitter food. As people age, their taste buds become less sensitive, and many therefore develop a taste for spicy food.

The sense of smell is also involved in our experience of taste and allows us to experience complex tastes. You may have noticed that when you have a cold, food seems to lack its usual taste. When your nasal passages are blocked, you can't smell the food, and this restricts your ability to taste the food. Just for fun, next time you are enjoying one of your favorite foods, try pinching your nostrils together with your fingers and see if you note any change in the taste.

How Do We Smell Odors?

Receptors for smell are located in the nose. The process of olfaction, or smell, begins when we inhale. As odors enter the nose, receptors in the upper nasal passages detect them. This triggers a neural impulse to the olfactory bulbs, which are connected to the receptors. A sensory code in the olfactory bulbs sends information about the odors to the brain by way of the olfactory nerve. The brain then interprets the neural impulses as a particular odor.

Animals use their sense of smell in the process of attracting and selecting a mate. At the appropriate time, their bodies give off **pheromones,** or odor molecules, that other animals of their species interpret as a sexual message. Some people believe that humans may also make use of pheromones to communicate sexual interest. But others think that even if this were true, pheromones would be just one of many factors involved in the complex nature of human sexual attraction.

Touch, Pressure, Temperature, and Pain

Our body's nervous system includes receptors in the skin that respond to the following stimuli: touch, pressure, temperature (heat and cold), and pain. These are called **somatic receptors.** Scientists have determined that although somatic receptors are found all over the body, their density varies in different areas.

Pheromones

People wonder if humans use pheromones to attract the opposite sex. Some researchers think not. Neurobiologist Emily Liman, in experiments with rats, identified a gene for tiny pores called *ion channels*. Pheromones cause a rat's olfactory receptors to open the ion channels, sending nerve signals to the brain. But Liman found that the equivalent gene in humans is mutated and nonfunctional. If this evidence is confirmed by further research, it suggests that humans do not respond to pheromones, although they may have done so at an earlier stage of human evolution.

The tongue, lips, face, hands, and genitals have much greater numbers of receptors and are therefore more sensitive to stimuli. Pain receptors are also found inside the body, so we sometimes experience pain in internal organs.

As with the other kinds of sensory receptors, somatic receptors convert stimuli to neural impulses and send them to the brain. In the brain the neural impulses are interpreted as specific sensations in the somatic sensory cortex.

Why Do We Have to Feel Pain?

All of us have at one time or another experienced pain. Think about an episode of physical pain you had to endure. Depending on the intensity of the pain, or how long it lasted, the experience was either mildly unpleasant, absolutely awful, or something in-between. Most of us try to avoid pain and would prefer never to experience it. And yet, we are actually lucky to be able to feel pain. Pain serves as a warning signal, providing us with vital information about illness or possible tissue damage. For example, pain lets us know if we burn ourselves or if we are suffering from an attack of appendicitis. Pain thresholds vary with each individual. Some people have a very low tolerance for pain, while others can withstand a great deal of pain. And some people have a rare condition that prevents them from ever feeling physical pain—but they are not to be envied.

How Does the Body Alleviate Pain?

People have long resorted to the use of various types of narcotic drugs to reduce sensations of pain. But the body also produces its own substances, known as **endorphins,** which can help reduce or eliminate pain. Various types of endorphins are produced and released by neurons in the upper spinal cord and in several regions of the brain. The endorphins bind to receptors in the brain, just as narcotic drugs do, to reduce or eliminate the pain.

Since we do not experience pain until the brain interprets incoming neural impulses as pain, some scientists believe that pain can be lessened by preventing some of the pain "message" from reaching the brain. The **gate control theory** suggests that we have a built-in gating mechanism in the spinal cord that can block neural impulses outside the brain. There are two types of pain fibers entering the spinal cord: large (fast conducting) and small (slow conducting). A message sent in one pain fiber can close the "pain gate" to a message from the other fiber. If only one pain message gets through to the brain, the result is that we feel less pain. Scientists suspect that this theory may explain how the ancient Chinese practice of acupuncture works. It may be that acupuncture needles inserted in the appropriate places in the body affect the functioning of our pain gates. When the acupuncturist twirls the needles, this may cause small, sharp pains which, when carried by small fibers, close the gates to more intense or chronic pain.

Sidebar

Managing Pain

There is much evidence that pain can be controlled by psychological methods. People suffering from intense pain experienced some relief when distracted by something else—for example by being shown colored slides and asked to describe aloud what they saw. If you were in pain, on what would you focus your attention to alleviate the pain?

CRITICAL THINKING

What Does Sensory Deprivation Prove?

To gain a greater understanding of how our sensory systems work, some researchers have conducted experiments in sensory deprivation. Read about one experiment and analyze it.

John Lilly, M.D., was interested in sensation and how our brains create a vivid impression of the external world based on neural impulses responding to various kinds of stimuli. Lilly wanted to learn more about the functioning of human sensory systems and how our senses allow us to survive in the external world. He suspected that depriving a person for a period of time of all incoming stimuli might reveal useful insights into the way we use our senses to connect with reality.

Lilly devised an experiment in which volunteers would spend varying lengths of time in an "isolation tank." They would be cut off from all outside stimuli. Floating naked inside the tank in body-temperature water, the volunteers also wore darkened goggles. With no sensations of vision, hearing, taste, smell, or touch, they

drifted in the silent darkness of the tank. At first their minds focused on their new environment and the condition of their bodies within it. Thoughts of the day would then occupy them. But soon, they began to lose track of time. And before long, many experienced vivid mental images that had nothing to do with outside stimuli. Lilly himself spent a lot of time in his isolation tank. He claimed to have left his body and visited other dimensions where he encountered "beings of higher intelligence."

While some volunteers found their experience boring and meaningless, others found it to be enlightening and profound, delightful, or scary. Some claim that this experiment demonstrates that when our senses are prevented from keeping us in touch with our ordinary sense of reality, our brains create an alternate reality.

THE PROCESS

1 Restate the argument. In your own words, give the rationale for conducting this experiment.

2 Provide evidence. List the evidence from the experiments that *supports* Lilly's belief that sensory stimuli help people connect with reality.

3 Give opposing arguments. What aspects of Lilly's experiment are *not conclusive?*

4 Look for more information. What else would you want to know about sensory deprivation? Make a list of your questions. Then research *Lilly* and *sensory deprivation* in

an encyclopedia, on the Internet, or in the psychology section of a library.

5 Evaluate the information. Make a chart with two columns:

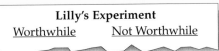

Lilly's Experiment	
Worthwhile	Not Worthwhile

Record the evidence and give each item a number from 1 to 5 to show its importance. Number 1 is most important.

6 Draw conclusions. Write one paragraph explaining your view of Lilly's experiment.

Our knowledge of the world comes to us through our sensory systems, which respond to various types of stimuli. We can see because sensory receptors in the retina of the eye convert light waves into electrical neural impulses, the language of the brain. The neural messages travel along the optic nerve to the visual cortex of the brain, where they are interpreted as images of the external world. Sensory receptors in the ear convert sound waves into neural messages that the auditory cortex of the brain interprets as sound. A similar process occurs with our other senses—smell, taste, touch, pressure, temperature, and pain. In each case, sensory receptors are activated by stimuli and then convey information in the form of neural impulses to the brain, where the information is interpreted as particular sensations.

Psychology WORDS TO KNOW

absolute thresholds—minimum amounts of energy that can be detected by the sensory systems. *p. 52*

auditory nerve—bundle of nerves that carries sound to the brain. *p. 58*

cochlea—tubular snail-shaped structure in the inner ear containing cilia, the main receptors for sound waves. *p. 58*

endorphins—substances produced by the body that can reduce or eliminate pain. *p. 62*

gate control theory—theory of a built-in gating mechanism in the spinal cord that can block neural impulses outside the brain. *p. 62*

perception—process in which the brain organizes sensory information to make it meaningful. *p. 52*

pheromones—odor molecules given off by animals that communicate a sexual message. *p. 60*

photoreceptors—neurons, or nerve cells, in the retina that are sensitive to light and convert it into electrical neural impulses. *p. 55*

receptors—nerve cells within the sensory organs that convert stimuli, such as light or sound waves, into neural impulses. *p. 52*

retina—light-sensitive lining at the back of the eye that contains rods and cones. *p. 54*

sensory adaptation—reduction in sensory response to an unchanging form of stimulation. *p. 53*

sensory coding—particular pattern of a neural message that a sensory organ sends to the brain. *p. 53*

somatic receptors—receptors in the skin that respond to touch, pressure, temperature, and pain. *p. 60*

visual cortex—part of the brain in which neural impulses are interpreted as visual images. *p. 55*

Perception

About three hundred years ago, the French philosopher René Descartes proposed a theory to explain human visual perception. He suggested that images of the outside world received by the eyes were transferred to a small screen inside the brain, where the soul could observe them. In the centuries since Descartes's time, many scientists have investigated various aspects of perception. The more that is learned, the more aware scientists become of the complexity of the human brain and sensory systems.

Scientists have established that receptors in our sensory organs transform stimuli from the environment into electrical neural impulses—the brain's "language." The brain processes all of the incoming neural impulses and constructs a picture of what's "out there," with sounds, smells, and tastes accompanying full-color images. Different scientists have proposed various theories to describe how this occurs. The mysteries of human perception continue to intrigue scientists.

What Is Perception?

In the previous chapter, we discussed how the brain receives sensory information in the form of electrical neural stimuli. Perception occurs when the brain organizes the sensory information to make it meaningful. Some researchers have referred to sensation and perception as two different phenomena, and in this book a separate chapter is devoted to each. However, in reality, the difference between the two is not always clear. Some people think of a perception as a complex type of sensation requiring a greater degree of awareness and an interpretation of the stimulus. According to this definition, awareness of a single flash of light would be an example of a sensation, while a series of light flashes might result in a perception of movement. At any rate, a **perception** is an experience caused by stimulation of the senses.

While the process of perception is still not fully understood, scientists have gained a great deal of knowledge about its various aspects. Because a thorough discussion of perception—perception of sight, sound (including perception of speech), smell, taste, and touch—could easily fill an entire book, this chapter will focus mainly on important aspects of visual perception.

Psychological Factors Influencing Perception

There is no absolute way to perceive the world. Each person is unique, with different experiences, memories, personal tastes, and expectations. These differences are the psychological factors that affect and influence a person's perceptions. For example, some people consider opera music to be nothing but loud, screeching noise, while others find it to be exciting and delightful music. In another example, a person who admires nature would probably enjoy driving through a forest, noticing many different shades of green, as well as other colors and textures. Someone else might drive down that same forest road thinking, "If you've seen one tree, you've seen 'em all." That person would possibly perceive the forest as a continuous dull greenish blur.

The Psychophysical Approach

Because perception involves psychological factors as well as a physical process, many researchers have explored the behavioral aspects of a response to stimuli, an approach known as **psychophysics.** Such scientists compare a person's response to different stimuli and different people's responses to the same stimuli. One result of the psychophysical approach was the establishment of absolute thresholds for the various sensory organs—the minimum stimulus that can be detected.

Researchers have also studied another kind of threshold known as the **difference threshold,** the degree of change in a stimulus necessary for a person to detect the difference. For example, the difference threshold for taste has been determined to be 1/5, or 20 percent. Suppose a cup of coffee has five teaspoons of sugar in it. To create a noticeable change in the sweetness of the coffee, you would have to add 20 percent more sugar, or one more teaspoon of sugar.

Studies of thresholds are useful in determining an individual's sensitivity to various sensory stimuli. The lower the threshold, the greater the sensitivity. Researchers noticed that people in an experiment may each have different reasons for their responses. Each person may be influenced by different aspects in their surroundings. Personal motivation also affects the response. For example, you might be reading this book right now while music is playing in your room and a younger sibling is playing in the next room. Do these sounds interfere with your ability to concentrate on your reading? Or can you block out these distractions? Do you have a test on this section in the near future? Or are you simply interested in the content of this book? The **signal-detection theory** takes into account your sensitivity to stimuli in your environment, your physical condition, and your motivation, mood, and attitude. According to this theory, someone's detection of a stimulus depends both on that person's sensitivity to the stimulus and on his or her response criteria.

Perceptual Constancies

Perception allows us to make sense out of our environment. As we go through life, we learn more and more about the world around us. We are constantly responding to stimuli and accumulating memories of our experience of the world. The brain becomes an immense storehouse of knowledge about details of our physical environment, such as the size, shape, and color of objects. Our memories play an important role in helping us interpret all new incoming stimuli and allowing us to perceive certain aspects of our world as constant, or unchanging. If this were not the case, the world around us would be an incredibly confusing place, because we are continually exposed to new stimuli. The following **four** constancies help us make sense of it.

❶ Size Constancy

Imagine you are traveling in a car on a long, straight stretch of divided highway. Way off in the distance ahead of you, you see a big truck heading toward you. It appears tiny, about the size of a little plastic toy truck. Because you have seen such trucks up close many times in the past, however, you have a fairly good idea of the true size of the truck. So even though the image of the truck appears tiny, you accurately perceive the truck as a huge rig, which will soon be hurtling by you on the other side of the divided highway. This phenomenon is known as *size constancy.*

Size

Step One. Hold an object, such as a pencil, a sheet of paper, or a book, with your hand extended at arm's length.

Step Two. Notice the size of the object.

Step Three. Slowly move the object toward you. What happens to the object's size? Does it appear to grow larger or smaller?

Step Four. Bring the object right in front of your eyes. How does its size appear now?

Analysis. Did the object actually change in size as it moved toward you? Of course not! Even though it appeared to grow larger, you know the true size of the object remained constant. So your perception of the object remained constant. This is what is meant by the term *size constancy*. When your brain knows the true size of an object, it knows that an object only appears to change size when its distance changes.

Shape

Step One. Look at a sheet of paper or book on your desk.

Step Two. Move your head to the side and look at the object again. How has its shape changed?

Step Three. Pick up the object and tilt it at various angles. Observe how its shape changes.

Analysis. Although its shape seems to keep changing, you know that it is rectangular and that its shape isn't really changing. So your perception of the object's shape does not change.

❷ Shape Constancy

Another perceptual constancy is *shape constancy*, an individual's ability to perceive an object as having a constant shape regardless of how it appears to change shape with a change in the observer's angle of view.

❸ Brightness Constancy

When you are familiar with the bright quality of a particular item—for example, a yellow raincoat—you will perceive its brightness to be at a constant level even though its surroundings may change. You will perceive it as bright even on a dark rainy day or when it is hanging in a closet. This phenomenon is known as *brightness constancy.*

❹ Color Constancy

Let's stay with the yellow raincoat a while longer. Since you know it is yellow, you will perceive it to be yellow whether you are seeing it outside on a bright sunny day or in the moonlight late at night—or even on a moonless night! The energy patterns—wavelengths of light—from the raincoat reaching your retina are very different at night than they are during the daytime. But *color constancy* allows you to perceive the yellow color of the raincoat no matter how the environment changes.

Perceptual Organization

Scientists have come up with different theories to explain how we organize perceptions. While the theories may vary a bit, one thing researchers seem to agree upon is that the perceptual process is extremely complex. The big question seems to revolve around the issue of how our brains continually process so many bits of information so quickly.

The Constructionist View

For a long time, the **constructionist view** prevailed among researchers. According to this theory, the brain constructs a perception out of a great many individual sensations. For example, when you meet someone and look at the person's face, your brain takes in countless sensations from each part of the face. A perception is then formed out of the sum of the sensations, and you "see" the face.

The Gestalt Psychologists

In 1912, Max Wertheimer, a German psychologist, formed a group known as the **Gestalt** psychologists. The Gestalt psychologists believed that the whole is more important than the sum of the parts and that each part affects every other. In other words, the brain immediately perceives a stimulus as a whole, rather than focusing on the individual sensations. The Gestalt psychologists focused on the interaction of the parts, observing how the brain uses certain perceptual cues to make sense of things. Based on their research, they developed what they called *laws of perception*.

The following **four** are the most important of these Gestalt laws:

1. **Law of Proximity.** We tend to group together things that are close to one another.

▲
Do you see the dots in vertical rows or horizontal ones? Your brain groups the dots that are closest together. Measure the distance between the dots in both directions.

2. **Law of Similarity.** We group together things that have some visual element in common, such as size, shape, or color.

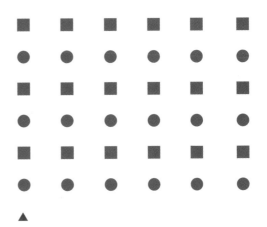

▲
Vertically, these objects are different from each other. Horizontally they are similar. Without conscious effort, your brain organizes these into horizontal rows.

3. **Law of Continuation.** We tend to see interrupted lines as continuous lines with something hiding part of them.

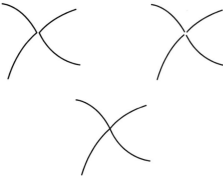

▲
Do the top two figures seem to be made of lines that cross?

4. **Law of Closure.** We tend to fill in missing details to complete a figure so that it has a consistent overall form,

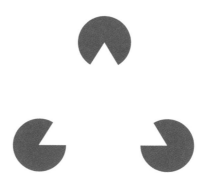

▲
What geometric figure is suggested by the broken circles?

Sidebar

Bottom-Up and Top-Down Processing

Bottom-up processing refers to a type of pattern recognition that begins with an analysis of small units or features and eventually results in a perception. *Top-down processing* involves a person's knowledge of the world. It starts with an analysis of higher-level information, such as the context in which a stimulus is seen. When you encounter something new, do you start by studying the details? Or do you look at the big picture?

Some bottom-up processors "can't see the forest for the trees." ▶

Figure and Ground

The Gestalt psychologists were also interested in an aspect of visual perception known as **figure-ground.** They realized that for us to perceive an object, we have to separate it from its background.

Here are the **three** Gestalt principles of figure-ground perception:

1. The figure is more "thinglike" and more memorable than the ground.

2. The figure is seen as being in front of the ground.

3. The ground is seen as unformed material and seems to extend behind the figure.

In one test of figure-ground perception, subjects are shown a Dalmatian dog against a background of black and white shapes. If they see a Dalmatian dog, they have perceptually organized the black and white shapes into a figure-ground pattern.

Look at the figure on the right. Do you see a white vase? Are you sure that is what you see? Look again. Perhaps you now see two profiles facing each other.

Notice that when you see the white vase against the black background, you cannot see the profiles. And when you see the profiles, you cannot see the vase. It is very difficult to see both profiles and vase at the same time. This is called a *reversible figure-ground pattern.* It was introduced by Danish psychologist Edgar Rubin in 1915.

Limitations of the Gestalt Approach

Many researchers today believe that the Gestalt approach, while useful as a way to describe certain aspects of perception, does not really explain how we perceive the world around us.

* Gestalt laws work best when applied to simple line drawings consisting of dots and lines on a page.
* Gestalt laws do not take into account the importance of recognition or prior familiarity with an object in forming our perceptions.
* Gestalt laws do not take into account our perception of depth in the three-dimensional real world.

Bodily Depth Cues

Several characteristics of our visual system work together to enable us to perceive depth. **Monocular cues** work if we look through only one eye. Other cues, known as **binocular cues,** require the use of two eyes. The following list describes **three** types of bodily depth cues.

1. **Accommodation** is the change in the shape of the lens that varies with distance. In this monocular cue, the lens in each eye bends or bulges to focus on objects as they come closer to the eye. The brain detects the sensation of this muscle movement and perceives the distance of objects closer than four feet.

2. **Convergence** is the way your eyes rotate inward and outward with changes in distance. In this binocular cue, the eyes have to converge to focus on an object closer than 50 feet away. To see how this works, hold a finger out at arm's length and focus your eyes on it as you slowly move it toward your eyes. When it gets close up, you will feel the sensation of muscles that control your eye movement.

3. **Binocular disparity** describes the difference between the images provided by each eye. Because our eyes are two and a half to three inches apart, each eye gets a slightly different view of the same scene. When our brain combines the sensations coming from both eyes, a convincing perception of depth results. Three-dimensional movies are based on this binocular cue. Such movies are filmed by two cameras several inches apart. Both images are simultaneously projected onto a screen. When the viewer wears glasses that filter out one of the images to each eye, each eye gets a separate image. And the brain is tricked into perceiving a two-dimensional scene as having a third dimension.

The Visual Cliff Experiment

Depth perception is necessary to survival. Without it, everything would appear flat, and it would be extremely difficult to judge distances. Driving on a highway in traffic would be suicidal since you wouldn't be able to tell how near or far the other cars were. Activities, such as baseball or basketball, would be impossible, though not life threatening. Imagine how difficult walking would be!

Because depth perception is such a vital skill, we acquire it when we are very young. Research has shown that infants begin to perceive depth at around three months of age, as their eye muscles develop and their eyes focus effectively. Depth perception is fully developed by six months.

In 1960 Elinor Gibson and Richard Walk devised an experiment known as a "visual cliff" to demonstrate that infants can perceive depth. Using a glass-topped table, they placed a sheet of patterned material directly beneath half of the glass and several feet below the other half. An infant on the table would crawl toward its mother when she stood near the "shallow" side. But when she stood near the "deep" side, the infant would refuse to crawl toward her, apparently afraid of "falling off a cliff," and thus demonstrating the ability to perceive depth.

Pictorial Depth Cues

Pictorial depth cues can give a two-dimensional painting, photograph, or movie the illusion of depth where none exists. All pictorial depth cues are monocular cues, since all of these can work even if one eye is closed. These **seven** cues exist in the real world as well as in pictures.

1. **Linear Perspective.** Parallel lines in the environment appear to converge as they move away from you. Perhaps you have stood near train tracks and noticed how they appear to come together in the distance, conveying a sensation of depth.

2. **Relative Size.** Objects that are known to be the same size will convey depth if one is smaller than the other.

3. **Relative Height.** Objects that are higher in a scene are usually perceived as being more distant, as long as they are below the horizon. Objects above the horizon appear to be closer if they are higher in your field of view.

4. **Overlap.** A sensation of depth is created when one object partially blocks another, because this means that one object is a certain distance behind the other.

5. **Texture.** Changes in texture can convey depth when the texture in the foreground contains vivid details that become less and less apparent as the texture recedes into the background.

6. **Atmospheric (or Aerial) Perspective.** Distant objects tend to look less sharp than close objects because the atmosphere often contains smog, fog, dust, or haze. A sensation of depth is conveyed because objects that are hazy and lacking in detail appear to be far away.

7. **Relative Motion.** This phenomenon can be seen by looking out the side window of a car as you are riding. Objects that are close to the car seem to be moving by very quickly, while objects in the distance, such as hills, appear to move slowly. This effect can convey the sensation of depth in a movie.

Perception of Motion

Our visual sensory system detects and perceives many different kinds of movement. A few examples are: a figure moving against a stationary background, objects at rest against a moving background, objects moving at different speeds in relation to each other, the observer's own movements in relation to his or her surroundings, and many different kinds of apparent movement where there is none. We can only marvel at the eye's amazing ability to sift through all the movement it encounters and the brain's ability to make sense of it all.

Induced movement, or the perception of movement of an object that is not moving, can be caused by the motion of nearby objects. For example, the moon often seems to be racing through clouds, when it is the clouds that are moving.

Our perception of movement in film is influenced not only by the physical movement on the screen but also by our past experience with moving objects and with watching films.

In the Eye

The eyes sense motion in **two** ways: detecting movement and tracking movement.

1. When the eye is still, the image of a moving object sweeps across the retina, firing a row of receptors in sequence. Neurons in the visual cortex, linked to the receptors, act as motion detectors.

2. When the retina locks onto a moving object and follows it in a tracking process, there is no movement on the retina, but the brain nevertheless perceives motion.

In the Brain

The brain perceives motion by **two** main processes, usually occurring simultaneously.

1. The short-range system detects movements without knowing what is moving, reacting only to changes in the patterns of light sensed by the retina. It operates automatically and is not influenced by attention.

2. The long-range system registers what is moving from one place to another. It can be influenced by attention.

Movement in Film

One of the most amazing illusions is something we have all experienced many times—the "motion" in motion pictures. In reality, movies consist of a sequence of thousands of still photographs projected onto the screen at a rate so fast that the gaps in motion between each frame are imperceptible. We perceive movement in the smooth flow of images on the screen.

Illusions

Most of us have heard the expression "Seeing is believing," and we accept it as an accurate statement. In other words, if you see something, you can believe that it is really there. But the fact is that when you see something, it is not simply the result of your eyes passively recording something. Rather, it is the result of your brain's interpretation of the stimuli reaching your eyes. What you see may not be what is really there; it may be what your brain believes is there. These inaccurate perceptions are called **illusions.** So instead of "Seeing is believing," perhaps a more accurate expression would be "Believing is seeing." It is our beliefs, based on prior experience of the world "out there," that sometimes causes us to perceive something inaccurately.

Psychologists are interested in studying how people respond to illusions. These inaccurate perceptions, caused by our attempt to make sense of the world outside, can reveal useful clues about the functioning of our system of visual perception. Because there are so many kinds of visual illusions, researchers have not yet been able to come up with one theory that can explain them all. In addition to Rubin's reversible figure illusion (page 71), the following **five** illusions are those most often used by psychologists.

❶ The Muller-Lyer Illusion

Which line appears longer? Measure them. Psychologists theorize that we misperceive the lengths of the lines because of our years of experience with straight lines, sharp edges, and corners.

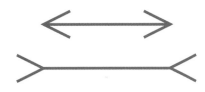

❷ The Ponzo Railroad Track Illusion

Which of the two horizontal bars on the railroad track is longer? Measure them. Why does the one on top appear larger?

CRITICAL THINKING

Do Some People Have ESP?

Researchers have conducted experiments designed to demonstrate whether or not extrasensory perception (ESP) exists in human beings. What do you think such experiments prove?

THE EXPERIMENT

Psychologist J. B. Rhine was interested in studying extrasensory perception. In 1933 he devised a special deck of cards. It consisted of 25 cards, each having one of five symbols on it—a star, three wavy lines, a circle, a square, or a cross. In one of his early experiments, he chose a subject, Pierce, who claimed to have ESP. He had Pierce attempt to identify the symbols on cards that were manipulated by an assistant in a building over 100 yards away. The assistant shuffled the cards and laid them facedown, one by one, so that the assistant himself did not see the symbol on the card. In 1,850 trials, Pierce scored 558 correct hits. Chance would have yielded 370 hits. The probability that Pierce would have identified by guesswork so many

cards above the chance expectation was less than one in a million times a million times a million times a million. Rhine believed he had demonstrated the existence of ESP, but many people remained skeptical. Over the years he carried out many ESP experiments. His critics pointed out that some of Rhine's experiments used badly printed cards on which a faint outline of the symbol showed through the back. At other times the experimenter knew the correct cards and may have unconsciously given subjects cues with his eyes, facial gestures, or lip movements. The performance of subjects on repeated tests has been inconsistent. So we are left with both believers in ESP and skeptics.

THE PROCESS

❶ **Restate the argument.** In your own words, explain what Rhine was attempting to demonstrate.

❷ **Provide evidence.** List the evidence from the experiments that *supports* Rhine's theory.

❸ **Give opposing arguments.** From the experiments and from your own experience, list the evidence that Rhine's theory was *not proven.*

❹ **Look for more information.** What else would you want to know before you decide whether ESP exists? Make a list of questions. Then research *J. B. Rhine* and *ESP* in an

encyclopedia, on the Internet, in the psychology section of a library, or in the index of a psychology reference book.

❺ **Evaluate the information.** Make a chart with two columns:

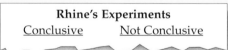

Rhine's Experiments	
Conclusive	Not Conclusive

Record the evidence and give each item a number from 1 to 5 to show its importance. Number 1 is most important.

❻ **Draw conclusions.** Write one paragraph explaining your thinking about the experiment.

③ The Necker Cube

There are two ways of seeing this cube. As you look at it, the cube suddenly seems to shift and another side seems closer to you. Then it shifts back again. Your brain is trying to decide which is the proper viewing angle, but not enough information is given for a conclusive interpretation.

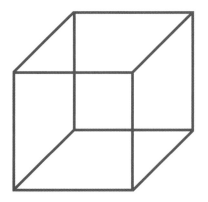

④ The Boring Figure

Designed by the American psychologist E. G. Boring, this ambiguous figure can alternately be seen as either a young girl or an old woman. Can you see them both?

⑤ The Ames Room

Designed by Albert Ames, this room appears to be a normal rectangular room when viewed from the front. But it is actually shaped so that the left corner is almost twice as far away from the viewer as the right corner. The viewer perceives the nearer person as being much larger than the other, although both are exactly the same height. The viewer has to decide if the room is an odd shape or if the people are odd sizes. Based on experience with the usual rectangular rooms, the viewer chooses the most probable interpretation—the people must be different sizes. This special room demonstrates that perception is an active process.

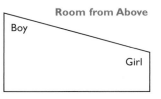

Room from Above

Boy

Girl

Observer

▲

This diagram above of the Ames Room reveals why the girl appears bigger than the boy.

Scientists do not fully understand how the brain processes incoming neural impulses to perceive the world. Perception, as opposed to mere sensation, is believed to involve a person's previous experience, memories, personal tastes, and expectations. Prior knowledge of perceptual constancies—such as size, shape, brightness, and color—helps us make sense of our environment. Scientists have proposed various theories to describe how perceptions are organized. Constructionists believe that the brain constructs a perception from a great many elementary sensations. The Gestalt psychologists believed that the brain perceives a stimulus as a whole, not as individual sensations. They proposed a series of Gestalt laws to describe the process. Our perception of depth involves certain bodily depth cues and pictorial depth cues. Our eyes sense motion in two ways—detecting movement and tracking movement. Illusions occur when we perceive something inaccurately.

Psychology

binocular cues—depth perception cues that require the use of two eyes. *p. 72*

constructionist view—theory that the brain constructs a perception out of a great many individual sensations. *p. 69*

difference threshold—degree of change in a stimulus necessary for a person to detect the difference. *p. 67*

figure-ground—separation of a pattern into a figure and a background; the figure is seen as being in front of the ground, which extends behind the figure. *p. 71*

Gestalt—organized whole shape or form. Gestalt psychologists developed principles of perceptual organization based on the brain's perception of a stimulus as a whole. *p. 69*

illusions—inaccurate perceptions. *p. 75*

induced movement—perception of movement of an object that is not moving; it can be caused by the movement of nearby objects. *p. 74*

monocular cues—depth perception cues that require only one eye to be processed. *p. 72*

perception—experience caused by stimulation of the senses. *p. 66*

psychophysics—study of behavioral aspects of a response to stimuli, such as absolute and difference thresholds. *p. 66*

signal-detection theory—theory for detecting sensory stimuli that takes into account not only the strength of the stimuli but also other elements such as one's mood and physical state. *p. 67*

CHAPTER 6

Consciousness

In this chapter, you will learn about:

- **how consciousness is described**
- **states of consciousness**
- **sleeping and dreaming**

Can we really explain why we do the things we do? Neuroscientist Michael Gazzaniga discovered that the conscious mind provides reasons for behavior that may not be real. Working with patients whose right and left brain hemispheres had been disconnected, Gazzaniga found that when a word such as laugh *was sent to the patient's right brain to process, the person would laugh. The patient's verbal left brain did not receive the message. However, when the patient was asked, "Why did you laugh?" the person responded with a logical reason, such as, "You guys are so funny." The left brain in this case made up a reason to explain the behavior.*

Consciousness consists of a complex collection of processes, such as waking consciousness, the subconscious, and the unconscious. In addition, there are various altered states of consciousness, such as daydreaming, meditation, drug-induced states, and perhaps hypnosis.

Sleeping and dreaming are among the most important states of consciousness—vital to the maintenance of one's health. Sleep disorders may affect the amount of sleep one gets or the psychological activity that occurs during dreaming. Fascinating and surprising information about consciousness continues to accumulate as research techniques improve.

What Is Consciousness?

What do you think of when you hear the word *consciousness?* A common definition of being conscious is being awake or aware, but science has a much more difficult time explaining what consciousness really is.

Consciousness may seem like a single experience. Yet, it is a highly complex phenomenon. It involves several physiological structures or processes and the interactions among them. We may understand the parts of the brain and nervous system that process sensory information, and we can trace the path that sensory information takes through the brain and into the centers of higher thought, but scientists don't agree on how those electrical signals result in our subjective experience of ourselves and the world.

We can observe events like chemical reactions and photosynthesis, but how can we study an internal experience such as consciousness? It is the scientist's challenge to understand the conscious mind. But how does a scientist get outside his or her own mental processes to study those same processes?

You can be conscious of a thought, a sensation, the behavior of others, and your own existence. For our purposes, we'll define **consciousness** as the awareness of one's self and one's environment.

Types of Conscious Experience

Here are some of the types of awareness that make up our consciousness.

* **External sensory perception** is awareness of sights, sounds, tastes, smells, and touch sensations in the environment.
* **Internal sensory perception** is the ability to internally experience sensory information from a remembered event or to create sensory representations of events we've never experienced, but only imagined.
* **Abstract awareness** involves the symbols we use to represent big ideas. We don't generally classify thoughts, ideas (about such things as freedom or peace), or emotions (such as disappointment or happiness) as sensory perceptions, yet we are conscious of them. Although we often describe or define such ideas without sensory references, some psychologists believe that we store everything in sensory images. These are often metaphors that carry the meaning of the more abstract term, such as an image of the Statue of Liberty for freedom or a feeling of relaxation or warmth for love.
* **Awareness of self** means you are aware of yourself as an individual apart from other individuals and objects in your environment. You not only have thoughts and feelings but are aware that you have them. You can have experiences and also observe these experiences from outside yourself. This is part of the puzzle of consciousness about which scientists theorize.

Early Ideas About Consciousness

One of the most influential ideas about consciousness arose in the seventeenth century with the French philosopher René Descartes. He concluded that the fact that he had thoughts proved his existence— "I think, therefore I am." Descartes believed in what is now called the mind vs. body duality, the idea that the mind was a separate entity, apart from the body. Even today, when scientists have discovered the biological basis of so many mental events and often insist that "the mind is what the brain does," we still sense the mind as something apart from the body.

During its early history in the eighteenth and nineteenth centuries, psychology frequently defined itself as the study of consciousness. But in the early twentieth century, William James questioned whether consciousness existed and suggested that there was no value in studying it because it couldn't be directly observed or measured. Behaviorist John Watson insisted that psychology "discard all references to consciousness," focusing instead solely on the observable behaviors of a person.

Levels of Consciousness

We typically think of consciousness in terms of what we are thinking or feeling at a particular moment in time. We may consciously work at a problem until we reach a solution. Yet sometimes ideas will pop into our minds—into our conscious awareness—fully formed. Where did these ideas come from? How were they processed?

Levels of Consciousness
Normal or Waking Consciousness
This state includes whatever we are aware of in the present. It can vary from daydreaming to intense concentration. Content is based, in part, on what we choose to attend to.
Subconscious
Thoughts, emotions, and behaviors are available to us, but not presently in our awareness. Some information is processed at this level of consciousness, such as the production and interpretation of language. Some theorists separate the subconscious into two subcategories. (Others simply use the term **subconscious** for both types of behaviors.)
In the **preconscious,** knowledge and memories are present in our minds but are not being accessed. For example: you can give your address if asked, but are unaware of that information unless your inner attention is directed toward it.
In the **nonconscious** are behaviors and thoughts that we process automatically, without conscious effort and sometimes without control. Examples include speaking, breathing, and blinking.
Unconscious
According to Freud, the **unconscious** mind contains desires, conflicts, or memories with which our conscious mind cannot easily deal. Although this theory is debatable, there does seem to be a part of the mind that serves as a well of resources, motives, or drives. When asked about some behaviors, we are often unable to explain clearly why we acted as we did. Freud would say that something in the unconscious was responsible for these behaviors.

Consciousness and Chronobiology

Chronobiology is the study of the effects of time on life processes. The timing of various biological events, including levels of consciousness, is regulated by a tiny piece of brain tissue, the suprachiasmatic nucleus (SCN), located near the intersection of the optic nerves from each eye. This **biological clock** programs activities in the body, such as changes in temperature and blood pressure, to occur at different times during a daily cycle. Biological clocks are almost always linked to some type of light-sensing cells. In other words, the amount of natural light influences each stage of each biological cycle.

Circadian Rhythms

Hundreds of the body's natural functions occur as cycles—from the time that you prefer to go to sleep and wake up to changes in body temperature, blood pressure, and hormone levels. These cycles are called **circadian rhythms.** *Circa dies* is Latin for "about a day." A circadian rhythm is a cycle that occurs in roughly a 25-hour period.

Each person has preferred circadian rhythms, particularly in the area of sleep. Some prefer to rise early and go to bed early—"early birds." Others prefer to rise later and go to bed later—"night owls." Many people experience a reduced alertness in early afternoon, related to decreased temperature and changes in hormone levels. In the circadian rhythm of temperature, many people's temperature reaches a low point at about 4 A.M.

Changes in Circadian Rhythms

If humans were permitted to establish a normal waking/sleep cycle in a cave into which no natural light could enter, they would settle into a free-running cycle of about 25 hours—the body's natural circadian rhythm. Because we normally live in a 24-hour cycle of light and darkness, our biological clocks set themselves to match that environment rather than the body's natural one. This is called **entrainment—the alteration of a natural cycle to fit a different rhythm.** Infants, who initially wake every couple of hours to be fed, gradually entrain their schedules to sleep through the night. Some changes in circadian rhythms can cause problems:

* *Shift Work.* Working during the hours when one would normally sleep may increase the risk of accidents and absenteeism and lead to poor job satisfaction, in addition to fatigue, stomach problems, and depression. Studies into the causes of the *Challenger,* Three Mile Island, Chernobyl, and *Exxon Valdez* disasters all found evidence of human error occurring on a night shift.
* *Jet Lag.* When you fly across a number of time zones, you may land where, locally, it is early morning. Your body, on a different geographical time, thinks it is bedtime. It may take several days to entrain to the new hours of daylight and darkness, during which time you may have difficulty sleeping at night and tend to be sluggish and unable to function as effectively as at home.

Altered States of Consciousness

While consciousness is often associated with a waking state, there are many variations on how aware or alert a person is or on the types of mental processes that may be going on in different levels of consciousness. States other than the common levels of consciousness are often called **altered states of consciousness**. Examples are shown in the accompanying table. In addition to the states described in the table, sleeping, dreaming, and a hypnotic state are also altered states of consciousness. These will be discussed in more detail later in this chapter.

Altered States of Consciousness			
State	**What Is It?**	**Effects/Uses**	**Other Issues**
Daydreaming	Fanciful imagery or unfocused thoughts that may be different from a person's reality.	Allows useful information from the subconscious to emerge and be processed. Enhances creativity. Can be a substitute for impulsive behavior. Can be restful in a stressful situation.	Problematic when time spent in daydreaming is excessive, when it is used frequently as an escape from reality, or when it interferes with normal, waking activities or responsibilities.
Drug-Induced State	The result of chemicals that alter the mental state, often through physiological changes and various effects on neurotransmitters in the brain. Stimulants (nicotine, amphetamines, and cocaine); depressants (alcohol, heroin); and hallucinogens (LSD and marijuana) all cause drug-induced states.	Some of these experiences are actually hallucinations or delusions—ideas that may seem real, but aren't, such as the ability to fly. Studies have shown that some drugs can permanently alter brain structure and/or chemistry, causing problems in later life.	Specific drugs will be discussed in Chapter 15. Some medications prescribed by doctors can reverse altered states of consciousness produced by mental illness. Improper use of prescription or illegal drugs is more likely to produce mental aberrations than to enhance mental processing.

more Altered States of Consciousness

State	What Is It?	Effects/Uses	Other Issues
Hallucination	Experiencing sights and sounds that do not occur. The person is unable to distinguish his or her perceptions from those produced by real experience.	In Western cultures, hallucinations are not considered useful because one is removed from reality and likely to make poor judgments. Some cultures value states in which people appear to access experiences outside of ordinary reality.	Hallucinations can arise from some mental illnesses, drug use, or through sensory deprivation—a situation in which incoming sensory information is greatly reduced.
Meditative State	A highly focused state of consciousness achieved by concentrating on a repetitive, peaceful stimulus (a sound or one's breathing).	Meditation can lower heart rate and blood pressure and alter metabolism and brain wave pattern. Can be used to counter stress.	The meditative state is entered consciously through deliberate relaxation.
State Induced by Biofeedback	The self-monitoring of one's physiological states to control certain bodily functions such as heart rate.	People can learn to reduce pain and tension by altering brain waves rather than by taking medication.	Some research indicates that biofeedback doesn't work as well under stressful (real-life) conditions as under controlled (laboratory) conditions.
Lucid Dreaming	Dreaming while you're aware that you're dreaming. One might control the direction of the dream. Lucid dreaming is learned through practice.	Can help overcome nightmares, provide rehearsal for waking experiences, and increase creativity and problem solving.	Studies have shown that lucidity was seven times more likely to make nightmares better than worse.

Sleep

Perhaps the most familiar altered state of consciousness and the most obvious circadian rhythm for us all is the state of sleep. The reasons why we sleep and dream are not well understood, although it is known that these functions are essential to our survival.

Why We Sleep

One way to explore reasons why we sleep is to observe what happens to people who have been deprived of sleep. Psychologists have recorded significant changes in body chemistry, perception, and the ability to think clearly and concentrate in those who go without sleep for several days.

Here are **three** theories about why we sleep:

1. **Physical and/or Mental Recuperation.** During sleep, the production of new cells is at its highest rate, and chemicals used up during the day in the brain and body are replenished.
2. **Consolidation of Thoughts and Experiences.** Although we think of sleep as down time for our conscious mind, the level of mental activity during some stages of sleep is extremely high. In fact, during some stages of sleep, some nerve cells fire five to ten times more quickly than during wakefulness!
3. **Adaptation.** Sleep is an adaptive behavior that kept our ancient ancestors quiet and unmoving during the hours of darkness, when predators were more likely to roam.

Stages of Sleep and Brain Waves

By monitoring brain waves, eye movement, and muscle tension during sleep, researchers have found that there are actually five stages of sleep—four nonrapid eye movement (NREM) stages and one **rapid eye movement (REM)** sleep stage. The average time it takes to move through the five stages is about 90 minutes. Therefore, we move through the cycle about five to six times each night.

The Stages of Sleep

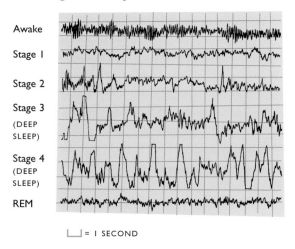

Awake
Stage 1
Stage 2
Stage 3 (DEEP SLEEP)
Stage 4 (DEEP SLEEP)
REM

⌞⌟ = 1 SECOND

The stages are based on differences in electrical activity of the brain, described in terms of the frequency and height or amplitude of the waves that are being produced at any moment in time. When you are awake and alert, your brain is producing *beta waves*—low amplitude waves with a frequency greater than 12 hertz (one wave per second). The table on the next page shows what happens during the stages of sleep.

The Stages of Sleep

Sleep Stages	Physiological Changes	Psychological Changes
Awake, but Drowsy	Body is relaxed, muscle tension low, heart rate slower than wakefulness.	Random, stream-of-consciousness thoughts and images—like light meditation.
NREM Stages		
Stage 1	Heart rate slows further and muscle tension decreases.	Light sleep, still in a transition phase. Sometimes associated with increased imagery.
Stage 2	Body relaxes further. Stages 1 and 2 together last about 30 minutes.	During this period, a person may talk in his or her sleep.
Stage 3	Transition into deep sleep. Stages 3 and 4 together last about 30 minutes and occur during the first 2 to 3 sleep cycles of the night.	Complete sleep. Somewhat difficult to awaken.
Stage 4	Considerable movement. Little perception of external sounds.	The person is deeply asleep and most difficult to awaken in this stage.
REM Sleep		
	About 90 minutes into the sleep cycle, people return quickly to Stage 1 and then begin REM sleep. In this state, people appear paralyzed, except for movement of the eyes.	When awakened from REM sleep, 85 percent to 90 percent of people report that they were dreaming and can recall contents of the dream. Periods of REM are longest during the last sleep cycles of the night.

Sleep Disorders

Sleep Apnea

* In one form, a person with sleep apnea experiences sudden and regular breathing stoppages during sleep.
* It is especially dangerous in young children. Devices may be used to signal parents when breathing has stopped.
* It is associated with snoring.

Sleepwalking

* Although deeply asleep, a sleepwalker may interact or talk with people.
* Sleepwalking occurs in NREM sleep.
* A person who is sleepwalking awakens with no memory of the activity.

Insomnia

* Insomnia is difficulty getting to sleep or staying asleep.
* A person with insomnia awakens unrefreshed, even after sufficient sleep.
* Causes of insomnia include diet, exercise patterns, sleeping environment, worry, or concern.

Hypersomnia

* A person with hypersomnia experiences chronic, excessive sleeping; irresistible drowsiness and napping during the day; and difficulty waking up.

SIDS

* Sudden Infant Death Syndrome (SIDS) is the sudden death of an infant under one year of age that remains unexplained after investigation.
* It is not technically a sleep disorder, although it often occurs when a child is sleeping.

REM Behavior Disorder

* A sleeper with REM behavior disorder may act out dream activity and in severe cases may endanger him or herself and others with movements.

Narcolepsy

* A person with narcolepsy falls asleep suddenly, unpredictably, and uncontrollably.
* It is thought to have a biological basis.
* The person may exhibit sudden loss of muscle control.

Night Terrors

* During night terrors, the sleeper will be terrified and may have eyes open but is not awake. When awakened, the person remains very frightened but in many cases does not remember why.
* Night terrors occur during NREM sleep Stage 4.

Nightmares

* Nightmares occur during REM sleep. Sleeper will often awaken and recall an apparently long and movielike frightening dream.

Sleep Deprivation

A recent poll by the National Sleep Foundation found that the average adult sleeps 6 hours and 58 minutes per night during the work week. Dr. Mary Carskadon of the Sleep Foundation is especially concerned about the sleep habits of children and teenagers. She says that teenagers need about 9.5 hours of sleep a night but get only 6.5 to 7.5. Because of the hormonal changes associated with puberty, the biological clocks of teens may not signal that it is time for sleep until 11 P.M. or later. Given that most teens must get up early for school, they are, according to Dr. Carskadon, ". . . among the most sleep-deprived in our society." Sixty percent of children ages 4 to 17 complained of feeling tired during the day. Data on automobile crashes show a high percentage of young drivers in sleep-related crashes. Dr. William Dement, head of the Sleep Disorders Center at Stanford University, warns that lack of sleep "is the most common brain impairment." Dr. Dement maintains that the national "sleep debt" is more important than the national monetary debt.

Dreaming

Although many people believe that dreams occur only during REM sleep, a significant percentage of people have also reported dreams when awakened during other sleep stages. However, REM dreams tend to be the longest and are primarily visual. Contrary to old views, a dream may take as long as the actual events would have taken and most dreams are about ordinary experiences and emotions.

People deprived of REM sleep often do not feel refreshed from sleep and often make up the deficit by having longer REM periods when they are allowed to sleep naturally.

Why We Dream

Scientists aren't certain why we dream. Freud suggested that dreams were the creations of the unconscious mind, producing in symbol what a person is unable to deal with consciously. Some contemporary theorists suggest that, during certain stages of sleep, neurons within the brain fire randomly. Dreams are the brain's attempt to make sense of the firings by weaving a story around them.

Have you ever watched a dog sleeping? Occasionally, although the dog's eyelids are closed, its eyes appear to be moving rapidly. The dog's paws may twitch and it may make sounds as if excited. Dreaming and REM sleep are as important for some animals as they are for humans, suggesting that the explanation for dreams may be biological, as well as psychological.

Dreaming and REM sleep have been shown to improve memory of information we try to learn just before retiring. Some theorists suggest that sleep and dreaming block out external stimuli that would require processing, thereby allowing the brain to consolidate information already there.

Although the functions of dreaming aren't fully known or understood, scientists do agree that REM sleep and dreaming are essential for good health. People deprived of this phase of sleep often feel as if they haven't had enough sleep and have difficulty concentrating.

What Do Dreams Mean?

Given that scientists are not even in agreement about whether dreams are psychological or biological, there are no reliable methods for interpreting dreams. Dreams may be random, they may be involved in consolidating information or in solving problems at the subconscious level, they may arise from the unconscious, or they may be responses to neural activity.

Sometimes, people feel that they understand the meaning behind a dream. Others worry about what a recurring dream may mean. But even if we are merely creating stories around random neural firings, it is likely that recent events or problems in our lives would be the most accessible in the production of those stories. Even when a reasonable interpretation is given for a dream, how would we be certain that it is correct?

CRITICAL THINKING

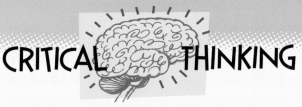

Why Do We Dream?

Some scientists believe that the reasons we dream are primarily psychological, while others believe they are primarily physiological. What can you find out?

THE ISSUES

Psychological Reasons for Sleep

Sigmund Freud believed that dreams reflected drives and wishes from the unconscious mind that people could not deal with when awake. Freud believed that because some wishes may be unacceptable or painful, they appeared in dreams as symbols. By interpreting these symbols, Freud tried to help a patient understand what his or her dreams really meant. People may dream about the same things, yet their dreams may have very different meanings.

Other psychologists believe that dreams are necessary to organize the day's experience and transfer it into permanent, long-term memory.

People often wake in the morning with answers to problems that seemed difficult the day before. When people have problems, they tend to sleep longer and have more dreams.

Physiological Reasons for Sleep

Those who believe that dreams are necessary for physiological reasons point to research with people who are awakened as soon as they enter REM sleep and are thus deprived of dreaming. The next day, these people often feel tired and unable to concentrate and report that their thinking is unclear. If allowed to sleep normally the next night, they will spend more time in REM sleep as if trying to catch up.

Some researchers suggest that the body physically recuperates during dreams and produces more of the biochemicals we use up during waking hours.

THE PROCESS

❶ **Restate the issues.** In your own words, state the two types of reasons.

❷ **Provide evidence.** From your own experience and from the information above, list the evidence that *supports* each of the theories.

❸ **Give opposing arguments.** From your own experience and from the information above, list evidence *against* each of the theories.

❹ **Look for more information.** What else would you like to know about why we dream? Make a list of your questions and search the Internet or the library for answers.

Include other ideas, such as animal dreams, how dreams occur in cycles, and immobilization of muscles during REM sleep.

❺ **Evaluate the information.** Put a plus sign beside the items in your lists that are the strongest pieces of evidence. Underscore the questions you think are most important.

❻ **Draw conclusions.** Write one paragraph explaining your answer to the question "Why do people dream?"

Hypnosis

Hypnosis is a process that allows a person to enter a trancelike state during which time he or she becomes highly suggestible. Encouraging a person to focus on a single stimulus and to relax may induce a hypnotic trance. With practice, many people can enter a light hypnotic trance on their own.

Some psychologists claim that hypnosis is not truly an altered state. It may simply be a relaxed and highly focused state. Others argue that a hypnotic state is very different from sleep or waking states, but brain wave analysis doesn't always support this argument. On an EEG, hypnotized people have much the same pattern as those in a normal, relaxed state of consciousness.

The hypnotic state has **five** qualities:

① Heightened Suggestibility

The person has a tendency to see, hear, or otherwise perceive what the hypnotist suggests. He or she may think or do what he or she is told but will generally not do things that are against his or her basic beliefs or moral code.

② Dissociation

Some theorists suggest that a hypnotized person becomes dissociated, or separated, from the sensations connected to external reality. Someone suffering from the emotions of a traumatic event may be able to talk about it and work through the problems associated with it. A person who can dissociate from the pain of a physical illness may experience relief.

③ Vivid Imagery

A person who is told that a pungent liquid such as ammonia is actually perfume will experience it as such. People may be led to believe that real objects don't exist or that imagined ones do.

④ Enhanced Memory

A person might mentally return to past events and describe these events in detail. These events might not be recalled in a waking state and they have not been proven to be more accurate than those recalled while awake.

⑤ Posthypnotic Suggestion

Suggestions made to a person during an hypnotic trance that may remain after the trance are called **posthypnotic suggestions.** This technique is often used to help people quit smoking, eat in a more healthy manner, or manage pain. However, posthypnotic suggestions tend to fade over time and must be periodically renewed to remain effective. There is, therefore, no evidence that hypnosis is more effective than other methods of behavior modification.

Some psychologists argue that people who are willing to be hypnotized are highly suggestible. They believe that any changes that occur as a result of hypnosis are the result of self-deception. In any event, some people do achieve their goals. Psychologists agree that, because of the potential for unexpected reactions, hypnosis should always be done by a trained professional.

Hypnosis and Market Research

Hal Goldberg, a consumer-behavior specialist, has a new use for hypnosis. Goldberg spent more than 20 years in the marketing business trying to determine the real reasons why people purchase specific brands. He realized that people in focus groups often gave him the information that they thought he wanted to hear or that might make them look good in the eyes of other group members.

Goldberg now runs focus group sessions with small groups of consumers who agree to be hypnotized. Under hypnosis, consumers appear less inhibited by what others might think.

"Imagine the last time you bought a sandwich spread in the grocery store. Do you see any brands?" asks Goldberg.

The consumer names one.

"And why did you buy that one?"

Goldberg then questions the consumer about the real reasons why the consumer chose that brand and about what factors in the packaging or advertising made the difference.

This is a type of qualitative research that focuses on individual thinking processes rather than on group tendencies. Manufacturers and advertisers have found it very helpful in their decision-making processes.

Hypnosis and Memory

Do people really recall more under hypnosis? Are repressed memories more likely to come to the surface when a person is in a hypnotic state of consciousness? Are these memories more accurate than waking memories? Despite the dramatic portrayals on TV shows, studies have shown that people who are not hypnotized are just as likely as people in a hypnotic trance to recall the details of a crime. Perhaps of more importance is that hypnotized people are just as likely to report incorrectly on what happened as those who are not hypnotized.

Age Regression Under Hypnosis

It is a common belief that memories of unpleasant events earlier in one's life can be more easily recalled under hypnosis. People might even act the age that they were asked to "go back to" in a process called *age regression.* However, research has demonstrated that people are not truly acting that age. They are acting the way an adult believes someone that age would act. Further, the memories that they recall are a mixture of fact and fantasy. The slightest hint in the tone of voice of the hypnotist can influence the answers of a hypnotized person. If the hypnotist asks, "Did something bad happen?" the suggestible person will agree that it did. For this reason, most courts today do not accept testimony acquired under hypnosis.

It is possible that more detail is recalled by some people under hypnosis simply because they are focused on a memory, rather than being distracted by outside thoughts. Further, our memories are only as good as they were at their formation. Many children misinterpret the meaning of certain actions and keep that misinterpretation in their memory. The recalled memory will still possess the faulty interpretation. In general, memories recalled under hypnosis have not been proven to be more accurate than those recalled while awake.

Current Theories of Consciousness

Theories about the nature of consciousness are plentiful. Psychologists and philosophers hotly debate everything from the definition of consciousness to whether animals are conscious. Newer theories of consciousness are described in books such as *Consciousness Explained* by Daniel Dennett, *How the Mind Works* by Steven Pinker, and *The Feeling of What Happens* by Antonio Damasio.

Damasio suggests that we actually have **two** types of consciousness:

❶ Core Consciousness

This type is that which gives one a sense of self in the here and now. It is a simple biological phenomenon that need not be exclusively human and doesn't depend on memory, language, or reasoning.

❷ Extended Consciousness

This type is that which "provides an organism with an elaborate sense of self—an identity and a person . . . and places that person at a point in individual historical time, richly aware of the lived past and of the anticipated future" and aware of the world outside of itself.

Damasio's is only one of many theories that attempt to explain what makes us human—and what gives us the awareness that we are human.

Consciousness is awareness of one's self and one's environment. It includes external awareness and an inner awareness that allows people to monitor and reflect on their thoughts and emotions. Consciousness includes waking consciousness, the subconscious, and the unconscious.

Altered states of consciousness are those other than normal waking consciousness. They include daydreaming, meditation, the state induced by biofeedback, hallucination, lucid dreaming, and drug-induced states.

Perhaps the most important altered state of consciousness is sleep, which includes dreaming. During sleep, a person passes through five different stages of brain activity. Hypnosis is an altered state that involves a suggestible, trancelike state.

Psychology WORDS TO KNOW

altered state of consciousness—state other than normal waking consciousness. *p. 84*

biological clock—structure within the brain that programs activities in the body to occur at different times during a daily cycle. *p. 83*

chronobiology—study of the effects of time on life processes. *p. 83*

circadian rhythm—cycle that occurs in roughly a 25-hour period. *p. 83*

consciousness—awareness of one's self and one's environment. *p. 80*

entrainment—alteration of a natural cycle to fit a different rhythm. *p. 83*

hypnosis—process wherein a person enters a trancelike state characterized by heightened suggestibility. *p. 92*

nonconscious—state in which we process behaviors and thoughts "automatically," without conscious effort and sometimes without control. *p. 82*

posthypnotic suggestion—suggestion made during hypnosis that remains when the person returns to normal consciousness. *p. 92*

preconscious—knowledge and memories that are present in the mind but are not being accessed. *p. 82*

rapid eye movement (REM)—stage of sleep in which there is rapid eye movement and during which dreams occur. *p. 86*

subconscious—below the level of waking consciousness. *p. 82*

unconscious—sum of wishes, memories, motives, or drives that influence behavior but are not consciously perceived. *p. 82*

CHAPTER 7

Learning

In this chapter, you will learn about:

- **how learning is defined**
- **theories of conditioning**
- **theories of cognitive and social learning**

In the early 1900s, Russian physiologist Ivan Pavlov was studying the role of the salivary glands in digestion. While measuring the amount of saliva produced in the mouths of dogs when various foods and other substances were placed in their mouths, he noticed something interesting. The dogs began salivating even before the food was placed in their mouths. In fact, they began salivating when the researchers approached them. Although Pavlov's main interest at that time was digestion, he was so fascinated with this observation that he wanted to understand why it occurred. The modern study of "learning" had begun.

Pavlov observed that animals learned to respond to a signal when it was associated with something to which the animal normally responded, such as food. The responses that an animal or person normally has to something in the environment became a key part of the study of learning.

Today, there are many different theories about how humans learn. While each theory focuses on a different aspect of learning, scientists are coming to realize that learning is a complex process involving many different factors.

The Study of Learning

Shipbuilders often build and test a model ship before constructing the "real thing." For a model to be of much use, it must be built of the same materials as the actual ship. An animal salivating at a signal associated with food helps us to understand how people learn because it provides a model of learned behavior.

Scientists observe learning in animals as a model for human learning. But to make this model valid, researchers must identify the same behavior in the animal as the human behavior they wish to understand. For example, animals can act as good models for many behaviors, such as simple learning, but they aren't good models to study why humans cry at a sad movie or laugh at a comedian's joke.

What Is Learning?

Learning is a word used to describe a category of behavior. The sorts of behaviors that fit into that category may be as different as learning to solve quadratic equations and learning to respond to a facial expression. Animals learn to respond to their names or to simple commands. Clearly, no one explanation will be found—no single process will be identified—to account for all types of learning.

Just as there are many types of learning, so there are many theories attempting to explain it. There are even disagreements about what the word *learning* means. With that said, how should we define it?

Learning is a relatively permanent change in behavior that results from practice or experience. Let's break down that definition to see why each word is important.

* *Behavior* can demonstrate learning. You might have learned a great deal about how to drive a car before you were old enough to drive—just by watching. Only after you took the wheel were the things you'd learned reflected in your behavior. Before that, it was potential behavior.
* *Change* is physiological in that new connections between neurons are formed or different chemicals are produced.
* *Relatively permanent* behavior means that there might be some variance in how you behave, but overall the change in behavior is permanent. States such as fatigue or a strong motivation might make you change your behavior on a particular occasion. If you revert to your normal behavior later, it isn't learning.
* *Practice* and *experience* are terms that are used to rule out changes that occur because of maturation or aging. A child removes something from a high shelf when he or she has grown tall enough to reach the shelf, not because he or she has learned to reach it. An older person's handwriting may change if arthritis produces pain in the hand—not because the person has learned a different writing method.

Two more terms are fundamental to an understanding of learning. A **stimulus** is some action that produces activity in an organism. A stimulus can be anything perceived by the senses, such as a smell, taste, or touch. It can also be a more complex action, such as a baby's cry or the smile on someone's face. A **response** is the reaction of an organism to a stimulus.

Aristotle's Laws of Association

Although Ivan Pavlov is credited with the beginnings of modern studies of learning, the idea underlying his work was suggested in the fourth century B.C. by the Greek philosopher Aristotle. Aristotle developed what he called laws of association. **Associations** are mental connections between two stimuli. Aristotle's laws state:

* Experience or recall of one object will produce a recall of objects that are similar or of opposite nature.
* Experience or recall of one object will produce a recall of things that were originally experienced at the same time.
* The more often two things are experienced together, the more likely it is that experiencing one will stimulate production or recall of the second.

Ivan Pavlov and His Dogs

Ivan Pavlov's research on digestion was already in the process of earning him a Nobel Prize when he became fascinated with the question of how dogs learned to associate various stimuli with an expectation of food. Pavlov is credited with the development of **classical conditioning,** which is learning through the association of a stimulus and response.

Pavlov recognized from the beginning that controlling the variables would be extremely difficult because dogs are so easily distracted by sounds and movement. He built a fortlike laboratory surrounded by a straw-filled trench to muffle sound. Once satisfied that he had limited any possible stimuli other than those being tested, he began his experiment.

Pavlov arranged his experiment in an attempt to limit the variables to the ones he wanted to observe. The dogs were strapped into a loose-fitting harness to reduce movement. A tube carried the dog's saliva to a measuring device.

Natural Response

Because salivating is the first step in the digestive process, it seems natural that the smell or taste of food would cause the dog's salivary glands to produce saliva. This natural response is called the **unconditioned response (UCR).** No condition or training is necessary to produce it, and it is involuntary. The food that produces the unconditioned response is called the **unconditioned stimulus (UCS).**

When Pavlov's students noticed that the dogs salivated in response to things other than food, such as the approach of the researcher, Pavlov tried to produce this response. He presented the dogs with an arbitrary stimulus that had nothing to do with food, such as a bell or buzzer. The dogs responded with an expectant "What is it?" look or perking up of the ears. Then, Pavlov paired the stimulus with the presentation of food within a few seconds. He did this repeatedly, eventually presenting just the bell without the food. The dogs salivated anyway.

Conditioned Stimulus and Response

When the sound and the food were paired, the dogs had learned to associate the sound with food. The involuntary response to food—salivating—was then transferred to the sound. Because the response was conditional on the experience of hearing the sound and being presented with food, it was called a **conditioned response (CR).** The sound that caused the response was the **conditioned stimulus (CS).**

When you react to someone's extended hand by reaching out your own to shake hands, you are demonstrating classical conditioning. Clearly, the animal model demonstrates a type of learning that is shared by humans.

"HE SALIVATES."

John Watson and "Little Albert"

John Watson, founder of behaviorism, believed that researchers ought to look for practical applications of conditioning. In a 1920 study, Watson tried to determine if he could condition an infant to experience the emotion of fear.

Watson presented the infant, known as "Little Albert," with a white rat. Unafraid, Albert wanted to play with the rat. Thereafter, every time he presented the rat, Watson immediately followed with a loud noise. On the eighth trial and those following, as soon as the rat appeared, Albert began to cry and try to crawl away. Later tests showed that Albert had generalized his fear to other white, fuzzy objects including a white rabbit and a white fur coat.

Watson had demonstrated that fear could be conditioned. But was his study ethical?

Pavlov's Observations

Convinced that in classical conditioning an organism learned to associate two stimuli and that this was what constituted learning, Pavlov continued to experiment to test the limits of conditioning. He and his followers explored **four** areas:

1. **Time Between CS and UCS.** When you feel a shock (the UCS), you involuntarily pull your finger back (the UCR). If a researcher is trying to condition you to pull your finger back in response to a sound (the CS), should the sound come before, during, or after the shock to produce a CR to the sound itself? Tests show that the sound should precede the shock by no more than .5 second to produce the strongest conditioned response.

After a number of trials, the sound alone produces the finger withdrawal. Apparently, the CS acts as a warning of the upcoming UCS. Does this make sense? If you were driving along and approached a dangerous intersection, would you want a warning sign to be placed way before the intersection, just before it, in the middle of it, or after it?

2. **Repetition.** Not surprisingly, the more often the CS and UCS are paired, the stronger the conditioned response. However, the greatest learning comes within the first set of repetitions, with each successive set showing less effect.

3. **Extinction.** If, after conditioning, the CS is presented repeatedly without the UCS, the CR eventually fades. This is called extinction. Extinction makes adaptive

sense. If an animal learns to associate a particular spot in the jungle with a predator it had once seen there and the predator never returned, it wouldn't be particularly useful for the animal to avoid that spot forever. Evolutionary theory suggests that extinction is a trait that was passed on in the genes of the most successful animals.

4. **Generalization and Discrimination.** In the real world, if you get an allergic reaction to tomatoes, you may avoid spaghetti sauce or pizza as well. As long as the CS is similar enough to the one learned, the CR will continue to occur. This is called stimulus generalization. Generalization is not always useful. A person who is afraid of tigers should be able to tell the difference between tigers and kittens. This is stimulus discrimination.

Applications of Classical Conditioning

Psychologists who work with individual clients sometimes use the principles of classical conditioning to help their clients. For example, if a child wets the bed at night, it is because the filling of the bladder doesn't wake him or her as it should. The child's bed might be wired so that the first hint of moisture causes a loud sound that wakes her. The filling of the bladder (CS) that initially didn't result in a response becomes associated with the sound (UCS) and the response of waking up (UCR).

Here are **three** ways in which classical conditioning can be used.

1. **Counterconditioning.** It's difficult to feel pleasure and fear at the same time. If a child fears small animals, a psychologist may present the child with a small animal at the same time that the child receives a favorite food. The child learns to pair the food with the appearance of the animal, replacing the fear with expectation of pleasure. This method of changing a negative response to a positive one is called counterconditioning.

2. **Flooding.** A client who fears being out among people (agoraphobia) tends to spend more and more time alone. Thus, he or she is never around people long enough to experience extinction of the fear response through discovery that most people are harmless. In flooding, the person is forced into contact with the feared stimulus to demonstrate the relative harmlessness of the stimulus. When the agoraphobic realizes that no harm occurs in the presence of people, the phobia may extinguish. One drawback to flooding is that, in some people, the fear is so great that further exposure to the stimulus makes it even worse.

3. **Desensitization.** If a client has a phobia of spiders, the therapist might use a sequence of events to gradually reduce the client's response to spiders. They might begin by looking at photos of spiders, then observing them at a distance, and finally up close. This method is called desensitization.

Operant Conditioning

In **operant conditioning,** a behavior is learned in connection with reward or punishment. Whenever you do something because you expect to receive some type of reward for the behavior (or avoid doing something to avoid punishment), you are demonstrating operant conditioning.

Thorndike and Trial-and-Error Learning

In early studies, E. L. Thorndike placed an animal, such as a cat, in a "puzzle box." The box contained a number of devices such as poles or chains. One of these devices, when clawed by the cat, would open the door to the box.

After clawing at the bars and other parts of the cage in an effort to get out, the cat began clawing at other things within the cage. When it clawed the key device, the door opened, and the cat left the box and got a food reward. After a number of trials, the cats stopped trying all of the unsuccessful behaviors and immediately clawed the door-opening device.

This trial-and-error learning, or what Thorndike called "selecting and connecting," is one example of operant conditioning.

Skinner's Research

B. F. Skinner, perhaps the most famous of the behaviorist psychologists, built on Thorndike's ideas and suggested that there were two types of behavior. The first, *respondent behavior,* like the UCR in classical conditioning, responds to some known stimulus and is involuntary.

The second type of behavior Skinner called *operant behavior.* Unlike respondent behavior, operant behavior represents a voluntary action on the part of the organism. Choosing to read a particular page in a book or to move one's hands is operant behavior.

Rather than study the stimulus that produced a response (behavior), Skinner preferred to study what happened next—whether the behavior would be repeated, and why. Skinner used reinforcement in his studies of behavior. **Reinforcement** is any event that encourages or discourages repetition of a behavior. It is the key to operant conditioning.

▲
1933 photograph of B. F. Skinner at work in the lab.

Operant Conditioning and Behavior	
Operant Conditioning to Encourage Behavior	**Operant Conditioning to Discourage Behavior**
Positive reinforcement—Following a behavior with something considered pleasant to encourage repetition of the behavior.	**Punishment I**—Discouraging a behavior by following it with unpleasant consequences, such as paying a fine for breaking the law.
Negative reinforcement—Following a behavior by stopping or taking away something unpleasant. It's important to note that this is not punishment because it results in a positive experience for the subject.	**Punishment II**—Discouraging a behavior by withholding something that is pleasurable, such as being "grounded" for staying out too late.

Principles of Operant Conditioning

* Any response that is followed by a reinforcing stimulus tends to be repeated.
* A stimulus is considered reinforcing when it increases the rate of an operant response.

What sort of action will be perceived as a reward and therefore a reinforcement? An employee who is "rewarded" for his or her efforts by receiving extra vacation time may perceive the reward as punishment if he or she is a workaholic who prefers to work rather than take time off. One way to identify reinforcements is to observe people and determine what stimuli increase the rate at which they perform a behavior.

Primary and Secondary Reinforcements

* *Primary Reinforcement.* In a typical Skinner experiment, when an animal (rat or pigeon) presses a lever, it receives food. A reinforcing stimulus that is tied to some aspect of survival—such as food, water, or a sense of security—is called a primary reinforcement. Primary reinforcements provide the strongest motivation to learn.
* *Secondary Reinforcement.* Money isn't essential to survival, but it is often associated with something that is, such as the ability to purchase food or shelter. Praise from an adult is linked to the need for love or acceptance and a sense of security. Money and praise are examples of secondary reinforcements.

Changes in Operant Conditioning

As in classical conditioning, the conditioned response in operant conditioning can undergo several different kinds of changes:

* *Generalization.* Jerry is really interested in math. He finds that he gets good grades on his math tests whether he studies or not. Jerry generalizes, believing that he can get good grades on any test without studying.

* **Discrimination.** When he fails his science and English tests, Jerry learns to discriminate. He learns to tell the difference between classes in which the behavior of not studying brings a reward and those in which it doesn't. His interest in math apparently made it unnecessary for him to study, but only in math.

* **Extinction.** If Jerry begins to get poor grades in math as well as other subjects, he may have to study for all tests because he now experiences punishment for the behavior of not studying. The conditioned response has undergone extinction.

Shaping

A common children's game involves hiding an object and having the child try to find it. One reinforcing method that parents often use is to tell the child, "You're getting warmer," as the child approaches the hiding place of the object. The phrase acts as reinforcement to keep the child looking.

When teaching an animal or a human a task more complex than simply pressing a lever for food, this same method is used. The learner is at first rewarded for any behavior that approximates the desired behavior. When teaching a small child to swing a bat at a baseball, any movement of the bat is initially rewarded with praise. As the learning proceeds, the child is rewarded only for swinging the bat more and more "correctly" until finally connecting with the ball—the desired behavior.

This process is called *shaping*—a method of refining a behavior by reinforcing behaviors that approximate it more and more closely. Shaping is particularly useful when a behavior is not something that an organism already does.

Chaining

Skinner believed that even in a complex series of behaviors, each is learned through conditioning. He was able to teach rats to perform a series of tasks, such as pressing a lever to release a ball, picking up the ball, and dropping it into a tube to release food. Each step was taught separately and then they were linked together in a process called *chaining*.

Dogs trained as companion animals for people with various disabilities are taught using a combination of shaping and chaining. Praise from their trainer or owner is often the only reinforcement needed.

"WHEN YOU SIT DOWN, YOU GET A SHOCK. OPEN A BOOK, YOU GET A SHOCK. WRITE SOMETHING, ANOTHER SHOCK. IT'S A TYPICAL PSYCHOLOGY CLASS."

Schedules of Reinforcement

How often must a person receive reinforcement for a behavior to continue? Every time the behavior occurs? In nature, that's unlikely. Animals don't always find food when they search a certain location, but they must continue to look. Workers aren't rewarded or praised for every job they do, even if they've all done well. Different schedules of reinforcement used in operant conditioning have different effects on behavior.

Schedules of Reinforcement		
Type of Reinforcement	**Example**	**Effect**
Fixed-interval (FI) schedule	Each day at 7 P.M., you turn on the radio to hear your favorite program. Your behavior is reinforced by hearing that program only if you turn on the radio at that time.	In this form of reinforcement, the person learns to engage in the behavior only when the appropriate interval has passed.
Variable-interval (VI) schedule	If a teacher walks around the room, randomly giving praise for various behaviors, the reinforcement to any one student's behavior occurs at different intervals.	In general, this results in the steadiest rate of responding—in this case, good behavior. One never knows when the pleasurable response—the praise—will come, so one is on good behavior most of the time.
Fixed-ratio (FR) schedule	A worker must produce 30 parts per hour to meet a quota that determines his or her pay.	The person engages in the behavior fairly consistently, with a brief rest after each reward.
Variable-ratio (VR) schedule	A person playing a slot-machine is rewarded only occasionally and after different numbers of "handle pulls."	To ensure the highest rate of reinforcement (wins), the player pulls the handle as fast as possible. Even if the machine never again pays off, the person keeps trying longer than on a machine on which he or she had never won in the first place.

The Biology of Conditioning

Some biological factors are important when looking at conditioning. Here are **two** examples.

1. **Taste Aversions.** Animals and humans often develop a dislike for a particular food when eating that food resulted in nausea or illness. On the surface, it looks like conditioning. However, conditioning generally requires repeated trials, while taste aversions occur after only one. This is called *biological preparedness.*

Learning to avoid a food that has made you ill is an adaptive behavior. If an animal required several trials to learn to associate the food and illness, it might not survive and reproduce.

2. **Instinctual Drift.** A raccoon instinctively washes its food before eating it. In one study, raccoons were taught to drop a coin in a slot to receive food. As the connection between the coin and food became stronger, the raccoons began washing the coins! Recognizing that such behaviors occur can help researchers avoid errors in their data and conclusions.

CRITICAL THINKING

Should Operant Conditioning Be Used to Control Behavior?

Wilhelm Wundt, the founder of experimental psychology, once berated his own students for their attempts to use what they were learning about the mind. He maintained that research should be used solely to understand the mind, not to manipulate it. You decide.

THE ISSUES

In 1956 behaviorist B. F. Skinner and humanistic psychologist Carl Rogers debated the issues of using what they had discovered about operant conditioning and learning to control human behavior. Skinner argued that people are already responding to the stimuli in their environment, so why not use what we know to affect them in some positive way. He wanted to apply conditioning principles to move people toward more appropriate behaviors. He saw this as enabling them to have better lives and more personal happiness. Principles of operant conditioning are used today in therapy to help people overcome phobias and anxieties and to assist in changing other undesirable behaviors.

On the other side, Rogers argued that such use of conditioning requires someone who must decide what "appropriate behaviors" are. Who, Rogers asked, can be trusted to make those decisions for someone else, since even researchers' behaviors are their personal responses to their own environments? Rogers maintained that we shouldn't be trying to shape people's futures and control their behaviors, but rather be trying to make them aware that they could assume their own control of those things.

Should operant conditioning be used to control behavior?

THE PROCESS

1. **Restate the issues.** In your own words, state the nature of the disagreement.

2. **Provide evidence.** From your own experience and from the information above, list the evidence *for* the use of operant conditioning to control human behavior.

3. **Give opposing arguments.** From your own experience and from the information above, list the evidence *against* the use of operant conditioning to control human behavior.

4. **Look for more information.** What else would you like to know before you decide? Make a list of your questions. On the Internet, in the psychology section of the library, or in the index of psychology books, research ways in which *operant conditioning* is used. Look up *behavioral psychology*.

5. **Evaluate the information.** Make a chart with two columns:

Using Conditioning to Control Behavior	
For	Against

   Record the arguments in each column and rank each column of arguments in importance from 1 to 5, with 1 as the most important.

6. **Draw conclusions.** Write one paragraph supporting your answer to the question "Should operant conditioning be used to control behavior?" Be sure to provide reasons.

More Than Conditioning

Several researchers have pointed out some behaviors that the theory of conditioning didn't seem to explain. In these cases, what goes on between the stimulus and response or between the behavior and the reinforcement?

Latent Learning

Edward Tolman suggested that as individuals interact with the environment, they form associations when two different stimuli are present. People might notice that whenever they respond in a certain way to a particular stimulus, a new stimulus appears. This leads to certain expectations about what behaviors will lead to changes in the environment. Tolman argued that organisms form **cognitive maps** of these associations, storing them for later use. Mice that explore a maze freely, but without reinforcement, later ran the maze more quickly for a food reward than mice who had never seen it before. Tolman called this *latent learning* because what they had learned was not obvious until it was needed.

Insight Learning

Wolfgang Kohler placed chimpanzees in a cage with bananas suspended from the ceiling. Also in the cage were several boxes. After trying all possible methods of jumping or climbing, the chimps seemed to study the boxes. Eventually, they would stack them beneath the bananas, climb up, and get the bananas. Clearly, this was more than Thorndike's trial-and-error and couldn't easily be explained by stimulus-response or reinforcement. Kohler referred to this type of learning as *insight learning*.

Cognitive Theories of Learning

With Tolman's and Kohler's experiments, psychology reached beyond behaviorist explanations into the realm of mental processes—cognitive psychology. **Cognition** includes such processes as thinking, memory formation, learning, and problem solving. One source lists nearly fifty different learning theories, most of them cognitive in approach. We'll address **two** of the major approaches.

❶ The Work of Jean Piaget

The work of French psychologist Jean Piaget is often considered to be the beginning of the great interest in cognitive psychology. Piaget's theory suggests that mental abilities develop as a function of biological development and experience. One major point in Piaget's theory involves the concept of the **schema,** a pattern that is recognized in experience or complex reality that helps to explain or deal with it. Similar to cognitive maps, schemas contain information about objects, actions, events, relationships, or just about anything pertaining to a particular content. You might have a schema for your morning routine, for dealing with parents, or for driving a car.

Piaget believed that children are born with a few schemas already in place—reflexes that allow them to suck, reach, look, and grasp. As a child begins to explore the world using these schemas, they develop more complex cognitive structures. The child becomes more dependent on thinking than on reflexive behavior. Piaget proposed that, at any stage of development, the child is dependent on the schemas he or she has available.

Piaget recognized a person's need to have his schemas match what goes on in the world. As we interact with the world, some experiences fit, and others don't. *Assimilation* is understanding something new in terms of existing schemas. We simply recognize or know about the new experience without questions.

When something isn't explained by our existing schemas, we are forced to modify or add to the cognitive structure so that it is capable of assimilating the new experience. This is called *accommodation*—roughly the same as learning.

❷ Information Processing Approach

Current technology is often used to understand processes in other fields. At one time, the brain/mind was described in terms of a telephone switchboard with a central "operator" making appropriate connections. It should come as no surprise that one new theory explains learning in computer terms.

Input and Output

In the field of human information processing (HIP), psychologists use terms familiar to computer users to explain human learning. They use *input* in place of *stimulus* and *output* in place of *response* or *behavior*. A primary interest of cognitive psychologists is what goes on between input and output. HIP psychologists describe Piaget's schemas in computer terms such as *storage, encoding, processing, capacity, programs,* and *subroutines.*

HIP psychologists may outline what they believe goes on in the brain/mind on flow charts similar to those written for computer programs. Here's an example showing how visual input, after associating with information from existing schemas, results in the output of identifying an apple. The diagram focuses on biological factors in processing, as each step involves a structure within the nervous system. Other flowcharts might focus on other types of processes.

Biological Factors in Processing

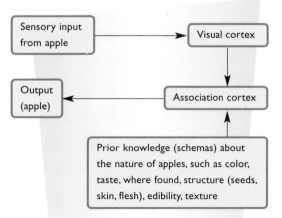

Factors Affecting Learning

In the HIP approach, a number of different factors have been identified as affecting learning.

Meaningfulness. Words or ideas that have personal meaning are learned more readily than those that are meaningless.

Transfer. At one time, psychologists believed that studying a difficult subject, such as Latin, would develop the mind's "mental muscles" and enable people to learn other subjects more easily. Although no support was found for this idea, information learned in one situation will transfer to another situation to the extent that the situations are similar. Latin may help you to understand word meanings in English, but it will not help you to understand algebra. To promote the greatest transfer, some cognitive theorists recommend what they call *situated learning*. This means learning a subject, such as math or science, as it is found in the world rather than as a theoretical body of knowledge.

Chemical Influences. Among the many chemicals that can affect learning, two of the most important are stimulants and depressants. Stimulants, such as the caffeine in colas or coffee, increase the production of brain chemicals and may allow for more rapid learning. However, too much of a stimulant, such as an amphetamine, will actually overstimulate the brain and cause loss of learning. Depressants, such as alcohol, reduce the firing of nerve cells and the potential for learning. In some cases, having a level of a chemical in their bodies can help people to recall something they learned under the influence of the same level of that chemical.

The TOTE Model of HIP

Cognitive psychologist George A. Miller proposed a theory that he believed should replace stimulus-response as the fundamental unit of behavior. It is called the TOTE model—Test, Operate, Test, Exit.

A TOTE unit consists of a goal and the behaviors necessary to achieve that goal. Let's say that your goal is to drive a nail into a piece of wood with a hammer. You first *test* to see if the nailhead is flush with the surface. If it isn't, you *operate* by hitting the nail with the hammer. This Test-Operate-Test sequence continues until the nailhead is even with the surface. At that point, you *exit*—stop hammering.

Do you know anyone who takes forever to decide what to order at a restaurant? Miller would say that the person's *exit* strategy is flawed. That is, he or she doesn't have a clear goal in mind that signals the end of the process. Does the diner want a light meal, a good-tasting meal, a food to really enjoy, or one that is filling? The person keeps running through all of these possibilities until, eventually, time becomes the exit goal.

Social or Observational Learning

Albert Bandura believes that organisms learn both by *direct experience* (doing something and experiencing the consequences) and *vicarious experience* (observing the outcome of the behavior of others). According to Bandura, observational learning, or what we learn by watching others, is of equal importance to what we learn through personal experience.

In the 1960s, Bandura demonstrated that children could learn aggression by observing aggressive behavior. Bandura had groups of children observe adults interacting with "Bobo," a smiling, life-sized plastic figure with a weighted bottom. The children observed an adult punching and hitting Bobo, which kept bobbing up with a smile on its face.

Then, one group saw the adult praised and rewarded for the aggressive behavior, a second group saw the adult punished for the behavior, and a third group saw the adult receive no consequences for the behavior. When each group was allowed to play with Bobo, the group that had observed the adult rewarded for the behavior tended to imitate more of the adult's behaviors than the other two groups.

Later, each group was again permitted to play with Bobo, and everyone was rewarded for imitating the aggressive behavior of the adult. Even children who had seen the adult punished now acted aggressively.

Processes in Observational Learning

Bandura proposed a number of different factors that affect observational learning:

Attention. When a child observes someone's behavior, to what parts of that behavior is the child paying attention? This will depend not only on age and development but also on individual interests.

Retention. How does the child store what he or she has observed? What associations has the child made? Has the child imagined what it would be like to duplicate the behavior (rehearsal)?

Motor Reproduction Processes. Is the child physically capable of reproducing the behavior? Can the child observe and adjust his or her behavior if it doesn't match the observed behavior?

Motivation. What reinforcement is available, either from outside or from inside the self, or by observing the original behavior being reinforced?

Violence in the Media

Observational learning suggests that media violence can foster violent behavior in those who observe it. Clearly, the factors mentioned previously must be considered, as well as any previous social learning that a child has acquired through interactions with family and friends. A person raised in a family where aggressive behavior is nonexistent or is punished or where loving and gentle behavior is practiced and rewarded may be much less likely to duplicate behaviors observed in the media. The issue is complex. Do you think that media violence should be eliminated until all of the factors are understood?

Current Approaches to Learning

The development of new research techniques in neurobiology, evolutionary biology, and cognitive processes has yielded much of interest to learning theorists. There is a growing awareness that mental processes, including learning, are sometimes better studied as systems influenced by biological, cognitive, emotional, social, and environmental factors than as isolated events.

Individuals differ in their use of cognitive processes. Some people more easily perceive the big picture, while others notice details. Some need a hands-on approach, while others prefer to think or reason about an idea.

In addition to cognitive preferences, people seem to learn more easily through different sensory modes, often called *learning styles*. One person may need to see a word spelled out, a second may need to hear the word spelled, and a third may prefer to write the word—to get the feel of it. Here are **three** examples of the many factors that influence learning.

❶ Emotional Influences

For some time, it's been recognized that a state of moderate emotional arousal is advantageous to learning. That emotion might be curiosity, humor, or sometimes even fear or anxiety. The key word is "moderate." If the emotion is overwhelming, little learning takes place.

Today, the role of emotion is proving to be even more important. Recent studies suggest that a lack of ability to experience emotion may affect reasoning and rational behavior. We'll learn more about this in Chapter 11.

❷ Evolutionary Influences

At one time, scientists believed that the presence of a harmful organism (an antigen) would cause the body to produce a chemical (an antibody) that would destroy the antigen. Now, scientists know that a tremendous variety of antibodies are present at birth—just waiting to be "turned on" by their matching antigen.

Similarly, some researchers suggest that our brains/minds contain, at birth, all the cognitive processes we will need throughout our lives. These processes are "turned on" by situations that we encounter in the environment. This theory, called *selectionism*, lends support to the idea that children learn best by interacting with the appropriate environment rather than by being "given" knowledge.

❸ Cultural Validity

Researchers are becoming aware of the importance of the culture in which a behavior occurs. Unless a process being studied is tested with people from a wide sampling of cultures in the situations in which it normally occurs, scientists may not be justified in saying that it is a fundamental human cognitive process. Differences across cultures in areas such as spatial perception, auditory acuity, or attention focus may significantly influence behavior.

Culture and social environment play important roles in learning. Here are some factors that may affect what is learned and how we learn it.

* *Cultural Values.* Learning is dependent on values. In a given culture how highly is learning valued beyond what is necessary for historical roles to be adequately filled?
* *Perceptual Processes.* Learning begins with perception. If survival depends on spotting a leopard among the jungle foliage or noticing different sounds when one steps on branches, those abilities might be more highly developed in a forest than in a culture where such events do not occur. Whether there is an actual difference in sensory ability or in the signals to which one pays attention, these factors are likely to affect perception in learning.
* *Intelligence.* Learning varies with intelligence. One definition of intelligence includes possession of "practical sense" and the facility of adapting oneself to circumstances. Might various cultures associate different behaviors with the possession of these qualities?

Unless psychological researchers are aware of these and other cultural factors, their research may lack environmental validity.

Psychologists are interested in understanding how human beings learn. They have identified four major ways in which learning takes place: (1) classical conditioning, which focuses on learning by making associations between stimuli and responses; (2) operant conditioning, which focuses on encouraging or discouraging behaviors through reinforcement; (3) cognitive learning, which focuses on the various mental processes that underlie behavior and learning; and (4) social or observational learning, which focuses on learning by observing and imitating others.

Current approaches help psychologists study different factors that may be involved in the learning process.

Psychology

association—mental connection between two stimuli. *p. 98*

classical conditioning—learning by associating various stimuli with a response. *p. 98*

cognition—processes of thinking, memory formation, learning, and problem solving, among others. *p. 108*

cognitive maps—Tollman's term for the mental processing of spatial relationships a person or animal experiences. *p. 108*

conditioned response (CR)—learned response to a conditioned stimulus that is not natural. *p. 99*

conditioned stimulus (CS)—stimulus that has been associated with a natural response. *p. 99*

learning—relatively permanent change in behavior resulting from practice or experience. *p. 97*

operant conditioning—encouraging or discouraging a behavior through reinforcement or punishment. *p. 102*

reinforcement—any event that encourages or discourages repetition of a behavior. *p. 102*

response—reaction of an organism to a stimulus. *p. 97*

schema—pattern that is recognized in experience or complex reality that helps to explain or deal with it. *p. 108*

stimulus—some action that produces activity in an organism. *p. 97*

unconditioned response (UCR)—organism's natural response to a stimulus. *p. 99*

unconditioned stimulus (UCS)—stimulus to which an organism has a natural response. *p. 99*

CHAPTER 8

Memory

In this chapter, you will learn about:

- the three tasks in memory formation
- various systems of memory formation and storage
- forgetting
- memory and learning

In the late 1800s, Hermann Ebbinghaus contributed to the growing experimental study of psychology with his studies on memory. Ebbinghaus made up long lists of "nonsense syllables" such as EOF, PEB, or RUV. He tried to memorize these lists under various conditions and tested himself on how long it took him to learn them and how well he remembered them. Although Ebbinghaus's most lasting findings were about how easy it is to forget rather than to remember, his work laid another cornerstone in the foundation of experimental psychology.

How do sensory impressions become memories? Is there a difference between your memories of the date of the signing of the Declaration of Independence and of how to play the piano? Why do you automatically remember some things and have to struggle to remember others?

Memory is a complex behavior that uses many different brain systems. There is still much to be learned about how and why we remember—and how and why we forget.

What Is Memory?

Memory is a mental process responsible for **encoding, storage,** and **retrieval** of information.

You may recognize these three terms as coming from the field of computer science. Once again, psychologists find familiar technology useful in describing mental operations. But keep in mind that computers and brains work very differently and that, at some point, the computer metaphor breaks down. After all, the software and hardware of the computer process information in a different way than does the "wetware" of the mind.

* **Encoding.** We can think of the encoding phase of memory as the process of taking input from the senses and converting it into a form that the brain can process. This would be like the computer taking input from the keyboard, mouse, digital camera, or scanner and converting it into the 1s and 0s of computer language.
* **Storage.** Encoded information can then be retained. This storage of information can be temporary or permanent, depending on its potential use. Some information might be temporarily stored in the computer files you presently have open and with which you are working. Once you save a file, it is stored on your hard drive—to be accessed as needed.

* **Retrieval.** At the appropriate time, the stored information can be accessed, either for its own usefulness, to be combined with other incoming information, or to be processed with other information from storage. This retrieval of information is like opening a file or an application that you want to use.

Stages of Memory

Where do each of the three processes occur?

The three-stage model of memory formation is often used to describe the steps of acquiring information, processing it, and either using it at the time or storing it for later use. This model is based on the following **three** stages of memory:

❶ Sensory Memory

Information from the outside world enters your brain through the senses. Each sense has a storage area for its particular type of information—visual, auditory, touch, taste, and smell. Information is held in **sensory memory** for a very brief time—a few seconds at most. We constantly scan our environment with our senses, so if information remained in sensory memory for very long, we'd experience blurred images, discordant blends of sound, or mixtures of tastes or odors.

❷ Short-Term Memory (STM)

From sensory memory, information goes into short-term, or working, memory. The information in **short-term memory** is what you are consciously aware of at any moment in time. Thinking about the last sentence you read, recognizing the face of a friend in the hall between classes, or holding a telephone number in your mind until you can dial it all take place in short-term memory.

❸ Long-Term Memory (LTM)

Long-term memory is like a hard drive, containing information you store for later use. You can access your LTM for answers to test questions, memories about your past or people you know, or procedures such as how to drive a car or use an index in a book.

Sensory Input and Sensory Memory

Our senses gather information from the environment and send it to different parts of the brain as sensory memories. The purpose of sensory memory is to hold information long enough for it to be recognized or attended to and then either ignored or passed on for further processing.

* *Visual Memory.* As you scan your surroundings, you make short-lived visual representations of what you see. The information is constantly changing, so your visual memory holds each representation for less than a second.

* *Auditory Memory.* Sounds that you hear are retained for a little longer, up to a couple of seconds. This may be because sounds generally occur only once, while visual information can be scanned several times a second. In addition, we may need to hold auditory information long enough to join successive sounds and identify them as words.

Similar brain regions store information on touch, taste, and smell, but much less research has been done on these sensory memory regions.

Attention and Recognition

If you processed everything entering your senses, you'd be overwhelmed with information. Attention and recognition determine whether something that enters sensory memory is ignored (forgotten) or sent along to short-term memory for further processing.

We tend to pay attention to something that is:

* Unusual, sudden, or dramatic—an adaptive behavior because we tend to notice things that could be harmful.
* An idea or pattern that we recognize.
* Relevant to our lives.
* Important to what we're presently doing.

Attention is the concentration of mental effort on sensory or mental events. Attention determines what information from the environment is sent on for further processing. People can consciously decide to attend to or ignore certain types of information, but often, unconscious values, beliefs, or emotions determine the process.

How do we recognize the personal importance of something? According to the diagram below, information doesn't make it to short-term memory (or long-term memory) unless we've paid attention to it or recognized it as something important. But without comparing the new input to something we already have in long-term memory, how do we know whether it is important?

The dotted line on the diagram shows this input from LTM to the process of recognition and attention. The connection may not be this direct. Theorists have suggested several ways that it might occur.

The Information Processing Model of Memory

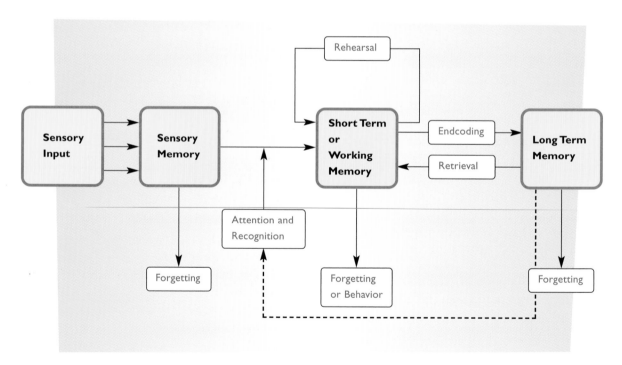

▲

The diagram shows an overview of the steps that cognitive psychologists believe we go through in memory formation.

Short-Term Memory

Short-term memory contains the things we are presently aware of. Short-term, or working, memory holds information, moves it from one place to another, and provides space for thinking and problem solving.

It is important to note that sensory input isn't necessary to have something going on in STM. When you're thinking about what you did last weekend or trying to decide what to cook for dinner, you may be drawing all the information you are using from your long-term memory. STM works on internal or external input similarly.

Encoding in STM

Information in short-term memory may be in the form of pictures (iconic), sounds (acoustic or echoic), or occasionally, meaning (semantic). For example, when trying to hold a telephone number in memory, most people hear it (acoustic encoding), although some people will see the number (iconic encoding).

One possible explanation for the acoustic preference in STM is that humans had spoken language before written language and so developed an efficient storage mechanism for sounds. What letter comes before *q* in the alphabet? Many people have to "say" the letters in order before answering. This suggests that the alphabet is stored acoustically rather than iconically.

There are **two** exceptions to the acoustic preference of STM.

1. Iconic images of extremely vivid or highly emotional memories seem to move through STM and into LTM relatively unchanged. This was once called "flashbulb memory." Studies have shown that, although people believe that such memories are more complete and accurate, the memories are actually as flawed as those of events stored in less emotional situations.

2. The second exception is called eidetic imagery—sometimes known as photographic memory. Some children and even fewer adults can record a scene or store pages of a book as images that can be recalled later without error.

Time Duration of STM

Information stays in short-term memory for less than 30 seconds unless it is rehearsed or elaborated upon in some way. **Rehearsal** is repetition, and **elaboration** is adding meaning to something by connecting it or organizing it with other information already in long-term memory.

If you look up a phone number, you probably keep repeating it to yourself until you reach the phone. If you don't, you may have to circle back to the phone book. If you do this long enough, the number may move on to LTM.

What methods might you use to link the name and face of a person you've just met?

Capacity of STM

In the 1950s, George Miller observed that STM is capable of holding only 7 plus or minus (±) 2 pieces of unrelated information. For example, most people couldn't hold a number such as 11749486712 in STM.

A process called **chunking**—grouping pieces of unrelated information—can overcome this limitation. By chunking the number to 1-174-948-6712, eleven pieces of information become four—the typical way we say a telephone number. In a study done over several months, one person was able to increase his memory from 7 digits to 72 simply by combining the digits into groups that were meaningful to him.

The 7 ± 2 "pieces" may be digits, numbers, words, familiar phrases, or ideas. Chunking is often used by experts to recall huge amounts of information in a particular field. Some chess players can hold an entire chessboard of pieces as one item in memory because they have a name for that particular alignment of pieces.

Storage in STM

Most of what has passed through your STM today has been forgotten. If the information wasn't important enough to be rehearsed or elaborated upon, the signal simply faded. This might be true of the sound of your alarm or the color of a towel you used. This reason for forgetting is called **decay.**

While reading the paper, you find an interesting article you plan to share with a friend. As you are rehearsing it, the phone rings, distracting you from the article.

When you hang up, thoughts of the article are gone! Any event that prevents you from rehearsing or elaborating information in STM is likely to prevent that information from being retained and passed on to LTM. This reason for forgetting is called **interference.**

Output of STM

What happens to information in STM?

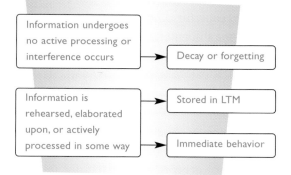

Information that is processed in STM may lead to an immediate behavior followed by decay or forgetting. Once you've decided what to make for breakfast, there's no real need to send that information to LTM. You may retain a memory of what you ate, but not of the process you used in deciding what to prepare.

"To find out if you're someone who could benefit from our Memory Improvement Seminar, please press 59736222582095217059."

Evidence for STM-LTM

Why do psychologists think that there are two different memory systems (STM and LTM) rather than just one? Continuing the work of Ebbinghaus, researchers ask participants to memorize and recall lists of nonsense syllables, such as ZOK or BIR. Participants are then asked to recall the syllables in order of their appearance on the list (serial learning) or in any order (free recall). Typical results are shown in the graph.

Participants tend to remember better the first syllables in the list. This is called the *primacy effect.* Researchers interpret this as resulting from more rehearsal time or chunking of earlier syllables and subsequent passage to LTM. In the middle of the list, there are too many syllables to rehearse, and they are coming too fast to chunk.

The ability to recall the last syllables—the *recency effect*—is attributed to their presence in STM. If the recall isn't requested until 30 seconds after the final syllable is presented—and during that time, the person is asked to perform an interference task such as counting backwards—the primacy effect remains, but the recency effect disappears. This lends support to the idea of two different types of memory.

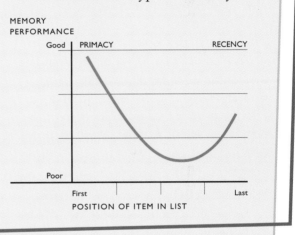

MEMORY PERFORMANCE

Good | PRIMACY   RECENCY

Poor

First   Last

POSITION OF ITEM IN LIST

Long-Term Memory

Long-term memory is not what it seems, because theorists believe that it is composed of several different types of memory—in terms of content, location, and the process of memory formation. Here is a general overview of the types of LTM.

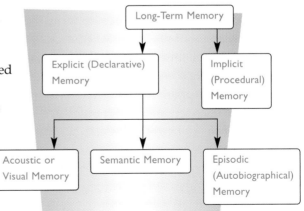

Explicit and Implicit Memory

Do you remember when and how you learned to walk or tie your shoes? Probably not. It would be difficult for you to describe in words how you acquired those skills. Memories that are difficult to put into words or that we don't remember acquiring are called implicit memories.

Memories of things that have happened to you and of things that you know—such as facts, concepts, and principles—can more easily be described. You can actively search for and find these memories. These are called explicit memories.

Procedural and Declarative Memories

Some theorists refer to implicit memory as procedural memory and explicit memory as declarative memory. Procedural memories are memories of perceptual and motor skills—"knowing how"—and are difficult to put into words. Declarative memory is "knowing what"—memories and thoughts that can be put into words or "declared."

Researchers proposed these two different types of memory after observing people with certain kinds of memory loss. Although unable to retrieve information about their lives or, in some cases, to form new memories about what happened each day, they were still able to perform many different skills. They were even able to learn new ones. Apparently, information could still be encoded and stored but not retrieved.

Encoding in LTM

As in short-term memory, information in long-term memory may be acoustic, visual, or semantic. Long-term memory may also be episodic. What's the difference between these types of information?

Acoustic Memories. Acoustic information may be sentences, thoughts, or sounds that we store "as is." The little song you sang when learning the alphabet or a parent's often-repeated "Clean up your room" are examples.

Visual Memories. These memories take **two** forms:

1. Imperfectly reproduced images of scenes, pages in a book, or other visual stimuli.
2. Cognitive maps by which we organize our environment. These may look like regular maps or may be made up of familiar landmarks. It's likely that we even have visual maps composed of symbols that represent concepts or relationships with people in our environment.

Semantic and Episodic Memories. What is your home address? How did you learn your home address? The answers to these two questions are different, as are the ways in which the information is encoded.

In general, semantic memories are memories of facts, concepts, and principles. They might include the capital of Illinois, the concept of truth, or the principle of supply and demand. Semantic memories can be acquired at any time and tend to remain stable over time.

Episodic (autobiographical) memories are memories of things as they are related to your life. What you had for supper last night, what the weather was like on Tuesday, and where you went on your last vacation—these are episodic memories.

We learn episodic memories in the sequence in which they happen. Episodic memories are more likely to undergo changes over time as memories adjust to more mature interpretations. An older person's memories of her childhood may be very different from what actually occurred.

Depth of Processing

One theory about the encoding of semantic memories is called Depth of Processing. The theory proposes that information processed at a semantic level—in terms of its meaning or relevance—is more effectively encoded, and thus retrieved, than information processed superficially.

Researchers presented participants with a list of words. On each trial, the participants had to answer a question about each word.

Physical Properties of the Word—Is the word in all capital letters? How many vowels are in the word?

Acoustical Characteristics of the Word— Does the word rhyme with _____?

Semantic Characteristics of the Word— Does the word mean the same as _____? Does the word fit into this phrase?

Researchers found that the more deeply (semantically) the word was processed, the more likely it was to be recognized on a later test of retrieval. They suggest that the deeper the processing, the better the memory. Another interpretation is that because semantic processing takes longer, time spent may be the key factor in efficient encoding and storage.

These findings would suggest that the more time you spend in organizing, associating, or giving other meaning to new information, the easier you will be able to retrieve it at a later time.

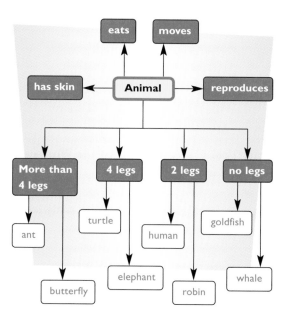

Duration of LTM

Assuming that information has been richly encoded and apart from the factors involved in forgetting, information will remain in long-term memory permanently.

Capacity of LTM

It was once believed that the capacity of LTM memory was limitless. Some researchers have tried to calculate the number of possible connections that a person could make, but without definite knowledge of how information is chunked, the size of the units stored, or the biological processes that help produce memory, these attempts are strictly theoretical. Others have tried to base the capacity of memory on the electrical power available in the brain. For all practical purposes, the number of things your memory will store is infinite—even if you sometimes feel as if you can't remember one more thing for that big test!

Storage of Semantic Memories

Early researchers believed that semantic memories were stored in hierarchical form. Below is a possible hierarchical structure for the classification of animals:

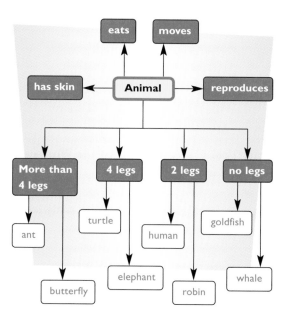

A network is one form of hierarchy that lets you make more complex connections among levels within. It models how you could connect a cat to mice, to witches, and to the idea of "nine lives."

A network can be pictured as a collection of items linked to one another in multiple ways. Here is a very simplified example of a network on the concept of *cat*. The network links obvious and not so obvious items (parrot) to *cat.*

There are many other ways in which information could be organized hierarchically. Animals could be divided into air, sea, and land creatures or into birds, mammals, and insects. The categories in the hierarchy will determine the ease with which a person can answer questions such as "Is a butterfly an animal?" or "Does a goldfish have skin?"

You can see how, if a person is asked to say whatever word comes into his or her head when you say "cat," the network could lead to "parrot" or "eats mice." In an actual network, some items are closer together or connected in multiple ways, so some answers (connections) are more likely than others are. The network model of semantic storage explains a wider variety of responses than the less complex hierarchical model.

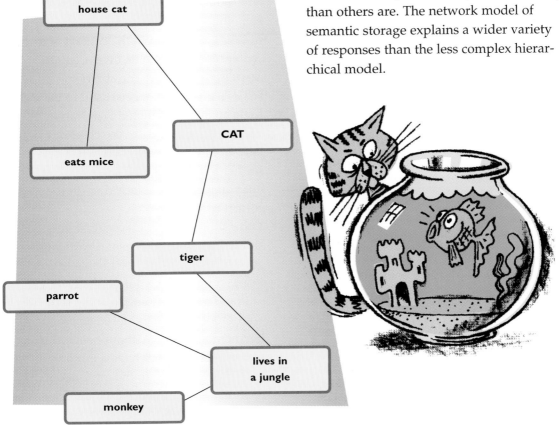

Memory Retrieval

Once information has been encoded and stored, how is it retrieved? Studies involving the retrieval of information are most often used in trying to understand memory. But memory retrieval is much more than just answering a question about what you know or what happened in the past.

Recall and Recognition

There are **two** ways in which previously stored information—sometimes called a *memory trace*—can be retrieved.

1. **Recall.** If you're asked the name of your fifth-grade teacher or the name of the sixteenth president of the United States, you must go into your LTM and hunt for the correct response—the particular trace that holds the information you need. **Recall** involves searching for and producing information from memory.

2. **Recognition.** Identifying teachers you've had from names on a list takes much less random searching through your databanks. **Recognition** is identifying whether or not you've encountered something, such as a person, thing, or word, before.

In general, recognition is easier than recall. You are given a cue about where to look in memory—an entry point into the network. Multiple-choice tests require recognition rather than recall, while essay tests generally require that you recall a body of information about a particular idea.

Tip of the Tongue (TOT)

At times, you might know the meaning of the word you want and be able to identify several examples, but you can't think of the word itself. You might say, "It's on the tip of my tongue," meaning that some of the information is there for you, but you just can't access the rest. This partial recall of related information suggests that memories aren't necessarily stored together.

Cueing Memory

Several other factors can affect your ability to retrieve information.

* **Context Dependence.** Context is the environment in which you encounter something. You may recognize the meaning of a word in the context of a sentence, but not on its own. *Context dependence* describes the ability to retrieve a memory more easily in the same context in which it was learned. You may not recognize the checkout lady from the grocery store when you see her in the mall. She looks familiar, but you just can't "place" her (in the correct context).

* **State Dependence.** Likewise, if you studied when you were in a particularly good mood, you may be unable to recall what you memorized if you're feeling sad or angry when you take the test. Your mood or state is stored as part of the memory trace. Without being in that same state, you may have a more difficult time "linking" to the information in memory. This influence on memory retrieval is called *state dependence*.

Forgetting

If you're asked a question and can't retrieve the answer from memory, is it because you've forgotten? Not necessarily. Consider the three stages it takes to form a lasting memory: it may be that you never encoded the information, that it was somehow stored incorrectly, or that there is a problem with the retrieval process. Assuming that the information has been properly encoded and stored and retrieval isn't a problem, there are still several reasons why a person may forget.

Reasons for Forgetting

* **Decay.** Early theories suggested that memory traces were electrical signals that moved through the central nervous system. If the memory wasn't activated over long periods of time, the signals would weaken and eventually disappear, or decay.

FORGETFULNESS —
The seven warning signs:

1.

* **Interference.** Interference might also contribute to forgetting. You've seen how interference can prevent a memory in STM from being rehearsed or elaborated sufficiently to move to LTM. Once in LTM, how can a memory be interfered with?

One theory regarding interference says that even after information has entered LTM, a consolidation period follows during which the information is settling in to its permanent location and connections are being strengthened. If you undertake another memory task during this time, new bits of information can interfere with one another and prevent the appropriate links from forming within the network.

Studies have shown that people who learn material just before going to sleep have better recall than those who learn during the day. One reason for this is that there is no chance for interference from other information. Other researchers have found that there's an increase in "fast-wave" sleep patterns after a learning task, suggesting that some memory consolidation may occur during sleep.

Amnesia

One serious reason for forgetting is amnesia. **Amnesia** is a temporary or permanent inability to remember. The study of people with amnesia has been one of the most important ways in which researchers have learned about memory. Amnesia has a number of possible causes:

* **Physiological Causes.** Brain tumor, head injury, stroke, or other trauma to the central nervous system can cause amnesia. Damage to parts of the brain produces different types of amnesia. Observing types of damage has helped researchers understand some of the processes involved in memory.
* **Substance Abuse.** Korsakoff's syndrome, a form of amnesia, is caused by chronic vitamin deficiency associated with alcohol abuse. Even after a patient stops drinking, the brain damage that was produced is generally irreversible.
* **Psychogenic Causes.** Although many people form vivid images of highly emotional events, others may become unable to recall the event except under hypnosis or when a similar event occurs. Many psychologists believe that some memories are repressed even among otherwise healthy individuals.

The two most common forms of amnesia are *retrograde* amnesia, in which a person loses the ability to form new memories after a trauma, and *anterograde* amnesia, in which the person cannot recall events that occurred just before a trauma. The latter is often irreversible and may indicate brain damage.

Amnesiacs may lose their ability to retrieve autobiographical memory but retain their semantic memory. They know the name of the president but not their own name. Others may learn new things but not remember doing them. The fact that many amnesiacs seem normal in every way except their specific loss of memory lends support to the idea that memory is a process separate from other cognitive functions.

Three-Stage Model of Memory Formation

Memory Stage	Sensory Memory	Short-Term Memory	Long-Term Memory
Time	Up to 2 seconds	Up to 18–20 seconds	Relatively permanent
Capacity	Full sensory impression	7 ± 2 units of information	Unlimited
Process	Holds sensory information briefly prior to processing	Works actively, consciously in processing, problem solving, preparation for long-term storage	Keeps information in long-term storage
Types	Input from each of the five senses	Information from senses or from LTM	Implicit/explicit (procedural/declarative), semantic/episodic, acoustic or visual

CRITICAL THINKING

Can an Eyewitness's Memory Be Trusted?

Many court cases hinge on the testimony of an eyewitness because juries are often persuaded by somebody who was present when the events in question took place. However, studies have questioned the accuracy and reliability of these reports. Should eyewitness testimony continue to play the same major role in the courtroom?

THE ISSUES

Most people think that nobody could give more accurate or complete information about an event than somebody who witnessed it. According to surveys, juries consider eyewitness testimony very important to their verdict decision.

However, many studies have shown that eyewitness testimony can be wrong. Eyewitnesses can only remember what they were paying attention to. They can miss important details at the crime scene without realizing it.

Another problem is that it is very difficult for human memory to avoid being influenced by new information. If a lawyer were to ask "Did you see the pipe on the ground?" a witness may be influenced into mistakenly remembering that a pipe was present when he didn't actually

see one. Studies show that when new objects are mentioned, eyewitnesses frequently add those objects to their original memories without realizing it.

Finally, juries are heavily influenced by witnesses that provide a large number of details and who appear confident in their testimony. Even when the details are irrelevant to the case, and the report does not seem to match up with the evidence, this sort of eyewitness testimony will have a significant effect on the jury.

Many lawyers say that there is no substitute for an eyewitness. However, some claim that in order to make the legal system more just for everybody, changes should be made in the way eyewitness testimony is used and presented.

THE PROCESS

1. **Restate the issues**. In your own words, restate the basic question presented.

2. **Provide evidence**. From your own experience and the information above, list the evidence *for* trusting eyewitness accounts.

3. **Give opposing arguments**. From your own experience and the information above, list the evidence *against* trusting eyewitness accounts.

4. **Look for more information**. What else would you like to know before you draw any conclusions? Make a list of your questions. On the Internet, in the psychology section of the library, or in the index of psychology books, research the way that

eyewitness testimony is used in court and studies on its reliability and accuracy.

5. **Evaluate the information**. Make a chart with two columns:

Trusting Eyewitness Testimony	
For	Against

Record the argument in each column and rank each argument in importance from 1 to 5, with 1 as the most important.

6. **Draw conclusions**. Write one paragraph supporting your answer to the question, "Should the way eyewitness testimony is used in a court of law be changed?" Give facts to support your conclusion.

The Biology of Memory

Memory is a complex process involving many different brain systems. Recent advances in imaging techniques, discussed in Chapter 2, allow researchers to observe regions of the brain that are particularly active during various mental tasks. Some of these regions are shown below.

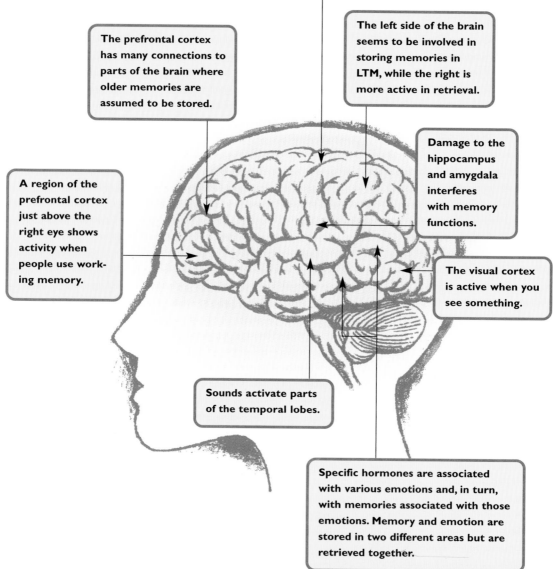

As information moves from one neuron to another, chemicals are released at the synapses. During and after memory, studies have observed changes in the synapses, the neurotransmitters, and in the physical structure of the neurons, dendrites, and insulating material around the neurons.

The prefrontal cortex has many connections to parts of the brain where older memories are assumed to be stored.

The left side of the brain seems to be involved in storing memories in LTM, while the right is more active in retrieval.

A region of the prefrontal cortex just above the right eye shows activity when people use working memory.

Damage to the hippocampus and amygdala interferes with memory functions.

The visual cortex is active when you see something.

Sounds activate parts of the temporal lobes.

Specific hormones are associated with various emotions and, in turn, with memories associated with those emotions. Memory and emotion are stored in two different areas but are retrieved together.

Memory and Learning

No learning takes place unless something is remembered. Memory formation and retrieval can be enhanced in a number of ways, such as the elaboration, organization, and context learning already mentioned. Here are **four** approaches to improving and understanding how we learn.

❶ Principle Learning

This useful technique involves learning the basic principles before trying to recall details. For example, if you first understand that the basic principle of dog training is stimulus-response, you can apply that principle to each new trick that you want to teach your dog.

❷ Schemas

As it is encoded and stored, information can become associated with a variety of schemas, or patterns the brain recognizes. For example, a word such as *honest* may be part of schemas for banking, working, shopping, or friendship. The word *honest* encountered in a new context will expand the schema and increase understanding of complex ideas.

❸ Mnemonics

Mnemonics are memory techniques based on active processing of information. For instance, if you have to memorize a list in an exact order, associate each word on the list with an object in the room—in the order in which you scan them. Then, when you go to recall the list, you mentally scan the room. Or, you might create a humorous or unique connection for list items, or tie together, in story form, the objects or words you have to remember. Again, the more unusual the story, the easier it will be to remember. You might also create a picture containing all of the objects on your list. Images can hold much more information than memories stored as words.

❹ Learning Curves

If you are learning something that requires the accumulation of information, the rate at which you learn will generally rise with more practice and will then level off. If you are learning something very unfamiliar, your rate of learning may be very slow. Once you've caught on, it may then rise quickly. Different learning tasks produce different learning curves.

Clearly, much remains to be understood about how we encode, store, and retrieve information. Here are just a few issues:

* *Repressed Memory.* Are some traumatic memories repressed? Can they be recovered? Should they be recovered?
* *Lab vs. Real Life.* Do the memory studies done in laboratories teach us anything about what we do in real life?
* *Reconstruction.* To what extent do memories reflect what actually happened? How do we change history?

Our memory systems encode, store, and retrieve information. One model suggests that there are three stages of memory formation: sensory memory, short-term (or working) memory, and long-term memory. Multiple system models suggest that long-term memory can be further broken down into explicit and implicit memory, procedural and declarative memory, and episodic and semantic memory.

Anything that will produce more active processing of information will tend to increase the probability that information will be encoded and stored effectively and be available for retrieval. Forgetting can occur because of decay, interference, or physical or mental trauma.

Memory processes can be linked to both structural and chemical processes throughout the brain.

Psychology

amnesia—temporary or permanent inability to remember. *p. 127*

chunking—process of grouping pieces of unrelated information. *p. 120*

decay—condition in which unrehearsed or unretrieved information is lost from memory. *p. 120*

elaboration—addition of meaning to information to organize it or make it more relevant and hold it in STM. *p. 119*

encoding—process of converting input into a form that can be stored in long-term memory. *p. 116*

interference—any event that prevents rehearsal or elaboration of information in STM. *p. 120*

long-term memory (LTM)—memory of information stored for later use. *p. 117*

memory—mental process responsible for encoding, storage, and retrieval of information. *p. 116*

recall—searching for and retrieving information from memory. *p. 126*

recognition—identifying something encountered before. *p. 126*

rehearsal—repetition of information to hold it in STM. *p. 119*

retrieval—process of getting stored information through recall or recognition. *p. 116*

sensory memory—memory of information very recently perceived by the senses. *p. 116*

short-term memory (STM)—working memory where information is consciously and actively processed. *p. 117*

storage—temporary or permanent retention of information in memory. *p. 116*

Thought and Language

In this chapter, you will learn about:

- the structures and processes used in thinking
- reasoning, problem solving, and decision making
- how language and thinking interact

Think of a moderately pleasant memory—perhaps when you did something you enjoyed. In your "mind's eye," make a picture of the memory. As you look at the picture, is it in black and white or color? Is it two- or three-dimensional? Is it a movie, a series of "slides," or a photograph? After noticing those qualities, change one of them—if the picture is in color, make it black and white; if it's a movie, make it stand still. What happens to your feeling of pleasantness?

Concepts, propositions, and language—along with mental images—are among the tools people use to process information. Specific steps in thinking can help in problem solving and lead to more accurate or useful decisions.

Can you think without language? Some researchers say that we can get a "sense" of a concept without having the words to describe it, just as a young child might have a sense of what a dog is before learning the word. How do language and thought interact?

What Is Thinking?

People use the word *think* to describe a wide variety of mental processes.

"I think I was four when that happened." (Memory)

"Think!" (Attention)

"I think UFOs exist." (Belief)

"I think that's a verb." (Statement of fact)

In addition to these examples, *thinking* is used to describe mental actions as diverse as reasoning, understanding, judging, supposing, pondering, and imagining. Mental processes are referred to as cognition.

Let's define **thinking** as a set of mental activities that results in the solution of a problem or the attainment of a goal. This definition focuses on goal-directed mental processes rather than the "thinking" we do when we are daydreaming or simply noticing our environment.

The Biological Basis of Thought

Cognitive neuroscience is the study of the biological basis of thought. Cognitive neuroscientists try to understand mental processes by studying how groups of neurons work together in specific regions of the brain to accomplish a given task and how these groups of neurons work together to generate higher mental processes.

The Thinking Brain

Although research in cognitive neuroscience is still in its infancy, **two** areas of the brain have been identified as playing important roles in thinking and higher mental processes.

1. **Association Cortex.** Nearly three-fourths of the human cortex is made up of association areas in which bits of information from the senses and previous experience are put together. Because humans have so much more association cortex than other members of the animal kingdom, scientists conclude that these areas are involved in higher thinking processes.

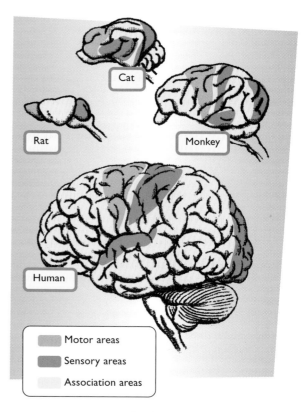

Motor areas
Sensory areas
Association areas

2. **Frontal Lobe.** The frontal lobe is responsible for giving humans the ability to think analytically, reason, and plan. Studies suggest that in this area of the brain different values are assigned to possible choices. People with frontal lobe damage are often unable to make decisions or make them unwisely.

The Psychological Basis of Thought

While there are many ways to organize the study of thinking, the graphic organizer below may be helpful as you study the various aspects of thought. As you read through the chapter, you may wish to create your own graphic organizer.

Structures of Thinking

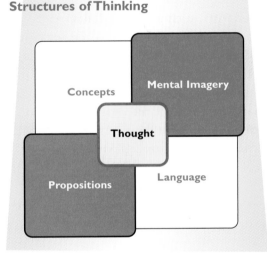

Processes in Thinking

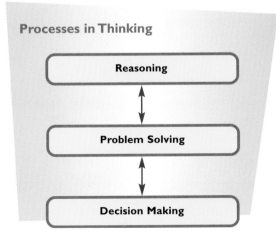

Structures of Thinking

Thinking is a complex process that uses many different methods. Concepts, propositions, and mental imagery are all methods used to bring structure to the thinking process.

What Are Concepts?

Imagine that each tree, each blade of grass, and each human or animal you encountered had to be processed as an individual perception. Fortunately, human minds are capable of grouping similar objects, actions, and experiences so that knowledge of one leads to knowledge or expectations of others with similar attributes.

The words *tree, grass, human, animal,* and *encounter* in the previous paragraph are all concepts. The first four words describe groups of objects with similar characteristics. *Encounter* describes a class of actions in the world.

Concepts are mental representations of classes into which we divide objects, actions, or events in the world. We use concepts to communicate, to predict, to reason—in short, to think.

The ability to form concepts is a highly adaptive behavior. Imagine the problems early humans would have had if they hadn't recognized concepts such as *tiger, food, shelter,* or *danger.*

Functions of Concepts

One important function of concepts is *cognitive economy*—the ability to sum up a lot of similar objects, actions, or experiences into a single, agreed-upon word, such as *book* or *enjoy*. Try describing your day without using any concepts!

For even greater economy, people combine concepts into larger groups. You may organize your geographic environment around a large concept of city or town, which is composed of neighborhoods. Within the neighborhood is your school, home, stores, and so on.

Where Do Concepts Come From?

In many cases, concepts are taught. When a child points to a dog, an adult says the word *dog*. If the child later misidentifies a cat as a dog, adults will correct the child. Eventually, the child learns to distinguish members of those concept groups, but how he or she learns to tell the difference isn't clearly understood.

Some theorists suggest that we begin by creating a **prototype**—an ideal example of the concept. When we see a spider, for example, we access our prototype for *bug* or *insect* and then compare the object we are looking at with characteristics of the prototype, such as *small* and *multilegged*. The more the new object has in common with the prototype, the more quickly we identify it. It takes us longer to identify a penguin as a bird than a robin because a penguin doesn't share many of the characteristics we commonly think of when we hear the word *bird*.

The meaning of a concept may differ from person to person. The spider concept of a person who fears spiders will contain different information than the spider concept of a person who collects them.

Social Concepts

Not all concepts refer to objects, actions, or experiences. Consider this example.

Social concepts deal with typical roles, personality characteristics, or other social descriptors, such as doctor, Italian, extrovert, or Catholic. Some social concepts can lead to stereotypical expectations or incorrect assumptions. While the ability to group people has cognitive efficiency, some people lose sight of the differences among individuals within the group. What does it mean to be a conservative or a liberal—a "jock" or a "nerd"—a college graduate or a self-taught individual? What images or expectations pop into your mind when you hear those concept terms?

I've mapped out the concepts I've already grasped to save you time.

Organization of Concepts

Concepts are grouped together in the mind in various ways depending on the object, action, or experience to which they apply. Here are **five** of the major organizing principles:

1. **Taxonomies.** A taxonomy is a hierarchical system of classification. Let's follow one branch of a taxonomy of the concept *transportation.*

Taxonomy of Transportation

Public
Private
    Single-passenger
    Multiple-passenger
       Trucks
       Cars
          GM
          Chrysler
          Ford
             Escort
             Taurus
          Toyota

This taxonomy could have many more heads and subheads. Other branches could describe features of each item in the taxonomy, such as number of wheels, color, or dimensions.

Taxonomies are useful for organizing fairly simple concepts and their features because they provide a great deal of cognitive economy. They help to answer questions such as "Is a Taurus a form of public transportation?"(No)

2. **Networks.** In Chapter 8, you saw how semantic memories could be organized into networks. For example, you'd expect that the concepts for *red, yellow, blue,* and *green* would be stored in a cluster around the larger concept of *color,* as shown here.

Network

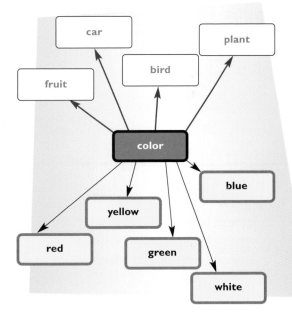

In turn, color could be linked to concepts whose features contain a color, such as "apples are red." Physiologically, one might imagine that each node is a set of neurons that responds in a unique way to the node's content—e.g., red. The closer together the nodes, the more quickly connections are made. "Is red a color?" will return a "yes" answer more quickly than "Can a car be yellow?"

3. **Schemas.** You may look at schemas as information about a concept gathered into a meaningful set. A schema about school would contain subschemas — concepts about classes, teachers, students, books, schedules, and other school-related information.

4. **Scripts.** A script is a concept dealing with a situation. Scripts contain a list of actions carried out for a particular purpose. You might have a "making breakfast" script, a "studying for a test"

script, or a "driving the car" script. The steps in the script contain concepts for objects, actions, and events.

5. **Cognitive Maps.** A cognitive map uses mental images to show spatial relationships among concepts. For example, you probably have a cognitive map for your house and for your room within your house. These maps vary from person to person since each person has unique interests and perspectives.

Evidence for Hierarchical Storage

Why do psychologists believe that some concepts are stored in a taxonomy? If someone asks, "Did Shakespeare have an elbow?" or "Did George Washington have two lungs?" you would answer "yes" in spite of the fact that you probably never thought of either of those relationships before. The specific relationship hadn't been organized or stored in your memory.

J. R. Anderson and G. H. Bower have argued that you reason to get these answers using your knowledge that both Shakespeare and Washington were humans and that humans have elbows and two lungs. This sort of reasoning is done using a hierarchical taxonomy.

They don't suggest that all information is stored in this way, but any relationships that haven't been previously learned appear to be accessible through this type of hierarchical organization.

What Are Propositions?

Statements called *propositions* are used in some forms of reasoning. A proposition is meant to represent a true statement—a representation of things as they are. One of the most important parts of good thinking is assessing the truth of the propositions one uses.

Truth is sometimes defined as a statement that represents the world as it really is. Because the way things "really are" is not always a matter of agreement, truth is more often an agreed-upon description of "reality." One need only read the letters to the editor in the newspaper to understand that the truth of a proposition can be hotly debated.

What Is Mental Imagery?

In addition to concepts and propositions, *mental imagery* plays a large part in our thinking. In a study by Stephen Kosslyn, participants were asked, "Do the ears of a beagle stick up above its head? How about a German shepherd?" Participants reported getting the answer by picturing the dog and "looking" at its ears.

Information About Space

We use mental imagery to represent information about objects in space. Spatial relationships, such as above, below, next to, and inside of, can be more easily visualized than represented as a network or taxonomy.

Which representation of a bear has greater cognitive efficiency?

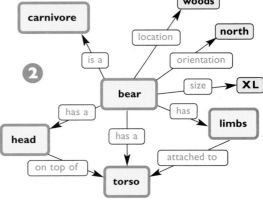

The diagram (2) is based on Steven Pinker's visualization of a network made up of separate propositions, such as "A bear is a carnivore" and "A bear has a head." Although the diagram is somewhat more organized than a list of sentences, it doesn't begin to "chunk" information as well as the drawing of the bear which represents all ideas about bear in a single image.

While you can picture things that no one has ever seen, such as a 500-pound polka-dot canary, you can't picture a pencil and pen next to one another where both occupy the same space. You can change the scale or color of an object, but you can't change fundamental concepts of spatial relationships.

Using Mental Imagery

Make a mental image of a room in your home. Notice the placement of the furniture, the colors, even the textures in the room. Now, move the furniture, change the color, rearrange or change other features in the room. Got it? Now, turn the whole room upside down!

In addition to re-creating, changing, or rotating objects in memory, mental images allow us to imagine things we've never seen. As you make plans for your weekend, you can imagine various scenarios before actually choosing among them. Here are some other uses of imagery:

* Many creative people get their ideas through imagery. Einstein described riding on a beam of light as a source of understanding.

* Images drive emotions. People have the same physical reactions when imagining emotional scenes as when experiencing them. When asked, many people report seeing pleasant memories in color, while unpleasant memories are black and white. Changing the color qualities changes the emotion.

* Ann is taller than Carol, and Carol is taller than Barbara. Who is the tallest girl? People may picture the relationship in their reasoning.

* Some people represent complex social relationships in mental imagery. Important people tend to be larger or closer. Less important people are farther away or less bright.

A picture may be worth a thousand words, but how do your mental images, along with concepts and propositions, ultimately result in ideas and thoughts?

Processes in Thinking

While thinking itself is a relatively seamless process, psychologists tend to look at reasoning, problem solving, and decision making separately.

What Is Reasoning?

Reasoning is manipulating information in a logical way to reach a conclusion. **Logic** is a method of thinking according to a fixed set of rules.

Deductive Reasoning. Reasoning from one or more propositions to a conclusion—from the general to the specific—is called **deductive reasoning**. Assuming that the original propositions are true and the rules of logic have been applied, the conclusion must be true. For example:

> All birds have wings.
> A sparrow is a bird.
> Therefore, a sparrow has wings.

Be careful, though, when you use deductive reasoning. If one of the original propositions is incorrect, then the conclusion may be false. For example:

> All birds can fly.
> Turkeys are birds.
> Therefore, turkeys can fly.

All birds might have wings, but that doesn't mean all birds can fly. The reasoning of the second example is faulty, since the first premise is incorrect.

Inductive Reasoning. What is the next number in the series 1, 2, 3, 4, __ ? Most people would say "5." In **inductive reasoning,** we reason from the perceived relationships among a set of particular instances—from the specific to the general. We assume that each number in the series is one more than the previous number ($f(x) = x + 1$). There are other, admittedly more complex, equations that will yield different answers that are correct according to that equation. Induction doesn't always lead to a single correct answer.

Formal Logic

Using formal logic, reasoning proceeds according to a set of fixed rules that, when applied correctly, will always result in a true answer. These rules help one avoid logical errors such as the "turkeys can fly" case of deductive reasoning.

Analogical Reasoning. In **analogical reasoning,** we reason by comparing information with similar information from another context. Early models of the atom compared it to the solar system. The motion of the planets around the sun (a visible system) helped people to imagine the motion of electrons around the nucleus (an invisible system).

Informal Reasoning. A headline reads, "A downtown jewelry store was robbed. A suspect was on a bus at the time of the robbery." People access the following "fact" in their semantic memory: People can't be in two places at the same time.

Based on this informal reasoning, most people might conclude that the suspect is innocent. Informal reasoning works on the basis of probability rather than rules of logic. It often results in correct conclusions, but it isn't infallible. Can you think of any way that the suspect might actually be guilty of the crime?

Cultural Differences in Reasoning

The processes of reasoning tend to be fairly common across cultures, but a number of factors can influence the results of reasoning. Results of reasoning—conclusions—may be limited or enhanced by their moral or ethical acceptability within the culture. The logical punishment for stealing in some cultures is having one's hand cut off—not an acceptable conclusion in most Western cultures.

What Is Problem Solving?

We spend a good part of our lives solving problems. **Problem solving** involves changing a situation from its present state to a desired state determined by some goal. Good problem solvers begin with **three** steps—often unconsciously:

1. Represent the problem.
2. Generate and evaluate strategies.
3. Generate solutions.

Represent the Problem

Successful problem solvers spend more time analyzing and representing the problem than they do generating solutions. Let's say that your problem is a cash shortage at week's end. Consider these **four** steps in representing the problem:

1. **State a Well-Structured Problem.** Unless you clearly define your present and desired states, it's easy to get off track. What is the present state? How much money do you have? What does "shortage" mean? What is the desired state? How will you know that you've reached the desired state?

2. **Concentrate on the Appropriate Variables.** Focusing on the amount of money you can earn baby-sitting or mowing lawns during the week is more productive than focusing on the possibility of a large inheritance.

3. **Eliminate Nonessential Information.** Focus your thinking on ways to solve the problem. What you'll do with the money when you get it isn't important at this stage.

4. **Identify Resources and/or Limitations.** What skills do you have that might help you increase cash flow? Do you have any time constraints that would prevent certain solutions?

Generate and Evaluate Strategies

A **strategy** is a systematic plan for generating solutions. The following chart shows some of the strategies typically used in problem solving.

Four Strategies to Problem Solving

Algorithms

An *algorithm is a step-by-step approach to problem solving.* Some algorithms involve simple trial and error. If X is a possible solution to a problem, the algorithm for a solution might be stated "Try X; if X works, then X = solution; if X doesn't work, then try next X." Clearly, this could go on as many times as there is another possible X. Algorithms guarantee a solution but can be very time consuming.

Heuristics

A *heuristic is a procedure that has worked in the past and is seen as likely to work in the future.* Heuristics are "rules of thumb" based on past experiences. If the light in your room goes out, you could check the fuse box, change the light bulb, check the wires in the wall or lamp, check the socket, and so on. Because experience suggests that the probability of the light bulb burning out is higher than the other choices, you try that first. Heuristics take less time than algorithms, but they may not result in a solution.

Means-End Analysis

Keep the final goal in mind while setting subgoals. In planning your study for finals, you might start with math but will set a time limit because you have exams in three other subjects. Will you need to spend the same amount of time on each? What exactly do you need to focus on?

Working Backward

Start from the goal state and work backward until you reach the present state. When a company wants to know how its competitor's product works, it will "reverse engineer" that product. This means beginning with the product and analyzing its construction to see what each part does. The company can then begin with its own parts and reconstruct a similar product.

Blocks to Effective Thinking

Human thinking isn't always based on fact and reason. Here are a few problems that affect our strategic thinking.

* *Mental Set.* A tendency to perceive or respond to something in a fixed way is a mental set. You have a corked bottle and a dime. The dime just fits through the opening of the bottle when it is uncorked. How can you put the dime in the bottle without removing the cork or breaking the bottle? Many people get stuck on this one because they have a mind-set that defines "removing the cork" as pulling it out. Try pushing it in!

* *Functional Fixedness.* The tendency to perceive an object only in terms of the use for which it is designed is called functional fixedness. One man, trapped in the trunk of a car, survived when he realized that he could let the air out of the spare tire when the breathable air in the trunk ran out.

* *Availability Heuristic.* The tendency to assign a higher priority to information we have encountered recently is called

availability heuristic. Let's say that your problem involves making a choice among various forms of transportation. If there have been several air disasters in the news recently, your heuristic might exclude air travel despite the fact that it is one of the safest modes of travel.

* **Confirmation Bias.** The tendency to perceive or seek out information that supports what a person believes and to ignore information that does not is called confirmation bias. For example, when people or organizations that support one side of a voting issue cite experts on the topic, they tend to quote only those experts who provide evidence for their position, not those who disagree. They may, in fact, not even look for evidence to the contrary because they are already convinced of their position. When confronted with contrary evidence, they will find reasons to discount it. "Don't confuse me with the facts. My mind is made up."

* **Representativeness Heuristic.** The tendency to think that a particular instance will be like the prototype for that category is called representativeness heuristic. You have a problem with your car. Your two possible sources of help are a man with dirty fingernails or a well-groomed woman. Most people would first approach the man for help. If it turns out that he knows nothing about cars, you would limit your solutions if you assumed that the woman couldn't possibly help you. Stereotypical expectations often limit problem solving.

Generate Solutions

Using whatever strategy or set of strategies you consider appropriate, you generate a set of solutions. Some solutions will be better than others in terms of possibility, probability, or their effects on other circumstances in your life. To solve your limited cash problem, winning the lottery may be a possible solution, but not a probable one. Working longer hours may be possible, but will certainly have an impact on your social life. So after generating solutions, the next step is to evaluate those solutions and make your decision.

Steps in Problem Solving

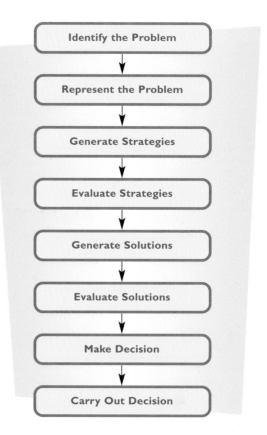

Identify the Problem

Represent the Problem

Generate Strategies

Evaluate Strategies

Generate Solutions

Evaluate Solutions

Make Decision

Carry Out Decision

What Is Decision Making?

In general, decision making occurs when you have a number of possible choices and you must settle on a single one. Selecting what to wear in the morning or what to eat for breakfast are forms of decision making.

Although decision making is listed as a separate process of thinking, it is also part of problem solving. After generating solutions, you must decide among them. Asking the right questions about your solution is as important as representing your original problem well. Before making a decision, ask the questions shown here.

Recall the problem at the beginning of this section—too little money left at the end of the week. Take that problem, or one that is presently important to you, and follow the steps to solve it. Remember to check for potential blocks to effective thinking that you might tend toward. After generating and evaluating your solutions, make your decision.

CRITICAL THINKING

How Can Other People Influence Your Thinking?

Are you more likely to buy a product that is good for you or one that tastes great? Are you more likely to vote for a candidate who stands for higher wages or protecting the environment? What words or phrases affect your thinking? Consider the issues and yourself.

THE ISSUES

You have read about a number of ways that people limit or distort their thinking. Another interesting behavior results from what's called the *framing effect*, the use of words or phrases that tap into people's values or preferences. Advertisers, politicians, and even parents may use the framing effect to influence the choices people make. For example, before an election year, political groups will conduct a poll to determine the major issues that concern people, such as the economy, jobs, education, or wilderness conservation. They'll then make sure that candidates use those catch words or phrases in their speeches. Basically, they're just repeating back what you've told them is important. Advertisers also do market research to determine why

people buy certain products. What words on a label or in a TV or print ad will make you want to buy the product? Should they use *hearty* or *filling* to describe soup; *lite* or *low-calorie* to describe salad dressing; *reliable, sleek,* or *exciting* to describe a new car? Depending on their values, different people will respond in different ways to such terms, but research will generally discover the catch words that "frame" a product or a candidate in a way that will appeal to a majority of people.

Smart parents know that to get a child to eat a particular food, telling the child that it is healthy isn't nearly as successful as describing how good it tastes.

How can other people influence your thinking?

THE PROCESS

① **Restate the question.** In your own words, state a question about words that attract you.

② **Provide evidence.** From your own experience and from the information above, list some catch words or phrases that influence your thinking *positively*.

③ **Give opposing arguments.** From your own experience and from the information above, list catch words or phrases that influence your thinking *negatively*.

④ **Look for more information.** As you watch TV or read print ads or articles about politics, notice which words or phrases appeal to you and which do not. Research *advertising*

psychology and the *framing effect* in the library or on the Internet.

⑤ **Evaluate the information.** Make a chart with two columns:

Words and Phrases	
Positive	Negative

Record the words and phrases in each column. Think about why each word or phrase affects your thinking as it does.

⑥ **Draw conclusions.** Write one paragraph supporting your answer to the question "How can other people influence my thinking?"

Language and Thought

Our ability to use language sets us apart from other animals. Humans use language not only to think but also to share the results of their thinking with other humans. Language conveys information about everything from concrete objects and events to abstract concepts such as truth and beauty.

Which Comes First?

Can we think about a concept without language? The human tendency to organize the world is at work even in the smallest child. The child has a sense of "dogness" before learning the word *dog*. When the child later uses the word *dog* to refer to a shaggy rug, adults can correct the misconception—again in language. Thought and language work together. The more complex the concept, the more precise the language we require to express it.

Elements of Language

There are several elements of language:

Phonemes. Because spoken language came before written language, the sounds that we are able to make become the units of language. These basic units of sound are called phonemes. Phonemes are strung together to make words. The one-syllable word *spoon* contains four phonemes—the /s/ sound, the /p/ sound, the /oo/ sound, and the /n/ sound. Humans can produce about 100 phonemes, although we only use a portion of them in speech.

Morphemes. Just as phonemes are the basic units of sound, morphemes are the basic units of meaning—words.

Phonemes must be combined in specific ways to become morphemes. A *bound morpheme* is a word that conveys meaning, such as *rest.* By combining morphemes with suffix or prefix phonemes, we can describe an event that is happening (such as "resting") or has happened (such as "rested").

Syntax—Phrases and Sentences. A phrase is a simple combination of words, such as "the blue coat," while a sentence is usually a complete thought. Syntax is the set of implicit and explicit rules by which we combine words, phrases, and clauses to produce sentences. These can be correctly combined in a number of ways to achieve the same meaning.

Semantics. At each level, from morphemes up, semantics is a set of rules and conventions for how to convey meaning.

The following illustration shows how the elements of language are related.

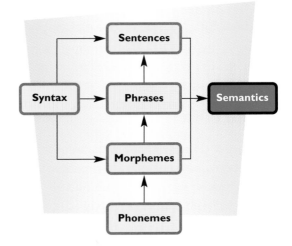

Languages differ in two ways. The lexicon of the language is the set of words used in that language. The grammar of the language consists of the rules for combining those words and for expressing semantic concepts.

Meaning and Understanding

Semantic factors that affect understanding include:

Context. You tell a friend that you met the President yesterday and she says, "Sure, and I won the lottery." Did she really win the lottery? No. She is matching what she perceives as an exaggeration with another exaggeration. As we gain more experience with language, we begin to understand the contexts in which it can be used.

Talking Up or Down. We may express an idea using "baby talk" to a young child and more complex language to an educated adult. Although we are using very different tone and words, with experience, people may perceive the same meaning in both forms of language.

Denotation and Connotation. *Denotation* is the agreed-upon definition of a word or phrase. *Connotation* carries extra meaning. While the term *crippled* denotes the same thing as *physically handicapped,* it connotes something that is considered inappropriate or insulting.

Nonverbal Communication. We interpret the same words spoken by two people in very different ways depending on the facial expression, tone, and body language

of each person. How do you know the difference between the word *Right* when said by a teacher after you answer a question correctly and *Right* spoken by a person who doesn't believe what you just said?

How Is Language Acquired?

In the 1950s and 1960s, psycholinguist Noam Chomsky and behaviorist B. F. Skinner debated about how children acquire language. Chomsky argued that human children are born with language ability and actively figure out language on their own. Skinner insisted that children acquire language through shaping and conditioning.

In *The Language Instinct,* psycholinguist Steven Pinker picks up Chomsky's argument. He points out that children typically grasp the rules of plurals and tenses very early in life. If *dog* becomes *dogs,* then *mouse* becomes *mouses*—just add an *s.* After you cooked dinner, you eated it—add *-ed* to make a past tense. Pinker asks where children learn these rules. A parent might correct a child who calls a dog a cat but may rarely tell him or her how to form plurals or past tenses. The child does that alone.

On Skinner's behalf, it's clear that a child's environment contributes to his or her vocabulary and grammatical repertoire. Studies have shown that a fetus may well hear and learn to recognize the inflections of his or her native language prior to birth. After birth, the infant shows a preference for speakers of that language.

Today, many believe that humans have an innate capacity for language in structures "hard-wired" into the human brain that provide the basic mechanisms for language.

The environment, particularly during the early years, fine-tunes the lexicon, grammar, and even our perceptions of sound.

As an example, the Thai language contains sounds English speakers call "half-tones"—pitches halfway between the tones that westerners normally use in speech. Researchers have found that, when western adults try to learn the Thai language, they are unable to perceive the half-tones, much less reproduce them. Although westerners are born with the capacity to hear those tones, their neurons have either been "tuned" to different tones or have disappeared because there was nothing in the environment to activate them.

Language and Concepts

Does language affect our ability to form concepts? Some languages have as few as two words to describe colors. Studies focusing on different aspects of color perception and recall have demonstrated that, regardless of the number of words a language has to describe colors, the ability to perceive colors is independent of being able to name them. One possible explanation for this is that all humans have the same physiological system for the perception of color.

What about other concepts that aren't dependent on a physiological system? For example, in English, we would say, "If I had the money, I would buy a car." In Chinese, this would be "If I have the money, I will buy a car." In English, you can conclude that you don't have the money. In Chinese, that conclusion isn't obvious.

It would appear that, in some cases, the lexicon and grammar of a language does affect the way in which a person is able to think.

What Must a Language Do?

Deaf people who use American Sign Language show that they are capable of the same complex cognition as people who use spoken English. While some form of language seems to be necessary for such cognition, it need not be spoken. It must, however, provide people with a way of communicating and of manipulating symbolic information.

Bilingualism and Culture

In the 1950s, linguist Benjamin Whorf proposed that language shapes the very ideas that people can have, as well as their perceptions. Here are **two** examples:

EXAMPLE 1: Cultures that live near and make their living from the ocean have many more words for ocean conditions—such as tides or waves—than cultures that live inland. An inland person doesn't need to use differences in ocean conditions to make decisions and, therefore, doesn't even perceive them.

EXAMPLE 2: English has many words to describe how one feels—self-focused emotions, such as anger or irritation. Japanese and other collectivist cultures have many words for emotions related to others, such as sympathy or concern.

Studies have shown that learning to think in the language of a culture that prioritizes concepts differently from your own helps you to understand more about your own thinking. Knowing another language also broadens one's outlook on how concepts affect perceptions and reasoning.

The ability to learn language is especially strong early in life. Second languages are more easily learned in childhood and adolescence.

Language Influences Thought

Although many scientists disagree with Whorf's proposition that language determines our thoughts and ideas, we can probably agree that language influences what we think. Today's concerns over "political correctness" in language demonstrate how our thinking changes when, for example, a female adult is referred to as a *girl* rather than a *woman.*

Language in Animals

While animals certainly communicate, questions remain about whether they truly use language. Attempts to teach human language to animals have been met with mixed reactions from scientists who disagree about how *language* is defined. Further, people who believe that the use of language separates us from other animals resist the idea that animals truly use language.

If we define language as the ability to manipulate symbols and use them to communicate, then it would appear that species such as dolphins, parrots, and chimpanzees use and understand language. They not only recognize and respond correctly to vocal and symbolic commands, but they use symbols to generate unique sentences.

Chimpanzees can be taught to use symbols representing objects and events in their environment. Some learn to use computer keyboards containing symbols to flash messages on a screen. Others have been taught sign language. One of the most famous, a female chimp named Washoe, has learned well over 200 different signs. Washoe combines the signs into meaningful sentences, such as "more banana" or "please sweet drink." Further, Washoe's baby quickly learned over a hundred of the signs from Washoe, and the two were seen communicating with each other using signs.

Although animals may use symbols to form meaningful sentences, they haven't shown the ability to use human language beyond the level of a young child. Further, animals learn the symbols themselves through operant conditioning. Using the symbols to generate new sentences correctly is reinforced with rewards, while human children seem to have an innate need for language. Whether animals are merely responding to conditioned behaviors or are truly using language to communicate will require more study.

Thought in Animals

With or without language, animals have shown surprising levels of thinking. Both chimpanzees and tamarin monkeys show evidence that they are aware of what another being knows or should know.

Chimps will warn another animal when they see something they realize the other animal hasn't seen.

A tamarin monkey will act surprised when a human behaves in a manner inconsistent with what the monkey thinks the person should know. For example, an apple is removed from under a box in the presence of both the monkey and the person. If the person later reaches under the box for the apple as if it were still there, the monkey adopts a position that researchers have identified as "surprise."

Research in animal thinking is restricted only by the cleverness of research methods that limit the interpretation to actual thought rather than stimulus-response or instinct.

SCRITCH SCRATCH

Current Research in Thinking

Linguist George Lakoff and philosopher Mark Johnson have recently combined research from multiple fields to suggest other ways of understanding thought and language.

Citing evidence from cognitive and evolutionary psychology, Lakoff and Johnson suggest that thought and reason are adaptations that are dependent on the nature of the body. Many concepts arise from our perceptions of the relationships of objects and events to our bodies. Examples include in and out, front and back, and large and small.

Lakoff and Johnson also maintain that our language is largely metaphoric, suggesting that we tend to think about even abstract ideas as objects that can be perceived and manipulated:

"Tomorrow is a big day."

"You're in trouble now."

"Give me your thoughts about that."

Is tomorrow really bigger than today? Is trouble a substance? Do you hand me your thoughts? Although none of the sentences is literally true, we easily understand them.

These are just a few of the ideas challenging cognitive psychology today. While the new tools of cognitive neuroscience and psychology have increased our understanding of thinking and language, much clearly remains to be learned.

Humans use concepts, mental imagery, propositions, and language in thinking processes. Information is stored in taxonomies, networks, schemas, scripts, and cognitive maps. Thought processes include reasoning, problem solving, and decision making. Good problem solvers either consciously or unconsciously follow a series of steps designed to identify and evaluate potential solutions or goal approaches.

Language is constructed from phonemes, morphemes, phrases, and sentences. By following explicit or implicit rules for the encoding and understanding of information contained in language, humans manipulate and communicate ideas. Even unspoken languages, such as American Sign Language, allow complex conceptual thinking.

Psychology

analogical reasoning—process of reasoning by comparing information with similar information from another context. p. 141

concepts—classes in which we represent and organize the world. p. 135

deductive reasoning—process of reasoning from the general to the specific, from one or more propositions to a conclusion. p. 141

inductive reasoning—process of reasoning from specific instances to a generalization. p. 141

logic—method of thinking according to a fixed set of rules. p. 141

problem solving—reasoning to change a situation from its present state to a desired state determined by some goal. p. 142

prototypes— "best examples" or most typical members of a concept class. p. 136

reasoning—process of manipulating information in a logical way to reach a conclusion. p. 141

strategy—systematic plan for generating solutions. p. 142

thinking—set of mental processes used for the purpose of solving a problem or attaining a goal. p. 134

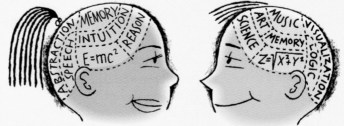

CHAPTER 10

Intelligence

In this chapter, you will learn about:

- theories for understanding intelligence
- intelligence testing
- the range of mental abilities from creativity and giftedness to mental retardation

Prompted by the achievements of his half-cousin Charles Darwin, Sir Francis Galton in the mid-1800s became interested in what accounts for individual differences. From his work emerged the concept of measuring intelligence. Because Galton believed that intelligence was inherited, his work also sparked a great deal of controversy, which has followed this field of study for over a century.

How much of intelligence is inherited, and how much is due to upbringing? What exactly is intelligence, and what do test scores mean? Why do some people with high IQ scores become underachievers, while others with average IQ scores become leaders? How does intelligence relate to creativity and artistic or athletic abilities?

Human beings are uniquely intelligent, and the form of that intelligence is unique in each of us.

What Is Intelligence?

Think of someone you recently met and ask yourself how you could tell if that person is intelligent. You may list things such as "catches on to new ideas quickly, speaks well, reads a lot." We think we can recognize intelligence—and its opposite! **Intelligence** can be defined as the ability to learn and to adapt to the environment. But not even psychologists who have spent their entire careers researching intelligence can agree on what intelligence really is.

Ask 25 experts in the field what intelligence is, as Robert Sternberg and Douglas Detterman did in 1986, and you'll get 25 different responses with little overlap. Here are a few replies:

* Different abilities to solve problems.
* Proficiency in mental performance.
* Knowledge and skills available at a single time.
* Independent abilities operating as a complex system.

Psychologists who study intelligence tend to fall into **two** general groups:

GROUP 1: believes that there is one measurable, general intelligence.

GROUP 2: proposes that there are multiple kinds of intelligence, such as musical, interpersonal, and practical intelligences, in addition to the logical-mathematical intelligence that is traditionally tested.

What Is Intelligence?
acquiring and using knowledge
solving problems
mental performance
juggling many ideas at one time
making sense of things
ability to reason, to understand complex ideas

The Origins of Intelligence Testing

While the controversy over what defines intelligence grows, people continue to search for ways to measure it. An entire field of psychology has developed around testing. **Psychometrics** is the field of psychology that measures psychological characteristics, such as intelligence. For much of the twentieth century, the psychometric view of intelligence has dominated. That view holds that individual differences in mental ability can be measured by tests and that intelligence can be defined by variations in test scores.

The first tests were developed before anyone had attempted to study the meaning of intelligence. The roots of some current theories on intelligence grew out of concerns that traditional intelligence tests weren't assessing all there is to being intelligent. Many psychologists feel that intelligence is more than a score on a test, though tests are still used to define intelligence. A history of intelligence testing is a good place to start to understand the current theories on the nature of intelligence.

The Grandfathers of Testing

The achievements in the study of evolution of his half-cousin, Charles Darwin, prompted the British aristocrat Sir Francis Galton (1822–1911) to try to measure intelligence. Galton, who was interested in individual differences, wrote *Hereditary Genius* in 1869. He claimed that intelligence was inborn. He applied statistical concepts (then used only in astronomy) to intelligence, plotting intelligence in a population on a bell-shaped curve, with the average intelligence at the top of the curve.

Galton's Bell-Shaped Curve

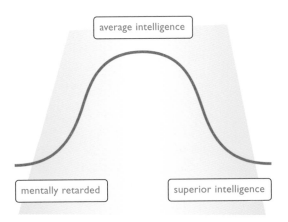

average intelligence

mentally retarded

superior intelligence

We sometimes say that someone who is overly confident has a "big head." French psychologist Alfred Binet actually began his explorations of intelligence before 1900 by measuring the size of people's heads. He thought at first that the bigger the head, the more intelligent the person, but this didn't prove to be true.

The testing movement grew out of Binet's studies when the director of public education in France asked for his help. Binet devised a test to measure the intelligence of Paris schoolchildren. He wanted to establish what was normal for each age from 3 to 11 years and to identify who would need special help. Binet had children put puzzles together, order objects by weights, define words, copy a figure from memory, and perform other activities that tested reasoning, judgment, persistence, and how well they could make adjustments to solve a problem. From his observations, he computed **mental age,** the age that he established was normal for a particular level of performance.

It was German psychologist William Stern who took this concept of mental age and developed a measure of intelligence called the **intelligence quotient: IQ =** mental age ÷ chronological age (how old you are) multiplied by 100. If the Binet test showed that 17-year-old Jane had a mental age of 20, her IQ would be equal to $20 \div 17 \times 100 = 118$. IQ is no longer figured this way; it is calculated by comparing a person's score against the average score of others of his or her age.

IQ Testing Takes Hold in America

You may not remember ever taking an intelligence test, since they are not given as routinely now, but at one time in the United States, every schoolchild was tested. There are several intelligence tests in use, but the two oldest are considered the standards against which any new tests are compared. They are the Stanford-Binet Intelligence Scale and the Wechsler Intelligence Scales.

The Stanford-Binet Intelligence Scale

Binet's scale had been translated and used in the United States at the turn of the century, but the popularity of intelligence testing soared after 1916 when Lewis M. Terman revised it. While working at Stanford University, Terman gave his revised test the name Stanford-Binet Intelligence Scale, which became the gold standard of all IQ tests that followed.

The test increased the number of tasks required from Binet's 54 to 90 and, unlike Binet's, used the intelligence quotient as the end result. The Stanford-Binet launched the era of mass testing of IQ.

The Stanford-Binet is an individual test, which means that a trained psychologist gives the test one-on-one to each test-taker. It scores in **four** areas of cognitive ability:

1. Verbal reasoning (understanding words and their use).
2. Abstract/visual reasoning (forming mental pictures).
3. Quantitative reasoning (using numbers and measurement).
4. Short-term memory (remembering things just taught).

The Wechsler Scales

The other major individual tests were devised by David Wechsler (1896–1981) to assess a person's "overall capacity to understand and cope with the world around him." He put the emphasis in his tests on factors that didn't require using words. Rather than one final score, the Wechsler gives **three** scores:

1. Verbal scale (language, reasoning, and memory skills as are found in the Binet test).
2. Nonverbal performance scale (spatial relations, such as putting puzzles together, sequencing, and problem solving).
3. Full score, calculated by adding the two scores together.

There are three Wechsler tests, each aimed at a different age group: preschool, children, adults.

Unlike the original Stanford-Binet, which used a ratio IQ (mental age divided by chronological age), the Wechsler tests based their scores on a deviation IQ. This means that a person's mental ability is scored in comparison with the average person of his or her age.

Scoring Intelligence
An IQ above 130 = superior intelligence
120–129 = very high intelligence
110–119 = bright normal
90–109 = average
85–89 = low average
70–84 = borderline mental functioning
below 70 = mental retardation

Group Tests

Individual tests such as the Stanford-Binet and Wechsler require a trained psychologist to sit at a table with the student, ask questions, observe responses and the reasoning behind the responses, and then score the test. This is acknowledged to be the most accurate method, but it is also expensive to implement. Group tests are given to many people at one time, are done entirely on paper, and are scored by a computer. They are much less expensive and are considered reasonably accurate, but they test only verbal, not performance, skills.

An example of a group test is the Scholastic Aptitude Test (SAT), which you may already have taken. Millions of students have taken it since it was developed in the 1920s. The SAT is not, strictly speaking, an intelligence test, but in testing your aptitude (ability) to do college work, it is also measuring aspects of intelligence. Originally all multiple choice, since 1994 the SAT has featured some short-answer questions as well.

Questions About Testing

Several issues surround IQ tests, each fertile ground for further research and debate.

What Makes a Good Test?

A good psychological test should be **reliable** and **valid.** A test is considered reliable if the results are repeatable each time it is taken by the same people. Reliability is established in **two** ways:

1. **Test/Retest.** The same person takes the same test at two different times, and the two scores are compared.

2. **Internal Consistency.** The same person responds to different questions that test the same concept to see if responses are consistent.

Validity is the true measure of a test's usefulness: Does the test score correspond to what it is supposed to be measuring? In the case of an intelligence test, is it an accurate measurement of intelligence? This is particularly hard to determine since there is no agreed-upon definition of intelligence. A great deal of work is being done on how to establish a test's validity. One way to check validity is to see if the test score corresponds with scores on more established tests—like the Wechsler—or with school grades. There is a growing sense that validation should also include an ethical question: Should the test be used for its proposed purpose?

What Do Test Scores Mean?

Psychologist Earl Hunt suggested that instead of thinking of intelligence tests as yardsticks, think of them as mental track meets. We should infer ability by combining scores within the test, much as athletic ability is inferred by combining the scores in a decathlon.

IQ has been strongly correlated to many important things that happen in life: schooling, occupation, and even whether someone follows the law. Much of life entails decision-making ability and reasoning power, which IQ is meant to predict. The higher your IQ, the more able you should be to deal with complex situations and decisions. A high IQ, however, no more guarantees success in life than a low IQ predicts failure. Intelligence is not the only factor affecting how you perform in school or on a job, but it may be the most important factor.

Other talents, abilities, and experiences are certainly essential to good performance in many jobs. Some psychologists in the field call these factors *personality traits* or *talents* and others call them *intelligences* (see the section on multiple intelligences later in this chapter).

Are IQ Tests Culturally Biased?

Intelligence tests are based on the premise that intelligence can be measured indirectly by testing people's knowledge and how they use it. But people have had different opportunities to obtain knowledge. And what knowledge is considered to be important in one culture, even within the United States, differs from what other cultures value. IQ tests have been criticized for having **cultural bias**—that is, favoring one culture—white, middle-class American culture—over other cultural groups.

This charge has created controversy in the field of intelligence studies, and recently federal and state courts have ruled that IQ tests cannot be used alone to make decisions about children's placement in particular schools or classes.

Heredity and Environment

Intelligence is considered to be the result of both genetic and environmental factors.

Effects of Heredity

Most psychologists believe that heredity plays an important role in intelligence. There is no single gene for intelligence, just as there isn't a single gene for personality or even height. There are many, as yet unidentified, genes involved.

An important way researchers have tried to tease out the genetic versus the environmental influences on people's differences in intelligence is through twin and adoption studies. Studying twins is a great way to get a handle on **genetic inheritability**—how much intelligence is due to genes—because identical twins have inherited the exact same genes from their parents. Fraternal twins and siblings share half of the same genes.

Effects of Environment

Environmental influences are usually divided into **two** categories:

1. **Shared Environment.** You and your brothers and sisters are influenced by your shared environment: you were all raised in the same family, in which such factors as socioeconomic status and the level of your parents' education was the same for each of you.

2. **Nonshared Environment.** Some things about your upbringing are unique to just you, such as the quality of attention you received from your parents; your friends; your life experiences; and the choices you make of activities, hobbies, and higher education. These are examples of a nonshared environment.

Twin Studies

There are **two** kinds of twins:

1. **Identical Twins.** These twins developed in their mother's womb from a single fertilized egg. They are both the same sex. They have exactly the same genes.

2. **Fraternal Twins.** These twins are as different genetically as any brothers or sisters. They developed in the womb from different eggs. They can be the same sex, or they can be of opposite sexes.

Researchers have found that identical twins who are adopted at birth by different people and raised apart have IQs more similar than fraternal twins who are raised together. This shows the power of genes over shared environment. Adoption studies have also shown that siblings raised in the same family (shared environment) are no more similar than siblings adopted away by different families. Genes are important, nonshared environment is important, but shared environment does not appear to be important at all.

Twin studies by Thomas Bouchard at the University of Minnesota and others have found that the effects of the environment on intelligence fade, rather than grow, with time. How much control have your parents and schools had in your life up until now? As you become more independent and make your own choices, it is your genetically influenced personality and preferences that may lead you to choose your experiences.

Recent Research

The American Psychological Association in 1996 appointed a task force of psychologists, chaired by Ulric Neisser, to examine what is known and unknown about intelligence and its measurement. They tried to distinguish sharply between scientific research and politics. As the report stated, "The study of intelligence . . . needs self-restraint, reflection, and a great deal more research." Here are some of their findings:

* Intelligence includes a genetic component, but just how genes contribute to individual differences in intelligence is not known.

* Environmental factors—such as attendance at school—are important to the development of intelligence, though it is not known what aspects of schooling are important.

* No important gender differences appear in overall intelligence test scores, though there are differences in specific abilities: males tend to score higher on visual-spatial and math skills, and females on verbal skills.

* Intelligence scores partially predict achievement in school—grade point average and number of years of education you complete—and to some extent what you accomplish outside of school, such as your career choice.

* Traditional tests do not sample all forms of intelligence, particularly not creativity, wisdom, practical sense, and sensitivity.

Exciting research continues to investigate the role of genes in intelligence. In May 1998, Robert Plomin of the Institute of Psychiatry in London reported the discovery of a gene variation that is statistically linked to high intelligence, perhaps by influencing the brain's metabolic rate. Reports in September 1999 claimed that scientists had genetically changed a protein in mice to make them more intelligent. Genes are not the whole answer to the question of what makes us intelligent. It remains to be seen how much of the answer they are.

Approaches to Understanding Intelligence

It pays to be smart, but we are not all smart in the same way. You may know every baseball score over the past five years for your home team but may be only average at math. You may be a talented musician but might not like to read books. Each of us is different.

Psychologists disagree about what is true intelligence and what are talents or personal abilities. As a result, different theories abound on what intelligence is. Experts on intelligence tend to fall into one of two camps: those who believe there is one general intelligence and those who assert that there are many different intelligences.

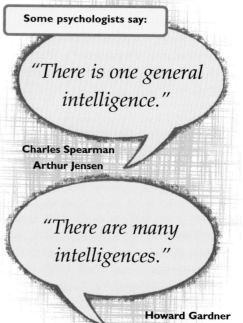

Some psychologists say:

"There is one general intelligence."

Charles Spearman
Arthur Jensen

"There are many intelligences."

Howard Gardner
Robert Sternberg
L. L. Thurstone

One General Intelligence

This approach to intelligence is the bedrock on which the industry of intelligence testing is based. Proponents say there is one factor for intelligence, called **G,** that can be measured with IQ tests and that predicts success in life. They point to data that show that people who do well on one kind of test for mental ability do well on others—whether it is a test using words, numbers, or pictures; and whether it is an individual or group test, written or oral. Those who do poorly also do so consistently on all tests.

Spearman's G

It was British psychologist Charles Spearman (1863–1945), at the turn of the twentieth century, who identified this consistent marker of intelligence and called it "G," using a statistical method called **factor analysis.** G is the factor isolated statistically that distinguishes those who are considered gifted, average, or retarded. Spearman also theorized another factor, called "s," for special factors: various abilities that together with G determine the depth and direction of intelligence. For example, how someone does in math is dependent on his or her G, general intellectual ability, and on his or her aptitude and education in math: s. But Spearman considered G by far the most important factor.

Artificial Intelligence (AI)

Simple tasks such as picking up blocks are easy for humans to do. But how do you get a computer to accomplish a task like that? It takes a complex number of steps to program a computer to accomplish those same simple tasks. Computer scientists have come a long way in their study of artificial intelligence (AI), which is the attempt to make machines and computers act or think as we expect people to. To mimic human thought, computers are being programmed to adapt and learn, detect patterns and draw conclusions, and improve upon themselves. A great deal about the workings of the human mind—learning, planning, explaining, perception, emotion, reasoning—has been learned in the process. AI technology is being used in medicine to assist doctors in making diagnoses of illnesses and in the banking industry to spot credit card fraud. Computers may someday be able to give advice, but will they have common sense? No one knows whether a computer will ever be able to think and feel like a human. But it is worth remembering that computers and robots are designed to help humans, not replace them.

Many intelligence theorists have cited the importance of G, although they don't necessarily agree on what this G actually means. Some describe it in terms of its statistical regularity, others as mental energy, general ability in abstract reasoning, or as an index for measuring neural processing speed.

Speed and Efficiency

Studies have shown a biological basis for general intelligence. The speed of nerve conduction is related to IQ: the brains of bright people use less energy during problem solving. The brain waves of people with higher IQs show a quicker and more consistent reaction to simple triggers such as clicks. This has led some researchers to suppose that differences in G result from differences in the speed and efficiency of information processing along nerve pathways of the nervous system.

Arthur Jensen and others have done simple reaction-time tests to see if there are differences among people with different IQ levels. In the simplest reaction-time studies, the person being tested places her index finger on a button and must immediately lift the finger and press a response button when a light comes on. The time between the light and the release of the finger from the first button is called the decision time: this is slightly faster in those with higher IQs. As the tasks are made more complex, an even stronger relationship between IQ and *decision times* develops. This relationship is the same across all age groups, racial-ethnic groups, and for both men and women.

Much other work on the biological basis of intelligence points to intelligence being the "efficient functioning of the brain," wrote Hans Eysenck in 1999. In his view, G is the energy of the brain that enables it to do its intellectual work.

Multiple Intelligences

L. L. Thurstone (1887–1955) was among the first to propose that a person can be intelligent in numerous ways. His Multiple-Factors Theory states that intelligence is made up of seven distinct mental abilities: verbal comprehension, word fluency, number facility, spatial visualization, associative memory, perceptual speed, and reasoning. He viewed them all as independent abilities that were not associated with one G factor.

Many others believe in more than one intelligence, claiming that traditional IQ tests ignore creative, artistic, and practical skills. Few agree, however, on how many or what these other intelligences are. J. P. Guilford constructed a three-dimensional cube that identified 150 intelligences! Daniel Goleman has made a case for a different way of being smart—emotional intelligence—which includes self-awareness, self-discipline, and empathy. And many alternative views to intelligence propose that it is learnable—that you can learn to increase your mental abilities.

Two theories that have received a great deal of attention are Howard Gardner's Theory of Multiple Intelligences and Robert Sternberg's Triarchic Theory.

Gardner's Eight Intelligences

Intelligence	Description	Examples in People
1. Linguistic intelligence	Using language; expressing what's on your mind and understanding people	Poets, writers, editors, journalists, speakers, lawyers
2. Logical-mathematical intelligence	Using numbers and quantities; reasoning well, understanding the underlying principles of things	Mathematicians, scientists, economists, computer programmers
3. Spatial intelligence	Forming a mental model of some kind of physical space	Navigators, chess players, architects, sculptors, cartoonists, hairdressers
4. Musical intelligence	Thinking in terms of music; hearing and recognizing patterns; creating music	Musicians, composers
5. Interpersonal intelligence	Understanding other people, perceiving their feelings, knowing how to communicate and work collaboratively	Group members, leaders, teachers, counselors
6. Intrapersonal intelligence	Understanding yourself, who you are, and what you can and can't do	Useful in any pursuit
7. Body-kinesthetic intelligence	Using your whole body or parts of your body to solve a problem, make something, or put on some kind of production	Athletes, performing artists such as dancers and actors
8. Naturalist intelligence	Recognizing and classifying landforms and bodies of water, plants, minerals, and animals	Mapmakers, farmers, hunters, botanists, chefs

Gardner's Theory of Multiple Intelligences

There is an old saying about developmental psychologists: when a developmental psychologist has one child, all children are seen as alike; when he or she has two children, the world is seen as split into two kinds of people: extroverts and introverts, masculine and feminine. But when a developmental psychologist has three children, all children are acknowledged to be different.

Howard Gardner, a developmental psychologist at the Harvard School of Education, has four children and does indeed believe that all children are different and shouldn't be assessed by one narrowly defined test of verbal and logical-mathematical intelligence. He doesn't deny that G exists, but he doesn't think it predicts much outside of formal schooling. He believes that the human mind has a range of intelligences, which allow us to solve the kinds of problems we are presented with in life. Each of us has differing abilities within these intelligences, and he believes that the purpose of school should be to encourage the development of all of our intelligences.

Gardner cites a biological base for his theory: when one part of the brain is injured, for example the area for musical abilities, the person can still talk; people who lose their linguistic abilities can still sing. There is not just one intelligence to lose, he maintains. In 1983 he identified seven intelligences, to which he added an eighth ten years later.

The Triarchic Theory of Intelligence

Robert J. Sternberg performed so poorly on his first IQ test in the sixth grade that school authorities had him retake the test with fifth-graders. This seemed so absurd to him that he didn't suffer from test anxiety and easily scored well. As a science project that year, he devised his own Sternberg Test of Mental Ability, a foreshadowing of his professional interest to come. He graduated from Yale, earned a Ph.D. from Stanford, and has been on the faculty of Yale's Department of Psychology ever since.

Good test-takers on traditional tests, he believes, tend to be great in analytical intelligence but not necessarily in the creative and practical aspects of intelligence. His triarchic theory proposes that there are **three** major intelligences that interact and are expressed in many different skills and abilities:

1. **Componential mental processes** together produce the ability to learn and use new knowledge effectively.

2. **Experiential intelligence** is illustrated by the use of past experience to gain insight for new situations. This intelligence is seen when someone adjusts well to new tasks.

3. **Contextual intelligence** involves matching one's activities to the environment wisely. (A study of Brazilian street children revealed they can do the math that they need to run their street businesses, but are unable to pass a math class in school.)

The Diversity of Mental Ability

Intelligence was once thought to be like a can of paint: a genius would have a gallon of it; the person with retardation would have only half a pint; the rest of us would have varying amounts between those extremes. But this is really only part of the story. Many other ingredients make intelligence what it is.

We all have intellectual gifts. We are all athletic and musical. But only to a degree. We don't all achieve at the same level. Not everybody can win an Olympic medal or a Nobel Prize, write a masterpiece, or come up with a scientific equation that will change the concept of life as we know it. Clearly, in the powers of intellect that we all possess, there are extremes.

Giftedness

Usually when we say that someone is gifted—as in "gifted musician" or "gifted athlete"—we know that person has exceptional abilities. But in terms of intelligence, there is much disagreement over the definition of giftedness. IQ is the standard means of identifying superior intelligence, and **giftedness** most commonly implies an IQ above 130 or 140 or that the child is in the top 3 to 5 percent of all students. But those theorists who criticize IQ testing as a measure of intelligence certainly don't believe in defining giftedness by IQ! Howard Gardner, for example, would say that someone could be gifted in any one or more of his eight areas of intelligence.

As the concept of intelligence has expanded, so too has giftedness to include not just superior intelligence but high performance in creativity, leadership, and performing arts. Giftedness shows up in children with excellent memories, vocabularies, or attention spans; exceptional imaginations, curiosity, or powers of observation; unusual abilities in music or the arts; and in the complexity and creativity of the ways they process information.

A major study started by Lewis Terman in the 1920s debunked many of the myths surrounding gifted children. They are not socially maladjusted loners, nor are they usually geniuses. These children are more likely to excel physically, emotionally, and socially in their lives. They become productive and accomplished as adults, but their achievements are not necessarily extraordinary.

Gifted children tend to thrive on encouragement. Young gifted children need intensive nurturing of their abilities to reach their potential. There is no consensus on how best to educate—or even how to identify—gifted children, however. Should gifted children remain in regular classes, or should they be placed in special classes? Parents and educators continue to debate this question.

A few who are gifted make great achievements in life, but perhaps only a few in every generation might be called geniuses, those with extraordinary intellect or creativity.

Intelligence and Mozart

Listening to Mozart may develop your enjoyment of classical music, but it will likely have little effect on your IQ. The weight of evidence is now against the existence of the "Mozart Effect," the IQ-boosting powers of a 10-minute sonata, first described in a 1993 study. The subjects in this study were college students, but the results were applied to many different groups of people. For example, based on that study, a whole industry of Mozart baby products sprung up. Pregnant women bought Mozart CDs to play to their babies even before birth. But soothing though classical music may be, two studies in the journal *Nature* in 1999 found it has no effect on intelligence.

Creativity

What is creativity? What role does it have in intelligence? Consider the role creativity played in the lives of these inventors.

* Edward Land was taking pictures of his family while on vacation when his young daughter asked, "Why do we have to wait to see the pictures?" Why indeed? thought Land, who, when he returned to his laboratory in Boston, invented the Polaroid camera and instant photography.

* While sitting on a hillside in Idaho at age 14, Philo Farnsworth had the inspiration that resulted in television. The neat rows on a nearby farm gave him the idea of creating pictures on a cathode ray tube out of rows of light and dark dots. He used this concept in a science project in school the next year and, when he was 21, demonstrated the first working model of a television.

* Albert Einstein started his work on relativity by imagining what things would look like if he traveled on a beam of light. For him, figuring out how to think about the problem was key to coming up with his Theory of Relativity.

There is a mystique about creativity. Where does it come from? Why do some people seem to have lots of it? How can we be more creative? **Creativity** is simply defined as the ability to develop ideas or products that are original, valued in a particular culture, and useful when completed. As you can see from the examples above, giftedness and talent often overlap with creativity.

Creative people are those who come up with new ideas or products, the creative process results in them, and a creative environment fosters their production. These three areas—creative people, the creative process, and the creative environment—are the major focus of research on creativity.

Creative Exercise

Rearrange five buttons so that each button touches every other button.

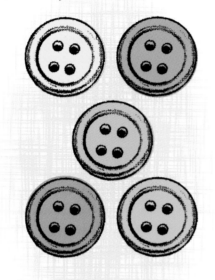

▲

Creativity is imagining different possibilities. It is seeing the same thing as others see, but seeing it in a new way. Turn the page to find a solution to this exercise.

J. P. Guilford spurred on creativity with his presidential address to the American Psychological Association in 1950. He presented the argument that traditional intelligence testing measures **convergent thinking,** the ability to choose a logical answer from a selection of possibilities, but not **divergent thinking,** a thought process that results in many original and different solutions or ideas.

For example, an airline pilot can be highly intelligent in terms of memory (knowing what all the dials and buttons mean), reasoning powers, and following routine instructions. But if a situation comes up for which the pilot was not trained—a terrorist has planted a bomb that will be activated when the landing gear goes down—an entirely new set of responses requires divergent thinking.

A flurry of work followed Guilford's presentation. At first people tried to develop tests of creativity and deductive thinking. E. P. Torrance, for example, devised a number of creativity tests for children and documented the relation between test scores and "creative" real-life performances decades later (starting a business, a journal, or an organization). But other researchers question whether testing high on divergent thinking really reflects all the mental processes that over a lifetime lead to genuine creative contributions.

Others have attempted to use mathematical or computer simulations of the creative thought process or have studied the lives of well-known creative people. Studies of creative people, for example, find that they have such traits in common as:

* Self-reliance.
* Sensitivity.
* Living on the fringes of the culture they inhabit.
* Behaving in a childlike way.

Creativity is not just useful in the arts. Scientists tap their creativity to make discoveries. Business executives want creative employees to develop new product ideas and innovations that will bring in more money. We could all benefit from more creativity in our lives. But only a few people in any generation break through with radically new ideas. The mental processes it takes to do this are still a mystery.

Solution to Creative Exercise

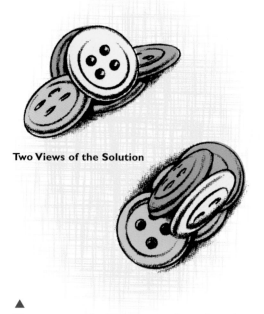

Two Views of the Solution

▲

You can arrange the five buttons so that each touches the other in this manner.

Mental Retardation

A person is defined as **mentally retarded** if his or her IQ is below 70 to 75 on either the Stanford-Binet Scale or the Wechsler intelligence scales and he or she is significantly limited in the skills necessary for daily functioning.

Mental retardation affects one out of every ten American families of every racial, ethnic, social, and educational background. It is caused by something that impairs the development of the brain before birth (abnormal genes, use of alcohol or drugs by the pregnant mother), during birth (oxygen deprivation), or in the childhood years (from disease, head injury).

IQ tests originally measured the various extremes of retardation from "borderline," "mild," "moderate," and "severe" down to "profound." But since 1992 when the American Association of Mental Retardation revised its classification system, the emphasis is no longer on establishing the level of disability. It is focused instead on what abilities an individual does have and what community supports he or she needs to improve daily living.

Savants

Savants are a prime example of the fact that intelligence is not a simple continuum from genius to mentally retarded. **Savants** have IQs below 70 but display extraordinary abilities in one area of competence: musical, memory, or math. Savant syndrome is often associated with *autism,* a psychological disorder first seen in childhood that is marked by social and language impairment and repetitive behavior such as rocking or swaying.

In the movie *Rain Man* (1988) Dustin Hoffman plays Raymond Babbit, an autistic savant who doesn't have a clue how to count money or survive in the world outside the institution he was placed in as a child. But tell him your birthday and he will tell you the day of the week you were born on. Ask him to multiply huge numbers and he can calculate them in his head.

The existence of savants means that at least in some circumstances, mental skills can be surprisingly independent and not controlled or limited to the person's general intelligence.

CRITICAL THINKING

Should IQ Tests Be Used by Society?
Are IQ tests useful tools or should they be discarded? Consider what they're good for. Then read about the issues and decide.

THE ISSUES

At one time in our society, IQ tests were considered so important that every child took them. Now they are rarely given.

Some psychologists argue that despite the controversy surrounding them, IQ test scores predict academic performance and future life, including careers. They measure very well the general mental ability necessary to reason, plan, solve problems, learn quickly, and understand complex ideas. IQ tests can identify children who need extra attention at both ends of the spectrum—the mentally retarded and gifted.

Other psychologists believe that IQ tests are culturally biased and that reliance on them to make decisions about children's education can harm rather than help them. They also argue that IQ tests don't measure creativity and other abilities or talents that are important to success in life. An individual's intellectual worth shouldn't be reduced to one test score.

Are IQ tests useful in our society, or should they be discarded?

THE PROCESS

❶ **Restate the question.** In your own words, state the nature of the disagreement.

❷ **Provide evidence.** From your own experience, and from the information presented in this chapter, list evidence that *supports* the usefulness of IQ tests.

❸ **Give opposing arguments.** List information that is *critical* of IQ tests.

❹ **Look for more information.** What else do you want to know about IQ tests? Make a list of questions and search the Internet, an encyclopedia, or the psychology section of the library.

❺ **Evaluate the information.** Make a chart with two columns:

> **IQ Tests as Tools of Society**
> Use Tests   Discard Tests

Record the evidence and give each item a number from 1 to 5. Number 1 is most important.

❻ **Draw conclusions.** Write one paragraph supporting your answer to the question "How Useful Are IQ Tests?" Be sure to provide evidence for your opinion.

Intelligence is a palette of colors we're born with, learn to use, and add to. Intelligence colors our lives. Our survival—but more than that, our enjoyment of life—depends on it.

Individual differences in intelligence can be measured through tests. IQ tests are powerful, but perhaps limited, barometers of intelligence. Some psychologists believe that there are other kinds of intelligences and that our value to society should not be reduced to one number, the IQ. Psychologists don't agree, and perhaps never will, on exactly what intelligence is. It is much more complicated than simply whether one is "smart" or not.

Psychology
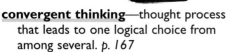

convergent thinking—thought process that leads to one logical choice from among several. *p. 167*

creativity—ability to develop original ideas or products that are valued and useful. *p. 166*

cultural bias—favoring of one culture group over others. *p. 158*

divergent thinking—thought process that results in many original or different solutions or ideas. *p. 167*

factor analysis—statistical technique that isolates what exactly a test is measuring. *p. 161*

G—Spearman's one measurable factor of general intelligence, shared by all mental processes. *p. 161*

genetic inheritability—way of plotting how much a trait such as intelligence is due to inherited genes. *p. 158*

giftedness—high intelligence; also includes high performance in visual and performing arts, creativity, leadership, and physical dexterity. *p. 165*

intelligence—ability to learn and to adapt to the environment. *p. 154*

intelligence quotient (IQ)—measure of intelligence level relative to others of the same age. *p. 155*

mental age—age Binet established as normal for a certain level of performance on his test. *p. 155*

mentally retarded—condition of having an IQ below 70–75 and significant limitations in the skills necessary to daily life. *p. 168*

psychometrics—field of psychology that develops and uses tests to measure psychological characteristics such as intelligence. *p. 154*

reliable—test condition characterized by achieving similar results from the same people. *p. 157*

savants—people whose IQs are below 70 but who have extraordinary abilities in one area of competence. *p. 168*

valid—test condition in which the test measures what it is supposed to be measuring. *p. 157*

CHAPTER 11

Motivation and Emotion

In this chapter, you will learn about:

- how and why people are motivated
- different types of motivation
- the importance of emotion in human behavior

The great humanistic psychologist Abraham Maslow once proposed that humans have a hierarchy of needs. These needs include not only the basic biological needs that we require for survival but higher needs such as recognition, achievement, and a sense of fulfilling our potential as human beings. These needs provide us with the motives for our behavior.

Other psychologists say that our basic biological needs produce drives that make us uncomfortable. We are motivated to act in a way that will relieve that discomfort and make us feel better. Motivation is a complex concept that involves the interaction of physiological, behavioral, and psychological factors.

One of the most important factors in motivation is emotion. The way we feel plays a key role in motivation and in other areas of cognition. Emotion may even be a necessary element in reasoning.

What Is Motivation?

Why does one person skip the biggest football game of the year to study for a math test, while another accepts a lower grade in math to attend the game? The answer is **motivation,** which is the incentive to act.

The Components of Motivation

Consider these components of motivation:

* *Motive*—a stimulus that moves a person toward a behavior designed to achieve a specific goal.
* *Need*—a lack of something that one requires or desires.
* *Drive*—a force that pushes a person to act.
* *Incentive*—a force that pulls a person toward a particular behavior.
* *Emotions*—the states of the body and mind associated with feelings.

Motivation is a concept that can't be directly observed or measured. It is a complex interaction among physiological and psychological factors. Motivation may be conscious or unconscious. "I need a good grade, so I'll study" is a conscious behavioral decision motivated by the need for a good grade. Nibbling on food while you're studying may be an unconscious behavior. Are you snacking because you're hungry? Or because you're nervous?

Needs, drives, incentives, and emotions interact to produce behavior. For example, a biological need for food creates a drive that pushes an organism toward the behavior of eating. If no biological need exists, the organism can still be pulled toward eating by the incentive of tasty-looking food. Both drives and incentives produce emotions that affect the behavior. The behaviors themselves produce different emotions, such as satisfaction.

Needs and Motivation

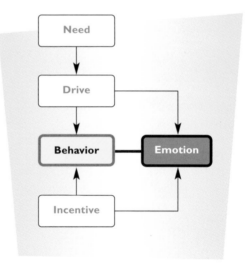

Primary and Secondary Needs

Primary needs are unlearned needs for basic things that affect the ongoing functioning of the body. If your body needs oxygen, food, water, or warmth, your body will respond to that need by producing a drive to fill it.

Although it doesn't involve maintenance of the body, sex is also a primary need. It is an essential need in a much wider sense because it ensures the survival of a species.

Secondary needs are psychological, not physiological. They may or may not have something to do with primary needs. Small children learn that having money allows them to buy treats. Later, this translates to the idea that money allows people to buy food or shelter, so a need arises to earn money. Depending on your culture or social environment, the need for money can vary and may even become an end in itself. Achievement and a sense of belonging are other secondary needs.

Processes That Affect Motivation

Homeostasis is a self-adjusting process that maintains a constant internal environment in an organism. The process responds to changes in both the internal and external environment of the organism.

Feedback is a process in which the output of one action becomes the input of another action. If exercise produces a rise in the body's temperature, that rise triggers cooling mechanisms in the homeostatic process. As the body cools, the temperature change causes the cooling processes to slow down or stop as the body returns to an acceptable temperature.

Homeostasis Motivates Behavior

Breathing is a homeostatic process that controls the amount of oxygen in your brain and bloodstream. When you exercise, your body needs more oxygen, so you automatically breathe more deeply.

When you get cold, you shiver and wrap your arms around yourself. The muscle action in shivering helps raise your body temperature. Keeping your arms close to your body reduces heat loss. Both of these actions take place automatically, working much like a thermostat to keep body temperature constant. They generally take place outside of your conscious awareness.

In humans, cognitive functions can work with the autonomic system. For example, when you are cold, you can build a fire or put on more clothes. If you are hungry or thirsty, you can choose what you want to eat or drink.

Homeostasis doesn't just control physiological functions such as breathing or body temperature. It also acts to keep our emotional states within acceptable limits. This process is reflected in our motivations toward pleasure and away from pain.

Theories of Motivation

Because motivation can't be directly observed, psychologists aren't in agreement about what it is and what causes it. Here are **four** theories to explain motivation.

❶ The Instinct Theory

An **instinct** is an innate, unlearned behavior. When stroked on the cheek, an infant will automatically turn toward the contact, looking for food. Mating behaviors, nest-building in birds, and a bee's "dance" to show hive members the direction of food are largely instinctive behavior. They seem to be "hard-wired" into the genes of a particular species.

At one time, psychologists believed that much of human behavior could be explained by instincts. If people bragged, they had a "self-assertion instinct." If they were humble, they had a "self-effacing" instinct. Such instincts were explained in terms of basic needs such as safety or socialization. The problem was that simply naming behaviors didn't explain them.

While scientists do agree that our behaviors have a genetic component, they no longer believe that instincts drive most motivation. If safety is an instinct, why are some people motivated to climb mountains or engage in "extreme" sports? Something else must be at work.

➋ The Drive-Reduction Theory

In the 1930s, psychologist Clark Hull suggested that the response an organism gives to a stimulus depends both on the stimulus and on factors within the organism, such as drives, prior training, and inhibiting factors. Hull maintained that animals (and humans) experience a drive as an unpleasant sensation. Drive-reduction theory says that an organism will do whatever is necessary to reduce the unpleasant sensation. It does this by filling the need that produces the drive.

Primary biological needs, such as hunger or thirst, are driven by homeostasis. Secondary needs—such as the perceived

Drive-Reduction Theory

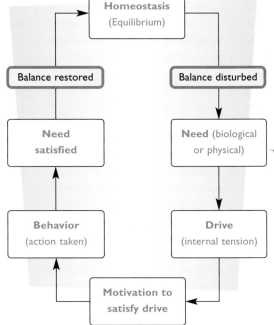

need for more money—also produce an unpleasant sensation, so drive-reduction also works for them.

One problem with this theory is that humans sometimes act counter to what drive-reduction might suggest. People will sometimes go on hunger strikes if they feel strongly about some cause. The motivation not to eat in this situation is greater than the biological motivation to eat.

➌ The Arousal Theory

Some psychologists feel that stimulation is a primary need. They point out that mice will explore a new environment even if no food is available. Infants investigate everything they can lay their hands (or mouths) on.

Too much stimulation causes stress, so homeostatic processes are working here as well. The comfortable level of stimulation seems to differ from individual to individual. Some people exhibit a drive toward high-risk situations and are uncomfortable without the adrenaline rush. Others are content to watch and would feel uncomfortable if they were forced to engage in high-risk behaviors.

❹ The Humanistic Theory

Humanistic psychologist Abraham Maslow proposed that humans have needs beyond those of survival and reducing drive tensions.

Humanistic psychologists believe that the need to do something important with one's life is as essential as the basic biological needs. They acknowledge that lower-level needs must be met before one would move on to higher levels and, eventually, to self-actualization. This list of lower- to higher-level needs is called the **hierarchy of needs**.

Maslow saw this hierarchy as a natural progression of motivation that would be limited only if the individual encountered obstacles that threatened lower-level needs, such as stability or security.

Critics of the hierarchy point to people who seem to show no interest in doing more with their lives beyond having security and meeting their basic needs. It is unclear whether they simply don't have the higher levels of needs or whether they have, indeed, encountered some obstacle that overcame the motivation to meet those needs.

Maslow's Hierarchy of Needs

* *Physiological Needs:* primary needs, such as food, water, shelter, and rest
* *Safety and Security Needs:* protection from threats in the environment, a sense of security, and a sense of stability
* *Social Needs:* a sense of love and belonging and acceptance by others
* *Ego, Status, and Self-Esteem Needs:* recognition, self-respect, knowledge, responsibility, prestige, and achievement
* *Self-Actualization:* fulfillment of one's potential—becoming the most that one can be

Cognitive Theories of Motivation

One can modify a biological drive through cognition. If you're on a diet, you may choose to ignore hunger signals or to eat less than might be necessary to fill you up. Other cognitive theories, such as the **two** listed below, attempt to explain secondary or higher-level motivations.

❶ Social-Cognitive Theory

According to this theory, a person has the mental model of a goal to work toward. At each point, the person compares his or her current situation with that mental model. The difference between the two provides motivation until the goal is reached. As long as there is a difference, the motivation remains.

In addition, progress made toward the goal may be perceived as reward or reinforcement. The anticipation of further reinforcement for success adds to the motivation.

❷ Cognitive Consistency Theory

This theory argues that motivation is the drive to maintain a balance between thoughts, beliefs, and behavior. When you behave in a way that seems to be at odds with what you believe, you feel a sense of discomfort called **cognitive dissonance.** At this point, you are motivated to get rid of this dissonance by:

* Making excuses for your behavior.
* Changing your behavior.
* Not thinking about your behavior (separating behavior from thought about the behavior).

According to the social-cognitive theory, what is the motivation for the person who finished second or third in this race? What might be the reward for either of those runners?

CRITICAL THINKING

Do All People Have Higher-Level Needs?

Some people talk about their "purpose" in life and are motivated to work toward some higher potential. Others seem to be concerned only with putting food on the table and keeping a roof over their heads. Do all humans have higher needs? What do you think?

THE ISSUES

Maslow and other humanistic psychologists maintain that self-actualization—fulfilling one's highest potential and doing something significant in the world—is the highest need of all humans. While acknowledging that a hungry person is more likely to be motivated toward finding food than worrying about self-respect, they maintain that these needs still exist. They point to people who go hungry rather than lose the respect of others by asking for help and to those who improve their minds even when living in poverty conditions.

Humanists argue that people who seem unmotivated may have encountered obstacles that have left them feeling threatened at a more basic level. Many people don't seem to be motivated beyond the levels of physiological needs, safety and security, and social affiliations. In fact, some seem to prefer work over exerting the effort to maintain a family or foster relationships with other people. Opponents of the humanists argue that, just as some people are motivated toward higher risk than others are, motivation toward self-actualization is an individual need rather than a universally human need.

Do all people have higher-level needs?

THE PROCESS

❶ Restate the issues. In your own words, state the nature of the disagreement.

❷ Provide evidence. From your own experience and from the information above, list the evidence *for* believing that all humans have higher-level needs.

❸ Give opposing arguments. From your own experience and from the information above, list the evidence *against* universal higher-level needs.

❹ Look for more information. What else would you like to know? Make a list of your questions. On the Internet, in the psychology section of the library, or in the index of psychology books, research the *Humanistic Theory of Motivation* and *Maslow's Hierarchy of Needs.*

❺ Evaluate the information. Make a chart with two columns:

Humans Possess Higher-Level Needs	
For	Against

Record the arguments in each column and rank each column of arguments in importance from 1 to 5, with 1 as the most important.

❻ Draw conclusions. Write one paragraph supporting your answer to the question "Do all people have higher-level needs, such as self-actualization?" Be sure to provide your reasons.

Physiological Motivation

Hunger and the sexual drive are **two** major physiological motivators that occur as a result of chemical, biological, and psychological factors.

❶ The Hunger Drive

Of all the physiological needs, hunger is probably the best researched of all. You may think of hunger as simply an uncomfortable feeling in your stomach and a desire to eat. Hunger actually arises from a complex mixture of internal and external factors, as you can see in the diagram below.

Factors That Affect Hunger and Eating

External Factors

* ***Stress.*** Stress causes an unpleasant sensation. Eating generally causes a pleasant feeling. Although the two are not related, a person may eat to counteract the negative feelings produced by stress. Eating certain foods, such as carbohydrates, releases the neurotransmitter serotonin, which has a calming effect.
* ***Eating Habits.*** In many families, you don't eat when you're hungry; you eat at fixed times during the day.
* ***Food-Related Cues.*** You might eat because the food is appealing to you, even though you are not hungry. For example, have you ever eaten a chocolate chip cookie even though your stomach was full?
* ***Presence of Eating Cues.*** If you always have a snack an hour or so before retiring, when the clock reaches that hour, it motivates you to go and get food—hungry or not.

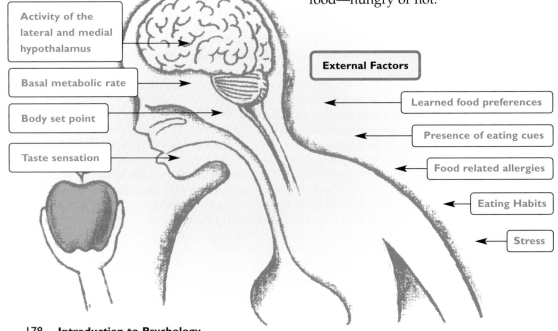

Biological Factors

Activity of the lateral and medial hypothalamus

Basal metabolic rate

Body set point

Taste sensation

External Factors

Learned food preferences

Presence of eating cues

Food related allergies

Eating Habits

Stress

Internal Factors

* ***The Hypothalamus.*** Two processes in the hypothalamus are related to hunger and eating. One monitors chemicals related to the amount of glucose in the body. When glucose drops below the accepted level, the hypothalamus produces the sensation of hunger. After the need has been met, other chemicals are released that signal the feeling that you are full. Another homeostatic system measures the amount of fats and amino acids stored in the body's cells. When their levels drop too low, hunger signals are switched on.

* ***Basal Metabolic Rate.*** Each person burns food at a different rate and expends energy with different efficiency. A person with a high metabolic rate can eat more without gaining weight than someone who is just as active, but has a lower metabolic rate.

* ***Body Set Point.*** Just as we have a temperature "thermostat" that keeps our body temperature within an acceptable range, one theory suggests that we have a weight "set point." Falling below that set point triggers biological processes that cause us to get hungry more often. Newer theories suggest that there is a "settling" point—a range of normal weights within which we can vary.

* ***Taste Sensation.*** Taste is an important factor when we first begin eating. It encourages us to continue. Before long, the taste buds begin to shut down so that we are willing to stop eating when we're full.

❷ The Sexual Drive

A second major source of physiological motivation is the sex drive. Just as the pleasure we feel in eating ensures that we will continue to give our bodies nourishment, so the pleasure that organisms derive from sex ensures that they will procreate, helping their species survive.

The sexual drive, like hunger, is a complex interaction involving chemistry, biology, and psychology. For example, researchers have discovered that, at their most receptive times, female moths release pheromones (biochemical odors) into the air. Moths fly mostly at night, so these odors help male moths find receptive females. Males follow the scent back to the females—sometimes as far as several miles!

The release of specific chemicals in the body triggers the emotions that we associate with the sex drive. When you say that there's a certain "chemistry" between you and another person, you may be right.

Cognition also plays an important role in mediating the sex drive. Just as cultural beliefs play a role in determining the foods one will eat or avoid, personal values and cultural customs are determining factors in when, how, and with whom one satisfies the sex drive.

Although it is a primary need, sexual activity is also associated with higher needs in Maslow's hierarchy, such as belonging, avoidance of loneliness, and self-esteem.

Human Pheromones

Studies have shown the importance of pheromones in the mating behaviors of insects and mammals such as mice and pigs. The detection of pheromones is linked to an organ within the nose called the vomeronasal organ, or VNO. Although humans have a VNO, scientists are unsure whether it is functional—or even linked to the brain.

Drs. David Berliner and Louis Monti-Bloch believe they have demonstrated that humans have functioning VNOs. In one study, a chemical purified from the skin of men significantly affected the mood in women when applied directly to VNO tissue.

Another study showed that a mother is able to identify a T-shirt worn by her infant from a pile of T-shirts. Although there is certainly chemical communication among humans, some researchers feel that it may be quite different from that in animals.

One theory suggests that mammals, including humans, may use scent to identify potential mates with different immune system capabilities from their own. Even within populations with very similar genetic backgrounds, both mice and humans have been shown to select mates with the least similar immune capabilities. This adaptive ability would ensure offspring with immune responses to the widest variety of factors—and the greatest chance of survival.

Psychological Motivation

In addition to the biological needs that we share with animals, humans have other needs that are not so easily explained in biological terms. Curiosity and the tendency to explore and manipulate our environment can be explained in adaptive terms—it is useful to know as much as possible about your surroundings in terms of what could and couldn't help or hurt you. But what about people who are motivated toward higher and higher goals and achievement?

Achievement Motivation

How long do you spend on a test question that has you stumped? Some people will continue to work at it until they figure it out. Others will just go on to the next question. The person who works longer seems to have a higher motivation for success. And that motivation works! Even if two people have equal ability, the one who sticks with it tends to achieve more.

Acquiring Achievement Motivation

The influence of parents and caregivers plays an important role in developing the motivation to achieve. Some things parents can do include:

* Demonstrating that they value accomplishment.
* Giving their children opportunities to solve appropriate problems and praising them for their efforts.
* Giving children the chance to have stimulating experiences.

Expectancy/Value Theory

The expectancy/value theory helps us to understand how adult behavior can influence future achievement motivation. The theory suggests that a person's perception of the inherent value of the behavior and his or her expectancy of success in carrying out the behavior are motivating factors.

Value is determined by:

* How the behavior fits into goals.
* How challenging the behavior is.
* How useful the behavior is.
* How interesting the behavior is.

Expectancy of success comes from:

* The difficulty of the task.
* Your past successes.
* A sense of control and competency.
* How your abilities fit the task.

When children have been exposed to appropriately challenging situations, have been given constructive feedback about their efforts, and have been given enough freedom to develop a sense of control and belief in their own abilities, they will look forward to challenges in later life.

Emotion and Achievement

Some children are praised for their accomplishments early in life. Their failures are treated as learning experiences rather than as lack of effort or ability on their part. These children learn that accomplishment feels good. These positive emotions may motivate them toward achievement later in life.

Extrinsic and Intrinsic Motivation

One type of performance toward achievement is reached through a series of specific goals. Once one goal is reached, another higher performance goal is set. A second type is more incremental. In this type of performance, the individual is always striving to do better or to improve abilities or knowledge. How do these goals affect motivation?

Extrinsic Motivation. For every *A* on his report card, a child receives $3. The money is a reward for a behavior—a reward that comes from outside the child. This is called an *extrinsic reward*. Behaviors leading to performance goals are often motivated by extrinsic rewards such as recognition, the approval of others, or prestige. **Extrinsic motivation** promotes behavior for external rewards or to avoid punishment from others.

Sidebar

Examining Your Motivation

In what contexts of your life do you feel the strongest motivations? Are the motivations intrinsic or extrinsic? What theories help you to understand your motivations? Where would you like to be more strongly motivated? What can you do about it?

Intrinsic Motivation. A child is praised for good grades and achievement, creating a positive emotion within the child. Later, the child realizes that the same feeling arises from the sense of accomplishment he or she gets in successfully completing a task. The reward is within the child—it is *intrinsic*. **Intrinsic motivation** promotes behavior for its own sake and for self-satisfaction. Behaviors leading to self-improvement are generally motivated by intrinsic rewards.

Studies have shown that people with intrinsic motivation are more likely to continue toward a goal, regardless of what other people do or say.

Cultural Factors in Motivation

The behaviors one selects to meet a given need are affected by the culture in which one lives. For example, many Americans wouldn't think of eating dog meat, but they eat beef regularly. Hindus consider cattle sacred and would go hungry before eating beef.

Some argue that biological needs will ultimately win out, even over deeply ingrained cultural taboos. During the Holocaust, fathers and sons in concentration camps were seen stealing food from one another. Cannibalism is unthinkable in most cultures, yet people have been known to engage in it in times of profound hunger.

Still other researchers maintain that culture is not the most important factor in motivation. In Mexico, traditional women's roles include being obedient wives and mothers. Modern Mexican and Mexican-American women continue to seek such roles where their own experience has shown the family situation to be a positive, pleasant one. If a girl's family situation was negative and unpleasant, she is much less likely to be motivated toward following the traditional role.

What Is Emotion?

Emotions are states of the body and mind associated with feelings. Emotions have physiological, behavioral, and cognitive components. When you hear a loud, unexpected noise, your heart rate and breathing increase, your adrenal glands secrete stress hormones, and your eyes widen. Your muscles tense and you take a defensive stance. Finally, your conscious mind has a chance to yell, "Fear!"

Types of Emotion

The ancient Chinese believed that there were four instinctive emotions—joy, fear, anger, and sorrow. Today, theorists have added a few more, such as love, surprise, disgust, and anticipation, but not everyone agrees. More subtle emotions such as irritation, terror, or tenderness are seen as either combinations of the more basic emotions or different intensities of those emotions. Humans can identify dozens of different emotions that may have only slightly different meanings.

The Value of Emotions

Psychologists explain which emotions they call *basic* by demonstrating their adaptive value:

* *Joy* helps to establish social bonds, an advantage in mating and healthy development of the young.
* *Anger* may actually prevent aggression. When a dominant male animal in a pack or herd stares down a challenging opponent, a fight is avoided.
* *Disgust* serves several purposes. It encourages the maintenance of a clean and healthy environment. In addition, vomiting after eating a "disgusting" substance may prevent poisoning, illness, or even death.

Physiological Aspects of Emotion

Think of something mildly depressing. Notice that your shoulders droop and your eyes—in fact your whole body—seem to be directed downward. Now, lift your chin and eyes and throw your shoulders back— and stay depressed! Chances are, you'll find it difficult to maintain a blue mood when you change your body's position.

Does the emotion of depression cause your body to take a "down" position, or does the position cause the emotion? Do they occur at the same time? Theorists have different ideas, but it is clear that your physiology is linked, in some way, to your feelings.

Arousal is a change in the physiological factors controlled by the autonomic nervous system (ANS). You sense your body's arousal when you feel fear, anger, or intense joy. By comparison, the emotions of compassion or dejection feel different.

The ANS has two parts—the sympathetic nervous system, which is responsible for arousal; and the parasympathetic nervous system, which calms the body. These two systems work in a homeostatic process to keep the body in an optimal state of arousal for the situation. Each emotion is linked to a specific level of arousal.

Researchers have identified specific portions of the brain that seem to mediate different emotions. For example, the amygdala in the midbrain has everything necessary to produce the emotion of fear. It can rapidly respond to stimuli from the senses, sending out the "flight or fight" response if needed, and has rich connections to the higher thinking portions of the brain in the cortex.

Theories of Emotion

Theories about emotion vary widely and focus on different components of emotion, such as the stimulus, the bodily responses, and cognitive factors. In your own experience of emotion, you may find examples that could be explained by each of the theories. Human emotion is highly complex, and it is unlikely that one theory will be found to explain it. Further, because emotions are subjective, the element of error in research on human emotions is difficult to control. There are several major theories about emotions, as the chart on the facing page presents.

Cognition and Emotion

Have you ever tried to "talk yourself" out of an emotion such as fear? Even if your conscious mind knows that there is no basis for fear, you may feel it nonetheless. It might be, like Little Albert's fear of white, furry things described in Chapter 7, the result of stimulus-response learning with little, if any, cognitive input.

More subtle emotions, such as depression or complex love/hate relationships, depend largely on how one interprets a situation. It's important to note that this interpretation doesn't have to be conscious. It is still cognitive, because unconscious thinking processes are at work. For example, a parent decides to help a teenager organize his room. The parent may see her efforts as helpful, while the teen may feel the parent is intruding or invading his space. Many of the issues for which people seek psychological help involve getting emotions under cognitive control.

The Necessity of Emotions

The same midbrain structures that affect the formation of memory mediate emotions. Research suggests that our experiences are stored in memory along with some "feeling tone"—a blend of emotions unique to each experience. Some scientists believe that it is this emotional blend that determines the value of a particular action or experience. They maintain that, without the ability to assign various values to behaviors, we would be unable to make rational decisions.

We know that emotional issues are more difficult to think about rationally and to decide upon logically. Although we try to eliminate emotion from our thinking, it may be a critical component of that ability.

Theories of Emotion

Name of Theory	General Principles	Pros	Cons
James-Lange Theory Stimulus ▼ Bodily Response ▼ Emotion	When we experience an emotion-evoking stimulus, our autonomic nervous system produces physiological changes that we experience as a particular emotion.	Assumes a different autonomic response for each emotion. The degree to which this is true varies from individual to individual.	Downplays the roles of both cognition and human values and choices.
Cannon-Bard Theory Stimulus ▼ Mental Processing ▼ Bodily Response AND Emotion	External stimulus is processed by the brain, which produces both the emotion and the bodily response simultaneously.	Argues that we experience the same bodily response to many different stimuli, so there must be cognitive recognition involved in identifying the emotion.	We respond to some situations before we recognize them consciously. At times, an emotion follows a "close call" rather than occurring with the body response.
Schacter and Singer's Two-Factor Theory Stimulus ▼ Bodily Reaction AND Cognitive Appraisal ▼ Emotion	The body responds to a stimulus. The brain appraises both the response and the situation. The appraisal gives rise to the emotion.	The quality of an emotional response changes depending on the situation in which it is experienced. The same experience can produce either fear or excitement.	Schacter's results have not been duplicated. Different studies yield different results, casting doubt on the theory.
Solomon's Opponent-Process Theory Stimulus ▼ Emotion ▼ Opposite Emotion ▼ Balance	Homeostasis is just as important in emotions as in the body. When one emotion is strongly experienced, the opposite emotion is soon experienced to bring balance back to the system.	Explains why anxiety over an event is often followed by relief when it occurs, leaving a sense of well-being.	Some people don't exhibit this sort of process, at least in an obvious way. In particular, joy doesn't immediately trigger a corresponding negative emotion.

Expression of Emotion

One of the most obvious forms of nonverbal communication is the expression of emotion. In seconds, most people can identify a basic emotion on someone else's face. In one example, students were able to tell if their teacher liked the student to whom she was talking by watching her face.

When people see photographs of people in other cultures, they are able to accurately identify emotions expressed on the faces. It would appear that facial expressions of emotion and their interpretation are universal and independent of cultural factors.

The Body and Emotions

Not only do we communicate emotion through our faces, but facial expression itself may affect the emotion. People report that they feel the emotion more deeply when they assume the appropriate facial expression. Try smiling and feeling sad at the same time.

In addition to the face, the whole body can affect emotion. When you say "I'm really up (or down) today," you are generally describing an emotion—but your posture might be erect (up) or slumped (down) as well. As you saw earlier, changing body position can change an emotion. Further, you can better understand what another person is feeling by assuming his or her expression and stance.

Culture and Emotion

While people of different cultures experience the same emotions, they may not respond to situations in the same way. For example, in many western cultures, which tend to be highly individualistic, people are primarily concerned with their own interests and will respond emotionally in terms of those interests. A potential threat to themselves or their livelihood evokes more emotion than a threat to their community or nation.

In collectivist cultures that emphasize interdependence among people, expressions of concern or respect are much more common than self-serving emotions that might disrupt the group well-being. Members of these societies feel more strongly about a perceived threat to their village, religion, or nation than about a threat to themselves.

Social Stereotypes and Emotion

Are women more emotional than men? Studies have shown that, in general, women are more sensitive than men to the emotions of others and are more willing to discuss their emotional states. On the other hand, the range of emotions expressed by either sex is much greater than the difference between the sexes.

For many years, researchers avoided the study of emotion as too subjective a topic. As science learns more about the biological basis of emotion and its interaction with cognitive processes, emotion is increasingly accepted as an integral factor in understanding the human mind.

RESEARCH

Emotion and Decision Making

Fascinated by the story of Phineas Gage (page 42), neurologist Antonio Damasio undertook a study of the role of emotions in reason.

Damasio treated a patient—Elliot—who'd had a portion of the frontal lobes of his brain removed because of a tumor. Elliot retained all of his intelligence, knowledge, and language abilities. But he felt and expressed no emotion. He felt no fear when driving in stressful conditions and although he still worked, he was unable to make the simplest decisions about what to do next or when to stop a particular task.

After many other studies, Damasio suggested that emotions produce the criteria by which we rank options. Without those criteria, there is no way to decide among the options. These studies reinforced the theory that emotion is a critical part of cognitive processes.

A behavior is what we do. Motivation is why we do it. Motivation is a complex combination of needs, drives, incentives, and emotions. Several theories have been proposed to explain emotion, including the instinct theory, the drive-reduction theory, the arousal theory, and the humanistic or hierarchy-of-needs theory. The social-cognitive theory and cognitive consistency theory focus on the role of cognition in motivation.

Hunger, thirst, and the sex drive are physiological motivations, while achievement and doing something "meaningful" are examples of psychological motivations. Motivations can be intrinsic or extrinsic.

Emotion involves physiological processes, expressive behaviors, and cognitive appraisal in generating feelings. The basic emotions of joy, anger, fear, and sorrow appear to be universal across cultures. Emotions may play an important role in cognitive functions such as reason and decision making.

Psychology — WORDS TO KNOW

arousal—change in the physiological factors controlled by the autonomic nervous system. *p.183*

cognitive dissonance—unpleasant feeling that occurs when your behavior doesn't match your beliefs or cognitive assessment. *p.176*

drive—force that pushes a person toward a particular behavior. *p.172*

emotions—states of the body and mind associated with feelings. *p.172*

extrinsic motivation—incentive to perform a behavior for external rewards or to avoid punishment from others. *p.181*

feedback—process during which the output of one action becomes the input of another action. *p.173*

hierarchy of needs—list of lower- to higher-level needs that humanistic psychologists believe all people possess. *p.175*

homeostasis—self-adjusting process that maintains a constant internal environment in an organism. *p.173*

incentive—force that pulls a person toward a particular behavior. *p.172*

instinct—innate, unlearned behavior. *p.173*

intrinsic motivation—incentive to perform a behavior for its own sake and for self-satisfaction. *p.182*

motivation—incentive to act. *p.172*

motive—stimulus that moves a person toward a behavior designed to achieve a specific goal. *p.172*

need—state of lacking something that one requires or desires. *p.172*

primary needs—unlearned needs for basic things that affect the ongoing functioning of the body. *p.172*

secondary needs—psychological needs—such as money and achievement—that may or may not have something to do with primary needs. *p.173*

Childhood

In this chapter, you will learn about:

- **a baby's beginnings**
- **how a child develops physically, cognitively, socially, and emotionally**
- **the influences of friends and family**

A "wild boy" was found living alone in the woods of southern France in 1799. Though he looked about 10 or 11 years old, he couldn't speak or understand language. He preferred to trot on all fours rather than to walk. Though he learned some words, he was never able to master language or social skills. Was it the lack of family and society that stunted his development?

A new belief took hold at the turn of the twentieth century: children need nurturing environments to grow properly. They need someone they can trust to keep them safe, to love and support them.

During childhood, play is work. The world is a learning laboratory. Everyone is a teacher. Each child is a melting pot of genetic and environmental influences, and though the exact amount of each is still debatable, the blend results in a unique individual.

Developmental Psychology: The Study of Change

Maybe your parents kept a record of your milestones of growth: smiled at two months old, sat up at six months, said "mama" at seven months, walked at a year, had a first friend at 15 months, were potty trained at two years, and on and on. These are the details that seemingly only a parent can fully appreciate. But psychologists too have put a magnifying glass to the thousands of changes that take place as infants grow into children, who grow into adolescents, who grow into adults. The result is a field of study called **developmental psychology.**

The study of human development can be broken down into **four** major areas:

❶ Physical Development

The actual growth of the body, its sexual development, the use of its muscles, and the changes in the brain and sensory organs (sight, hearing, taste, and smell) are called **physical development.**

❷ Cognitive Development

The changes in the way we think, reason, learn, acquire language, and use knowledge are called **cognitive development.**

❸ Social Development

The changes in how we relate to other people and develop our own sense of self are called **social development.**

❹ Emotional Development

Changes in feelings and emotions and the development of personality are called **emotional development.**

A child's development is an interactive process that occurs in the mostly predictable steps of **maturation.** Heredity and environment interact continuously throughout our lifetimes. Similarly, as a child physically grows up, the development of his or her emotional life, development as a social being, and cognitive development all interrelate. Just because someone is maturing physically, however, it does not mean that emotional maturity proceeds at the same pace.

Childhood growth occurs in stages that are broken down by age group: prenatal, infants (birth to 1½ years), toddlers (1½ to 3 years), preschoolers (3 to 5 years), school-age children (6 to 11 years), and adolescents (12 to 20 years). Some predictable changes occur within each age group, though there is individual variability.

Life Begins

We refer to a baby's entrance into this world as the miracle of birth. It is certainly a dramatic entrance! From a fertilized egg—no bigger than the head of a pin—emerges a functioning baby. Miraculous as it may seem, the birth of a child is actually the result of a steady process of development that occurs before birth, a nine-month process of **prenatal development** that can be divided into three-month segments called *trimesters.*

Prenatal Development

* ***The First Trimester.*** During this time the fertilized egg, holding genetic information from the father (23 chromosomes) and the mother (23 chromosomes), grows from what is called an *embryo* (which looks like a tadpole) at 8 weeks into a *fetus* three to four inches long—about the size of a fist. It has formed (though not developed) all of the major organs of the body.
* ***The Second Trimester.*** During this time the fetus starts to move. The gender of the baby is determined at the time of fertilization, but now the fetus is visibly a boy or a girl. By the end of the sixth month, it is fully formed but only about 14 inches long.
* ***The Third Trimester.*** The baby grows larger and puts on weight until at 40 weeks it is considered "full term," generally weighing about six to nine pounds. The lungs have matured, and the baby is ready to be born.

The Newborn

Safe in the womb one day, the next day the baby has to breathe on his or her own, maintain body temperature, get used to new sights and sounds, and learn to make his or her needs known. Though equipped with instincts to survive, the baby is rather helpless and depends on the parents for safety, warmth, hygiene, food, and love.

The newborn's development during the first year can be seen in the chart on page 192. The timing of the stages varies from baby to baby, however, and some even skip a step. For example, some babies never actually crawl; they go from dragging themselves across the floor to walking. But almost all children go through most of these changes in behaviors and skills.

The development of these behaviors and skills depends largely on the growth and maturation of the infant's central nervous system. The brain develops rapidly from just before birth and continuing through the first three years of life (and even into adolescence). Science is just beginning to understand how the nerve cells and the trillions of synaptic connections in a child's brain are organized in those first three years so that a child learns to talk, to read, and to solve problems.

For the first few months of life, the lower areas of the brain—the brainstem and midbrain—control most of a baby's activities: breathing, digestion, sleeping, and wakefulness. Newborns, for example, sleep an average of 16 hours a day; by six months old, they sleep 13 to 14 hours and, by age two, 11 to 12 hours a day.

First-Year Milestones			
Timeframe	**Physical Development**	**Cognitive Development**	**Social-Emotional Development**
1–3 months	Sleeps most of time; range of focus increases; begins to lift head slightly.	Has survival reflexes but is uncoordinated and fairly helpless; central nervous system still developing.	Not sociable; cries a lot; depends on nurturing behavior from adults.
4–6 months	Repeats actions; can focus on distances; begins reaching; rolls from back to stomach; sits up with support.	Starts cooing, playing with sounds; listens intently; can coordinate use of hands, eyes, ears, and mouth; by sixth month, uses hand as a tool to reach things.	Smiles a lot; laughs; responds when spoken to; prefers parents and siblings to others.
7–8 months	Starts exploring; crawls or somehow propels self forward; bangs and shakes objects; claps hands.	Understands simple words, own name; stays on a task for more than a few seconds; may say first meaningful word; interested in cause and effect, such as pulling a string to move a toy.	May have fear of strangers.
9–10 months	Pulls to stand; may even walk while holding onto something; can climb on stairs and furniture.	Remembers short sequence of events; out of sight is no longer out of mind.	Starts to show affection; is more of a partner in play such as peekaboo and pat-a-cake; recognizes self and mother in mirror.
11–12 months	Explorations continue with increased mobility; may begin to walk; may bring spoon to mouth.	Solves simple problems; understands more words; may say first words; develops sense of humor; remembers things that happen.	Uses verbal and nonverbal ways to get attention and approval from caregivers; develops strong relationship with primary caregiver.

Born to Perceive

Babies are born with all their senses functioning, though these senses develop over time. Newborns can see, although they focus best at 8 to 14 inches away, the perfect distance to see mom's and dad's faces. Their range of focus is better by three months old. Over the next several months—as they interact more with the world—they will follow movement and people with their eyes. As they gain greater control over their bodies and develop hand-eye coordination, they can reach for and grasp dangling objects and eventually are able to grab them.

A baby's ability to hear begins in the womb. Human voices and music from those months may even seem familiar. Soothing tones help infants stop crying. They begin to coo and babble, sounds that will soon evolve into real words.

From birth, babies prefer sweet tastes. They cry or turn away if given something bitter or sour (as something poisonous might taste). Touch is very important to babies; they like to be wrapped snugly in a blanket and to be hugged.

Though in many ways newborns are helpless, their new world is not a confused blur, nor are their minds blank slates. In 1961 Robert Fantz, M.D., showed that newborns prefer to stare at real faces or patterns with clearly defined edges and high contrast—such as white stripes on black—rather than at colors. These preferences lay the groundwork for the visual stimulation infants seek and set the stage for their later explorations.

Survival Instincts

Researchers are growing more aware of how sensitive these seemingly helpless beings are to their environment. A newborn's reflexes ensure survival. The gag reflex helps a baby spit up mucus from the mother's womb so he or she can breathe. The sucking reflex enables the infant to get nourishment. If you touch the cheek of a newborn, he or she will turn in that direction in an effort to locate mother's breast. A newborn will startle in response to a loud noise or a sudden change in position and grasp your finger if you stroke the palm of his or her hand.

When they are first born, babies tend to be cross-eyed because they have little control over their eye muscles. As they get older, their eye muscles develop and, by the time they are six months old, they have developed the ability to perceive depth.

Attachment and Temperament

The birth of a baby is the beginning of a love affair between parent and child that lasts a lifetime. Studies show that something about the physical appearance of babies fosters attachment to them. Shown pictures of babies, with their cute faces, chubby cheeks, and large round eyes, adults react physically—their hearts beat faster and their eyes dilate. Even babies are interested in other babies!

Emotional Bond

Attachment is the term developmental psychologists use to describe the emotional bond between infants and one or more adults, usually parents or primary caregivers. Attachment is a security blanket. It allows infants to venture out and explore, returning to the adult as a safe haven. It is a building block for later relationships and for the development of the child's personality.

Fathers can respond just as sensitively to their children's needs as mothers, though it is most often mothers who provide the physical care—soothing, feeding, and holding their infants. When distressed, babies turn to the person who satisfies their needs.

Most infants display a secure attachment: a balance of exploration and play with the desire to remain near their mothers or caregivers in an unfamiliar setting. Through various studies, secure attachment has been linked to confidence, successful relationships with friends, and doing well in school. It can even override the effects of an unstable home environment. According to a 1996 report of the National Institute on Child Health and Human Development, secure attachment is not affected by being in child care more than 20 hours a week.

Some infants, however, resist separating from their mothers, are anxious in unfamiliar settings, and may even strike out at their mothers when they are reunited after a separation. Some children even actively avoid their mothers when upset, readily separate from them, and are friendlier to strangers. A very small number of infants approach a reunion with their mothers after separation with blank, even depressed looks.

These different forms of attachment were first described by Mary Ainsworth in 1962 and have been verified or built upon by psychologists since then. Ainsworth also found that the quality of a child's attachment depends on how sensitive the parent is to the infant's need for contact and comfort. Mothers who are depressed or addicted to drugs, for example, do not always attend to their children's needs, and these children may develop an insecure attachment to their mothers.

Children with no attachment at all— such as babies left in orphanages who were rarely picked up or responded to— do not learn to cope with the stresses of everyday life.

The Roots of Personality

Sarah is an easy-going baby, quick to smile and not at all bothered if her mother brings her to a crowded, noisy restaurant or puts her in a new swing at the playground. Ben has been loud and often irritable since birth. He sleeps irregularly and cries if brought into a roomful of new people.

Every child is born with a certain **temperament:** an individual style of responding to events or situations. This includes how sociable, irritable, emotionally responsive, distractible, adaptable, and active a child is. Some see temperament as a biological—perhaps even genetic—root from which grows a person's personality.

The modern study of temperament began in the 1950s with Alexander Thomas and Stella Chess's New York Longitudinal Study. They followed 100 children from infancy through early adulthood to see if individual differences influenced the way the children developed through life. Besides identifying three temperament types (easy, difficult, slow to warm up), they examined "goodness of fit": the extent to which a child's temperament fits with the values, expectations, and style of the child's family. How sensitively a parent responds to a child's needs (and thus how well a child attaches) can depend on the child's temperament and the "goodness of fit."

Temperament tends to persist over time, though it is not necessarily unchangeable. Jerome Kagan at Harvard University, for example, has studied inhibited children (shy, timid, and cautious) and uninhibited children (bold, sociable, and outgoing). He found that three-year-old children who were extremely inhibited were more likely to be inhibited as adults than three-year-olds who were sociable. But he has also found that many children who began life with one of these tendencies changed their behavior as a result of experience. Successful social interactions can reduce shyness, while constant stress or rejection may make an uninhibited person shy.

Physical Development

Your parents may have made marks on the wall every year to plot your growth in height. You couldn't wait to be taller! Growth in height and weight are the most obvious measures of physical development. Growth can occur gradually over time or in sudden spurts. You may even remember as a child waking up with pain in your legs—"growing pains"—as your body adjusted to quick growth. Each person grows at his or her own rate to a height influenced by both genetics and nutrition. After learning to walk, a child is literally off and running.

* **Toddlers** (about 1 to 3 years) are still a little top heavy and take quick short steps; they "toddle" in the walk for which they are named. As the proportion of fat to muscle and bone changes, their bodies become leaner. A major physical milestone in these years is bowel and bladder control, which enables them to be potty trained.
* **Preschool children** (3 to 6 years) pick up speed, running, chasing, and climbing. They start to master the fine-motor skills necessary to cut with scissors, color and paint, and zip up a jacket. As their center of gravity lowers, they can begin to balance. They can throw and catch balls—not an easy feat since you have to watch and time exactly when to close your arms around a ball!
* **Ages six to nine** show continued steady physical growth, though at a slower pace. With increased strength and muscle coordination, boys and girls can play more complicated sports such as basketball. Rates of growth vary considerably

by preadolescence. Some children's bodies mature more quickly than others, with children becoming noticeably taller and going through puberty at age nine or ten, while others might not experience these changes until a few years later. Children become self-conscious at this age, and how they feel about themselves fluctuates widely.

Cognitive Development

The baby in the high chair is a magician and a scientist. Baby throws down a spoon and mother picks it up; baby throws it again and mother picks it up again, maybe with a scowl on her face this time. What will happen if baby does it again?

Words, baby also discovers, have magical powers. "Mama," says the child, and mother appears to give care. "Ba-ba," says the child, and father offers a bottle of milk. Baby's first learned words serve immediate needs, much as an English-speaking adult learning Spanish for travel might start with the words necessary to get a hotel room or a meal.

Dramatic gains in cognitive ability occur in school-age children (6 to 12 years). By second grade they can add and subtract, are proficient readers, and tell jokes. Their play no longer has to be supervised. By fifth grade, children pay attention to details, organize the information they are learning, think more logically, and understand situations with increasing objectivity. With the support and encouragement of parents and teachers, children become competent and confident.

Approaches to Understanding

It is not easy to understand children's cognitive or intellectual development, particularly when children are young and can't tell us what they know or think. Developmental psychologists focus on how babies and toddlers use language and how their visual perception changes as they increasingly prefer complex images. Psychologists also watch how toddlers and preschoolers play, becoming skilled at pretending and playing different roles.

Information-processing theories—an approach first used to study the adult thought process—have influenced the study of cognitive development in children as well. These models assume that the mind is a system for storing, processing, and responding to information, much like a computer.

But the theory most profoundly influencing education and understanding of changes in a child's thinking has been Jean Piaget's stages of cognitive development.

Jean Piaget

The Swiss psychologist Jean Piaget (1896–1980) observed that children have different levels of understanding at different ages. They don't think the way adults do. And their response to a situation depends on their level of understanding at that point in time. Ask a three-year-old girl, whose thinking is still self-centered, what her mother wants for her birthday, and she is likely to say a doll. She can't yet understand that another person has different desires from her own.

Piaget theorized **four** stages of cognitive development:

1. **Sensorimotor Stage (birth to 2 years).** Children learn to coordinate sensory and motor activity; explore their bodies; manipulate objects; and begin to understand that people and things exist even if they can't see them.

2. **Preoperational Stage (2 to 7 years).** Children use language and try to make sense of the world; test thoughts; have a self-centered view of the world; and start to classify objects and learn to count.

3. **Concrete Operational Stage (7 to 11 or 12 years).** Children collect things and use logic to solve problems. A Piagetian experiment illustrates this stage: A child is shown two equal balls of clay and watches as one is rolled out into a snake. A preoperational child will think the two balls now have different amounts of clay, but the child who has mastered concrete operations will know that they have the same amount despite the change in shape.

4. **Formal Operational Stage (12 years to adult).** Children use abstract thinking; can form hypotheses without physically moving objects and test them mentally; and can think about thinking.

Russian psychologist Lev Vygotskii, a contemporary of Piaget, criticized Piaget's theory on the grounds that it represented the child as intellectually on his or her own, working things out through his or her own actions. Vygotskii felt that culture, society, and adults were important to the development of a child's thoughts. Though much of Piaget's theory has stood the test of time, increasing evidence since the 1970s suggests that some of the methods Piaget used to test children may have led to underestimating some of their abilities.

Paying Attention to ADHD

Attention-deficit hyperactivity disorder (ADHD) is so common it is sometimes referred to as the common cold of psychiatry. More than 2.5 million children have been diagnosed with ADHD, and in 10 to 50 percent of the cases, the symptoms continue into adulthood. Children with ADHD have trouble paying attention, they act and speak impulsively, and they can't seem to sit still. They usually have normal intelligence yet have trouble in school and in relating with other children.

There have been disputes among experts and parents about ADHD. Some claim that ADHD is overdiagnosed and that too many children are taking medication to treat it. Some experts question whether ADHD even exists. Recent research has come a long way in answering these questions. A brain scan, for example, is now being investigated as a tool to help in the diagnosis of ADHD.

Although the exact cause is not known, it is now thought that ADHD involves the disruption of the neurotransmitters norepinephrine and dopamine. It also appears that ADHD has a strong hereditary component.

A large study conducted by the National Institute of Mental Health reported in 1999 that stimulant drugs such as Ritalin were more effective than behavioral therapy for ADHD symptoms. The combination of both drug and behavioral therapy didn't help ADHD symptoms much more than drugs alone, the six-center study found. However, the combination did help treat the other mental disorders that are often seen in children with ADHD, such as depression, learning disorders, anxiety, or defiant behavior.

Acquiring Language

Hannah, age two, is alone in the kitchen while her mother talks on the telephone. She sees a carton of eggs on the table and happily begins to plop the eggs one by one onto the linoleum floor. Her mother returns and hears Hannah saying to herself as each egg splatters, "No, no, no, bad." She anticipated her mother's response, but it didn't stop her from breaking the eggs!

When Hannah is a little older, words will have enough meaning to stop her before she touches the eggs. The development of thought and reasoning processes depends on learning words and how to manipulate words into language. Words also provide the first key to impulse control and development of a conscience.

Learning language is an immensely complex task, yet children seem to master it in a relatively short period of time. By age five, children have acquired most of the language abilities of an adult—with some rough edges, such as incorrect grammar!

There are two parts to language: what we understand and what we can say. If you've taken classes in a second language, you know that what you can understand often is more advanced than what you can say. This is true for babies learning their native language, too.

Babies in the first year coo, babble, combine syllables, and start saying their first words. They begin to change the pitch of their words, raising the tone at the end of the word as if asking a question. "Mi?" with a raise of tone at the end conveys the question, "Can I have milk?" "Dat?" means, "What is that?"—a question asked over and over again when babies about 14 to 18 months old realize things have names. Primitive sentences take form at about 18 to 24 months old: "No eat," "Me go," "Me want." These youngsters are learning to use words to communicate.

Children learn a great deal from the responses of the adults around them. When parents answer a child's babbling with "baby talk," the child learns the give and take of conversation: First I say something, you answer, and so on. They get clues about the meaning of words from the context. "Wave bye-bye to grandma," the parent says as grandma leaves the house and gets into her car. The child follows the parent's gaze and learns something new watching grandma drive away.

There are different theories about how language develops. Do children gradually learn to speak and understand language because they learn to imitate sounds and are reinforced for doing so? Or are they born, as linguist Noam Chomsky theorizes, with some sort of innate language acquisition device, a genetically inherited ability to discern grammar, the basic principles of language?

One question key to language acquisition as well as other areas of child development asks whether there are **critical periods,** specific times during development when something is learned or it doesn't happen at all. Eric Lenneberg, for example, agrees with Chomsky that we're born with principles of language, but he believes there is a deadline for applying them. If our first language is not acquired by puberty, it may be too late.

Lorenz and Imprinting

The study of critical periods in animals led to a search for similar periods in human development. In 1952, animal behaviorist Konrad Lorenz showed that in ducks there was a critical period for "imprinting," when the ducks were programmed to respond to the image of their mother. If the mother wasn't there at the critical time, Lorenz demonstrated that the ducklings would follow him or another substitute.

Isolation

The critical period hypothesis was put to the test when a horrendous case turned up in California in the early 1970s. A 13-year-old girl was discovered who had been locked up alone in a barren room tied to a potty-chair for most of her life, with virtually no exposure to sounds or voices. She could barely talk or walk and was completely uncivilized. Doctors at first were optimistic that with a nurturing environment and loving care she could overcome her nightmarish past.

A linguist who worked with her commented that this girl they called "Genie" wanted desperately to recode her world with words, pointing to objects to get their labels. The words she first learned were different from words babies first learn; she learned words for emotions—*angry, sad, excited*—and for colors and shapes. She learned to read simple words.

But after a while, her progress slowed and she never really learned to talk. She couldn't seem to put words together in a normal grammatical way; she would say, "Applesauce buy store" for "We need to buy applesauce at the store."

The same thing happened in the case of the French "wild boy" mentioned in the introduction to this chapter. After early progress, neither child ever completely learned to talk or become "civilized." Does that mean that they missed a critical period in the development of language acquisition, attachment, and other aspects of child development? Were they retarded at birth or retarded by years of isolation? These cases and others like them provide evidence for, but can't prove, the critical period hypothesis.

Social and Emotional Development

Such extreme cases of isolation do, however, underline the importance of human contact in infancy and early childhood. A caring connection with a parent brings trust, attachment, and nourishment of mind and body. It is the emotional foundation from which self-control, self-esteem, understanding right from wrong, curiosity, and motivation emanate.

Piaget said little about a child's emotional life, since his focus was on intellectual growth, but he did write that every intelligent act is accompanied by feelings of interest, pleasure, and effort. These feelings provide the motivation that sparks intellectual growth.

A prime example of the way children's cognitive, social, and emotional development interact is in the way they play.

Child's Play

Play has a purpose. It encourages interpersonal relationships, creativity, exploration, and the joy of living. It enhances learning and the use of language. Watching children at play—what they say and do and what they paint or draw—provides psychologists with insights about what is on children's minds.

A child who pushes a boat around is the captain. The child is in charge and acts out his or her own ideas. The child, not the parents, is in control of his or her play. If there is a new baby in the house, a child may use dolls or stuffed animals to act out his or her feelings. A child can use playtime to explore the natural world by sifting sand from one container to the other. A child can learn how to concentrate by patiently placing one block on top of the other. A child can get pleasure by knocking over the blocks, and he or she can learn to deal with anger when another child knocks them down.

Through play, children gain confidence. Though at 18 months their play is mainly solitary, they like to have other children around them. By three, children play together, learn to get along, take turns, and share. They learn to use words and not actions (such as hitting and biting) to show anger. Play is the magic elixir of child development.

Pretending and imagination are important aspects of playing. Toddlers enjoy sipping tea with a favorite doll or talking with stuffed animals. They make airplane noises while pretending to fly around the house. Preschoolers love to dress up in costumes or play kitchen or store. They act the part of mommy or daddy going to work and coming home again to see their children. Their play often models the behavior of the adults around them.

A child's first friends often are parents and siblings. They play peekaboo and "this little piggy went to market," and they make funny faces at each other. Friends start to take on importance by age four or five. By the time children start school, they can actively choose with whom they will play. Children usually become less self-absorbed and more social as they interact more with others in school.

Social Competence

Children learn to give and receive, express their feelings and ideas, and make choices. This helps them develop **social competence,** mastering the social, emotional, and cognitive skills and behaviors that are needed to succeed as members of society.

The social skills and self-confidence needed to form friendships with other children are critical to social competence. Most of the time, difficulties getting along with others are short-lived, but some children have chronic problems forming friendships. Other children find these children's behavior annoying. It might be bossy, self-centered, or disruptive. Such children get angry easily or don't follow the rules of a game. How a child handles the social interaction necessary in games with rules predicts popularity.

Early problems with social competence often predict future problems in school, poor self-esteem, and mental health disorders. It is critical to help children who display such behavior. The ways to help a child develop social competence vary with the age of the child. Methods often include training in social skills, such as how to enter a group, how to be a fair player in games (follow rules, take turns), how to have a conversation, and how to solve problems and get what is wanted without anger.

Socialization

Play is also a means of **socialization,** in effect introducing a child to the accepted way of doing things in a given society. In the United States, for example, we encourage independence of thought and competitiveness. We start children very young at playing team games, and we cheer them on to win. In a cross-cultural example, the children of Tengu in New Guinea play games that don't end in one team winning; the end of the game comes when the two sides have achieved equality.

Society also influences differences in **gender roles,** which are attitudes and activities associated with each sex. Boys and girls are socialized to play in different ways and with different kinds of toys. Despite a conscious effort on the part of parents and teachers to reduce gender-role stereotyping, boys and girls are treated differently from birth. Girls are treated more gently and encouraged to be expressive and nurturing; boys are encouraged to be more independent, competitive, and outgoing.

There seem to be some inborn differences in addition to the biological sex differences. Boys tend to be more physically active and aggressive, preferring noisy play that requires large groups and spaces. Boys may not play house or play with a doll in the same way as girls do, but when told it is okay, they enjoy dolls, too. Action figures are typically dolls with male cartoon-character themes. Alternatively, girls can be just as rough-and-tumble as boys.

As the roles of men and women have changed at home and in the workplace, many parents and educators have attempted to neutralize socialization along gender lines. Children may see both their mothers and fathers go to work, they may see both parents cooking, cleaning, and shopping for groceries. Yet somehow it is still conveyed to them that there are different expectations for boys and girls.

Becoming a Moral Person

With so much violence on our streets, in our homes, and even in our schools, never has the issue of how a child learns right from wrong, good from bad, seemed so important. The study of **moral development**, how children develop the system of values on which they base their actions in life, has been a focus of psychologists since Lawrence Kohlberg (1927–1987) expanded on the thoughts of Piaget in the 1970s.

Among several approaches to the study of moral development are the following **three** theories:

Sidebar

TV as Teacher

Childhood is disappearing, argues psychologist Neil Postman, as a result of the new media environment: television, rock videos, computers, and film. These media erase the dividing line between childhood and adulthood, exposing young children to adult issues such as sex, illness, death, and war. Children learn from TV, but the lessons are not age-appropriate.

Think of some of the ways that television serves as an agent of socialization.

1. **Behavioral/Social Learning Approach.** People develop morality by learning the rules of acceptable behavior; they are born with no moral sense.
2. **Personality Approach.** This theory focuses on how the factors involved in personality development also affect moral development.
3. **Cognitive Development Approach.** This theory focuses on the development of the reasoning powers necessary to be moral.

Kohlberg, a cognitive psychologist, proposed six stages of moral judgment. They start with an emphasis on avoiding punishment and getting rewards, progress to a level where winning approval from friends and conforming to laws and customs is important, and finally advance to a level where a personal moral code is formed.

Kohlberg's work spurred other theorists to fill in missing pieces. Carol Gilligan, for example, pointed out that in western cultures, girls and women may respond to moral dilemmas differently from boys and men, tending to add an aspect of caring as a moral value.

Theorists who study the development of morality differ over the question of whether people are born with any moral sense. Some psychologists believe that the emotions that form the basis of morality are present at birth: empathy, caring, admiration, outrage, shame, and guilt. A child as young as 18 months can show concern when mother is crying by approaching and hugging her. Certainly a young child feels the sting of injustice when he or she cries, "That's not fair." These natural emotions help children define and redefine their values, testing them through other social interactions.

Morality isn't developed in isolation. Children's positive moral feelings need to be encouraged by the adults in their lives and their negative urges need to be redirected. These adults need to be role models demonstrating not just "Do as I say" but "Do as I do." Few children, or adults for that matter, do the right thing all the time. It is lifelong work to be a moral person.

The Psychological Theory of Development

A profoundly influential theory of how a child develops into a social being was unveiled in 1950 with the publication of Erik Erikson's *Childhood and Society.* Erikson broke with the views of the famous Sigmund Freud that held sway until that time. Rather than seeing a child's development as a series of sexual conflicts, as Freud had, Erikson viewed it in terms of social/emotional conflicts. Erikson, who had studied psychoanalysis under Anna Freud, Sigmund Freud's daughter, saw development as a lifelong process, with significant stages well beyond Freud's emphasis on the first few years of life.

Erikson's psychosocial theory of development consists of eight stages, each focused on resolving a conflict. (See the chart on the next page.)

The Fabric of Family

The birth of a child is like a revolution in the household. Nothing will ever be the same again. Sleep is disrupted. Everyone is uncertain about what to do. No one appears to be in control, except maybe the new baby, who seems like a tyrant with insatiable needs!

In the best of circumstances, when two parents are involved, it takes a lot of hard work to care, love, and guide this new child. With compromises by all involved— parents, grandparents, other relatives, and siblings—a fabric of family is woven.

Erikson's Psychosocial Theory of Development

Age	Psychosocial Conflict	Description
Infancy	Trust versus mistrust	Basic needs must be met through trusting relationships or child will learn to mistrust the world.
Toddler (1 to 3 years)	Autonomy versus shame and doubt	Child learns control over body functions and own activities; starts making choices.
Preschooler (3 to 5 years)	Initiative versus guilt	Child actively explores; tests limits of self-assertion.
School age (6 to 12 years)	Industry versus inferiority	Child overcomes feelings of inadequacy; masters new tasks and skills.
Adolescence (12 to 19 years)	Identity versus role diffusion	Adolescent experiences confusion among various role models; solves "identity crisis," a term Erikson coined.
Young adulthood (19 to 25 years)	Intimacy versus isolation	Young adult commits to an intimate relationship and/or career direction.
Adulthood (25 to 50 years)	Generativity versus stagnation	Adult creates something enduring, such as children or work.
Maturity	Ego integrity versus despair	Adult has resolved the conflicts of previous stages; has gained the wisdom and strength to face frailty and death without despair.

Parenting Style

The parent-child relationship is one of the most important—if not the most important—relationships in our lives. Studies over the past 30 years point to features of this relationship that are linked to a child's psychological development: how responsive the parents are and how demanding they are. The best profile seems to be parents who are responsive—warm, accepting, and are able to see things from the child's perspective. Parents need also to be moderately demanding and offer consistent standards for behavior.

Couples may find they have different ideas about the best way to parent. They may disagree about how much television they should allow, what religion to raise their children in, and how to discipline. Differences are inevitable, and couples must work hard to communicate and nurture their own relationship as well as their relationship with their child.

Many pressures beset families these days: long work hours, fatigue, juggling work and family, endless chores, and so forth. Often relatives don't live close together and aren't available to offer their love and support on a frequent basis.

Divorce

Half of all marriages end in divorce, a difficult emotional experience for parents and their children. It is likely that you or a friend of yours has had first-hand experience with divorce.

How children react to divorce depends on their age and ability to understand and express what they're feeling. Young children need consistency in their lives and are concerned about losing their home, friends, and contact with both parents.

Psychologist Judith Wallerstein, an authority on the effects of divorce on children, proposes that children of divorce have the following psychological tasks to face:

* Come up with a realistic understanding of the divorce.
* Get enough distance from the situation to continue with their lives.
* Handle their anger.
* Deal with guilt (the belief that the divorce was their fault).
* Face the fact that divorce is permanent.
* Be optimistic that in the future they can have a happy relationship or marriage.

Studies link the effects of parents' divorce with emotional and behavioral problems, school drop-out rates, trouble with the law, and difficulties forming intimate relationships. Yet psychologists also acknowledge that it may be more damaging for a child when a troubled marriage continues.

Another adjustment hurdle after divorce is the remarriage of parents to others. For children, remarriage of parents and the blending of families raises a new set of problems, particularly for young adolescents who are coming to grips with their own changes.

Death in the Family

Almost every child faces the death of someone close—relative, friend, or pet. In fact, 5 percent of children under age 15 will lose one or both parents. Death means different things to different children, depending on their age, how close they were to the person who died, and the family's religious beliefs.

Just because a small child hardly seems to notice the loss does not mean he or she hasn't felt it. Even school-age children, who understand death, may act as though nothing happened because they are so overwhelmed. Others may have physical symptoms—a headache or a stomachache—or behavior changes, such as not wanting to go to school or letting their schoolwork suffer.

Research suggests that, beginning between ages five and seven, children should participate in the rituals surrounding death, such as funerals. Death should be openly acknowledged and children should see their parents grieve.

Effects of Poverty

In the United States, money is the key to opportunity. It may not be the key to happiness, but if you don't have enough to put food on the table at the end of the month when the bills are due, this is irrelevant.

Nationwide in 1998, 18.9 percent of all children under the age of 18 were living in poverty, defined by federal guidelines as an annual income below $16,660 for a family of four. Many of these children live in single-parent homes, often with never-married mothers.

Poverty affects all areas of a child's life. Children living in poverty are more likely to suffer health problems; poor nutrition; physical, mental, and learning disabilities; lower self-esteem; and more violence and stress in their lives. Poverty is related to both academic failure and extreme delinquency.

Child Abuse and Neglect

Child abuse and neglect violate all we know about what a child needs to thrive in this world.

Blame it on drugs or alcohol, cycles of poverty, a violent society, or poor parental role modeling. The fact remains that one million children annually are victims of abuse or neglect, usually by parents or a family member.

Children who have been abused often show signs—either right away or years later—of **post-traumatic stress disorder,** which means they may feel emotionally numb, guilty or fearful; they may relive episodes of abuse; or they may develop depression. Children who were abused tend to abuse their own children. But the cycle of abuse can be broken, as numerous studies have shown. Egeland, Jacobvitz, and Sroufe in 1988, for example, identified some factors shared by women who had been abused as children but who didn't abuse their own children. These women:

* Had emotional support from a non-abusing adult in childhood.
* Had undergone therapy at some point in their lives.
* Had a satisfying relationship with a mate.

Resilience

Despite the odds, despite the bad things that can happen to children—abuse, poverty, death in the family, mentally ill or drug-addicted parents—many clearly do all right. They grow up to lead productive lives. Research has shown that most of us are born with a potential for **resilience**, a protective resistance to the negative messages and events that happen in life.

To tap into this resilience, people need social competence and the problem-solving skills to plan and seek help. It takes an awareness on the part of the child that something really major is wrong, that he or she is not to blame and can have control over his or her environment. It often depends on the presence of at least one caring person: a relative, a teacher, or someone in the community. Resilience ultimately means having a sense of purpose and optimism.

CRITICAL THINKING

Can Violence Be Stopped?

Aggressiveness in early childhood is the single best predictor of violent behavior later in life. What can be done to stop it? Read about the issues below and suggest solutions.

THE ISSUES

Violence in the streets and the schools of our nation appears to be on the rise. Looking through the magnifying glass of the media, we are left each time wondering how a violent incident could have been foreseen and prevented.

Research shows that aggression is a learned behavior that develops through observation, imitation, experience, and rehearsal, according to an American Psychological Association policy paper on preventing violence. Helping a young child to find alternatives to aggressive behavior is an important step in preventing later violence. Children need role models, emotional support, and strategies to control their anger and frustration and to learn to deal more effectively when conflicts arise with other children. They can learn that there are other ways to get what they want besides aggression.

But is preventing violence as simple as this might seem? What kinds of factors that lead to violent behavior later in life might be left out of this approach?

THE PROCESS

❶ **Restate the issues.** In your own words, state the question.

❷ **Provide evidence.** List different *sources of violence in childhood* and other factors that might lead to violent behavior.

❸ **Give opposing arguments.** List factors that affect violence that may be *unchangeable*. Consider the evidence about the roots of aggression in the brain.

❹ **Look for more information.** Use the Internet, newspapers, and books to learn more about *aggression* and *violence* in our society and what can be done to prevent it. Add to your list.

❺ **Evaluate the information.** Where does the strongest weight of evidence seem to be? Underline these factors in your lists.

❻ **Draw conclusions.** Write two paragraphs describing your suggestions for preventing violence. Be sure to support your ideas with evidence.

Childhood is a magical time. From genetics, influences of family and friends, and life experiences emerges a young individual. Children progress through fairly predictable stages as they grow physically, cognitively, socially, and emotionally. The end result, however, is as different as each of our thumbprints. These are difficult times for families, for some more difficult than others. But most people have the potential for resilience that carries them forward with purpose and optimism to a bright future.

Psychology WORDS TO KNOW

attachment—emotional bond between infants and their parents. *p. 194*

cognitive development—changes over time in the way we think, learn, reason, and acquire language. *p. 190*

critical periods—times in development when the environment has the greatest impact for specific learning. *p. 199*

developmental psychology—field that studies the many changes that occur as an infant grows into an adult. *p. 190*

emotional development—changes that take place over time in feelings and emotions and the development of personality. *p. 190*

gender roles—expressions of the identity associated with maleness or femaleness. *p. 202*

maturation—orderly, predictable process of growing up. *p. 190*

moral development—how children develop the system of values on which they base their actions in life. *p. 203*

physical development—growth and development over time of the body. *p. 190*

post-traumatic stress disorder—symptoms felt by someone who has experienced or witnessed such traumatic events as child abuse, violence, or war. *p. 207*

prenatal development—growth that occurs before birth. *p. 191*

resilience—ability to bounce back and do well despite the things that go wrong in life. *p. 208*

social competence—mastery of the social, emotional, and cognitive skills necessary to succeed as a member of society. *p. 202*

social development—changes in how we relate to others and form our own sense of self. *p. 190*

socialization—process by which children learn the beliefs, values, and accepted behaviors of their society. *p. 202*

temperament—an individual's style in responding emotionally to situations. *p. 194*

Adolescence

In this chapter, you will learn about:

- how adolescence is defined across cultures
- the biological and cognitive development that sets the stage for psychological changes
- the social context in which adolescents develop
- challenges and possible crises facing adolescents today

Adolescence is a relatively new term, having first been used in 1904 by a psychologist named G. Stanley Hall. Before the twentieth century, young people commonly passed from childhood into adulthood after whatever schooling they received. Their work was a valuable commodity for their families and the economy. Hall's research developed during the Industrial Revolution, when the labor market shifted in emphasis from rural work to urban factories and service industries. Adolescence is identified as a stage between childhood and adulthood and is primarily a phenomenon of the Western world today.

What Is Adolescence?

Adolescence is the period of life between about 12 and 20 years of age. The beginning of this time in the life span is typically marked by bodily growth and sexual maturation. The end of adolescence, however, is more difficult to pinpoint because it is influenced by individual maturity as well as social factors.

When is a person ready to assume the role of an adult? One determining factor may be education. In many developing countries, a high school education is a luxury. In these societies, children experience little time between childhood and a life of work, and working brings adult status.

What is an adolescent today? According to developmental psychologist John Santrock, adolescents in our culture are achievement oriented, are likely to work at a job, experience adult roles earlier than in the recent past, show more interest in equality between the sexes, and are heavily influenced by the media. Does this sound right to you?

How do you think the North American mix of ethnic and economic differences figures into this description? As you read this chapter, use what you learn to think critically about this important phase of your life cycle and its psychological impact.

Two Phases of Adolescence

Because of the diverse changes that a young person experiences over the course of adolescence, it helps to break down the study of adolescence into **two** phases:

1. **Early:** Middle school and junior high years; includes most changes of puberty.
2. **Late:** High school up to about age 20; includes concerns about career, dating, and identity, according to Santrock.

A Time of Change

Adolescence is a time of change on at least **four** levels:

1. Biological, or physical.
2. Cognitive, or intellectual.
3. Social, including peers and family.
4. View of self, including self-esteem.

Changes in emotions occur, too, but emotional changes reach across all four levels.

A Time of Challenge

Psychologists differ on ways of looking at adolescence. Here are **three** points of view:

1. According the Erik Erikson, the primary challenge for adolescents is forming an adult **identity.** This means developing a sense of yourself, who you are as an adult, what you believe in, and what you value. It is difficult work and it takes a long time—eight years or longer. Erikson's personal experiences growing up in a Jewish, immigrant family and his work with Native Americans and with soldiers returning to civilian life

after World War II gave him insights into the "crisis" that people experience as they develop their sense of self.

2. Another popular notion, actually the original notion put forth by G. Stanley Hall, is the "storm and stress" point of view, which suggests that biological changes largely account for apparent turmoil.

3. Other researchers disagree with views 1 and 2. Anthropologist Margaret Mead, who studied adolescents in non-Western cultures, observed no major turmoil in the societies she studied. In these societies, roles and expectations were well defined, which may explain why people had a smoother transition into adulthood. Mead's research may suggest that, within cultures like that of the United States, where roles are less well defined and expectations of one's life's work are largely unformed, adolescents can face some significant challenges and may react accordingly.

Each of these three different points of view lends some insight to the study of adolescence, but we are still far from a definitive understanding of this period of life.

Biological Changes

Researchers see changes in the brain and motor development of adolescents as well as the very clear physical changes that come at this age. Two major physical changes in adolescence are the **growth spurt** and **puberty,** or sexual maturation. These changes occur simultaneously.

The Growth Spurt

Can you recall when you noticed your body beginning to change? Suddenly you were taller, heavier, more muscular. Boys may have developed broad shoulders, girls may have developed wider hips. You eat constantly, it seems. Your voice changes. Perhaps your skin breaks out. You need new clothes.

Before any noticeable growth happens, greater amounts of hormones start to kick in—estrogen in girls, testosterone in boys. These hormones stimulate the production of an increased amount of **growth hormone (GH).**

For girls, the growth spurt might begin around age 10-1/2, peak at about age 12, and slow down at about 13. The growth spurt for boys might begin at around age 12 or 13, peak at age 14 or 15, and slow down at 16 or so. Keep in mind, though, that the rate of physical change varies from person to person. Just look around the halls of any junior high or high school for an endless array of body shapes and sizes.

Boys experience bigger growth spurts than girls because testosterone has an effect on muscles and bones that estrogen does not have.

Genetics has a lot to do with an adolescent's growth, but good (or poor) nutrition can also play a role.

Puberty

During puberty, girls and boys develop secondary sex characteristics, which simply means the appearance of adult genitalia, pubic hair, and increased breast size in girls. With sexual maturity, girls menstruate and are able to conceive children, and boys can physically father children. Again, this happens at varying individual rates; there is no rule as to when all aspects of puberty happen to everyone.

Differences Between Boys and Girls

Each person experiences changes during adolescence. But is it the same experience for everyone? Researchers who study this experience have set out the following pattern:

* Girls who physically mature earlier than other girls in their class experience self-consciousness.
* Boys who mature earlier tend to be proud of their physical changes.
* Girls who mature later seem to be satisfied with their rate of development.
* Boys who mature later tend to suffer from a lack of self-confidence.

Note that the pattern of the girls' responses are opposite the boys' responses.

Differences Do Even Out

Many young people are concerned that they are maturing at a rate different from their friends. Differences in physical development eventually even out and can even reverse themselves as life continues.

Young people who worry about the physical changes they are experiencing can do several things to help ease their minds.

They can talk about their concerns with friends or their doctor. They can also learn about the normal physical changes from health-care providers. It is usually better for people to talk about any concerns they might have, instead of worrying about them alone.

RESEARCH

What Happens to "Bad Girls"?

Writing in 1997, researcher Kathleen A. Pajer described Jennifer, a 16-year-old girl who had threatened her mother with a knife during an argument about telephone privileges. Other problems included a history of truancy, shoplifting, and assault. "What happens to girls like Jennifer as they mature into women?" Pajer asked. Pajer analyzed twenty studies on the adult outcomes of girls with antisocial behavior or criminal behavior in adolescence. The subjects had committed one or more offenses (such as assault or running away) which resulted in their entering the juvenile justice system. After a follow-up period (average 15 years), the studies investigated whether the subjects had committed crimes as an adult or were exhibiting other antisocial behavior.

Pajer found that females who behaved in an antisocial manner during adolescence had higher mortality rates, were 10 to 40 times more likely to commit crimes as adults, and had a variety of psychiatric problems. The antisocial adolescents were also more likely than a control group to have adult substance abuse problems, more likely to raise children who would be arrested, more likely to be divorced, and less likely to attain education beyond high school.

Pajer's research suggested that if she did a 10-year follow-up on Jennifer, she would find that Jennifer "has not graduated from high school, has had multiple unstable relationships, is using drugs and alcohol, uses aggression to solve conflicts, has received psychiatric and social services, has been in jail, and has had difficulties caring for her children." Sadly, this pattern, long known to be true for boys as well, is all too familiar.

Cognitive Changes

The work of Jean Piaget heavily influences understanding of adolescent cognition. Psychologists have also commented on how adolescents—as compared to younger children and adults—process information, pay attention, perceive, remember, and use language.

Sidebar

Quiz Your Cognition

Try this quiz to see where you are on Piaget's scale.

1. Can you imagine a world with more justice, less poverty, or a cleaner environment?
2. Do you think people can do much right now to achieve a better world?
3. Can you solve an algebra problem, read a map, or make a plan?
4. Have you written an organized essay or term paper, engaged in a debate, or used logic in an argument?

If you answered yes to these questions, you are thinking according to what Piaget calls "formal operations." The abilities to 1) imagine hypothetical scenarios, 2) think idealistically, 3) understand abstract thought, and 4) use logic and organizational skills are all signs of this stage.

Piaget on Adolescence

According to Piaget, children and adolescents move through stages; patterns in thinking are shaped at each stage by a particular view of reality. (This was first discussed in Chapter 12.) The stage that applies to older children is the formal operational stage. At this point, a person is able to think in abstract and hypothetical terms. Most researchers agree that the start of adolescence does not immediately signify this formal stage. Rather, it means that the door is open to more advanced thought processes as individuals distinguish their "inner selves" from the outside world.

On the other hand, an awareness of self as apart from others and the rest of the world can also mean self-consciousness, which sometimes leads to anxiety.

Adolescent Cognition	
Aspect of Cognition	**What's Happened Since Childhood**
Information Processing	Improves throughout childhood until early adolescence.
Perception	Changes most from infancy to childhood.
IQ	Stays relatively constant over a relevant 10-year period, such as age 8 to 18.
Attention	Improves through childhood and early adolescence; strategies become more "planful"; adolescents can screen out irrelevant information better than younger children.
Memory	Use of such memory strategies as rehearsal and organization improves. Adolescents can express or describe memories more easily.
Language	Reflects abstract thinking abilities; shows increased sophistication, such as in the use of irony and humor.

Moral Reasoning

Lawrence Kohlberg's study of moral development in children showed that moral reasoning evolves well into adolescence and young adulthood. Kohlberg presented the subjects of one experiment with a story of a moral dilemma in which a man has a choice of stealing a drug to save his wife's life. He evaluated the reasons the subjects gave for deciding that the man was right or wrong to steal and found a pattern related to age. Kohlberg's stages are not completely based on age, however, and not every person reaches the highest moral level.

Kohlberg's stages of moral reasoning are summarized in the table that follows. In the right-hand column of the table, only one alternative is given for each of the stages. Think about the reasoning for alternatives not provided. For example, in Stage 2, what would be the "self-serving" reason the man might use *not* to steal the drug? What would be the Stage 4 reason *to* steal the drug?

Kohlberg's Stages of Moral Development		
Stage	**Motivation**	**Reasoning and Actions**
Preconventional Morality		
Stage 1	Punishment and obedience	Consequences determine morality. The man should not steal the drug because he could go to jail.
Stage 2	Naïveté and hedonism	Rules are all-important; morality is self-serving. The man should obey the law. Or he should steal to get something for himself—his wife lives to help him.
Conventional Morality		
Stage 3	Pleasing other people, receiving approval for behavior	Decisions for what's right are based on what helps others or gains approval. The man loves his wife, so stealing the drug is not wrong.
Stage 4	Good of society, maintenance of law	Respect for law dictates that stealing is wrong. The man should work "within the system" to help his wife.
Postconventional Morality		
Stage 5	Distinction between legal and moral	Choices are based on weighing circumstances and evaluation; it is wrong to steal but more wrong to let a person die. The man should choose life over property and steal the drug.
Stage 6	Individual conscience	Choices reflect an evolved, complex personal belief system. The man loves his wife and wants the drug for her but believes what's right cannot be defined for one case but rather relates to what is good for humankind; hence he chooses not to steal the drug.

Connecting the Study of Morality and Adolescence

Adolescents think idealistically, critically evaluating their world and looking for better answers. In understanding adolescence, it helps to consider how a framework for moral thinking develops. Theorists after Kohlberg shed further light on the complexities of moral decision making. **Four** areas emerge.

As you read, apply your own idealistic thinking and form a critical view. Try to reach a personal belief about each role, then discuss your conclusion with others. What ideas do others have to add that change your thinking?

❶ The Role of Culture

A comparison of Indian Hindu Brahmin children and U.S. children ages 5 through 13 reveals how concepts of right and wrong can differ significantly between two cultures.

Brahman children believe the following acts are right: hitting a disobedient child, eating with your hands, and having your father open a letter addressed to you. They think the following acts are wrong: calling your dad by his first name, eating beef, and cutting your hair soon after your father's death.

William Damon, director of the Stanford Center on Adolescence, found that in some cultures such as that of India, where special practices have social or religious meaning, a definition of morality includes maintaining tradition. In Western cultures, people emphasize the abstract concepts of justice and social welfare.

❷ Gender Differences

Kohlberg's theory has been criticized as failing to include the views of women, who see caring for others as a high moral value. On the other hand, in recent studies women have scored similarly to men on Kohlberg's scale, suggesting that they perceive justice as morally valuable in the same way that men do.

❸ The Role of Parents

Martin Hoffman compared **three** parental approaches to discipline:

1. Love withdrawal.
2. Power assertion.
3. Induction, or explaining why a behavior is wrong and how it affects other people.

Only induction was shown to be effective in helping children develop moral maturity. It provides a framework for children to use to evaluate their own behavior, promotes sympathy toward others, and offers a model for future better behavior.

❹ The Role of Schools and Other Institutions

All in all, how has society helped or hindered the development of morality in young people? What roles have our institutions—our schools, churches, and synagogues—played? You may want to come back to this question after you explore the rest of this chapter.

Social Development

Adolescents develop within contexts provided by the family, the peer group, and schools. Gender and sexuality are also meaningful contexts of adolescent development.

The Family

The family is meant to be a unit of caring in which older members provide shelter, love, and training for the young. Close family relationships serve as models for the individual throughout his or her life span. Socialization—the process by which the values, beliefs, and behaviors of the older generation are transmitted to the young—is an important role of the family.

Changes Within the Unit

Do you and your family really change that much when one member is going through adolescence? The answer is yes; the entire family is affected. Relationships are constantly changing anyway, and the onset of adolescence adds to and magnifies these changes. Here are some ways in which your family relationships can change during this period:

* As an adolescent, you use your more advanced cognitive skills. For example, you use logic to question discipline, and others react.
* Because you think idealistically, you may compare your parents or family to an ideal situation (and be disappointed).
* Family members' expectations of you may continue to be shaped by your behavior as a child, which may create misunderstanding.
* Your parents are likely to be in middle adulthood, undergoing their *own* changes (see Chapter 14), which interact with yours.
* You show increased independence from the family—and again, your parents are likely to react to your changed behavior.

Why All the Conflict?

You're not imagining it—often there is more conflict in the parent-adolescent relationship than in the parent-child relationship. The most intense time for conflict is in early adolescence, the period of striking changes in physical growth and sexual maturation.

Research has shown that even though conflict may increase, it is usually focused on everyday life—messy rooms, what to wear, with whom to go out, when to be home, and so on.

Conflict isn't necessarily a bad thing. It can promote a healthy separation between parent and adolescent and encourage autonomy. As teenagers test their understanding of their identities and their goals, they may also be rejecting relationships and changing their behavior in ways that catch others off guard. Why is she suddenly dressing that way? Why won't he spend more time with the family? Why must they come home just after curfew, instead of just before? This type of conflict in the family can result in healthy maturation of the adolescent, and parents can help the process by leaving the lines of communication open.

Still, conflict is not much fun, and it is often difficult to keep focused on the ultimate goal: the development of healthy and self-reliant young adults within the family unit.

Two-Way Communication

Your Adolescent, a guide for parents published by the American Academy of Child and Adolescent Psychiatry, has the following advice for parents:

"Remember that communication is a two-way activity. Teens who don't seem to want to communicate may have parents who cut them off, who won't tolerate dissenting views, and who ridicule their friends or jump to conclusions. Communication is more than simply answering and asking questions. Communication is about giving and receiving. It's about talking and listening."

This is good advice for both parents and adolescents. Parents most often want to reach out to their children but don't know how to do it. Young people can make a world of difference by letting their parents know the most effective ways to communicate with them.

The Peer Group

Adolescents generally spend an average of 22 hours a week with their friends, not including time spent in school; that's a lot more time spent with friends than with family. Although adolescence is a time of increased importance of the **peer group**, research has shown that peers—those of the same age and social group—are a key influence at all stages of the life span.

Importance of Peer Influence

How important are peer influences? Researcher Harry Harlow has focused on this question in his well-known work with rhesus monkeys. In these studies, Harlow and his associates raised two groups of monkeys: a "mother only" group and a "peer only" group.

Those in the first group, attended to only by their mothers, experienced no interaction with young monkeys. They were antisocial and behaved aggressively when later coming into contact with peers. The second group, raised with same-age peers and without mothers, tended to cling together and became easily "stressed out" over small disturbances. As adults they showed unusual aggression to monkeys outside their peer group.

Developmental psychologists also learned a great deal from the work of Anna Freud and Sophie Dann. They studied a group of six orphans who, in 1945 at age three, were discovered raising themselves in a Nazi concentration camp. The children first displayed intense hostility to the adults who cared for them at the end of the war. They couldn't bear to be separated and were extremely considerate of each other.

These studies suggest that both the family—for security—and the peer group—for socialization—are vital to human development.

Is Peer Influence Positive or Negative?

Because teenagers spend so much time with other teenagers, the influence peers have comes as no surprise. But how strong is this influence and is it positive or negative?

Peer influence is more likely to encourage positive behavior than negative behavior. Researchers have found that teenagers choose friends with similar values.

More Facts About Peers

Briefly, here are some more facts about peer influence from the American Academy of Child and Adolescent Psychiatry:

* Peer influence reaches its height in early adolescence.
* Girls may be slightly more susceptible than boys.
* Adolescents who are not confident about their social skills are most likely to be influenced.
* Even those most susceptible are less likely to follow friends into antisocial behavior than they are to follow neutral or positive behavior.

Conflicts and Pressures

Difficulties that crop up in adolescence may have something to do with reactions to the conflicts between the values of parents and those of peers. Some adolescents form cliques and engage in deviant behavior, or behavior that most people find unacceptable. However, youths who engage in deviant behavior tend to alienate most other teenagers as much as they alienate the older generation. In addition, the number of adolescents who actually engage in deviant behavior is small, compared to the adolescent population as a whole.

The majority of adolescents do not suffer much from conflicts between peer values and those of family and society at large. Why? One reason may be that the influence is spread across very different areas of an adolescent's life.

For example, peers win out when it comes to fashions to follow, clubs to join, and places to go. But parents and other adults have influence over life goals such as where to go to college, what to do after college, and other big decisions.

School has a significant influence on children and adolescents, if only because they spend so much time there between preschool and high school graduation. Hours spent in school add up to about 10,000 total. But research has not provided a completely clear picture of just how school affects adolescents.

Transitions in Schooling

Transitions in schooling are important to adolescents. The transition from elementary school to middle school or junior high can be a tumultuous time. That is likely because this transition is happening along with so many other life changes, from physical changes to social relationships. Positive aspects, on the other hand, include more freedom from family and time with peers, as well as intellectual challenge.

The transition to high school presents challenges, too. The "top-dog phenomenon" occurs when students literally move from being the oldest in middle school to being the youngest in high school. Back at the bottom of the pecking order, they have to get used to a new school with new policies, new teachers, and new students. This phenomenon can affect self-esteem, discussed later in this chapter. And guess what? It happens again with the move to college, and then again in the world of work.

Gender and Sexuality

The transitions of adolescence also involve the complex issues of gender identity and sexuality. Psychologists distinguish between gender, which is simply the state of being male or female within a society, and sexuality, which is one's physical and emotional feelings and behaviors surrounding sex.

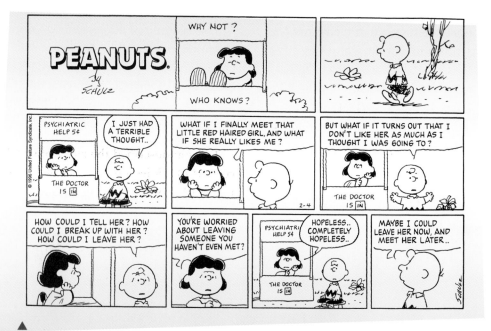

▲ Worry about boy-girl relationships is universal in adolescence.

Different societies treat sexuality in many different ways. Adults in Western cultures tend to restrict the information on sex they give children in an attempt to protect them. As adolescents search for answers to their questions about sex, however, they are often exposed to misinformation. Against a backdrop of sexual references and images in the media, the result can be extremely confusing.

Male and Female Perspectives

Some of the differences in the way boys and girls feel deserve attention. From a psychological perspective, it is important to evaluate the motivation behind certain behaviors, as well as how healthy these behaviors are.

Girls value emotional connection and intimacy. As a result, they are more likely to want a long-lasting relationship. Boys tend to be more concerned with physical pleasure itself and less focused on commitment to any one person at this age.

Many factors influence a young person's decision-making process. Peers influence how teenagers experiment with sexual behaviors. In addition, our culture is filled with sexual suggestions. Families can also greatly influence a young person's decision regarding sexual behavior. It is important to recognize that while many factors may be at work, responsibility for the decisions regarding one's sexual behavior are the individual's alone.

Teenage sexuality is a serious issue. Engaging in sexual intercourse carries the risks of AIDS, sexually transmitted diseases, and teenage pregnancy. In addition, feeling pressured to do something one is not ready to do causes stress, and the negative feelings of regret can damage self-esteem.

Psychological Challenges

Forming an identity is a critical task in adolescence. The work of Erik Erikson and James Marcia illuminate this process.

Identity and the Self

"What do I want to do—now, this afternoon, or with my life?"

"What are my special talents and skills? What are my values and beliefs?"

"What am I going to do when I'm older?"

These are just some of the questions most of us try to answer as we work to discover who we are. During adolescence, these questions can seem especially overwhelming, because we may be considering them seriously for the first time.

Erikson described the psychological conflict of adolescence as "identity versus role confusion." This conflict is resolved in adolescence. This means that by the late teens or early twenties, people have a good idea of who they are. Erikson called the sense of confusion and anxiety that may accompany this work "the identity crisis."

Professionals widely agree with Erikson that attaining "identity achievement" means reaching a healthy place. Higher self-esteem and less self-consciousness are happy benefits.

What happens to people who do not achieve identity formation? Erikson believed they become depressed and drift through life or form a negative identity as "black sheep" or "losers." He believed that on some level people feel it is better to have a negative identity than to have no identity.

Identity Development

James Marcia outlined **four** stages in identity development. Each stage relates to how the individual is tracking in four "real world" areas: career and other achievement goals, values and religion, sexual orientation, and politics.

1. **Identity Diffusion.** The person has not thought about major life choices and is nowhere near committing to a course in life. "I just haven't thought about my values; I don't know what I think."

2. **Foreclosure.** The person does not question his or her life choices but instead bases them on those of parents. "I guess I have the same values as my parents—that's the way I was brought up."

3. **Moratorium.** The person is taking the time to think, question, and experiment with life choices. "I am working on my own sense of right and wrong; I see some good things in the way I was brought up, but I am considering other choices as well."

4. **Identity Achievement.** The person has made some personal commitments to his or her own choices. "I know what I believe and what's right for me."

James Marcia found that adolescents in the moratorium stage generally feel better about themselves than people in the identity diffusion or foreclosure stages. In other words, it is normal to be open to alternatives, to be engaged in a searching process.

The Identity Process

Here are some important points to remember about the process of forming identity:

* The identity process moves through the stages progressively, although a person starts out with either identity diffused or foreclosed.
* Forming identity takes time. Erikson was probably optimistic in stating that the identity stage is commonly resolved by age 18. Instead, the process typically continues well into the college years.
* The process is uneven. One may have a great sense of identity about religion, for example, but almost none about politics; a finely honed sense of self in terms of sexuality, but no career goals.
* Adults continue to struggle with identity; stressful life events such as divorce can cause an adult to reopen whole areas of their lives and re-evaluate them.

The Role of Self-Esteem

Self-esteem in adolescence has been studied with interest. Some psychologists theorize that people value themselves less during this challenging time than at other stages of life.

Life experience is broadening, and with it come new areas of evaluation. By age eight children can evaluate how well they perform physically, academically, and socially. In adolescence, success in work, friendship, and attractiveness to the opposite sex matter as well. Once again, there is much to measure up to, and it is normal to have some feelings of doubt.

Declining Self-Esteem

Erik Erikson believed that a decline in self-esteem comes with all the challenges of the teen age. Other researchers have come to the same conclusion, particularly during school transitions and the top-dog phenomenon. Mary Pipher, in her book *Reviving Ophelia*, discusses the risks to self-esteem adolescent girls face in a culture that does not value their gifts. Boys tend to show more self-esteem than girls do in early adolescence, perhaps because of the boost they receive from increased freedom.

Increasing Self-Esteem

It is difficult to say when feelings of self-esteem even out, since it varies so much from person to person. In fact, studies show modest increases in self-esteem throughout the teenage years. Perhaps the most encouraging fact from all the self-esteem studies is that most adolescents arrive at adulthood feeling pretty good about themselves. This ties in with Erikson's identity achievement concept: once you do the work, you're on your way.

Challenges and Crises

The identity crisis is not the only crisis some adolescents go through, unfortunately. While most adolescents react normally to life challenges during this time, some succumb to harmful or antisocial behaviors.

Substance Abuse

Substance abuse affects the largest number of people of all categories of psychological problems. It is one of the most serious problems in our society. Unemployment, school dropouts, crime, domestic abuse, and child neglect all result from it. Adolescents are particularly vulnerable.

What Is Substance Abuse?

Substance abuse is the use of any substance to the detriment of your health—including psychological and social health. While alcohol, tobacco, and drugs are what most people think of when they hear this term, it also includes substances such as glue or paint thinner, which can cause a "high" when sniffed but also serious damage to the vital organs of the body.

Causes of Substance Abuse

Teenagers and adults may use drugs and alcohol initially for pleasure or to "fit in" with others. Then they may begin to think they are using them for other reasons: to "manage" anxiety or sadness or to "cope" with pressure—according to the American Academy of Child and Adolescent Psychiatry. But adolescents who abuse substances are not managing or coping well. They have more trouble than others their age in dealing with all the normal challenges of life. As a result of substance abuse, they may have trouble in school, on a job, or with relationships, and they are more likely to become involved in accidents.

Perhaps it is no surprise that when parents abuse drugs and alcohol, their children are more likely to do so as well. Both genetic and environmental factors may play a role. Children of abusers should be aware that they are at risk of developing addictions.

How to Cope

Addressing the life stresses that lie beneath adolescent substance abuse is key to finding a way out. Discovering alternative, healthier ways to cope can be a solution. Treatment often includes a therapy program for the family as well as the individual.

Delinquent Behavior

The term *juvenile delinquency* may sound a little dated, but it has meaning in the study of adolescent development. Juvenile delinquency covers a range of behaviors, from "acting out" and antisocial behaviors to threatening and criminal acts. It usually refers to a pattern of destructive and illegal behavior, and unfortunately it is increasing.

In 1993, more than one in three students reported gangs in school, nearly half knew that weapons were being brought to school, half had witnessed violence at school, and one-quarter worried about becoming a victim of violence at school. Statistics indicate the situation is worsening today.

Psychological Factors

Many psychological factors contribute to delinquency:

* ***Having a "negative identity"*** is Erikson's term for the desire to be "someone everyone thinks is bad" rather than "nothing at all." If you can't be a good guy, you might as well be a bad guy rather than a zero.
* ***Experiencing difficulty with self-control*** means not being able to "delay gratification" or wait for what you want—stealing instead of working to buy a CD, for instance.
* ***Having "inadequate standards of conduct"*** means not being able to see that wrong is wrong and not being able to stop before committing a wrongful act. This person doesn't recognize it is wrong to steal and doesn't stop himself when tempted.

CRITICAL THINKING

What Can We Do About Juvenile Deliquency?

Once, the term juvenile delinquent *conjured up a leather-jacketed tough kid straight out of a fifties movie. Juvenile delinquency has changed over the years. Today, some adolescents are committing serious crimes and are a danger both to society and to themselves. How should society address juvenile delinquency?*

THE ISSUES

Why do some adolescents exhibit delinquent behavior while others do not? While the answers are complex, the way a child is raised can make a difference. Many delinquent adolescents were punished harshly by parents as children or were given "mixed signals" about their behavior, which can promote an inconsistent sense of right and wrong.

Influences come from outside the family as well; as children witness the world's real violence (war, crime in their neighborhood), along with a reflected violence in the media, they may become desensitized, especially if they are susceptible in other ways.

Preventing delinquent behavior is not easy. Here are a few facts:

Programs need to include many approaches and methods for helping adolescents; there is no "magic bullet."

The quality of education matters, and schools play an important role.

The burden of "reform" cannot be placed strictly upon the individual; society's institutions need to change.

Attention to at-risk children needs to start early in their lives with individual attention.

Group counseling, "scaring straight" programs, vocational training, and the juvenile justice system have not limited delinquency. Neither have such school practices as suspension, expulsion, detention, or the presence of security guards.

THE PROCESS

1. **Restate the issues.** In your own words, state the nature of the issue.
2. **Provide evidence.** List the ways you believe professionals, parents, and peers *are addressing* the problem of delinquent behavior *constructively*. With what ideas do you most strongly agree?
3. **Give opposing arguments.** List ways of addressing delinquent behavior that *seem negative* or counterproductive. Has anything been left out of the picture that you believe would help?
4. **Look for more information.** What else would you like to know before you form an

opinion? On the Internet, in the library, or in the index of psychology and other social science books, research *juvenile delinquency, parenting and juvenile delinquency, violence in society,* and *discipline problems in schools.*
5. **Evaluate the information.** Is the information you've gathered cohesive, contradictory, or confusing? What are the main themes that seem to be emerging?
6. **Draw conclusions.** Write a paragraph supporting your answer to the question "How can we constructively address delinquent behavior?" State reasons, not just opinions.

Eating Disorders

While many of us probably feel we overeat from time to time, the term *eating disorders* refers to much more severe reactions to psychological stresses. For a person with an eating disorder, food may represent something entirely different from just good-tasting nourishment. Instead, eating or refusing to eat can become a control issue for adolescents as they cope with changes in their lives. *Anorexia, bulimia,* and *binge eating* are **three** eating disorders teenagers may face.

1. **Anorexia.** One in every 200 teenage girls (as compared to 1 in 2,000 boys) in the United States develops anorexia nervosa ("nervous loss of appetite"); up to 10 percent of those may die from the disorder. Symptoms include significant weight loss, continuing to diet even though very thin, and preoccupation with food. Many anorexic teenagers are classic "good girls" who struggle for a sense of control. Treatment includes helping the sufferer regain self-esteem and take some control—to "nourish" herself in other ways—as well as to encourage parents to exert less control.

2. **Bulimia.** More common than anorexia, a person suffering from bulimia (or bulimia nervosa) binges, or eats large amounts of food in one sitting, and then purges by vomiting, using laxatives, or even exercising extremely vigorously.

Many bulimic sufferers may look only slightly underweight or even overweight. Symptoms include many digestive disturbances and conditions related to poor nutrition, as well as damage to tooth enamel from the effect of stomach acids. In recovery, bulimia sufferers must address issues of self-esteem and may realize that they are clinically depressed. Often, however, people with bulimia may not realize that they have a problem and therefore may not seek help.

3. **Binge-Eating Disorder.** Perhaps most common and least recognized as serious, a binge eater uses food as comfort. This individual needs to seek help in addressing underlying psychological problems. Binge eaters often are overweight, and their problems can be lifelong. The distinction between a person with a real problem and someone who may just need to improve his or her diet is that the binge eater has a crisis in self-esteem that underlies his or her destructive behaviors surrounding food.

Solutions include therapy for the individual and the family. Family therapy has been identified as an important step in recovery for young people who suffer from eating disorders.

Teenage Pregnancy

Teenage pregnancy affects almost one million girls a year in the United States, and about 29,000 of them are under the age of 14. The problem is deeply rooted in social and economic causes.

Some Important Facts

The American Academy of Child and Adolescent Psychiatry reports that:

* Most teenage girls who have babies drop out of high school and never go back.
* Most teenage mothers live below the poverty level.
* Only about one in five teenage mothers receives support from a teenage father.
* Teenage fathers are less than half as likely to complete high school as their peers.
* Teenage mothers face more serious medical complications giving birth and have a 60 percent higher death rate than mothers first giving birth in their twenties.
* One-third of teenage mothers 16 years and younger have a second child within two years.

Suicide

Romeo and Juliet are perhaps the most famous pair of teenage suicides. Their story is beautiful and poetic and heartbreaking—and completely fictional. Suicide is not beautiful or romantic in real life.

Almost half a million teens in the United States attempt suicide each year, and suicide has crossed the mind of 1 in 10 teenagers. It is now the third leading cause of death for high school students in this country.

What brings a young person to this desperate point in his or her life? Pressures, crises, rejections—all sorts of problems combined with depression and difficulty in coping can lead to a suicide attempt. All too often people are not aware that feelings of despair and hopelessness can be temporary. They have a difficult time imagining that they will ever feel better. Most people who commit suicide have earlier shown friends or family members it was on their minds. Mental health experts advise you must always take someone's comments about doing away with himself or herself as a sign of trouble and get help.

Heading Off Crises

If this section on crises seems sobering, remember that most adolescents do make it to adulthood with many problems solved—and, most important, with the tools to solve many others. Erikson's idea of forming an identity recognizes that adolescence is a time of overcoming obstacles and gaining the inner strength to continue doing so as an adult.

Psychology teaches that when you are facing a crisis, the best thing to do is find a way to ask for help. And finding help may be as simple as talking it out with another person. The study of psychology also demonstrates that challenges are a part of everybody's life. Developing methods to cope with and learn from challenges—developing inner strength—is in itself extremely satisfying.

Culturally, people experience adolescence, the period in human development between about ages 12 and 20, differently around the world. Some things are the same everywhere, however: all early adolescents experience significant biological changes as they undergo a growth spurt and complete puberty. And the cultural and social contexts of adolescence, whatever they may be, contribute to setting the stage for, adding to, or smoothing out the key psychological challenges. The process of forming an adult identity is the key psychological challenge of childhood. Despite bumps in the road, most adolescents emerge with self-esteem intact and ready to face the challenges of adulthood.

Psychology

growth hormone (GH)—hormone stimulated in early adolescence that controls the growth spurt. *p. 214*

growth spurt—active physical growth taking place in early adolescence; starts at about age 10½ for girls and about age 12 for boys. *p. 214*

identity—sense of who one is, what one believes in, and what one values. *p. 212*

peer group—people of the same age and social status; influences socialization in important ways. *p. 222*

puberty—time of sexual maturation, the point at which adolescents develop secondary sex characteristics and begin to be capable of reproduction. *p. 214*

CHAPTER 14

Adulthood and Aging

YiKES!!

In this chapter, you will learn about:

- **the stages of adulthood**
- **physiological and cognitive changes in adulthood**
- **concerns related to aging**

Adulthood continues the process of psychological development, but more slowly. Psychologists are redefining the stages of adulthood. Some propose that by the year 2020, we may see six Eriksonian stages of adulthood, ranging from youth (18–25 years) to "very old age"— 100 years and over.

During each stage of adulthood, various physical and cognitive changes occur. How much these changes affect a person is determined by a number of factors, not the least important of which is expectation or attitude.

In 1999, 91-year-old comedian Milton Berle was honored for his lifetime of work. "In 1951," he quipped, "I signed a lifetime contract with NBC. It expired 20 years ago!" More and more often, people once considered "very old" are producing remarkable accomplishments. A branch of psychology known as gerontology now studies the effects of aging and the concerns of older people about living out their lives with meaning and facing death with dignity.

What Is an Adult?

Childhood describes a span of years during which tremendous changes take place within an individual. Adulthood is very much the same, though it can be more than three times as long, lasting from about age 20 through the end of life. Today, that can easily come well into one's eighties or nineties.

The changes in childhood are obvious. An individual grows from a tiny infant to a fully formed adult. Psychologically, the changes are just as profound. The changes in adulthood take place more slowly and less obviously, but they are there, nonetheless. Just as there are important developmental tasks at each stage of childhood and adolescence, adults also have tasks to accomplish.

Individual Differences

At the beginning of a marathon, all the runners are bunched together. Soon, however, considerable distances may open up between individual runners. The same is true of life. By the time we reach adulthood, many of the psychological traits that define us have already developed. Some individuals still seem rather young, while others seem very mature in their behavior.

You may know people who seem "old" at 30, while others appear "young" at 70. Our perceptions about people are due as much to their attitudes about life, their expectations, and their openness to change as they are to their physical appearances.

Periods in Adulthood

Because individual development differs greatly—a difference that often increases through the years of adulthood—it is difficult to clearly define stages within the adult years. Some studies indicate that people perceive their lives as having periods of stability, followed by periods of change. These may or may not occur in the same age ranges.

It is helpful, however, to have a framework for considering the tasks or developmental challenges that individuals face as they move through their adult years.

Stages of Adulthood
Early Adulthood—Erikson: Stage 6
20–40 years. Decisions are made about relationships, marriage, and parenthood; physical health peaks; sense of identity continues to grow; career choices are made; intellectual abilities increase.
Middle Adulthood—Erikson: Stage 7
40 to 60–65 years. Search for meaning in life assumes greater importance; some physical deterioration occurs; gender characteristics may become less defined; wisdom and problem-solving ability increase.
Late Adulthood—Erikson: Stage 8
60–65 years and older. Most people are healthy and active mentally and physically, although some abilities decline; they cope with physical/health limitations, loss of loved ones, retirement; they reflect on life and its successes.

Early Adulthood

Early adulthood is often described as the period between ages 20 and 40. In the early stages, people may "try their wings"—to begin to do things a bit differently from their parents. Many need to become independent—to move away from home and begin a life of their own. For some, establishing a career becomes the focus. Others focus on forming close relationships.

Intimacy vs. Isolation

In his stage six, early adulthood, Erikson suggests that the primary task is the development of intimacy. **Intimacy,** to a psychologist, does not describe a physical relationship but refers to one's ability to relate to another human being on a deep, personal level.

In adolescence, relationships are often an exploration of one's identity—a role that one "tries on" to see how it feels. Relationships in young adulthood are less about one's self and more about the larger satisfaction that can be experienced through the close interaction of two individuals. This includes the formation of close friendships as well as marriage, companionship, and family life.

Commitment may be difficult for a person who hasn't yet come to terms with his or her own identity. The intimacy of young adulthood is different from earlier relationships, in that the focus is not on what you will get in return for your participation. In a general sense, love is the willingness to give without expecting anything in return.

The inability to achieve this sort of intimacy with others results in a form of **isolation.** The individual feels separate from others and lacks the advantages of the strength and support people gain from close relationships.

Work

Freud once said that a healthy adult is one who can love and work. In early adulthood, people explore career choices and decide what they will do to feel productive and to support both their independence and a family.

Someone who attended college or other training beyond high school may have already decided on a career. It is, however, becoming more common for people to reevaluate their work after a number of years. In some cases, people may be attracted to newly created professions. In other instances, people may embrace opportunities that they previously avoided for economic or practical reasons.

And sometimes the family structure changes so that one or the other parent can return to the work force.

Marriage

Finding a marriage partner with whom to bear and raise children is important to most people in early adulthood. This makes considerable biological sense. The commitment of marriage encourages couples to stay together and cooperate to nurture children to adulthood, thus increasing the likelihood that one's genes will be passed on.

Marriage in America

Only about a quarter of Americans over 18 have never been married. Worldwide, 90 percent of adults marry. With many young Americans focusing on educational and career goals, the average age at the time of a first marriage has risen from 23 to 27 for men and from 21 to 25 for women.

In the 1600s and 1700s, parents arranged most marriages. Arranged marriages were based on the social or monetary benefits to the families involved and were intended to provide a stable home for children of the marriage. Since the 1800s, most Americans have based their marriages on romantic love.

In many successful marriages, companionship and intimacy—in both the physical and psychological senses—are the primary goals. Married people have a sense of security, as well as the opportunity to share their successes and problems with someone who cares for them.

Choosing a Spouse

Some of the factors that influence one's choice of a spouse are:

* Religion.
* Level of education.
* Social status.
* Age.
* Ethnicity.
* Attitudes toward health.
* Attitudes toward life goals.
* Attitudes toward having children.

Most people choose a spouse with whom they share some or most of these attitudes. Marrying someone with whom one has grown up is fairly common, perhaps because of the likelihood of sharing similar attitudes and attributes.

Marriages between people with similar interests and goals have a greater chance of success, partly because fewer opportunities for disagreements arise as the marriage is developing. Further, a sense of working together toward and achieving a common goal may help to strengthen a marriage.

Family Life

As people become more settled in their career choices and within a marital relationship, the natural tendency for many is to start a family. Because people are marrying for the first time later in life, they are also having children later in life. Today many people, for example, begin having children when they are in their thirties.

Against this backdrop, it is not unusual for both parents to work outside the home and share parenting responsibilities. This is a much different scenario from a generation or two before, when gender roles were much more clearly defined. Typically the mother stayed home to take care of the children while the father worked outside the home. Today no scenario is typical, since any combination of responsibilities for each parent is possible.

Whatever the roles and responsibilities of each parent might be, the important result should be for children to feel loved and secure.

"Let's try getting up every night at 2:00 AM to feed the cat. If we enjoy doing that, then we can talk about having a baby."

Divorce

Many marriages end in divorce. Divorce rates are high when people marry at a very young age. Because teenagers' identities are not fully established and their reasons for marriage may be shortsighted, many teenage marriages end in divorce. Even marriages among people in their early twenties have a higher divorce rate than among adults on the whole. Marriages among adults in their late twenties and those who are better educated tend to stand a greater chance of surviving.

Reasons for Divorce

Most people say that they believe in marriage for life. Why, then, do more than 40 percent of all first marriages in the United States end in divorce? At one time, people stayed in marriages because of their commitment and a sense of responsibility, but today's societal norms make divorce more acceptable. And where a spouse once had to have a reason such as abuse, abandonment, or infidelity before filing for divorce, today's "no-fault" divorces allow the courts to rule in favor of dissolving the marriage if both participants are willing.

Here are some other common reasons for divorce:

* Unrealistic expectations that marriage will always be romantic or gratifying and that disagreements won't occur are not met.
* As people reassess their careers and life goals through their twenties, they may think that the marriage no longer fits their new goals.
* Women or men able to support themselves (and their children) leave unhappy or abusive relationships.

Physical Changes in Early Adulthood

For most people, physical attributes such as muscle strength, cardiac output, sensory sharpness, and reaction time are at their peak during the twenties. Unless people have abused their bodies through excessive sports training, work, or unhealthy habits such as drug or alcohol abuse or poor nutrition, they are at their physical best during these years.

Cognitive Changes in Early Adulthood

Because cognitive abilities are often linked with physical health and well-being, young adulthood also represents a high point in a person's creative and intellectual abilities.

Much of the work done by leading researchers in the sciences, for example, is done before they are 40. One theory suggests that only the "relatively young" can take full advantage of new ideas. As individuals age, their ideas become more set, prejudices increase, and fear of peer disapproval overcomes the drive for new and different ways of approaching problems.

Developmental Tasks of Early Adulthood

* Becoming independent.
* Forming a social network.
* Developing intimate relationships.
* Adjusting to sharing one's life with another person.
* Assuming the responsibilities of a family and home.
* Engaging in a career or job.
* Assuming some responsibility within the larger community.

RESEARCH

Adulthood and Moral Development

Lawrence Kohlberg's stages of moral development (see Chapter 13) suggest that, during adulthood, people may reach two stages of morality beyond the fourth stage achieved by most adolescents. In stage five, people behave as they do because they respect others, respect social order, and prefer living under legally determined laws. While people respect individual rights and acknowledge that society has agreed upon a set of appropriate behaviors, they reserve the right to work toward a change in that system if they see it as flawed.

In stage six, individuals are motivated by a sense of universal ethics—"I did it because it was the right thing to do." What is "right" in this case is determined by one's conscience and is based on universal principles of justice, human rights, and the dignity of human beings as individuals. It is suggested that only a small percentage of people actually reach this final stage of morality.

Critics of Kohlberg find his experimental methods flawed and suggest that he was biased against women or did not include them in his studies. Some argue that ethical behavior changes from context to context. A person may achieve stage five or six behavior with family but only stage three or four with the rest of society.

Middle Adulthood

Middle adulthood—or what is commonly referred to as "middle age"—spans ages 40 to 60 or 65. In the early part of this century, many people didn't live long enough to enjoy this period of their lives. Men who worked the land or in mines and factories often died in their late forties. Once children had been raised and sent out on their own, women felt that their life role had been fulfilled. Even if they lived longer, it would never have occurred to most of them to take on a new role at that point in their lives.

Today, the middle years focus on meaning in one's life. People reassess their goals and recognize that some of them may never be achieved. In every growth process, acquiring new abilities comes with the loss of something. Focusing on the loss rather than the new possibilities is a danger during the middle years.

Generativity vs. Stagnation

The middle years of adulthood comprise Erikson's seventh stage. During this time, the challenge is generativity.

Generativity includes the following tasks:

* Caring for and guiding the next generation.
* Creating, originating, and producing something meaningful for one's self and the next generation.
* Doing something for the betterment of the world in general.

Erikson suggested that if one did not become generative during the middle years, the alternative was stagnation. **Stagnation** is a failure to develop and grow, and it can result in feeling that life is empty and meaningless.

Midlife Crisis

At one time, researchers believed that people in middle adulthood went through a period when they thought their lives were meaningless. They became dissatisfied with their careers or jobs and grew uninterested in their marriage partners. The recognition that one was not just starting out and that the years available to fulfill one's dreams were dwindling were believed to trigger these feelings.

More recent research has found little, if any, evidence that such a crisis actually occurs. Rather than age triggering events, the events themselves may trigger a change in outlook and a reorganization of one's life goals. Children leaving home, a change in career or job, divorce, relocation, or retirement are all important events in middle adulthood. They can occur at a variety of ages and have different effects on the people who experience them. Instead of experiencing the "empty nest" syndrome—a feeling of being useless and of having nothing more to do after the children leave home—many people undergo a **midlife transition** and undertake new projects, become more active in the community, or tackle a new career.

Physical Changes in Middle Adulthood

During middle adulthood, physical capacities may have less to do with age than with a person's general health and lifestyle habits. Those who have maintained healthy habits such as good nutrition and regular exercise are often in better physical condition, and capable of more activity, than younger people who have relied on their youth to maintain their bodies and minds.

Here are several important factors in physical aging:

* Exercise is important in keeping bodily functions, such as the heart's pumping capacity and lung volume, at their maximum potential.
* Genetics plays an important role in overall health, but genes do not predetermine an individual's health in later life. That depends on many factors interacting with a possible genetic predisposition.
* Expectations play a critical role in maintaining a healthy life. They affect the choices we make in activities, challenges, or job changes. "I'm getting too old to do that" can become a self-fulfilling prophesy. When one doesn't remain active or doesn't accept new challenges, the capacity to do so declines.
* Hormonal changes can affect both men's and women's bodies as they age. Many myths are associated with these changes, myths that can cause more harm than the physical changes involved.

Female Menopause

Menopause is defined as the cessation of a woman's menstrual cycle. Research has shown that menopause is not as traumatic an experience for women nor the source of depression and many physical ailments as earlier myths held.

Expectations play an important role in the changes that occur with menopause. If a woman perceives it as a loss of her identity or grieves over her inability to bear children, the onset of menopause can result in depression. If she expects the physiological changes that her body undergoes during menopause to be debilitating, they can be. But if she perceives menopause as a normal progression of age, and if she considers it as liberation from fears of pregnancy or the responsibilities of raising children, it may be the beginning of a new and potentially exciting phase of life.

Male Menopause

While there is no obvious menopause in males equivalent to the cessation of the monthly cycle in women, men do experience a gradual reduction in their hormonal levels. For a few men, this triggers physical reactions similar to those of female menopause.

The hormonal changes men experience may be tied to other age-related changes such as weight gain, lower energy levels, and decreased fertility. The psychological reactions to hormonal changes can be more limiting than any actual physical change.

Cognitive Changes in Middle Adulthood

There is some debate about the mental and intellectual changes that occur with age. Studies show that the ability to recall information declines during middle adulthood. However, the ability to recognize that same information increases throughout life. Some believe that while some cognitive abilities decrease, other ways of coping or processing information may actually increase.

Different types of studies yield different results. Cross-sectional studies (in which researchers test people of various ages at the same time) suggest that mental abilities decline as a person ages. Longitudinal studies (in which the same people are tested over a period of years) suggest that mental abilities increase until sometime in the sixties. They then decrease—but to a much smaller degree than cross-sectional studies would suggest.

What is being tested is an important variable in these studies. An older person with weaker vision may not complete an IQ test—not because he or she couldn't, but because of trouble reading the print. In addition, some suggest that "wisdom" acquired throughout life is not the same as the "intelligence" tested.

It is fairly well established that if a person continues to use and challenge his or her mental capacities, they will, in many cases, remain sharp. "Use it or lose it" is an appropriate instruction for both physical and mental faculties.

The Sandwich Generation

As the population ages and parents live into their eighties and nineties, many people in middle adulthood find themselves responsible for their parents' well-being. At the same time, there is a trend toward children who have been out on their own for a time to return home. They may be trying to save money for a business or to reevaluate the direction of their lives. This double responsibility puts both a psychological and economic burden on people in midlife at a time when they typically are reevaluating their own goals and finally feeling the freedom to take on new challenges.

Developmental Tasks of Middle Adulthood

* Assisting one's children to become successful and happy adults.
* Establishing and maintaining an appropriate economic stability.
* Achieving civic and social responsibility.
* Making decisions about one's identity in later life.
* Developing healthy leisure activities and strengthening social relationships.
* Adjusting to the aging of parents.

Cultures and Attitudes Toward Aging

Attitudes toward the role of elder members of society differ from culture to culture. For example, in China, a woman is forbidden to have another child once she has become a grandmother. In Ladakh, Pakistan, when the eldest son marries, the parents move to a smaller home to prepare themselves for a life of prayer and what they call a "reduced worldly authority." In Israel, members of the kibbutz (collective farm or settlement) are encouraged to work as long as they are able to maintain a meaningful social role in the community. In India, the mother-in-law makes the decisions about the household and directs the wives of her sons living in the same home. In Poland and Italy, the grandmother fills this role.

Late Adulthood

In 1900, only about 4 percent of the population of the United States was 65 or older. By 1990, that figure reached 12.5 percent. By the year 2020, advances in health care and new attitudes toward aging will push Americans over 65 to 20 percent of the population. The average life expectancy of adult females will be about 88 and of adult males about 83.

Physical Changes in Late Adulthood

Even though people are living longer and staying much more active, the human body continues to age in recognizable ways:

* Wrinkles and folds appear in the skin as it loses its elasticity.
* Senses can become less sharp.
* Bones can become more brittle as they lose calcium, making the risk of fractures greater.
* The immune system may weaken, making older people more prone to disease.

What Causes Aging?

Several theories regarding aging have been proposed. One suggests that we have biological clocks that move ahead at a programmed rate. That rate is determined, in large measure, by the genes we inherit. Cells may be programmed to divide a certain number of times and no more. In addition, cells are less capable of repairing themselves in later life. Another theory suggests that environmental damage may influence aging. Depending on the number and type of potentially damaging agents, such as pollutants or carcinogens (cancer-causing agents) in our environments, cell damage may occur that can no longer be repaired. In addition, our bodies produce substances known as *free radicals* during digestion. These substances may also contribute to the destruction of healthy cells.

Aging is a complex biochemical and psychological process. Perhaps the healthiest approach is to select activities and foods that are known to be healthy and to be aware of and avoid the potential hazards.

Cognitive Changes in Late Adulthood

The great majority of older people have no serious reduction in intellectual capacity. Unless some illness or malfunction damages the brain, they retain the ability to learn and can develop new cognitive skills, such as using computers or other technologies.

Myths of Aging	
Myth	**Reality**
People will age the same way their parents aged—either in good or poor health.	Although genetics plays a role in health, many seniors are now living more healthy lifestyles than did their parents, resulting in fewer illnesses and longer lives.
People should just accept the fact that their bodies are old and shouldn't expect to feel good.	While people should not deny that their bodies are aging and slowing down, poor health is not inevitable.
Most older people lose their intellectual capacity.	Most older people have no serious reduction in intellectual capacity.
After a certain age, people can't change.	People can and do change at every stage in life. Consider the senior sites on the Internet and seniors who begin new careers in their seventies.

Senile Dementia and Alzheimer's Disease

Some older people suffer from a serious loss of mental ability known as **senile dementia.** It can produce problems with memory, concentration, and decision-making ability. Dementia is caused by a malfunction in the brain—not by aging. The very fact that people are living longer increases the probability that a malfunction may occur. Dementia occurs more often in people in their eighties or older.

Alzheimer's disease is the primary cause of senile dementia. It involves the deterioration of cells in the brain. Heredity seems to play a role in the disease, and a number of different treatments are being tested. The other major cause of senile dementia is blood vessel damage due to stroke.

Ego-Integrity vs. Despair

Erikson believed that in late adulthood people recognize that their lives have had meaning. They are satisfied with themselves as they are and feel fulfilled. Erikson called this reflection on and acceptance of one's life **ego-integrity.**

Confronting the end of life without ego-integrity can result in despair. One might feel that time is running out and that not all of one's achievements have been made. The person in despair might be angry at or deny physical limitations. It is understandable that older people in good health or in comfortable economic positions are more satisfied with their lives than others.

Social Changes in Late Adulthood

As people age, they must adjust to changes in their social situations. People often eagerly anticipate retirement as an opportunity for more free time. However, once retired, some may begin to feel less productive and less connected to society as a whole. To increase productivity and interact with others, many seniors turn to volunteerism, community projects, visiting with friends, or even part-time work.

Family dynamics, too, change as we age. Grandparenting can be a very different experience from parenting. Without direct responsibility for their grandchildren, grandparents enjoy them in ways they couldn't enjoy their own children.

Developmental Tasks of Late Adulthood

* Reflecting on and acknowledging the meaningfulness of one's life.
* Adjusting to physical and health changes and remaining active.
* Adjusting to the loss of friends and loved ones.
* Establishing affiliations with other members of one's age group.
* Remaining active in social and civic organizations.
* Adjusting to retirement and financial changes.
* Shifting interest from work to leisure, social, or volunteer activities.

Research in Aging

Gerontology is a branch of psychology that studies the effects of aging. **Thanatology** is the study of death and the ways of coping with it. Both of these fields will become increasingly important as a larger percentage of the population enters late adulthood.

As attitudes toward aging change and new research challenges the myths of aging, more and more people live rewarding and happy lives in their later years. Validating one's role in life, refocusing on goals that are appropriate for one's age, and continuing to maintain a positive outlook and accept new challenges are as important in later life as they are for the young.

Death and Dying

At some point, everyone reaches the end of life. As people grow older, they experience the loss of parents, friends, brothers, sisters, or even spouses. Part of ego-integrity is the acceptance of death as a natural part of life. Some people accept imminent death in stages. Elisabeth Kübler-Ross theorized that these **five** stages are common, although not everyone experiences all of them:

1. **Denial:** "The doctor must be wrong. I'm not that sick."
2. **Anger:** "It's not fair. Why me and not someone else?"
3. **Bargaining:** "If I get better, I'll give all my money to charity."
4. **Depression:** "Why bother going on if I'm going to die anyway?"
5. **Acceptance:** "I've had a full and rewarding life. I'm ready to move on to the next step."

Facing Death with Dignity

One of the greatest fears for some people is losing their dignity as they age. Images of people being kept alive by machines or of losing control of their bodily functions can be frightening. It is important to treat old or dying people not as helpless infants but as mature adults who have earned dignity and respect.

At one time, elderly or terminally ill people had little choice of where they would die: either at home or in the hospital. Today, hospices provide an alternative. A **hospice** offers terminally ill patients and their families physical and emotional support to help them cope with death. It encourages family and friends to visit or stay with the dying person for as long as they want or need to.

Some people choose to execute a **living will** to express their wishes about being kept alive by artificial means. Not only does this reduce the personal indignity that a person might experience, but it also gives older people a sense of control over their lives—and deaths.

Funerals

A funeral is a traditional way to say good-bye to a member of a family or community. While the specifics of a funeral depend on religious or spiritual beliefs, the process serves a number of functions. It is a symbolic way to separate the living from the dead. This provides those who remain behind with a way of closing that chapter in their lives. Funerals also provide a way to celebrate the deceased person's life and to acknowledge the legacy he or she leaves behind.

CRITICAL THINKING

Should We Try to Extend the Average Life Span?

Many people are thrilled that advances in medicine and psychology promise longer life spans, but extensive resources are being used to accomplish this. Is this the best use of these resources? Read about the issues and form your own opinion.

THE ISSUES

Some say that, by the year 2020, advances in medical diagnoses, organ transplantation, gene therapy, and lifestyle management will enable more people to live into their eighties, nineties, and even hundreds. People will have more time to realize their dreams and to accomplish more in their lifetimes. Families may include four and five generations. People in their fifties may go back to school and enter new careers in their sixties and seventies. The demographics that have driven product development and advertising will shift from the young to more mature buyers.

But the resources necessary to accomplish this are also extensive. Millions of dollars and large amounts of medical resources are being used to extend the average life span. Some people feel these resources should be spent on ways to improve the average person's quality of life, not the length of life. What good is longer life if you're burdened with poor health? Use those resources to find cures for disease instead, they argue.

Some people fear that an increasing number of older, active people will remain in a work force that is, even now, difficult for some young people to enter. If older workers aren't forced to retire, fewer and fewer jobs will be available. Perhaps these opportunities should go to younger and potentially more productive people.

Should resources be used to extend the average life span?

THE PROCESS

1. **Restate the issues.** In your own words, state the nature of the issue.

2. **Provide evidence.** From your own experience and from the information above, list the evidence *for* increasing the expected life span of humans.

3. **Give opposing arguments.** From your own experience and from the information above, list the evidence *against* increasing the expected life span of humans.

4. **Look for more information.** What else would you like to know before you form your opinion? Make a list of your questions. On the Internet, in the psychology section of the library, or in the index of psychology books, research *life span, euthanasia,* and *gerontology.*

5. **Evaluate the information.** Make a chart with two columns:

Increasing the Human Life Span	
For	Against

Record the arguments in each column and rank each column of arguments in importance from 1 to 5, with 1 as the most important.

6. **Draw conclusions.** Write one paragraph supporting your answer to the question "Should resources be used to extend the average life span?" Be sure to state reasons, not just opinions.

The stages of adulthood include early adulthood, from 20 to 40 years; middle adulthood, from 40 to 65 years; and late adulthood, age 65 and older. Each period of adulthood carries with it certain challenges. Young adults have the challenge of intimacy vs. isolation; middle adults, of generativity vs. stagnation; and older adults, of ego-integrity vs. despair.

Each period of adult life entails certain tasks of development. In early adulthood, those tasks include establishing committed and open relationships with others, identifying a career, and becoming independent. In middle adulthood, tasks such as making a home, starting a family, and forming a commitment to the good of society are major concerns. Older adults must adjust to changes in their lives and continue to challenge themselves while coming to terms with their mortality.

Psychology

ego-integrity—reflection on and acceptance of one's life as it has been and is. *p. 244*

generativity—ability to create and produce throughout one's life. *p. 239*

gerontology—branch of psychology that studies the effects of aging. *p. 245*

hospice—facility or program for terminally ill patients. *p. 245*

intimacy—ability to relate to another human being on a deep, personal level. *p. 235*

isolation—feeling of separateness from others and a lack of the strength and support gained from close relationships. *p. 235*

living will—legal document that expresses what someone wants done if he or she becomes incapable of making decisions about health care. *p. 245*

menopause—cessation of a woman's menstrual cycle. *p. 240*

midlife transition—change that occurs as a result of life events during which one may undertake new activities. *p. 239*

senile dementia—condition of aging that produces problems with memory, concentration, or decision-making ability. It is caused by a malfunction in the brain, such as Alzheimer's disease or blood vessel damage due to stroke. *p. 244*

stagnation—failure to develop and grow resulting in feeling that life is empty and meaningless. *p. 239*

thanatology—study of death and the ways of coping with it. *p. 245*

CHAPTER 15

Stress and Health

In this chapter, you will learn about:

- causes, effects, and ways of coping with stress
- behaviors that promote health
- behaviors that endanger health

Your teacher announces that each person in the class is responsible for designing and leading a class activity related to healthy living. How do you feel about the task—challenged or threatened? Any type of change is a stressor—a factor that may produce a stress reaction, such as increased heart rate, nervousness, or anxiety. People cope with stress in different ways—actively or defensively.

Health involves a complex balance among the brain, mind, and immune system. Medical diagnoses now take into account information about lifestyle and social relationships in addition to physical symptoms as doctors are influenced by the biopsychosocial model of medicine.

Some people, particularly those who have a genetically low tolerance for stress, may engage in negative behaviors, such as substance abuse, aggression, or self-deception. These negative behaviors may actually increase stress.

What Is Stress?

The word *stress* can be used in several ways. Rather than defining stress in general, let's separate its meanings by using the following terms:

* **Stressor** describes an event or circumstance that produces change in a person's internal or external environment. "My job is so stressful" identifies a stressor—in this case someone's job that causes stress.
* **Stress reactions** are the physical and psychological responses of the body and mind to stressors. "I'm so stressed out" describes a reaction to stress.

Stress Involves Change

A stressor is any physical or environmental change, real or imagined, to which you are exposed. Hosting a party, getting a poor grade on a test, having a fight with your best friend, catching a cold, or getting a promotion at work are all stressors. Each may produce a stress reaction.

Although we generally think of stress as something to be avoided, the fact is that not all stressors are bad, nor is all stress damaging to your health or sense of well-being. The physiological changes accompanying the challenge of a new job or anticipation over an upcoming move may increase motivation or make you more alert. This "good stress" is called **eustress**.

Some people thrive on changes in their lives; they're always looking for new challenges. Others become a "basket case" at the mere thought of changing some part of their routine.

Inherited tendencies, psychological coping mechanisms, and one's social support system are all factors in how a person handles stress. Further, unrelated stressors occurring at the same time may combine to produce stress in even the most "laid-back" person.

Types of Stressors

Stressors include daily hassles, minor and major life changes, and unexpected disasters or catastrophes.

Stressors
Daily Hassles
Physical hassles, such as noise, air pollution, weather extremes, overcrowding, an annoying commute, or a temporary illness. Mental factors, such as worry about one's job, finances, relationships, responsibilities to family.
Minor Changes
Changes that may not seem stressful, but that alter the pattern of life: moving, graduation, change of grade in school, new family members, or a change in one's job.
Major Changes
Marriage, separation or divorce, a chronic or major illness, loss of one's job, alcohol or drug abuse, serious financial difficulties, serious conflicts with employer or family member.
Disasters/Catastrophes
Natural disasters, such as fire or flood, loss of home, death of a loved one, a major or life-threatening illness in self or a loved one, serious accident.

Physiological Responses to Stress

In the 1920s, American physiologist Walter Cannon reaffirmed that responses to stress are the result of the interaction of mind and body. That is, both physical and emotional or psychological stressors produce much the same biological responses—namely, a release of epinephrine (adrenaline) and norepinephrine (noradrenaline). These stress hormones enter the bloodstream and prepare an individual for what Cannon called "fight or flight." Cannon pointed out that being prepared to escape from or respond to a potential threat was an adaptive behavior.

General Adaptation Syndrome (GAS)

Canadian scientist Hans Selye spent 40 years researching animals' reactions to various stressors, such as shock, surgical trauma, or restraint. He maintained that the body's adaptive reaction to stress is similar regardless of the stressor—like a defensive posture that one might assume regardless of the nature of the threat. He called the response the **general adaptation syndrome (GAS)**.

Selye proposed that GAS has **three** phases:

1. Alarm.
2. Resistance.
3. Exhaustion.

How GAS Works

Imagine that you've just discovered that a loved one has a life-threatening illness. At first, you feel anxiety and concern—alarm. When the worst happens and the person actually dies, you experience grief and feel depressed. You feel tired all the time and have to force yourself to move through the days following the death—resistance. After dealing with the funeral and the concerns of family members during the mourning period, you feel drained of energy—exhaustion. If you try to continue to carry on without giving your body and mind time to recover, you may become seriously ill yourself.

Psychological Responses to Stress

How do you know that you are stressed? Our perception of stress is a combination of the biological reactions discussed above and various psychological responses.

* The flood of hormones in the alarm ("fight or flight") phase of stress is accompanied by feelings of fear or anxiety.
* In the resistance phase, people may experience forgetfulness, irritability, anger, guilt, poor concentration, low motivation, low productivity, mood swings, and other negative states that may, in turn, produce even more stressors.
* During the exhaustion stage, depression and withdrawal may occur. Some people exhibit irrational behavior and may abuse alcohol or drugs.

Cognitive Effects of Stress

The optimal level of stress appears to vary from individual to individual. The heightened response to stressors is sometimes called arousal. The Yerkes-Dodson Law describes the relationships among the level of arousal, performance, and task difficulty.

Think about how you feel as you are about to take a test. Your attitude may vary between ho-hum and excessive concern and anxiety. Your performance on the test will be best if your attitude lies somewhere in between those extremes—that is, if you are sufficiently "up" for the test, but not overly concerned. This optimal level of arousal varies inversely with the difficulty of the task. Because a high arousal level makes concentration difficult, you would tend to do better on a more difficult test with a lower arousal level.

TICK
Tick
TICK
TICK

Factors That Influence Stress

A number of factors affects the way in which you respond to stressors:

* **Personality.** Openness to new experience is a major personality trait. Some people perceive change as a challenge—others as a threat. People who tend to see change as a threat are more likely to experience negative stress responses.
* **Stress Tolerance.** About 10 percent of the population inherits low stress tolerance—the inability to deal with stress that most people handle with few or no problems.
* **Perception of Control.** Some people become overwhelmed by the irritations of daily life because they believe these factors to be out of their control. Others *choose* the things that they allow to "get to them." The more control one perceives in a situation, the healthier one's response to stressors.
* **Self-Efficacy.** People who believe themselves capable of achieving what they set out to do are less affected by stressors. Research has shown that self-confidence actually reduces adrenaline levels in the bloodstream in potentially threatening situations.
* **Social Support.** People with supportive family and friends tend to be less affected by stressful situations.

What's Your Stress Level?

Think about the last 12 months of changes in your life. Identify each stressor in the table below that you've experienced and then add up their values. If you've experienced total stress within the last 12 months of 250 or greater, even with normal stress tolerance, you may be overstressed. Persons with low stress tolerance may be overstressed at levels as low as 150. This scale was first proposed in 1967. What types of modern stressors might be added to the scale?

Stress Scale for Youth	
Stressor	**Event Values**
1. Death of parent, boyfriend/girlfriend	100
2. Divorce (of yourself or your parents)	65
3. Puberty	65
4. Pregnancy (or causing pregnancy)	65
5. Marital separation or breakup with boyfriend/girlfriend	60
6. Jail term or probation	60
7. Death of other family member (other than spouse, parent, or boyfriend/girlfriend)	60
8. Broken engagement	55
9. Engagement	50
10. Serious personal injury or illness	45
11. Marriage	45
12. Entering college/beginning next level of school (starting junior high or high school)	45
13. Change in independence or responsibility	45
14. Any drug and/or alcohol use	45
15. Getting fired at work or expelled from school	45
16. Change in alcohol or drug use	45
17. Reconciliation with mate, family, or boyfriend/girlfriend (getting back together)	40
18. Trouble at school	40
19. Serious health problem of a family member	40
20. Working while attending school	35
21. Working more than 40 hours per week	35
22. Changing course of study	35

Stress Scale for Youth *(continued)*

Stressor	Event Values
23. Change in frequency of dating	35
24. Sexual adjustment problems (confusion of sexual identity)	35
25. Gain of new family member (newborn baby or parent remarries)	35
26. Change in work responsibilities	35
27. Change in financial state	30
28. Death of a close friend (not a family member)	30
29. Change to a different kind of work	30
30. Change in number of arguments with mate, family, or friends	30
31. Sleeping less than eight hours per night	25
32. Trouble with in-laws or boyfriend's or girlfriend's family	25
33. Outstanding personal achievement (awards, grades, and so forth)	25
34. Mate or parents start or stop working	20
35. Beginning or ending school	20
36. Change in living conditions (visitors in the home, remodeling house, change in roommates)	20
37. Change in personal habits (start or stop a habit, such as smoking or dieting)	20
38. Chronic allergies	20
39. Trouble with the boss	20
40. Change in work hours	15
41. Change in residence	15
42. Changing to a new school (other than graduation)	10
43. Presently in premenstrual period	15
44. Change in religious activity	15
45. Going in debt (you or your family)	10
46. Change in frequency of family gatherings	10
47. Vacation	10
48. Presently in winter holiday season	10
49. Minor violation of the law	5
Total score =	

Conflict

One of the major stressors is conflict—feeling pressures from opposing forces or motives. Psychologists describe four different types of conflict.

Stress is greatest when motives are the strongest, such as when there are conflicting moral or ethical questions.

Types of Conflict

Approach-Approach Conflict

A conflict in which both choices have a positive outcome. Should you go to a movie or to a party with friends? Even after you decide, you'll feel stress until you're sure the choice worked out for the best.

Avoidance-Avoidance Conflict

A conflict where neither choice is particularly appealing. Your boss wants you to work this Saturday night. If you stay at home, your parents want you to baby-sit your little sister.

Approach-Avoidance Conflict

Choices have both good and bad outcomes. Should you agree to tutor your little sister in math on Saturday mornings? You don't want to give up that free time, but it makes you feel good to help her.

Multiple Approach-Avoidance Conflict

Among several alternatives, each has advantages and disadvantages. How will you spend your time after school? Try out for a sport and commit to practice every day? Get a part-time job? Leave the time free in case something comes along that you want to do? Each choice has a positive and a negative outcome.

Coping with Stress

While eustress, or good stress, can add anticipation and excitement to life, even enjoyable changes can eventually build to the point where they can threaten health. When a person is exposed to stressors to the point where he or she begins to experience negative physiological and psychological effects, he or she is overstressed. How does one cope with overstress?

Active coping can be an effective way to manage stress. With active coping, you can choose behaviors that support health, such as good nutrition, exercise, relaxation, and meditation. Here are six specific ways you can use active coping.

① Be Aware

Before you can cope with stress, you must be aware of it. The first important coping strategy is simply to notice what factors in your life strongly affect your emotional and physical reactions—your stressors.

The word *distress* comes from Latin words meaning "to stretch apart." Allowing yourself to "stretch apart" too far may cause you to snap. Don't ignore your distress—your responses to stressors. Acknowledge them. Ask "What am I telling myself about the meaning of these events?" For example, what do good grades, lots of friends, or a well-paying job *mean* in terms of your life or self-image? Often stress reactions are caused because we give too much importance to events.

❷ Make Changes

Recognize what you can change and what you can't. Which of your stressors can you avoid or eliminate from your life? Can you reduce the intensity of the stressor by better planning of your time? What kind of time and energy would be required to make changes in your life that would reduce or eliminate some of your stressors? Are you willing to make those changes?

❸ Take Control

Take control over your stressors. Decide which of the factors that produce stress are valuable to you and which aren't. For example, holding on to anger or resentment against a person or situation occupies a portion of your brain and produces stress. It is your choice whether to allow that person or situation control over part of your brain.

Do you tend to overestimate the importance of situations? Do you think that you have to please everyone? Do you tend to overreact or insist on "winning" in everything you do? Those reactions are within your control once you become aware of them and analyze their effects on your stress level.

❹ Moderate

Learn to moderate your physiological reactions to stress. Learn and use relaxation techniques, such as slow, deep breathing and deliberate release of muscle tension. You can even learn to control your heart rate and blood pressure with training.

❺ Take Care of Yourself

You can maintain your physical reserves by:

* Exercising regularly.
* Eating well-balanced, nutritious meals.
* Maintaining your ideal weight.
* Avoiding stimulants such as nicotine and caffeine.
* Taking periodic breaks.
* Getting enough sleep.

You can maintain your emotional reserves by:

* Developing mutually supportive friendships and relationships.
* Pursuing realistic goals that are meaningful to you, rather than goals set by others.
* Expecting and responding calmly to some frustrations, setbacks, or sorrows.
* Caring about and for yourself.
* Laughing!

❻ Get Help

If you feel overwhelmed by your responses to stress and are unable to make the necessary changes yourself, get help! You're not alone. Stress-related disorders, including both physical and psychological issues, account for 60 to 90 percent of office visits to health-care professionals.

A health-care professional can teach you ways to cope with various kinds of stress and can help you to understand why certain events are stressors for you but not for others. Getting help with problems is a wise choice when you are so caught up in feelings of stress or anxiety that you can't think as clearly as you are able.

The Psychology of Health

For many years, an illness for which a doctor couldn't find a cause was termed *psychosomatic*—an illness caused or aggravated by some psychological factor. Some sufferers pegged it a polite term for "It's all in your head." Although the person actually experienced symptoms, they were often considered less important than "real" symptoms for which "real" causes—such as bacteria, viruses, or failure of body systems—could be found.

Today, a new field of study known as *psychoneuroimmunology (PNI)* is emerging.

What Is PNI?

Psychoneuroimmunology is a field of study based on research showing that the brain, the hormone-producing endocrine system, and the immune system are all linked together by "messenger molecules." Researcher Candace Pert calls these molecules *neuropeptides*, or "information substances."

Stress, Health, and Humor

You've seen how stress can affect heart rate, breathing, and blood pressure. Many studies also demonstrate that stress can negatively influence the immune system. But now, research shows, laughter may indeed be the best medicine.

In a 1990 study of college students, Herbert Lefcourt and his colleagues measured levels of a specific chemical in saliva—one indicator of a healthy immune system response. He also measured the students' ability to respond with humor in various situations and the likelihood they would use humor in stressful situations.

Lefcourt found higher levels of the chemical in students who had been exposed to a humorous video versus a control group who had experienced a regular class. Levels were even higher in those students who tended to use humor when stressed.

In more recent research, Lefcourt has found that women who intentionally use humor as a means of coping with stress have lower blood pressure than those who don't. The results are opposite for men. Lefcourt hypothesizes that women tend to make fun of themselves in response to stress, thereby relieving tension. Men tend to make fun of others—a method of maintaining position in the social hierarchy, but one that may actually increase stress.

In her book, *Molecules of Emotion*, Pert describes PNI as the study of a bodywide communications system that regulates our physical, psychological, and emotional health. The importance of one's psychological state to one's biological health can no longer be disputed as studies demonstrate the correlation between anger and arthritis, between stress and high blood pressure, and between cancer and "taking control of one's life."

A New Approach to Health

Today, when a person trains to be a doctor, that training is likely to be based on a **biopsychosocial model** of health. This model acknowledges that a person's body, mind, and social environment all play a part in maintaining good health or succumbing to illness and disease.

When a doctor interviews a patient, questions now extend far beyond physical symptoms. They include potential stress factors in the person's life, lifestyle, and information about the person's family, friends, and relationships.

Stress and the Immune System

The **immune system** is a complex system that defends the body from the attacks of bacteria, viruses, and other foreign substances.

When the brain produces stress hormones, the number of disease-fighting cells in the immune system is reduced. Findings from studies related to the immune system reveal the effects of stress:

* When exposed to a cold virus, almost double the number of people leading stress-filled lives developed colds than those who reported low stress levels.
* The immune systems of *Skylab* astronauts were depressed following the stress of reentry and splashdown.
* Stress due to exams lowers the immune system's response to certain viruses, such as Epstein-Barr.
* Depression and grief tend to lower immune system responses.

The Relationship of Stress and Illness

This table shows how stress is related to the development and progress of a few significant illnesses. It is often possible to take control of many of the psychological stressors.

Stress and Illness

Illness	Physiological Symptoms and Causes	Psychological Factors	Treatments
Headaches	* Muscle tension. * Increased blood pressure. * Change in size of blood vessels in the head, which compresses nerve endings and produces pain.	* Stress may produce muscle contraction and increased blood pressure. * Pain causes stress.	* Progressive relaxation and biofeedback may reduce both stress and physiological factors. * Medication generally blocks pain receptors.
Cancer	* Rapid and atypical growth of abnormal cells * Abnormal cells develop in everyone, but are generally disposed of by the immune system. * Risk factors include environmental pollutants and some behaviors, such as sunbathing, smoking, and a diet high in fat and low in fruits and vegetables.	* Stress, anxiety, and depression reduce immune system efficiency, allowing the growth of cancerous cells. * Being diagnosed with cancer increases stress. * Behaviors that increase risk are often a matter of choice and/or habit and can be changed.	* Some cancer patients have found that actively taking control of their lives leads to remission. * Social support from family, friends, and particularly from others who share the illness has been shown to have positive effects.
Heart Disease	* People with a family history of heart disease have a greater risk of developing the disease. * Risks include obesity, high cholesterol, high blood pressure, and lack of exercise; and behaviors such as smoking, heavy drinking, and unhealthy eating habits.	* Risks include intense or driven personality type; tendency toward anger and hostility; strain and frustration from work, financial, family situation; any high-level stressor(s) with which a person doesn't adequately cope.	* Although surgical and medical treatments are available, people suffering from heart disease often benefit from changes in unhealthy behaviors and the addition of healthy behaviors.

The Chemistry of Stress

The body's complex chemical systems contain messenger molecules, some of which make you feel "up" and others that calm and quiet you. When life is running smoothly, messages from the two types of chemicals are in balance. But when serious stressors are present, the production of "up" molecules—serotonin, noradrenaline, and dopamine—is reduced and the balance is disrupted. Let's take a closer look at these molecules.

Serotonin is critical in the healthy functioning of your body clock. When you feel stressed, your body produces cortisol, a hormone that prepares your body for battle. As serotonin increases and you move into the sleep cycle, the amount of cortisol produced normally drops and you can rest. Because serotonin is one of the first chemicals to be affected by stress, an inability to sleep is often the first symptom of overstress. Cortisol levels remain high, and your body has no time to "come down" from its alert state.

Noradrenaline sets your body's energy level. Without sufficient noradrenaline, you feel exhausted and tired all the time—unwilling to do much of anything.

Dopamine is the brain's natural pleasure/pain regulator. It regulates the release of endorphins—chemicals that help us to control our response to pain as well as to feel good about our lives. When stress depletes the dopamine function, we not only are more sensitive to pain, but we don't derive much pleasure from things that are normally pleasurable.

Behaviors That Support Health

PNI studies suggest that the body and mind constantly strive for balance. If the behaviors that we choose support that balance, our chances for a healthy life are enhanced. Behaviors that support balance include:

* Eating well-balanced and nutritious meals that are low in cholesterol and fat, contain vitamins and minerals that contribute to the body's chemical balance, and do not exceed the demands of the body's metabolism.
* Engaging in regular exercise to regulate weight and metabolism.
* Avoiding toxins in the atmosphere, especially smoking.
* Reducing stress through positive coping mechanisms such as relaxation and meditation; recognizing, analyzing, and dealing with stressors; and working to change compulsive or negative behaviors.
* Developing a strong social support system.

Unhealthy Behaviors

Not all methods that people use to cope with stress are healthy. **Defensive coping** involves reducing stress through:

* *Avoidance:* Withdrawing from a stressor because of fear or an inability to cope in any active way.
* *Self-deception:* Lying to oneself about the seriousness of a situation.
* *Aggression:* Taking out one's stress on another person, which often increases the stress.
* *Substance Abuse:* Attempting to use drugs or alcohol to alter moods.

Mood-Altering Drugs

Drugs that people misuse to cope with stress fall into **three** categories:

1. Stimulants ("up" drugs).
2. Depressants ("down" drugs).
3. Hallucinogens.

Some substances may *temporarily* replace the "up" molecules, boost the body's energy, help relieve aches and pains, or make a person feel better. They include:

* *Caffeine:* The "wake-up" ingredient in coffee, cola, or a hit of chocolate.
* *Alcohol:* Provides a *temporary* "fix" to problems of mood and inability to sleep; diminishes pain sensations and increases pleasure. Abusers use alcohol to fall asleep, to wake up, to feel more assertive, to feel more relaxed.
* *Nicotine:* Another chemical that can both calm anxiety and reduce pain sensitivity, as well as boost alertness. Nicotine and other drugs alter the body's own natural chemistry.
* *The Body's Own Adrenaline:* People who engage in high-risk or high-demand activities are often overstressed and are using their body's own adrenaline to keep them "high."
* *Other Drugs:* Marijuana, cocaine, amphetamines, and heroin also temporarily replace the functions of the body's natural "up" molecules.

The Down Side of "Up" Drugs

Using drugs to balance the body's chemistry is, according to Dr. Steve Burns, like using a bulldozer to level the dirt in a flowerpot. There's simply no control. All mood-altering drugs cause a condition known as *rebound*. The drug may make a person feel better quickly, but when it wears off, the user will feel bad just as quickly—the crash.

Just as the eyes adjust to an increased amount of light, the body adjusts to an increased amount of the drug. Some drugs work by reducing or increasing the amount of natural chemicals that the body produces. The body fights back—trying to rebalance a system that is even more out of balance. More of the drug is needed to get the same "up" feeling. Instead of regaining the balance of good health, the person hitches a ride on an emotional roller coaster whose hills get higher and whose valleys get deeper.

Drugs and Side Effects
Stimulants
Increase heart and breathing rates; diminish appetite, further throwing the body chemistry off.
Depressants
Suppress brain functions; reduce inhibition; slow reflexes; impair judgment.
Hallucinogens
Distort perception; may have unexpected, sometimes permanent psychological impact.

CRITICAL THINKING

How Should People Cope with Stress?

Various stressors affect each individual differently. It might then appear that different people would find different coping mechanisms useful. What is a negative mechanism for one person may work very well for another. What do you think works best?

THE ISSUES

Active coping involves changing circumstances, situations, and behaviors in your life to remove or lessen stress or to change your attitude toward it. Methods include:

* Changing what you think by monitoring your "self-talk," such as "I'm so stupid," and changing it to "I blew that one, but I can do better the next time."
* Learning to use relaxation and meditation when stressed.
* Changing your physiological state through exercise, which makes it difficult to "hold onto" stress.

Defensive coping involves reacting to stress rather than actively managing it. One might react by:

* Taking a time out.
* Holding back expression of angry or hurt feelings.
* Eating a big slice of cake.
* Denying that the stressor exists.

Sometimes active coping may not be effective and defensive mechanisms may be, at least temporarily, effective.

What are the advantages and disadvantages of active and defensive coping mechanisms? Under what circumstances might a person choose each of these mechanisms?

THE PROCESS

① **Restate the choices.** In your own words, state the difference between the choices.

② **Provide evidence.** From your own experience and from the information above, list the *advantages and disadvantages of active coping mechanisms.*

③ **Give opposing arguments.** From your own experience and from the information above, list the *advantages and disadvantages of defensive coping mechanisms.*

④ **Look for more information.** What else would you like to know about these coping mechanisms? Make a list of your questions. On the Internet, in the psychology section of the library, or in the index of psychology books, research *stress, coping mechanisms,* and *defensive mechanisms.*

⑤ **Evaluate the information.** Make a chart with four columns:

	Active		Defensive	
	Adv.	Disadv.	Adv.	Disadv.

Record your thoughts in each column. Under what circumstances might you choose defensive coping rather than active?

⑥ **Draw conclusions.** Write one or two paragraphs that compare and contrast the advantages and disadvantages of active and defensive coping mechanisms. Under what circumstances might each be used? Be sure to state reasons, not just opinions.

Addictions

In addition to the roller coaster effect, many drugs are addictive. Addiction is a complex biopsychosocial issue. It often involves lasting changes in brain chemistry and structure. Critical changes in brain circuitry then affect the way we process information and the choices we have. Addictions add even more stressors to an already overstressed brain.

"Down" Drugs

When some people feel stress, they go to their doctors for medication to help them sleep and relax. These depressants include tranquilizers, such as Valium, and barbiturates. Although these "down" drugs affect the brain differently from the "up" drugs, users experience the same cycles of rebound and crash. Typically, the drugs only work for one to three months. By that time, quitting them can cause such severe withdrawal symptoms that a person finds it difficult to stop taking them even though they are not working.

Side Effects

In addition to rebound and adaptation, many drugs' side effects add stressors of their own.

Health Management

Just as the immune system adapts to and protects us from environmental stressors, the mind must respond and adapt to psychological stressors. Both are defense systems, and failure in either system makes one vulnerable to attack.

If we are exposed to small amounts of a potential allergen over a long period of time, our immune system may learn to adapt to it or develop resistance against it. In the same way, if we learn to deal with the small stressors in our lives through active coping at an early age, they may not bother us as much in later life, or we may develop stronger resistance against them.

For most individuals health maintenance is certainly within their control—in terms of the healthy habits they develop and the ways in which they choose to deal actively and positively with potential stressors.

People feel stressed when the stressors in their lives exceed their ability to cope effectively with them. Stressors include daily hassles, frustrations, life changes, illness, grief, and changes in social relationships. About 10 percent of the population suffers from low stress tolerance—a genetic inability to deal with stressors that the rest of the population handles with relative ease.

Many major illnesses, such as cancer and heart disease, are related to stress. Good mental and physical health are the result of maintaining balance in nutrition, exercising, reducing stress with active stress coping mechanisms, and engaging in healthy behaviors.

Negative coping mechanisms—such as aggression, self-deceit, and substance abuse—often increase stressors and make a person even more vulnerable to illness.

Psychology

active coping—managing stress by choosing behaviors that support health. *p. 254*

biopsychosocial model—model that acknowledges a person's body, mind, and social environment all play a part in health. *p. 257*

defensive coping—managing stress through such behaviors as avoidance, self-deception, aggression, and substance abuse. *p. 259*

eustress—"good" stress that may increase anticipation or prepare one to meet a challenge. *p. 249*

general adaptation syndrome (GAS)—generalized response to stress consisting of alarm, resistance, and exhaustion. *p. 250*

immune system—complex system that defends the body from the attacks of bacteria, viruses, and other foreign substances. *p. 257*

overstress—condition in which a person begins to experience negative physiological and psychological effects of stress. *p. 254*

psychoneuroimmunology (PNI)—new field of study that recognizes links among the brain, the hormone-producing endocrine system, and the immune system. *p. 256*

stressor—event or circumstance that produces change in a person's internal or external environment. *p. 249*

stress reactions—physical and psychological responses of the body and mind to stressors. *p. 249*

Yerkes-Dodson Law—generalization that task difficulty and arousal interact such that low levels of arousal improve performance on difficult tasks; high levels of arousal improve performance on easy tasks. *p. 251*

Personality

In this chapter, you will learn about:

- **what personality is**
- **several different theories of personality**
- **how various theories compare**

Hippocrates, an ancient Greek physician, suggested that the differences among people's thoughts, actions, and feelings were the result of different blends of four basic fluids in the body. Yellow bile was associated with a quick temper (choleric). Blood was responsible for a warm, happy temperament (sanguine). Phlegm produced a cool demeanor (phlegmatic). Black bile was associated with thoughtfulness or melancholy (melancholic). Physicians at the time focused on balancing these fluids, or humors, in the body.

Since the time of Hippocrates, many psychologists have attempted to describe and explain personality. They have based their theories on the words we use to describe one another and ourselves, on the unconscious, on reinforcement, on the "self," and on our interactions with others.

Through a variety of approaches, psychologists are trying to understand why people are different and how these differences develop. Predicting a person's behavior in a specific situation is another goal of personality theories.

What Is Personality?

A psychologist once said, "What personality is, everybody knows; but nobody can tell." Personality has been variously described as a unique pattern of traits, individual differences, and behavioral predispositions and the sum of our behavioral tendencies. For our purposes, we will define **personality** as the relatively stable patterns of thinking, feeling, and acting possessed by an individual.

Psychology and Personality

Although Hippocrates addressed certain aspects of personality, it wasn't until the 1930s that it became a major topic of study in psychology. In his book *Personality: A Psychological Interpretation*, psychologist Gordon Allport maintained that psychology had ignored individual differences in an attempt to explain how people were alike. Psychologists of that time were much more interested in theories that might enable them to make explanations and predictions about people in general.

Allport believed that the study of individual differences should be the basis of psychology rather than just one of many topics of study within the field.

How Personality Is Studied

Given the many different ways that personality is described, it should come as no surprise that the theories describing it take very different approaches. Personality may be studied:

* In clinical observations, ranging from a psychologist working with a particular problem in a person's life to serious mental illnesses.
* In experimental psychology where participants may be observed under a variety of conditions.
* Using tests and measurements of various personality factors.

Depending on a psychologist's preferences, these methods will differ in what content is observed and what form of investigation is seen as most appropriate.

Theories of Personality

In this chapter, we'll look at **five** different theories of personality. (See below.)

Theories of Personality	
1. The Psychoanalytic Approach	Focuses on the role of the unconscious in the development of personality.
2. The Trait Approach	Focuses on characteristic behaviors and conscious motives.
3. The Behavioral Approach	Focuses on behaviorism and social learning.
4. The Humanistic Approach	Focuses on self-awareness and the development of the "self."
5. The Sociocultural Approach	Focuses on the roles of gender, ethnicity, and culture on the development of personality.

The Psychoanalytic Approach

The psychoanalytic approach suggests that inner conflicts and struggles of which people are unaware affect their personalities. Freud claimed that everyone is born with biological drives such as sex and aggression. These drives conflict with society's rules and laws. One's behavior at any given time is determined by these conflicts.

Freud proposed that the mind is like an iceberg. The conscious mind floats above the water and contains our conscious awareness. Below the water is the much larger unconscious mind containing thoughts, feelings, and desires of which we are mostly unaware. At times, some of the contents of the unconscious enter the preconscious mind, where the conscious mind can retrieve them.

Freud believed that the mass of unacceptable passions and drives in the unconscious are repressed because the conscious mind can't deal with them. However, he believed the unconscious exerts an important influence over our everyday behaviors. He described a series of psychosexual stages of development based on sexual drives.

Id, Ego, and Superego

Freud proposed **three** systems that take part in the conflict between our inner drives and external restraints.

1. **The Id.** The **id** is the largest portion of the iceberg—hidden from view and from the conscious mind. The id contains the basic drives to survive, reproduce, and engage in mastery over others. If the id had no restraints, it would satisfy all of its needs. This is called the **pleasure principle.** For example, when an infant is hungry, it cries—demanding immediate attention to that basic need. Because a child is unaware of any social restraints, the id is in full control of his or her behavior.

2. **The Ego.** The **ego** contains our conscious perceptions that develop with maturity. It operates on the **reality principle**—tempering the needs of the id with the reactions of the real world. For example, the ego understands what would happen if the id's drive for sexual satisfaction or aggression were reflected in one's behavior without restraint. The ego tries to ensure that the individual will experience pleasure rather than pain resulting from society's reactions to unacceptable behaviors.

3. **The Superego.** As a child absorbs the values of parents and society, the **superego** develops. Rather than focusing on internal wants and needs, the superego is driven by what it perceives as ideal—right. The superego operates from the **morality principle**—a combination of conscience and a chosen self-image of ourselves as moral persons. When the ego engages in behaviors that the superego considers inappropriate, feelings of guilt may be experienced.

Defense Mechanisms

According to Freud, one of the ways that the ego avoids pain or reduces anxiety is by using **defense mechanisms** to distort reality.

* *Repression* pushes anxiety-producing ideas into the unconscious. When a person "explodes," repressed thoughts may have broken into consciousness.
* *Rationalization* involves making up a reason for your behavior or explaining away that of others. Denied a raise, a person might say, "I really didn't need the money."
* *Projection* involves placing the cause of your problems on someone else or seeing your own faults in other people. You assume there's tension at home due to your sibling's behavior, when it is really your behavior causing the tension.
* *Displacement* is the emotional version of "passing the buck." You're angry with your teacher, so you yell at your best friend.
* *Denial* is refusing to accept something that is upsetting. A smoker may deny the risks of lung cancer.
* *Reaction formation* is acting contrary to your true feelings. You are "extra nice" to someone you can't stand.
* *Sublimation* is finding acceptable outlets for your feelings or desires. An aggressive person might transfer that aggression to sports.
* *Regression* is reverting to earlier, immature behaviors that once got you what you wanted. You throw a temper tantrum to get your way.

Freud believed that a person with a strong ego could balance the id and superego and rarely needed defense mechanisms.

Neo-Freudians

Some of Freud's followers accepted the id, ego, and superego and Freud's focus on the importance of the unconscious mind in personality. However, they disagreed with his emphasis on sexual and aggressive drives. Further, some of Freud's ideas were clearly biased against women. *Psychodynamic* or *neo-Freudian* theories grew out of the work of Alfred Adler, Karen Horney, Carl Jung, and Erik Erikson.

Alfred Adler believed that we are all born with feelings of inferiority. Striving for superiority is the main motivational force in the development of personality. We do this by actively developing talents, working toward improvement, and learning to cope with any weaknesses. Some of Adler's terms are still popular today. **Overcompensation** describes the acts of people who are fanatical in their drive for perfection. **Inferiority complex** results when a person's conscious thoughts are dominated by an inability to succeed.

Karen Horney agreed with Freud that childhood experiences play a large role in the development of personality, but she believed that it was social influences rather than sexual drives that were most important. Horney studied basic anxiety, which she claimed could be overcome by learning to adjust to and cope with the social world. She said that people suffering from basic anxiety move toward, away from, or against people—all of which can be problems if taken to extremes.

Carl Jung, although he was a close friend of Freud, broke with psychoanalysis and founded what he termed *analytic psychology.* Rather than the unconscious, Jung emphasized what he called the *collective unconscious*—a rather mystical region to which we all have access as a result of being human. Contained within the collective unconscious are various **archetypes**—universal forms that we encounter in our lives, such as mother, father, god, hero, or leader. Archetypes tend to recur in a society's literature and art.

Jung believed that being in touch with the archetypes within us is important to a healthy personality. For example, women may experience their masculine side and men, their feminine tendencies, in appropriate situations. Jung spoke of our **persona** as the image we present to others. Your real self can be very different from the persona that you allow others to see. Jung suggested that when the persona and real self were substantially different, serious anxieties and emotional problems could occur.

Erik Erikson, like Horney, believed that social relationships, such as that of the mother and infant, were of very great importance in personality development. Erikson gave more credit to the ego than Freud and believed that people were quite capable of making choices. As you have seen in earlier chapters, Erikson proposed eight stages of development that focused on developmental tasks rather than on Freud's sexual forces.

Evaluation of Psychoanalysis

Freud was a brilliant neurologist and the true father of modern personality theory. Many of his principles remain important to this day:

* Focus on the unconscious.
* Interest in cognitive and symbolic behavior.
* Belief in the importance of basic drives of sexuality and aggression.
* Assumption that early experiences underlie later behavior.
* Development of psychoanalytic therapy as a treatment for behavior disorders.

Psychologists who came after Freud analyzed his work and used the flaws they found in it as starting points for their own. Among the weaknesses of Freud's approach are these criticisms:

* He placed too much importance on the unconscious and not enough on the influence of social relationships.
* Because Freud worked primarily with white, middle-class individuals, his ideas may not apply across a more general population.
* Because Freud had very definite ideas about what caused certain problems, he may have influenced what clients said, or his interpretations of what they said might have been biased.
* Modern research has demonstrated that many of Freud's explanations for events, such as "Freudian slips," dreams, and sexual repression, can be explained in other ways.
* Freud's ideas about the natural superiority of men have been criticized and are now considered sexist.

The Trait Approach

A **trait is a characteristic of personality that remains fairly stable over time**. Traits may describe:

* Physical characteristics, such as black hair or brown eyes.
* Social characteristics, such as shy or humorous.
* Moral characteristics, such as honest or trustworthy.

Trait Theorists

Trait theorists believe that social and moral characteristics are relatively unchanging and that they determine our behavior during various situations. Leading trait theorists include Gordon Allport, Raymond Cattell, and Hans Eysenck.

Allport's Classification of Traits
Cardinal Trait
A trait that an individual exhibits in all situations
Central Trait
A trait exhibited in most situations
Secondary Trait
A trait whose presence in an individual depends on the situation

Gordon Allport used an unabridged dictionary in the 1930s to identify words used to describe a person. Initially, he identified about 18,000 words, which he then narrowed down to about 4,500. Allport classified the traits in several ways. A common trait is one that is shared by most people, such as honesty. The preceding chart shows another set of classifications that Allport used. Individuals who exhibit cardinal traits are fairly rare. Secondary traits seem to be fairly common as behaviors change from one situation to the next.

Raymond Cattell used statistical methods to analyze the huge amount of information on traits that Allport had gathered. He first reduced the number of traits to about 200. Cattell identified traits that seemed obvious, such as truthfulness, tidiness, or friendliness. He called these behaviors "surface traits." He then noticed that these traits seemed to fall in clusters—individuals who exhibited one trait in a cluster also exhibited the others. From that, he determined that each cluster was the result of a single, more fundamental trait—a "source trait." Source traits are those believed to be at the core of personality. They correspond roughly to Allport's central traits.

Cattell listed 16 personality source traits. The list is bipolar—that is, it shows the two extremes of each trait. People generally fall somewhere between the two poles of each trait. See the chart on the next page.

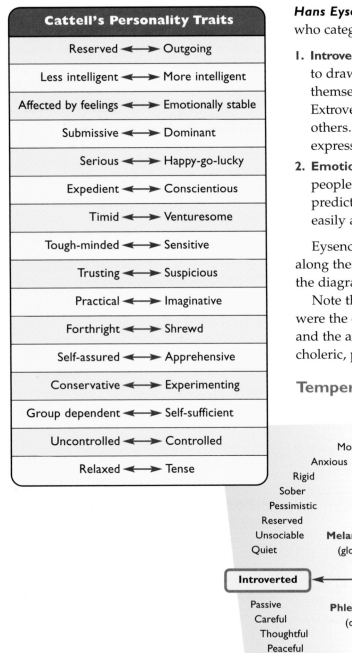

Cattell's Personality Traits

Reserved ⟷ Outgoing

Less intelligent ⟷ More intelligent

Affected by feelings ⟷ Emotionally stable

Submissive ⟷ Dominant

Serious ⟷ Happy-go-lucky

Expedient ⟷ Conscientious

Timid ⟷ Venturesome

Tough-minded ⟷ Sensitive

Trusting ⟷ Suspicious

Practical ⟷ Imaginative

Forthright ⟷ Shrewd

Self-assured ⟷ Apprehensive

Conservative ⟷ Experimenting

Group dependent ⟷ Self-sufficient

Uncontrolled ⟷ Controlled

Relaxed ⟷ Tense

Hans Eysenck was a British psychologist who categorized traits in **two** dimensions:

1. **Introversion-Extroversion.** Introverts tend to draw their ideas and energy from themselves and are often imaginative. Extroverts get their energy and ideas from others. They tend to be active and self-expressive. Jung first proposed this idea.

2. **Emotional Stability-Instability.** Stable people tend to be calm, rational, and predictable. Unstable people can become easily agitated and be unpredictable.

Eysenck arranged personality traits along these two dimensions, as shown in the diagram below.

Note that the central "temperaments" were the classic ones used by Hippocrates and the ancient Greeks—melancholic, choleric, phlegmatic, and sanguine.

Temperaments

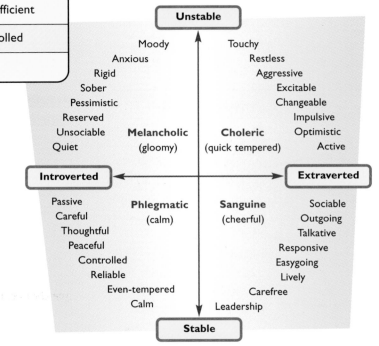

Unstable

Moody	Touchy
Anxious	Restless
Rigid	Aggressive
Sober	Excitable
Pessimistic	Changeable
Reserved	Impulsive
Unsociable	**Melancholic**	**Choleric**	Optimistic
Quiet	(gloomy)	(quick tempered)	Active

Introverted ⟷ **Extraverted**

Passive	**Phlegmatic**	**Sanguine**	Sociable
Careful	(calm)	(cheerful)	Outgoing
Thoughtful			Talkative
Peaceful			Responsive
Controlled			Easygoing
Reliable			Lively
Even-tempered		Carefree
Calm	Leadership

Stable

More recent research supports the theory of five major personality traits. Researchers disagree about all five, and newer theories propose more than five.

The chart below shows the Big Five most commonly mentioned. As you can see, two echo Eysenck's traits. The descriptions are again bipolar.

The Big Five Personality Traits	
Emotional Stability	Calm ←→ Anxious Secure ←→ Insecure
Extroversion	Fun-loving ←→ Serious Affectionate ←→ Reserved
Conscientiousness	Careful ←→ Careless Responsible ←→ Irresponsible
Agreeableness	Trusting ←→ Suspicious Helpful ←→ Unhelpful
Openness to New Experience	Variety ←→ Routine Imaginative ←→ Practical

Evaluating the Trait Approach

Identifying a person's traits can be useful in matching people to jobs or predicting success in various situations. But research has shown that, despite a definition that describes traits as "relatively permanent," individuals rarely exhibit the same trait under every circumstance. As situations vary and change, so do behavior and the traits it reflects. Despite earlier hopes, identifying traits is only mildly useful in predicting behavior.

The major criticism of the trait approach is that, while it describes personality traits, it doesn't explain where they come from.

The Behavioral Approach

Since the work of Pavlov, the behaviorists have focused solely on the effects of the environment on people's behavior. Behaviorists claim there is no need to consider personality or traits because they are created by reinforcement (positive or negative) in the environment. John B. Watson, B. F. Skinner, and Albert Bandura are among the best-known behaviorists.

Behaviorists

John B. Watson theorized that we behave as we do because early behaviors have been

Can Personality Change?

Personality is assumed to be a relatively permanent set of traits and behaviors that is unlikely to change to any great extent over the life of an individual. Yet, the purpose of therapy is to create changes within a person. Does this make sense?

Paul Costa and Robert McCrae cite several different "levels" of personality. Psychophysical systems are *basic traits*—tendencies and abilities of the individual that may be inherited or acquired through experience. During maturation, these tendencies interact with external influences to produce *characteristic traits*—behavior

and thought, typical habits, attitudes, and relationships. For example, if a child with a basic ability in music is never given the opportunity to develop it, his or her characteristic behavior will not exhibit that basic trait or ability.

Even if a person appears to change in radical ways, it may be because that person was open to change—one of the basic Big Five personality factors. In deciding whether change does or does not occur, the level at which the change appears to occur is of utmost importance. Characteristic traits may change, but whether basic traits can change is still open to research.

---

reinforced. Pointing to experiments such as those with "Little Albert" (page 100), Watson claimed that by controlling a person's entire environment from birth, you could make a person into anything you wanted. He pointed particularly to ways in which people create fearful associations to objects or events—associations that can affect or limit our choices in later life.

B. F. Skinner agreed that behavior is the key to understanding personality and that looking into people's minds is not profitable. He claimed that the behaviors of later life were learned as children go through the process of socialization, of learning what behaviors are acceptable and lead to reward and what behaviors

are unacceptable and are punished.

In Skinner's ideal society, everyone is happy because they have learned to contribute to society and, therefore, receive its benefits—rewards. Skinner insisted that our behaviors aren't freely chosen but are actually shaped by the environment. According to Skinner, an idea like free will doesn't explain anything.

Albert Bandura stressed in his "social learning" theory, the role of observation in the development of personality. He demonstrated this in the Bobo doll studies (page 111). Social learning theorists believe that people have free will, which allows them to act on and influence their environments. Further, people are motivated to

Behavior and Internal Factors	
Skills	We have certain innate social and physical abilities.
Values	We determine the relative worth of any behavior.
Goals	We decide what we will work toward and how we will do it.
Expectations	We predict what will happen as a result of a behavior.
Self-efficacy	We have certain beliefs about our own abilities to accomplish a task or reach a goal.

learn more about that environment and about ways to control it. Behavior is based both on what we observe other people doing and on the internal factors charted above.

Evaluating the Behavioral Approach

Undoubtedly, we learn to engage in some behaviors and to avoid others through reinforcement and by observing others. Learning theory is helpful in understanding those behaviors and in helping people to solve problems that they produce. But learning theory doesn't help much in understanding our myriad internal experiences. It diminishes the role of human thought and choice. Although behaviorism and social learning focus on internal feelings and processes, they are limited in their ability to explain individual personalities.

The Humanistic Approach

The humanistic approach is about 180 degrees away from the behavioral approach. While behaviorists refuse to look inward and attribute all behaviors to reinforcement from the environment, humanistic psychologists emphasize internal positive factors in motivation and personality that they see not only as uniquely human, but as unique to each individual. Abraham Maslow and Carol Rogers are major exponents of this theory.

Humanists

Abraham Maslow focused on an individual's desire to reach his or her full potential—and his or her awareness of that desire. He believed that individuals must find their own paths to that goal. Unlike many earlier psychologists, Maslow studied healthy people who coped efficiently with the world and seemed fulfilled.

Studying successful people, Maslow determined that they shared certain characteristics. They were self-aware, open and friendly, and not unduly affected by the opinions of others. People such as Abraham Lincoln, Thomas Jefferson, and Eleanor Roosevelt had a secure sense of who they were and tended to focus their energies on a single task that they perceived as their mission in life. Maslow termed these people *self-actualized.* This state describes the highest need in Maslow's hierarchy, and he considered it the goal of every individual. (See page 175.)

Carl Rogers, in his work in psychotherapy, noted that many people have conflicts between what they perceive as the ideal person and their real selves. He suggested that unrealistic standards might have been imposed on these individuals as children. As adults, they never feel able to live up to those standards. Rogers suggested that parents should give a child **unconditional positive regard.** While a parent may disapprove of a child's behavior, the child should always receive the parent's love independent of any behavior that the child does or does not exhibit.

Believing that individuals can consciously shape their personalities, Rogers emphasized **self-concept, our thoughts and feelings about the type of person we are.** Rogers believed that our self-concept and our experience in the world must be congruent (in agreement or consistent) for us to be happy and healthy.

Rogers also emphasized self-esteem, one's respect for one's self. Self-esteem arises, in the beginning, through the *esteem, or regard,* in which others hold us. Parents help children establish self-esteem by giving them unconditional positive regard. Conditional positive regard would lead a child to believe that he or she is worthwhile only as a result of certain behaviors.

For Rogers, the key to self-actualization is self-reflection—knowing and understanding your feelings and needs and behaving in a manner consistent with them.

Conditional Regard

If I get the answer right, does that mean you'll like me?

Evaluating the Humanistic Approach

Because humanistic psychology encourages people to grow and progress over time, it has a lot of personal appeal. It stresses control over one's life and happiness and focuses on the rich experiences we have in our lives. But some critics point out that, because conscious experience varies from one individual to the next, one can't apply scientific theories to it. The humanistic approach is criticized for several reasons:

* Focusing solely on one's own needs and happiness may result in individuals who are selfish and have little regard for others. Humanists argue that self-actualized, effective people are concerned with the greater good.
* The concepts in the theory are vague, subjective, and not open to testing.
* The theory ignores the human capacity for evil.
* Like the behavioral approach, humanistic theory doesn't adequately explain how personality forms or where specific traits come from.

CRITICAL THINKING

What Is the Role of Free Will in Personality?

Behaviors are manifestations of personality. Early behaviorists claimed that a person's behavior is totally controlled by reinforcement from the environment. Humanists say that our choices are made from within ourselves. What do you think? Read about the issues and develop your own opinion.

THE ISSUES

Watson and other early behaviorists insisted that we can be completely "conditioned" by external positive and negative reinforcement and that, even if we think we are freely choosing a behavior, we are not. Instead, the behavior we "choose" is the result of prior conditioning. Behaviorists might point to the ease with which individuals can become "brainwashed" or develop sympathy with terrorists who capture them.

Humanists, on the other hand, argue that we are human because we are aware of having a higher potential and of our desire to reach it. We exert free will when we choose the manner in which we'll move toward that potential. They point to common characteristics among famous people who have accomplished a great deal and who seem to have reached a stable, happy, and committed "personhood." What role does free will play in our personality?

THE PROCESS

① **Restate the issues.** In your own words, state the nature of free will.

② **Provide evidence.** From your own experience and from the information above, list the evidence *for* free will in choosing behaviors that manifest our personality.

③ **Give opposing arguments.** From your own experience and from the information above, list the evidence *against* free will in choosing behaviors that manifest our personality.

④ **Look for more information.** What else would you like to know before you decide? Make a list of your questions. On the Internet, in the psychology section of the library, or in the index of psychology books, research *free will, behaviorism,* and *humanistic psychology.*

⑤ **Evaluate the information.** Make a chart with two columns:

> **Free Will in Choosing Behaviors**
> For   Against

Record the arguments in each column and rank each column of arguments in importance from 1 to 5, with 1 as the most important.

⑥ **Draw conclusions.** Write one paragraph supporting your answer to the question "What is the role of free will in personality?" Be sure to state reasons, not just opinions.

The Sociocultural Approach

Basic dimensions of personality identified by personality theorists aren't directly applicable across cultures. The sociocultural approach focuses on the effects of ethnicity, gender, and culture on the formation of personality. Dutch social scientist Geert Hofstede analyzed 117,000 responses from participants in 50 countries to identify several cultural dimensions of personality.

In the United States and other Western cultures, **individualism** is a valued trait. People are encouraged to work toward individual achievement and think in terms of individual identities —"I am honest" or "I am a teacher." People from Africa, Asia, and South America tend to define themselves in terms of a group—**collectivism**. Their goals are those of the group, and people feel complete only in terms of social relationships to family, nation, or religious affiliation. They might say "I am a citizen" or "I am a mother."

Power distance is the extent to which less powerful members of a culture expect and accept unequally divided power. Having an assertive personality wouldn't be valued if you were a member of a "lower caste." This dimension also affects self-concept and self-esteem.

Uncertainty avoidance is the extent to which members of a culture feel threatened by uncertain or unknown situations. One would be unlikely to develop an innovative personality in a culture that mistrusts and avoids uncertainty.

Comparison of Major Personality Theories

	Freudian Psychoanalysis	Neo-Freudian Psychodynamics	Trait Approach
Major Theorists	Freud	Adler, Horney, Jung, Erikson	Allport, Cattell, Eysenck
Major Personality Factors	Unconscious conflicts among id, ego, and superego.	The unconscious and social factors.	Early years fix traits.
Healthy Personality Factors	Balance among the needs of inner drives, social constraints, and ideals.	Recognition and adequate conflict resolution between unconscious and social factors.	Recognition of strengths and weaknesses of one's traits and consistent behavior.
Criticisms	Existence of unconscious cannot be confirmed. Theory based on limited cultural sample.	Concepts such as collective unconscious and stages of development may be difficult to confirm.	Descriptive rather than explanatory. Disagreement exists over the number of "basic" traits.

Masculinity/femininity is the extent to which a culture has distinct roles for men and women—such as, men are more assertive, tough, and responsible for material gain, while women are modest, tender, and concerned with quality of life. If the roles are strongly maintained, a person's gender will highly influence the personality characteristics that are developed.

Long-short-term orientation is the extent to which a culture values future rewards and determines personality traits such as perseverance and thrift.

Research suggests that people who are bicultural are more likely to be emotionally stable and have high self-esteem. How might you explain this in terms of the cultural factors listed above?

Evaluation of the Sociocultural Approach

There can be little doubt that the norms of our culture and the expectations of our gender play an important role in shaping our personalities. In most cases, we aren't even aware of the depth of their impact on our behavior.

Attending to ways in which ethnicity, culture, and gender affect personality will no doubt yield insights into the behaviors of individuals within a given culture. However, we still need to study personality outside of any cultural setting. Scientists may yet be able to understand the basic mental processes and behaviors that humans of any culture, ethnicity, or gender are likely to demonstrate.

Behavioral Approach	Humanistic Approach	Sociocultural Approach
Watson, Skinner, Bandura	Maslow, Rogers	Hofstede
Rewards and punishments felt and observed.	The unique potential within each individual.	The way an individual's culture perceives various factors.
External reinforcement, over which the individual has little control.	Self-actualization and development to the fullest potential.	Happiness and fulfillment within the constraints of cultural determinants.
Weak in explaining traits and personality. Ignores internal experience and denies free will.	Said to be self-centered and unrealistically optimistic. Weak in explaining personality.	Does not address basic personality tendencies that may be culture free.

Other Theories

In addition to the major personality theories described in this chapter, other theories are growing in importance and replacing the older theories. They include:

* *Social Cognitive Approach.* This focuses on the context or situation in which behavior occurs. One important aspect of personality is one's sense of personal control—whether one's life is controlled by the individual or from outside.
* *Evolutionary Approach.* This focuses on the role of adaptation in the development of personality.
* *Biological Approach.* This focuses on the role of genetics in the development of personality.

As among the multiple approaches to psychology itself, it may well turn out that each approach contributes something of value to our understanding of personality.

Personality Types

In most bookstores, as well as on the Internet, you can find books and web sites offering to help you determine your "type." A personality type is a set of traits that an individual typically demonstrates. One well-known personality test is the Myers-Briggs Type Indicator, which places individuals in one of 16 categories or types. The important thing to remember is that not all "type" tests have much, if any, research data to back them up. Some, in fact, are based on unscientific factors such as your favorite color or the number of letters in your name. Even some of the scientific tests fail to take context or situation into account. They imply that a person behaves in the same way in all situations—something that research has demonstrated is not true.

We'll learn more about the Myers-Briggs and other personality tests in the next chapter.

Chapter 16 Wrap-up
PERSONALITY

Personality is defined as the relatively stable patterns of thinking, feeling, and acting possessed by an individual. The major theories of personality include Freudian and neo-Freudian psychoanalysis, the trait approach, the behavioral approach, the humanistic approach, and the sociocultural approach. Each theory focuses on a different aspect of personality and suggests a different fundamental source of behavior consistent with an individual's personality.

Other theories of personality take a social cognitive approach, an evolutionary approach, or a biological approach in attempting to explain what personality is and how it develops. Each of the theories contributes to psychology's total understanding of personality.

archetypes—Jung's term for the universal forms that we encounter in our lives, such as mother, father, god, hero, and leader. *p. 268*

collectivism—trait wherein one works for the goals of a group. *p. 276*

defense mechanisms—devices used by the ego to avoid pain or reduce anxiety. *p. 267*

ego—Freud's term for the cognitive and perceptual processes that are in touch with reality. *p. 266*

id—Freud's term for the part of the unconscious mind containing the biological and sexual drives. *p. 266*

individualism—trait wherein one works for personal and individual goals. *p. 276*

inferiority complex—mental state that occurs when a person's conscious thoughts are dominated by an inability to succeed. *p. 267*

morality principle—principle upon which the superego acts; a combination of conscience and a moral self-image. *p. 266*

overcompensation—behavior that is more than what is required to overcome a sense of inferiority. *p. 267*

persona—according to Jung, the image of ourselves that we present to others. *p. 268*

personality—relatively stable patterns of thinking, feeling, and acting that an individual possesses. *p. 265*

pleasure principle—drive to satisfy needs and avoid pain; principle upon which the id acts. *p. 266*

preconscious—part of the mind from which information from the unconscious can be retrieved by the conscious mind. *p. 266*

reality principle—recognition of the real environment; what the ego tempers the needs of the id with. *p. 266*

self-concept—our thoughts and feelings about the type of person we are. *p. 274*

superego—Freud's term for the part of the mind that engages in ethical decision making and moral reasoning. *p. 266*

trait—characteristic of personality that remains fairly stable over time. *p. 269*

type—set of traits that an individual typically demonstrates. *p. 278*

unconditional positive regard—love given by a parent regardless of the behavior of a child. *p. 274*

unconscious—according to psychoanalysis, the part of the mind that contains thoughts, feelings, and desires of which we are mostly unaware. *p. 266*

CHAPTER 17

Psychological Assessment

In this chapter, you will learn about:

- **how and why personality is assessed**
- **objective and projective assessments**
- **aptitude, achievement, and interest tests**

In the ancient world, people were selected for various positions in government on the basis of physical tests, mental abilities, and their knowledge of the law and the world. The practice of using tests for hiring is still alive and well. Today, tests are used for everything from diagnosing mental disorders to college admissions to choosing a career.

Other methods used for psychological assessment include interviews and behavioral observations. Interviews may be either informal or highly structured, in which the interviewer asks a specific list of questions in a particular order. With behavior-rating scales, observers can identify behaviors that a person frequently or rarely uses.

Test taking sometimes causes anxiety. You can use a number of methods to improve test-taking ability and reduce anxiety. Because tests are used today for so many purposes, it pays to know how to take them effectively and with relatively little stress.

Psychological Tests

Early in the twentieth century, people believed in predicting the moral character or intelligence of a person by looking at physical characteristics, such as the height of the forehead, the distance between the eyes, or body weight. Since then, we've come a long way in testing intelligence, personality, potential achievements, and interests.

History of Assessment

Although some psychological testing was done in the early 1900s, most of it focused on intelligence, aptitudes, achievements, and interests, with little attention paid to personality traits. In the mid-1940s, psychologists at the Menninger Foundation promoted a different approach through a group of tests designed to determine various personality factors. Using these tests was termed *psychodiagnosis.*

Throughout the forties and fifties, clinical psychologists became highly skilled in the use of psychodiagnostic tests. However, a split occurred between those who argued for the study of traits and their relationship to behavior and those who thought of personality as a whole system that couldn't be understood in terms of the presence or absence of one or more traits.

The popularity of behaviorism, which maintained that there was no such thing as personality and, therefore, nothing to be measured, compounded the dispute. Although psychological tests have greatly improved over the years, some psychologists still won't use testing.

Uses of Assessments

A **psychological test** measures an individual's intelligence, feelings, behaviors, cognitive functioning, goals, or aptitudes. Different psychological tests can be used to measure intelligence, achievements, abilities, interests, and various personality traits. Psychological tests are used in a variety of ways, chiefly for clinical assessment of people with psychological problems with self and others or behavioral or mental disorders. Such tests can:

* Diagnose problems.
* Uncover causes of problems.
* Predict the course of symptoms.
* Suggest treatment.
* Assess the degree to which the problem has impaired the functions of a person.

Personality assessments are a type of psychological test sometimes used when hiring or considering a person for a promotion. They measure:

* Problem-solving ability.
* Job suitability and work style.
* Values, attitudes, and work ethic.
* Work behavioral style.

Other types of tests can help identify the type of work for which one is best suited or has the greatest aptitude. These differ, though, from tests that help identify the type of work a person is most interested in. And, of course, there are the various intelligence tests discussed in Chapter 10.

Types of Assessment

Psychological testing may range from informal interviews to observation in familiar settings to standardized testing.

Interviews. Interviews may be informal, allowing conversation to flow freely and comfortably for the interviewee. Information about the person's background, upbringing, family relationships, schooling, and career may be discussed. Emphasis is placed on any problems the person may have had in these contexts.

Some interviews are much more structured, with the psychologist asking a specific list of questions in a particular order.

Behavioral Observations. Interesting behavioral information can be collected by observing people in their typical surroundings. For example, if a teacher were being observed, the observer might count the number of times that the teacher asks questions, how long he or she waits for the answers, and how the teacher behaves toward particular members of the class. This type of observation is often used to help people be more aware of their own behavior and personality style.

Standardized Testing. As you'll see in this chapter, some of the most common tests are written. Test takers might answer a variety of true/false statements, complete sentences, rank themselves on a scale of how likely they are to engage in a behavior, or do other tasks.

Ethical Concerns

Your grade on the next math or history test may worry you, but it isn't likely to have a long-term effect on your life. The result of a psychological test carries that possibility. It is therefore important to understand and assess the circumstances of any such test. Some of the ethical issues that surround the taking of psychological tests include:

* You (or a parent or guardian if you're a minor) must give permission for the test. You should always know the reason for taking the test.
* The person giving the test must respect your privacy. It is, however, important to recognize that the law permits access to results of psychological testing in some cases. If you have serious psychological problems, it may be worth this risk, particularly if you have confidence in the person administering the test.

* If tests are given for scientific research, you should be fully informed not only of the purpose of the test but also of how the results will be handled and who will have access to them.
* Recently, the use of computer-scored and- interpreted tests has become a cause of concern. In some cases, computer interpretations have not been adequately tested. Furthermore, people with insufficient training may use these interpretations.

In general, people should make sure they know and trust the psychologist performing any assessment.

The Results of Testing

If you take a psychological test that could have significant impact on your life or on your future, and you feel that there is some doubt about the results or interpretation of the test, ask to be retested. Some tests, such as an IQ test, may be attached to your permanent school records and will follow you through your schooling.

In some cases, test questions might make test takers feel as if there is really something wrong with them. Keep in mind that there is a very wide range of "normal" psychological behaviors. Further, if a psychologist tells you that you have a problem, there's nothing wrong with consulting someone else. While training in the use and correct interpretation of psychological assessments is extensive, psychologists are human, too. Answers to test questions, particularly those that must be interpreted, are open to misinterpretation. Under certain circumstances, even standardized tests aren't accurate.

Results of a single test are less valuable in understanding psychological problems than the results of a **battery** of tests—a set of tests that assesses information about a variety of behaviors and cognitive processes in different ways. For serious psychological problems, a battery of tests administered by a highly qualified professional can be extremely beneficial.

Arguments for Testing

John Exner conducted a survey of several hundred psychologists to gather information about the use of assessments. Of those who responded, a full 25 percent didn't use standard assessments in diagnosing their clients. Exner suggested that assessments would lead to better treatment.

Exner cited two women in their early thirties who both complained of frequent anxiety and panic attacks. He claimed that the typical treatment for this complaint includes the prescription of anti-anxiety medication and some sort of stress management control. Exner then described the results of psychological assessment of the two women. The underlying causes of their anxiety were remarkably different. With this information, it is likely that *different* treatments might have been more effective for the two women.

States and Traits

When selecting a test, it is important to distinguish between a trait, a relatively stable personality characteristic, and a **state,** a person's present mental and physical condition. How, for example, can we know if a person demonstrating anxiety on a test is reacting to certain factors that caused test anxiety in that situation or actually has the trait of anxiety?

The diagram below shows how external anxiety-producing factors might cause an anxious state that affects mental processing and test performance. Even a person with a low anxiety trait can grow anxious if external pressures become great enough. It is critical, therefore, to be certain a test is measuring traits, not states. How is this done?

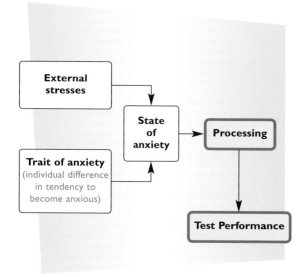

Testing the Test

Although there are a variety of available psychological tests, any test that is truly diagnostic must meet certain conditions.

Reliability

The consistency of a test is called its reliability. This means that the results on a test should be replicable. There are several different types of reliability:

* **Test-Retest Reliability.** A high correlation between the scores a person gets on the same test taken at different times is called test-retest reliability. This type of reliability can be an indication of whether someone's state affected his or her score. If the results vary greatly, either the test is not reliable or the person's state affected the results.

* **Internal Consistency.** An estimate of the degree to which each item or subpart of a test measures the same thing as the rest of the test items or subparts is called internal consistency. Items or subparts that are designed to measure the same characteristic should yield similar results.

* **Equivalent-Forms Reliability.** Sometimes, when a test is retaken, a person will remember something from the first test. This can affect the score, so different forms of the test are used. With equivalent-forms reliability, each test yields the same results when administered to the same individual at different times.

Validity

Validity is whether a test measures what it is supposed to measure. As with reliability, there are several forms of validity:

* **Content Validity.** To be valid, the words and ideas used in a test must have the same meaning across cultures, ages, and genders. What one culture might identify as normal behavior, another might call aggressive. Tests must be validated across a representative cross-section of the population. This is called content validity.

* **Construct Validity.** The extent to which a test accurately identifies the presence or absence of a quality or characteristic is called construct validity. If you design a test to measure a person's aptitude for learning a foreign language, you might give this test to a group of students entering a foreign language class. Then you would wait until they had completed the class and compare their results on the test with their achievement in the class. If there was a high correlation, your test would have construct validity.

* **Predictive Validity.** Once your test has been shown to be valid in measuring foreign language aptitude, it might be used to predict the success of a particular student in a language class. This use of a test to predict the success of someone in a particular situation is called predictive validity.

Sometimes a number of related questions are interspersed through the test. The answers to these questions should be consistent if the test taker is answering honestly. If he or she is not, the test administrator might question the rest of the answers. This is another way of measuring the validity of test results—this time, in terms of the honesty of the test taker's answers.

Standardization

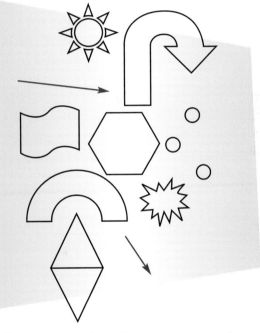

Suppose that these figures appear, each on a separate card, on a psychological test. Person A is told to "Copy these figures, placing them all in some pattern," while person B is told simply, "Copy the figures the best you can." It would be impossible to tell how much of each of the final drawings is the result of the instructions and how much is due to intellectual abilities, perceptual-motor skills, or personality differences between the test takers. To avoid such problems, many tests are standardized.

Reliability and the Myers-Briggs Type Indicator

The Myers-Briggs Type Indicator (MBTI) is a test that attempts to identify a person's "type" based on his or her preferences in four different bipolar dimensions of personality. Those dimensions are shown in the table.

MBTI Personality Dimensions	
Preference	**Person chooses to**
Extrovert (E) vs. Introvert (I)	Focus energy on the outer world (E) or the internal world of ideas (I)
Sensing (S) vs. Intuition (N)	Perceive using the senses (S) or through intuition or "hunches" (N)
Thinking (T) vs. Feeling (F)	Reach conclusions by objective thinking (T) or subjective feeling (F)
Perception (P) vs. Judgment (J)	Use his or her mind primarily to become more aware of things, people, etc. (P) or to come to conclusions about what has been perceived (J)

The preferences are interpreted as suggesting other aspects of personality. For example, a *judger (J)* prefers order and structure, and a *perceiver (P)* tends to be more spontaneous and flexible.

The test includes questions such as "Are you more logical or intuitive?" "Do you prefer being alone or with other people?" These are called "forced choice" questions because you must choose one or the other, even if you feel that both are true during different situations or contexts in your life. From your answers, you are placed in one of 16 personality types. Each type supposedly indicates the primary and secondary strengths that people bring to different situations in their lives.

Although many people like the MBTI, it does not pass the test-retest reliability standard. Some people's choices have changed depending on their state at the time of the test. For this reason, some psychologists refuse to use the test in professional settings until more research is done.

Standardization is the administration and scoring of tests according to established rules. By ensuring that each person who took the test heard or read the same set of instructions and that the tests are all scored in the same manner, one can rule out those factors as affecting the results of the test. The Scholastic (or Standard) Assessment Test (SAT) is a written standardized test used by many colleges to help them select applicants. Both the Stanford-Binet and Wechsler intelligence tests are given individually. The test administrators are trained to ask the questions and to interpret the answers in a standard manner. If a test contains essay questions, graders are trained to score the answers based on the presence or absence of specific information.

Norms

Once you have developed a test and given it to many different people of various ages, genders, cultures, and socioeconomic groups, you will have a sense of how most people in each of those groups typically answer each question. These standard patterns of test answers are called **norms.** When a person's score on a psychological test is compared to the norms of a similar group of people, it can be judged as average, high, or low. A high score isn't always positive. Whereas a high score on an intelligence test would suggest higher than average intelligence, a high score on a test of aggressive behavior might indicate a psychological problem.

Scoring well off the norm doesn't always indicate a problem. It may reveal a unique personality or particularly creative characteristics.

Objective Tests

The two main types of psychological tests used in test batteries are objective and projective tests. **Objective psychological tests** are objective in the sense that the scoring of the test requires no interpretation and can, in fact, be done by computer. These tests often take the form of a questionnaire composed of standardized test items. Because the items limit the test taker to specific choices, such as true/false or multiple choice, the test results can be compiled by computer, but a highly trained examiner must do the final interpretation.

The first important objective personality test—the Minnesota Multiphasic Personality Inventory (MMPI)—dates to the 1940s. The California Psychological Inventory (CPI) is another frequently used objective personality test.

The Minnesota Multiphasic Personality Inventory (MMPI)

The MMPI is the most frequently used measure of personality traits. It was designed to help diagnose psychological disorders such as depression, paranoia, schizophrenia, hysteria, and intro/extroversion. A newer version of the test, the MMPI-2, replaced the original test in 1989. Gender biased and out-of-date language was replaced.

The test consists of 567 true/false items that can be scored by computer and compared to norms stored in the computer's memory. Most psychologists believe that the results of the test should be verified and enriched by observation and interviews.

What the MMPI Measures

The MMPI is a self-report test. That is, the person provides personal information about symptoms, experiences, and behaviors. Statements are along the lines of "My head hurts a lot of the time," "I think shoplifting is okay," or "I hear things that other people don't hear."

Items are criterion-keyed. That is, for scoring they are grouped according to the way people answer them, not by their content. If a certain question is typically answered "true" by "normal" people and "false" by people with a certain psychological disorder, it can be used to distinguish the two, regardless of the reason why the difference occurs.

Criterion-keying produces 13 primary scales on the MMPI, three of which are used to determine if the person appears to have answered the questions honestly, has exaggerated complaints or answered items carelessly, or has denied potential problems. The scales are not foolproof, because some people with serious psychological disorders may have highly distorted self-perceptions.

Why Would People Lie?

There are several reasons why people might not answer test questions honestly or why the results may be misleading. If, for example, the test is being given as part of a child-custody case, a person might lie to look like a better parent. Someone might claim excessive problems if he or she were taking the test as part of a personal injury lawsuit.

The California Psychological Inventory (CPI)

While the MMPI and MMPI-2 diagnose psychological and behavioral disorders, the California Psychological Inventory is designed to measure "normal" traits such as sociability and responsibility. Like the MMPI, the test contains three validity scales for measuring "faking good," "faking bad," and careless test taking.

The CPI has a higher degree of validity than the MMPI-2 because a much larger group was used for the norms and there was greater concern for controlling age, socioeconomic, and geographical factors. The CPI also has higher test-retest reliability. The CPI is often used to predict management potential, reactions to stress, and success in school and work.

The 16 Personality Factor Test (16PF)

The fifth edition of Cattell's 16PF test of 16 primary personality factors is a multiple-choice test designed to describe personality as a whole rather than diagnose psychological problems. The 16 traits are grouped into five global factors: extroversion, anxiety, tough-mindedness, independence, and self-control. This test, published in 1994, is widely used by human resources professionals in many companies worldwide to measure the aspects of personality related to career development.

The NEO Five-Factor Inventory (NEO-FFI)

A relatively new test, the NEO-FFI has 60 five-point rating scale items based on the Big Five personality traits described on page 271.

CRITICAL THINKING

Should MMPI Test Results Be Used in Diagnosis?

The MMPI is among the most widely used psychological diagnostic tests, not only in the United States, but also in other countries. Yet, some claim that it contains major faults. To what extent should the results be used?

THE ISSUES

Proponents of the MMPI point to its long history of use and recent changes to upgrade language and remove gender bias. Some suggest that computer scoring of the test can produce more reliable reports and diagnoses. They maintain that problems arise because people are not sufficiently trained in interpreting the many scales and subscales available in test reports.

Opponents say that psychologists are so in awe of computerized results that they fail to question if the results are sufficiently supported by research. The computer gives an impression of scientific precision to test data that unfairly impresses the lay public, especially in court cases.

Critic Peter Merenda points to the following:

1. In test-retest reliability trials at intervals of one day to one week, as few as 50 percent of the questions are answered the same.

2. The characteristics listed on the 10 scales are obsolete and misleading.

3. The use of true/false items is highly questionable.

4. No provisions for cultural differences are made when the test is translated into other languages. Statements such as "I prefer to work with women" may be meaningless in some cultures.

5. The norms are skewed so that only extremely different results are interpretable.

THE PROCESS

❶ **Restate the issues.** In your own words, state the nature of the disagreement.

❷ **Provide evidence.** From your own experience and from the information above, list the evidence *for* using test results to diagnose psychological problems.

❸ **Give opposing arguments.** From your own experience and from the information above, list the evidence *against* using test results to diagnose psychological problems.

❹ **Look for more information.** What else would you like to know before you decide? Make a list of your questions. On the Internet, in the psychology section of the library, or in the index of psychology books, research *psychological assessment, reliability and validity of testing,* and *computer scoring.*

❺ **Evaluate the information.** Make a chart with two columns:

Using Test Results in Diagnosis	
For	Against

Record the arguments in each column and rank each column of arguments in importance from 1 to 5, with 1 as the most important.

❻ **Draw conclusions.** Write one paragraph supporting your answer to the question "To what extent should MMPI results be used in diagnosing psychological problems?" Be sure to state reasons, not just opinions.

Projective Tests

Projective psychological tests have no specific answers. The simplest form of such a test might ask the test taker to state, "My greatest fear is . . . ." Other projective tests ask people to interpret drawings of vague shapes, inkblots, or pictures of people engaged in various tasks. In some cases, answers are simply used as a point of discussion in informal interviews, but some projective tests are much more sophisticated.

The term *projective* comes from the belief that people will project their internal thoughts, feelings, problems, or personality traits onto relatively meaningless external objects such as inkblots. From the way the client interprets the object, the psychologist attempts to determine underlying processes.

Can Projective Tests Be Objective?

It is important to recognize that, although a projective test is open-ended, it can still be standardized and normed. One of the earliest projective tests—the Rorschach or inkblot test—uses images like the one shown.

▲
What does this figure look like to you?

Swiss psychiatrist Hermann Rorschach first used inkblots such as this when he became curious about whether mentally ill patients would interpret them differently from normal people. In the 1920s, Rorschach published a set of 10 cards that are still used today.

Because this test has been given to so many people and has been the subject of so much research, it has become highly standardized and normed. Norms are determined by:

* The region of the card to which the person responds—to the whole picture or some detail.
* Whether the person responds to texture, color, or shading.
* The actual content of the interpretation—animal, human, or bizarre, and whether this is typical of the way most people would perceive the figure.
* Recurrence of interpretation across cards.

While the test is a good predictor of a person's current emotional state, it would never be used alone to diagnose or treat a person's problems, in part because of questions about its reliability and validity.

The Thematic Apperception Test (TAT)

Originally developed in the 1930s for studying achievement motivation, the TAT consists of a number of illustrations of people and things. The test taker is asked to tell a story with a beginning and an end about each illustration. The stories are then informally analyzed for content and quality.

What story might you tell about this picture? You may find it interesting to compare stories with your classmates.

▼

Who Uses Which Tests?

Not surprisingly, the types of tests a psychologist chooses to use are determined by the theory to which that psychologist subscribes.

* Trait theorists tend to select objective tests of traits such as MMPI-2, CPI, or 16PF.
* Psychoanalytic theorists tend to select projective tests such as TAT.
* Behavioral theorists tend to observe behavior in natural settings.
* Humanistic theorists use questionnaires that ask people to describe their real self and their ideal self. Descriptions that are similar indicate a healthy personality.

Although the TAT is not standardized for clinical use, it is often used in conjunction with other clinical or vocational assessments. The stories can also be used as interesting starting points for discussing problems.

As stated earlier, the TAT was first used to measure achievement motivation. Psychologists who use the TAT are trained to identify motivation scores from the stories.

Limits of Projective Testing

Some psychologists criticize the interpretation of projective tests because of the unfortunate eagerness of some test administrators to assume psychological problems and assign diagnostic labels. Critics maintain that one tends to find what one is looking for and question whether the projection is that of the client or the psychologist.

"ROnschach! WHAT's To BECOME OF YOU?"

Aptitude and Achievement Tests

You are probably more familiar with aptitude and achievement tests than with projective or objective psychological tests. For many people, a test is a test. You've taken plenty of them in your years in school. But all tests are not created equal. An **aptitude test** attempts to *predict* your ability to learn something new. An **achievement test** is designed to assess what you have already learned.

Intelligence Tests

Intelligence tests are among the most famous aptitude tests. The Stanford-Binet gives you a score based on your performance compared to the average performance of others of the same age. The Wechsler Adult Intelligence Scale— Revised (WAIS-R) scores individuals on separate verbal and nonverbal tests based on 11 different subtests.

If used appropriately, intelligence tests can help teachers or employers focus on a person's strengths rather than limitations.

College Aptitude Tests

The SAT and ACT are familiar tests for most college-bound students. A person's score on the SAT, or Scholastic (or Standard) Assessment Test, is used by many colleges and universities to predict academic performance. The test includes separate scores for verbal and mathematical aptitudes. Colleges also use the American College Testing (ACT) exam score to predict academic success. The ACT tests "educational development" in English usage, mathematics, reading, and science reasoning.

Aptitude or Achievement?

Although the SAT and ACT are called aptitude tests and are used to predict future academic success, they are, to a large extent, achievement tests. Both assume significant achievement in the use of the English language and grammar and a working knowledge of algebra and geometry. Other countries rely on a student's academic record, which demonstrates both aptitude and the student's motivation to succeed.

Some people argue that it is impossible to test aptitude without testing achievement of some type. Others claim that it is possible to test for aptitudes such as mechanical ability, motor skills, or clerical accuracy without testing achievement.

Achievement Tests

In general, the tests you take for your classes are achievement tests. They measure the amount of material you have learned (or, more accurately, remembered) from your classes.

The Medical College Admissions Test (MCAT) must be taken for admission to medical schools. Other tests include the Graduate Management Admission Test (GMAT) for business schools and the Law School Admission Test (LSAT) for law school admission. Passing the General Educational Development (GED) test gains a high school diploma for those who haven't completed high school.

Vocational Interest Tests

Many people take the most popular tests of vocational interest and/or aptitude, and studies demonstrate that the tests have high validity and reliability ratings. As such, they are very useful in predicting success in various careers. With so many occupational choices, you can get a head start in deciding upon a career by taking a vocational interest test.

The Strong-Campbell Interest Inventory

Although some of the questions on interest tests seem obvious—"Would you rather design a building or teach students?"—many others are much subtler. Questions range from items where the test taker indicates a "like" or "dislike" for a behavior or activity to statements with which the test taker must agree or disagree. A computer will compare the choices you have made on the test with choices made by thousands of people who are successful in many different professions. It is just as important to know what you don't want as what you do.

For example, if it turns out that the majority of teachers who took the test would also like to be a librarian, and you would hate that profession, that is important even if many of your other choices agreed with teacher choices. From the test results, you can judge in what professions your interests are most likely to serve you well.

The Kuder Preference Record

Another widely used vocational interest inventory is the Kuder Preference Record. This is a forced-choice test, where you must choose one of the answers, even if all or none of them seem to apply. You might be asked if you would rather a) plant a garden; b) sing a song; or c) read a book. Results on this test indicate how interested a person is in such areas as literature, art, music, science, engineering, or nature.

Interest inventories don't predict a person's success in a given occupation. They just indicate the areas in which the person demonstrates the greatest interest.

Taking Tests

Students may have trouble on tests because they don't understand the material or don't know how to study or because they have **test anxiety**—difficulty retrieving what they know in a test environment. This anxiety increases with the relative importance of the test. Here are a few tips for test taking:

* Learn everything you can about a test beforehand. Ask the teacher or students who've taken the class before what the tests are like. Ask to see earlier versions and examples of good answers to essay questions.
* Make up test questions for yourself similar to those that might be on the test.

* Use practice tests for "big" tests such as the ACT and SAT.
* Begin studying well in advance of the test. Study a limited amount before going to sleep at night so that memories can consolidate.
* Study until you know everything really well. You will be more confident about your ability.
* Be prepared. Don't add to your worries by forgetting your pencil or a calculator.
* Think positive thoughts. Instead of telling yourself that you will fail, remember times that you've succeeded. Focus on your strengths.

Tips for Various Test Types	
Multiple Choice	1. Answer the question before looking at the choices. 2. Read all the choices. 3. Rule out obvious wrong answers. 4. Choose the best of the remaining choices.
True/False	1. Do not mark TRUE unless every part of the statement is true. 2. Watch out for statements containing *always, never,* or *all.* They are usually false. 3. Longer items with more information tend to be true—but not always!
Short Answer	1. Answer in brief, complete sentences. 2. Include relevant and important terms. 3. Select the most important points for discussion.
Essay	1. Read the key word, such as *compare, evaluate,* or *prove.* 2. Be sure that your answer does that. 3. Organize your thoughts on a separate sheet of paper before beginning to write. 4. Support your statements with examples where possible.

Psychological tests are used to diagnose problems, for hiring and promoting workers, and to assess abilities, achievement, or interests. The major types of tests are objective, projective, intelligence, aptitude, achievement, and vocational interest tests. Interviews and behavioral observations are also used to assess personality and other psychological factors. Various tests are chosen depending on the theory a psychologist prefers. A battery of tests is of more value than any single test.

Every formal test must possess four factors: it must be standardized, normed, and have been tested for reliability and validity. A person can use a number of methods to be more at ease during tests and to have a better chance of test-taking success.

Psychology

achievement test—test designed to assess what one has already learned or can do. *p. 292*

aptitude test—test that attempts to predict ability to learn or do something new. *p. 292*

battery—set of tests that assesses information about a variety of behaviors and cognitive processes in different ways. *p. 283*

norm—standard pattern of results on a test given to many people. *p. 287*

objective psychological tests—tests that can be scored without interpretation. *p. 287*

projective psychological tests—open-ended tests that ask a person to interpret ambiguous drawings or to complete sentences. *p. 290*

psychological test—measurement of personality factors such as intelligence, feelings, behaviors, cognitive functioning, goals, or aptitudes. *p. 281*

standardization—the administration and scoring of tests according to established rules. *p. 286*

state—person's present mental and physical condition. *p. 284*

test anxiety—state in which a person in a test environment has difficulty retrieving what he or she knows. *p. 294*

validity—test standard in which a test measures what it is supposed to measure. *p. 285*

Social Psychology: Cognition

In this chapter, you will learn about:

- how self-perception forms
- how attitudes and prejudices form
- how interpersonal attraction develops

"What a good girl!" "Big boys don't cry!" "Spend more time on your math and science." "You'll never be any good at art." We are the targets of comments about who and what we are or aren't—who and what we should or shouldn't be—from the time we first comprehend language. How important are these comments to the development of our idea of self? In what ways do they influence our sense of future possibilities or our belief in our limitations? This chapter will explore the importance of other people to the development of our self-perception.

The important people in our lives—our reference group—also help to shape our attitudes and beliefs. Through our natural cognitive process of categorizing the world, we develop stereotypes, and sometimes prejudices. Where do these come from?

Are there universal standards for what makes a person attractive? Why do people develop an attraction for one another? And what's love got to do with it?

What Is Social Psychology?

Social psychology is the study of how people influence and are influenced by others. Unlike sociology, which emphasizes group processes, social psychology emphasizes the individual. In this chapter, we'll examine how social situations and interactions with others affect our thinking. In the next chapter, we'll look at how those same factors affect behavior.

The Self

The *self* is what we perceive ourselves to be—an insider's view of our personality. The development of our concept of self depends heavily on our relations with others. Many of the concepts that we develop, such as generosity, kindness, or love, come from our experiences with the behaviors of others.

Social Interaction and the Role of Others in Self-Concept

Theories about the importance of social interaction to the development of the concept of self are numerous. Here are a few of the ideas proposed:

* We are born (preadapted) expecting another being (generally our mothers) to be tuned to our needs.
* Establishing relationships is a need second only to seeking pleasure and avoiding pain.
* Establishing relationships is the primary motivation in our lives.

Several theorists go so far as to claim that we are aware of ourselves only because others are, or have been, aware of us. In other words, there is no self without others!

Social psychology is a fairly new approach to understanding the individual. For that reason, it is not surprising that theories about how others influence individual development vary widely. Here are just **three** of the theories about the role of others:

1. We make the thoughts, feelings, and behaviors of certain others a part of ourselves and claim them as our own. Children, for instance, often assume the preferences, values, and beliefs of their families and cultures.

2. We use the thoughts, feelings, and behaviors of others as a way to manage our own motivations, control, self-evaluation, and self-defense. For these purposes, we carry representations of others in ourselves. Depending on the situation, we may remember a parent's admonition to "be careful"; recall that someone else did a task better; emulate a mentor's actions; or think about how we are viewed by our peers.

3. We view representations of others as parts of ourselves. To the extent that maintaining a relationship with a parent, loved one, employer, or coworker is part of how we define ourselves, representations of those people will remain as working parts of ourselves. This differs from the second theory because it focuses on the "whole other" rather than on just the characteristics, beliefs, or actions of others.

Developing Self-Concept

A child's view of his or her competencies combines some parents' views, teachers' views, views of peers, and his or her own direct observation. A person's self-concept may also include images or fantasies of other people. As the child matures, the views of others play different roles in the initiation, maintenance, and evaluation of his or her actions. You may find it interesting to think about how you have internalized the ideas of others in developing your sense of self.

Who Am I?

Researchers are only now exploring the exact mechanisms by which the thoughts, feelings, and behaviors of others influence self-concept. R. A. Shweder suggests that our culture provides answers to a number of core self-knowledge questions, including:

* What is me, and what is not me?
* What is male, and what is female?
* What is grownup, and what is childlike?
* Who is "of my kind," and who is not?
* What is "our way," and what is not?
* What determines the hierarchy in acquiring benefits or bearing burdens?
* Am I independent, dependent, or interdependent?
* What do I want, and what does the group want?
* How can I avoid the violence of person vs. person?

How are such questions answered and how do they become part of a person's sense of self? Certain studies show that some of the answers are transmitted through day-to-day conversations with children. For example, children regularly hear statements such as "Boys don't cry," "That's not fair" "What do you want to be when you grow up?" or "Good little girls don't do that." Because children are searching for the answer to what it means to be a person, they absorb these adult—and sometimes peer—values, making them part of their "selves."

Other researchers argue that imitating the actions and values of significant others is merely part of a larger process. They say that an individual absorbs what others have to offer and, with effort, shapes it into forms consistent with his or her own personality and valuable to his or her own purposes.

Self-Schemas

As a child develops language, he or she labels various experiences and makes them more concrete. Words such as *good, funny,* or *creative* describe only a small part of a child's internal experience. As children recognize that their perceptions of themselves are, in some ways, different from others' perceptions, or that *good* may be different for various people within their world, they begin to generate schemas that integrate their experiences with the views of others.

As you've seen, *schemas* are the large views we hold about objects, actions, events, and relationships that all pertain to a particular content. **Self-schemas** are cognitive structures that allow people to differentiate themselves from others. Schemas become more detailed as people advance in age and experience, as follows:

* Young children's self-descriptions generally contain family members or playmates.
* Adolescents' descriptions of self remain interpersonal as they describe themselves as "friendly," "easy to talk to," or "loyal."
* As self-schemas become more enriched, an adult develops an "expected" self, perceiving how he or she would behave in various circumstances.
* Self-schemas can also include "possible" selves that may be either desired or ideal images of self, or feared and unpredictable ones.

Reference Groups

Children are aware that others may have a different opinion of them than they have of themselves. The appraisal of others plays an important role in a person's self-perception in situations without objective feedback, such as grades, athletic ability, or peer appraisal. Unfortunately, children are not very accurate in their perception of what others think of them.

Those people or groups of people whose opinions we care about are called **reference groups.** One theorist says that we see ourselves in terms of "generalized others." We think about "What do *people* think of me?" rather than "What does *my teacher* think of me?"

Social Comparisons

We not only come to see ourselves as others see us, but we come to see ourselves differently depending on the "others" who are around at a given time. Comparing self to others is called **social comparison,** and it has two functions: *normative* and *comparative.* In normative comparison, an individual learns the typical values and behaviors of the group. The comparative function allows an individual to see how he or she differs from the group. There are three different purposes of comparison.

Why Compare?
Self-Evaluation
Diagnosing information about one's abilities.
Self-Improvement
Determining what, if any, of one's characteristics need work.
Self-Enhancement
Enhancing self-esteem by recognizing ways in which one is unique or different.

The Social Identity

Personal identity is composed of an individual's thoughts and emotions, particularly self-knowledge and evaluation. **Social identity** is based on the impressions someone makes, what others think of that person, and his or her attractiveness or popularity within a group. Several theorists maintain that someone with high social identity and low personal identity will try to get along with others. Those with high personal identity will work for personal achievement.

It would appear that a balance between the two would hold the greatest promise of success in both personal and interpersonal situations.

Sidebar

Protecting the Positive Self

It is important to psychological good health to keep a positive view of oneself. We do this through a process called *reality negotiation*. We think of behaviors as being "good" or "bad" compared to our perception of our ideal self—I do "good" things and I don't do "bad" things. When we perform a behavior that we perceive as "bad," we have mechanisms to protect our positive sense of self.

Here are **four** of these mechanisms:

1. **Decreasing our connection to the behavior**

   EXAMPLES: "I didn't do it," "I only did it once," "I didn't mean to do it."

2. **Decreasing our responsibility**

   EXAMPLES: "Yes, but . . .," "Everybody's doing it," "It was too hard. Nobody could have done it right." Another way to decrease responsibility is blaming it on someone or something else. This argument is presented in court cases when lawyers suggest that upbringing or other circumstances should be held accountable for the accused's behavior.

3. **Self-handicapping**

   EXAMPLES: "I wasn't feeling well at the time," "I was upset (or angry or not myself)." The handicap is responsible for the behavior—not the person.

4. **Reducing the "badness" of the behavior**

   EXAMPLES: "It's not as bad as it looks," "It was just a small piece of pie," or the Robin Hood defense—"I did it for a good cause"—or blaming it on the victim—"he just got what he deserved."

How Others Perceive Us

The way we perceive one another grows with our experiences of others. Each perception, in turn, affects our expectations and perceptions of the next person we interact with. Our own schemas are partly responsible for the ways we perceive other people. If our schemas about social interactions are based on many positive social experiences, they include the assumption that the next interaction with a person will be positive. On the other hand, negative schemas will cause us to predict negative interactions.

Positive schemas result in our responding to positive or pleasant cues when we meet another person. People with negative schemas will interpret exactly the same cues—the same facial expressions—in an entirely different, and negative, way.

The Function of Schemas

We use schemas to structure our perception of events, make predictions about the future, and decide on goals and plans. Schemas are modified as new experiences provide new or different information about the world. However, schemas that could be too easily changed wouldn't be of much value in bringing stability to our world. We become efficient at fitting people into our schemas as we mature.

First Impressions

The first impression is one tool we use to place people in our schemas. This helps to explain why first impressions are so important and why their effects are so long-lasting.

Even people who believe themselves to be nonjudgmental are affected by the way they first perceive another individual. Numerous studies demonstrate that physical attractiveness plays a large part in the impression we form of a person. When applying for a job, you are encouraged to wear your best clothes and be well groomed because, like it or not, employers will often base their impressions on an applicant's looks. Because people tend to believe that their first impressions of others are correct, other qualifications you demonstrate later may take on less importance to the employer.

It has been estimated that it takes about four minutes for the average person to size up another individual—to decide if that first impression is positive or negative. Some of the factors that people use in that decision are:

* Cleanliness.
* Eye contact.
* Voice quality.
* Facial expression.
* Color of the skin.
* Gender.
* Age.
* Personal space.
* What you say and how you say it.

People judge your intelligence from what you say and how you say it. Depending on the impression you want to make, using or avoiding slang or making jokes can attach you to a peer group or alienate you from a potential employer.

The Effects of First Impressions

If, in a first encounter, someone spends the entire time telling you how important he or she is and generally suggests that you're lucky to become acquainted, how eager will you be to spend more time with that person?

If, on the other hand, a person smiles, asks you about your own interests, and is friendly and warm, you'll probably be more open to a possible friendship. That first impression affects your behavior in regard to that person.

Because first impressions tend to be lasting additions to an individual's schema, they are difficult to overcome. People must generally work much harder to "prove themselves" if the first impression they produced in others was negative.

Self-fulfilling Prophesies

If you're being interviewed for a job and the employer's body language, facial expression, and questions suggest that he or she isn't particularly impressed with you, what would your reaction be? Keep in mind that as a person is forming a first impression of you, you are also forming one. We tend to react positively to smiling, friendly people and negatively to cold or unfriendly people. If the employer acts negatively because of a poor first impression, you are more than likely to confirm that impression in your response to his or her negative behavior. This is called a **self-fulfilling prophecy.** The employer is getting the expected behavior from you, but largely because he or she expected it!

Attribution Theory

A teacher you really like yells at you for something that normally receives little or no reaction. What reason would you give for this behavior? What if a teacher you didn't like berated you?

Attribution theory suggests that people tend to explain the behavior of others in terms either of the person's personality traits or of external factors such as the situation. If you attributed the first teacher's behavior to a bad mood or irritation at something else, those are external factors. If you said that the second teacher acted out of meanness, you're attributing the behavior to a personality trait.

You yell at your best friend. Why? Research shows that we more often attribute negative behaviors in others to personality traits, while in ourselves, we see the cause as external.

The adaptive character of such behavior can be seen in this example. If you get a poor grade on a test, are you more likely to say that it was because you're not smart enough or because you hadn't studied enough, didn't feel well, or that the material hadn't been explained clearly enough in class? Attributing the cause to such external factors helps you to protect your positive self.

You don't have the same responsibility for the self-image of others that you have for your own, so you are not as prone to look to external factors for causes of their behavior.

How We Make Attributions

The attributions that we make to the behaviors of others and to ourselves depend on:

* What we already know, believe, or have experienced with regard to the person or situation.
* The behavior itself.
* The consequences of our attribution.

Your previous experience with one teacher was positive and with another was negative. You're more likely to attribute the behavior to external events for the "positive" teacher and personality traits for the "negative" teacher. The consequences of the attribution would have simply confirmed your impression of the teacher. When attributing a cause to your own behavior, you tend to attribute "good" behavior to internal personality traits and "bad" behavior to the situation or external influences, thereby maintaining a positive self-concept.

Other Factors in Attribution

Harold Kelley devised a model of attribution based on several possible dimensions of a behavior that can range from high to low.

Let's say that it is the first day of class and a student stumbles walking through the door to the classroom. We don't see any reason for the stumble, but a number of other people also stumble as they enter the room. The behavior can be viewed in several different ways:

* *Consensus.* If a person behaves in the same manner as many other people in the same circumstances, we are more likely to say that it is the external situation, rather than some personal trait, that causes the behavior. This is called *consensus.*

CRITICAL THINKING

Do We Know Why We Do Things?

According to attribution theory, humans strive to explain behavior—both their own and that of others. As you've seen, we often fall victim to various biases in attributing causes to our own behaviors. Can we know the true causes of our behaviors? What do you think?

THE ISSUES

We assume that we have a good reason for almost everything we do. Even a simple act, such as making a choice from a restaurant menu, can be explained in terms of likes and dislikes, the mood we're in, what we've eaten in the past few days, how hungry we are, or the cost of the meal. Sometimes, the reason we give is some combination of those factors. If asked, we can usually generate a set of reasons that appears logical and reasonable.

Michael Gazzaniga and others involved in split-brain research have suggested that schemas or "modules" outside of our conscious awareness actually generate many of our behaviors. Often, we are totally unaware of the reasons for those behaviors. Gazzaniga argues that, when asked, our conscious mind—the "interpreter"—looks at the behavior and generates reasons based on our self-perception and the "rules" of social behavior. If such reasons make sense to others and ourselves, we are satisfied.

Can we know the true causes of our behaviors?

THE PROCESS

❶ **Restate the issues.** In your own words, state the nature of the issue.

❷ **Provide evidence.** From your own experience and from the information above, list the evidence *for* people knowing the true causes of their behaviors.

❸ **Give opposing arguments.** From your own experience and from the information above, list the evidence *against* people knowing the true causes of their behaviors.

❹ **Look for more information.** What else would you like to know before you decide? Make a list of your questions. On the Internet, in the psychology section of the library, or in the index of psychology books,

research *hemisphericity, Gazzaniga, right and left brain modules,* and the *interpreter.*

❺ **Evaluate the information.** Make a chart with two columns:

Knowing the Causes of Behavior	
For	Against

Record the arguments in each column and rank each column of arguments in importance from 1 to 5, with 1 as the most important.

❻ **Draw conclusions.** Write one paragraph supporting your answer to the question "Can we know the true causes of our behavior?" Be sure to state reasons, not just opinions.

* **Consistency.** If that same student stumbles through the door on other occasions, this is called *consistency*—repetitions of the same behavior in the same situation. While you may begin to attribute the behavior to clumsiness, you may still give the benefit of the doubt if you don't see the person stumbling anywhere else.
* **Distinctiveness.** If the same student stumbles or bumps into people around the school, this is called *distinctiveness.* You're now likely to attribute the behavior to the trait of clumsiness.

Attribution Bias

How might your inference differ if a Democrat criticizes a Republican or if a Democrat praises a Republican? Depending on whether you're a member of the National Rifle Association or someone who despises guns, you attribute school violence to "bad kids" or to guns. Conservatives might blame poverty on lack of motivation of the poor and unemployed, while liberals might attribute it to external circumstances. Employers might attribute poor production to lazy workers, and workers, to poor working conditions. The complex causes of behaviors are often ignored in favor of the following types of attribution bias:

* **Fundamental attribution error** is the tendency to underestimate external reasons and overestimate personality traits as causes of people's behavior.

* **Actor-observer bias** is the tendency to attribute the behavior of others to internal or personality factors and our own behavior to external factors.
* **Self-serving bias** is the tendency to attribute your own positive behaviors to internal causes and negative behaviors to external causes.
* **Gender bias** is the tendency to attribute positive behaviors in men to internal traits and in women to external causes.

It is interesting that, in some studies, women exhibit gender bias more than men do. When asked to review a book, women tend to give more positive reviews to a book by John Jones than to the same book by Joan Jones. People tend to attribute the success of a woman's book to external factors rather than to intelligence or talent, as they would for a book by a male author.

Attitudes

A belief is something that we assume to be true. Beliefs are often both unconscious and unexamined—that is, we are unaware that some things we think or say are not proven facts. They are something we have come to accept as true without much thought or consideration of evidence. **Attitudes** are beliefs and feelings about people, objects, or events that cause us to behave in certain ways. Attitudes are often stated as propositions or statements of fact that are unquestioned—"That's how those people are," "Don't bother trying that. It never works," "Everyone is out to get me," "Capital punishment is wrong."

Often, people aren't aware of their attitudes or of how those attitudes developed. But the attitudes themselves determine what we perceive in our surroundings, how we act toward others, and what we expect to happen as a result of our behavior.

How Attitudes Change

Whenever an inconsistency occurs between an attitude and a behavior, we feel uncomfortable and are motivated to change either the attitude or the behavior. This is called **cognitive dissonance.** Let's say that you believe what you've heard and read about the risks of smoking. You even tell a friend that smoking is unhealthy, yet you continue to smoke. This produces a level of discomfort that can be reduced either by not smoking or by mentally reducing the risks and trying to persuade yourself that it can't happen to you. The more addicted you are to the behavior, the more likely you are to change the attitude rather than the behavior.

How Attitudes Develop	
Conditioning	When a child says or does something that agrees with what a parent or other adult believes, the child is positively reinforced through praise, a smile, or a nod. Behaviors such as sharing, studying hard, or helping others, when reinforced, develop into attitudes about those behaviors.
Observational Learning	We learn and develop attitudes by watching others. If you see a classmate who is popular and attractive, or popular and engaged in sports, you may develop an attitude that one must be attractive or athletic to be popular.
Cognitive Evaluation	Some attitudes develop as a result of evaluating information and deciding what to believe—cognitive evaluation. This might be the case when you decide that exercise is good for your health or that smoking isn't. When someone's behavior doesn't fit your expectations, you may use cognitive evaluation to change your attitude about and your expectations of the person.
Cognitive Anchors	Some of the earliest attitudes that you form act as fundamental and lasting beliefs around which you shape your world. These cognitive anchors not only shape your perception and interpretation of the world, but also may prevent you from accepting other attitudes that form later in life.

Using Social Schemas to Develop Attitudes

Our social schemas include the ideas we have formed about various groups. When you meet a new person, you automatically process and absorb that person, into existing schemas. You then use the schemas to make predictions about the person. Notice that this involves nothing of the actual characteristics or personality of the individual being assessed. Those tend to be ignored or overlooked.

Sell the IBM, but wait until it hits 190, then, about the Digital...wait, my parents are home... "He DIDN'T !!... like WOW!... really CooL".

For many adults the word *teenager* brings certain social schemas to mind. If a person's experience with teenagers is limited to representations in the media, the schemas may include a chatty, silly girl or a silent, brooding boy.

Do all the teenage girls and boys you know fit into these schemas? It is likely that they don't.

Stereotypes

In social psychology, a **stereotype** is a set of distorted, generalized beliefs about a group of people. This generalization comes through in statements such as "Girls are gossips" or "Boys are unfeeling." In analyzing absolute statements like these, it becomes clear that they are false. Individuals use stereotypes because:

* They are an efficient, although largely incorrect, way to organize information about other people.
* Individuals assume that people who are not like themselves are somehow alike.
* Traits seen in some members of a group are assumed to exist in all members of the group.

Effects of Stereotypes

Stereotyping assigns people to social schemas based on such factors as physical characteristics, age, gender, socioeconomic group, dress, or ethnicity. Rather than being perceived as an individual, a person is seen as a caricature—an exaggerated version of the supposed characteristics of the "group." Many stereotypes tend to focus on negative characteristics of a group, although some positive stereotypes, such as that attractive people make better leaders, also exist.

It takes a lot of evidence for people to redefine the stereotypes they've developed. Even when you get to know someone from another group as an individual—as a person who does not exhibit stereotypical characteristics—you may consider this person the exception rather than admit that your stereotype may be incorrect. Contrary information tends to be assimilated into the stereotype rather than used to change the stereotype.

Stereotypes unfairly limit the potential of members of certain groups. Even a positive stereotype may put an unfair burden on group members. Many "honors" students are familiar with this problem.

Prejudice and Discrimination

Prejudice, from the word *prejudge*, is an unfounded and generally negative attitude toward a group of people. It involves prejudging an individual based on the stereotypical characteristic of his or her group. Prejudice is a mixture of stereotypical beliefs, negative emotions, and schemas that predispose individuals to act. Some people might believe that politicians are corrupt, and they might feel disgust for politicians' behavior. As a result, these people don't go to the polls because "All politicians are crooks, so why bother."

Consider these **five** causes of prejudice:

1. **Categorization.** Being able to quickly identify members of one's own social group can be interpreted as an adaptive behavior. As we've seen in earlier chapters, categorization is one of the primary tools of thinking.

2. **Exaggeration of Differences.** We tend to prefer those who are similar to ourselves in age, socioeconomic level, and attitudes—our "in-group." We assume that members of "out-groups" are more different than they really are.

3. **Justifying Economic or Role Status.** The traits that we assign to various groups are used to justify their status or the roles they play in society. If one family is less economically successful than another, someone might justify the difference by assuming they must not work as hard.

4. **Observational Learning**. Along with attitudes and beliefs, children learn to imitate their parents' biases and prejudices.

5. **Scapegoating.** When problems are too complex for an easy solution, we tend to find someone to blame—a scapegoat. Having an easy though unjust solution allows us to feel less threatened and more in control.

Discrimination is the unfair treatment of individuals because they are members of a particular group. People are predisposed to discriminate because of prejudice. Classic cases involve separate schooling for blacks and whites; better education for boys than girls in some cultures; the right to vote afforded to males and not females in the early history of the United States; refusing to employ a person who is overweight or disabled; and firing people because they've reached a certain age.

Cases of discrimination often create self-fulfilling prophecies. If people are discriminated against because they are disabled, for example, they may have a greater chance of being unemployed, thus reinforcing the stereotype that the disabled don't really want to work. In addition, victims of discrimination tend to have lower self-esteem. This results in lower expectations that, in turn, reduce their opportunities for success.

Overcoming Prejudice

Prejudice is difficult to overcome, but not impossible. Increasing contact among groups, speaking out against prejudice, and making a conscious effort to seek out nonstereotypical qualities within another group can help to reduce prejudice.

Unconscious Prejudice

Researchers at the University of Washington and Yale University have developed a test to measure the unconscious levels of race and age prejudice, gender stereotyping, and self-esteem. The Implicit Association Test (IAT) revealed that 90 to 95 percent of people demonstrate associations that indicate implicit or unconscious prejudices.

In a computer version of one part of the test, people are shown faces that they must quickly identify as young or old. They are then shown words, such as *pleasure, evil, peace,* and *friend,* and are asked to press keys to indicate whether each word is good or bad. Finally, faces and words are shown randomly and the terms "young or good" and "old or bad" are the choices. Then the terms are reversed—"young or bad" and "old or good." Making this choice takes much longer! Nearly 80 percent of people show a strong preference for young over old.

The researchers believe that unconscious prejudice may occur despite people's wishes and regardless of the culture in which they live. They hope that awareness of these roots of prejudice may help people overcome these apparently biological tendencies.

Interpersonal Attraction

Attraction, like prejudice, is an attitude. Just as there is a biological tendency to classify self and others, there is a biological necessity to be drawn toward friendship or love of others.

Factors in the formation of friendships or groups include:

* **Similarity.** People are drawn to those with similar physical or cultural features and commonality of belief or attitude.
* **Proximity.** People who live or work closely together tend to interact more frequently and share common issues.
* **Reciprocity.** People tend to enjoy the mutual exchange of feelings or attitudes. Studies show that we are more comfortable with people who appear to like us.

In general, common interests and attitudes lead us to find others attractive.

Physical Attractiveness

People from various cultures find different physical traits attractive. However, there does seem to be some universal appeal in large eyes, high cheekbones, and narrow jaws. No such universal standard of body type exists. Some cultures value a full-bodied look in women as indicative of childbearing potential. Some cultures value a lean look in men, while others value a more muscular shape.

Physical attractiveness, in general, is a stereotype that carries positive expectations. What are some examples?

Love, Sweet Love

The word *love* is used to describe everything from feelings toward a mate or a child to feelings toward a food, one's country, or a good movie. Most commonly, *love* describes strong feelings of attachment, affection, and mutual attraction shared by two people. Psychologist Robert Sternberg has proposed a triangular model of love, as shown in the diagram below, based on **three** characteristics:

1. **Intimacy**—Closeness, mutual concern, and a sharing of feelings.
2. **Passion**—Feelings of romantic or sexual attraction.
3. **Commitment**—A couple's recognition of and dedication to the desire to be together "for better or worse."

He then went on to define six types of love based on various combinations of these three characteristics. *Infatuation*, Sternberg said, was passion alone. *Empty love* was commitment alone. *Liking* was intimacy alone. *Compassionate love* occurs when intimacy and commitment are both present. *Romantic love* is the combination of intimacy and passion. Finally *fatuous love* is the combination of passion and commitment. You could say that true love exists when all three characteristics are present in both partners.

The role of others in the development of a sense of self is complex and, some would say, essential. As children mature, they look to reference groups for answers to questions such as "What are my personal boundaries?" "Who is 'our kind' and who is not?" and "What do I want vs. what does the group want?" Our schemas related to social interactions continue to become enriched through language. Those schemas determine what we perceive in an interaction, how we behave, and what we expect to happen in the interaction.

We attribute causes to our own behaviors and those of others and develop beliefs and attitudes about others. Some attitudes can become prejudices and lead to discrimination. More positive attitudes include attraction and love.

Psychology

attitudes—beliefs and feelings about people, objects, or events that cause us to behave in certain ways. *p. 305*

attribution theory—theory that we tend to explain behavior in terms of internal personality traits or external factors. *p. 302*

cognitive dissonance—emotional state that results when a person's attitude and behavior are not consistent. *p. 306*

discrimination—unfair treatment of individuals because they are members of a particular group. *p. 309*

personal identity—sense one has of oneself as different from others, it includes thoughts and emotions, particularly self-knowledge and evaluation. *p. 300*

prejudice—unfounded and generally negative attitude toward a group of people. *p. 308*

reference groups—those people or groups of people whose opinions we care about. *p. 299*

self-fulfilling prophecy—an expectation that is met as a result of itself. *p. 302*

self-schemas—cognitive structures that allow us to differentiate ourselves from others. *p. 299*

social comparison—comparing of ourselves to others to learn the typical values and behaviors of a group and to determine how we differ from the group. *p. 299*

social identity—how one is known in the world. It is made up of the impressions one makes, what others think of him or her, and attractiveness or popularity with a group. *p. 300*

social psychology—field that studies how individuals influence each other. *p. 297*

stereotype—set of distorted, generalized beliefs about a group of people. *p. 307*

Social Psychology: Behavior

In this chapter, you will learn about:

- how being part of a group influences the way individuals behave
- why people cooperate with and help others
- what factors contribute to aggressive behavior and violence

On April 20, 1999, two high school students walked into Columbine High School in Littleton, Colorado, where they had already rigged a number of bombs. Once inside, they opened fire on teachers and students, killing 13 and wounding more than 20 others before taking their own lives. In the wake of this tragedy, psychologists and the rest of the American public asked, "What caused these boys to want to harm so many people?"

Humans are social beings. Much of our behavior involves interactions with other people. When and why do we help others? When and why do we try to harm others? How does being part of a group cause us to behave differently from the way we do when we're alone? Social psychologists study how we interact with other people, how other people influence our behavior, and how we act in response to others.

Society and Group Influences

In the course of a day, you probably find yourself in a number of different types of social situations. Whether you realize it or not, the society in which you live as well as the different groups to which you belong have a big impact on how you behave. In Chapter 18, you discovered how other people influence the way we think. In this chapter, we'll discuss how other people influence the way we behave.

What Is a Group?

Have you ever said or done something because of the people you were with? If you have, you know that your behavior can be influenced by a group. In social psychology, a group is more than just a collection of individuals who happen to be in the same place at the same time. To be a **group** in this sense, two or more individuals must:

* Interact with each other.
* Share a common goal.
* Have a relationship that is fairly stable over time.
* Be interdependent.
* Recognize a relationship between themselves.

You may belong to a number of groups—your family, a sports team, your school chorus, a church group, or an after-school club. Each group has certain standards of behavior called *norms.*

Norms

Norms are spoken or unspoken rules that tell us how we should behave—that is, how others expect us to behave. We rely on social norms to help us act appropriately in social situations. For example, while waiting in line to see a movie, we know that others expect us to wait our turn rather than to push to the front of the line.

Norms affect how we dress, talk, and act. Work norms might require us to dress conservatively, talk politely, and be punctual, while the norms of a social group might include dressing in a current style, using slang, and arriving "fashionably late." Following norms helps keep social interactions running smoothly.

You probably follow some norms without realizing it. For instance, when you're talking to a friend, you both have a similar idea about how close together you should stand. If you step closer, you are likely to find that your friend steps backward to maintain the "proper" amount of space.

◀ The "Dance of the Eye Contact" happens as the characters try to obey social norms regarding eye contact.

Norms in Different Cultures

Social behavior varies among cultures because different cultures have different social norms. For example, American culture places a high value on being on time. Many other cultures have no such value. In Russia, people value a sense of seriousness—even tragedy. People who smile too much appear "out of it." In many cultures, individuals are expected to demonstrate their emotions, while in others, emotional displays may be seen as a sign of weakness. Norms include everything from dating habits to ideas about modesty to child-rearing practices.

When people from different cultures come together, they may experience a "culture clash" because they have different expectations about how people should behave.

Would You Conform?

Psychologist Solomon Asch did a series of experiments to explore what happens when the pressure to conform to social norms conflicts with a person's perception of reality.

In his experiments, Asch staged a fake experiment regarding visual judgment. Seven college students were shown a line drawn on a card and three lines drawn on another card. They were asked to identify which of the three lines was the same length as the single line.

Six of the students were actually Asch's accomplices. The true objective of the experiment was to see whether the seventh student would believe his or her own eyes—and publicly admit it—even when the rest of the group gave a different, incorrect answer.

Asch found that 75 percent of the students he tested went along with the incorrect majority opinion at least some of the time. However, when students wrote their answers in private instead of saying them aloud, they were much less likely to conform. They were also less likely to conform if even one other participant supported their opinion.

Asch's experiment has important implications for social living because it shows how powerful the desire to conform is. Indeed, this desire to conform is so strong that we may find ourselves publicly supporting attitudes or behaviors that we don't really agree with—perhaps even when we believe them to be morally wrong.

Conformity

Conformity refers to adopting attitudes or behaviors that reflect the social norms of a group. Groups can exert an enormous pressure to conform. Although social norms might seem to limit our choices and our self-expression, most people conform to most social norms. Why do we feel a need to "go along with the crowd"? Psychologists cite **two** reasons we conform:

1. We want to be liked.
2. We want to be right.

Why Do We Conform?

If you think that conformity by definition is a bad thing, consider what life would be like without it. Team or club members who do not conform to some norms would have a difficult time working together. Here are some powerful reasons to conform:

* We conform when we acknowledge rules of fair play or discussion, keeping our interactions from chaos.
* By behaving toward others as we are expected to, we promote group harmony.
* Dressing as others do, laughing at the same jokes, or even supporting the same political views often helps us feel that we "belong."
* Agreeing with others, even if they are wrong, prevents us from being wrong by ourselves.

Sidebar

Handling Peer Pressure

The pressure to conform to others like yourself is called **peer pressure,** and it can be positive or negative. It can help you do things like maintain good study habits, or it can cause you to do harmful or illegal things that you later regret. The following tips can help you to resist negative peer pressure.

1. Consider what the consequences of your actions will be.
2. Ask yourself what decision you would make if you had a choice. Then remember that you *do* have a choice.
3. Don't believe that "everyone is doing it." Like you, many other people are able to think for themselves.
4. When you are asked to do something that makes you uncomfortable, don't be afraid to say no and to repeat yourself as needed to make your point.
5. Avoid situations in which you'll be asked to do something that makes you uncomfortable.
6. Look for friends who share your values and who will exert *positive* peer pressure—the kind that helps you make good choices.
7. Don't pressure others to do things that make them uncomfortable.

Why Do We Choose Not to Conform?

In spite of the pressure to conform, most of us sometimes refuse to do as others do. Although we crave a sense of belonging and a desire to be like others, we also want to feel we are individual and unique. The act of emphasizing our individuality is called **individuation.** When we recognize that we're pressured to adopt attitudes or behaviors in which we do not believe or that we feel may be harmful, we may choose to change groups rather than conform.

Conforming can certainly be harmful. In 1988, C. S. Crandall studied the eating habits of women in two college sororities. In his study, he found a link between social pressure and binge eating.

When Are You Most Likely to Conform?

Solomon Asch's research and that of other psychologists has identified some factors that affect the decision to conform:

* We are more likely to conform if we like the people exerting the influence and want to be liked by the group.
* The larger the group, the more likely we are to conform to it.
* We are less likely to conform if the group is not strongly unanimous, so that we may find support for a differing view.

Conformity Factors

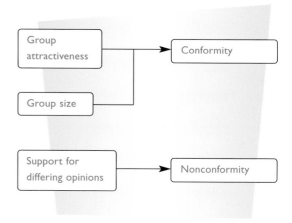

Cooperation and Competition

Cooperation and competition are important dimensions of human interaction. Consider your classroom. You, your classmates, and your teacher cooperate with each other so that you and your fellow students can learn. You cooperate when you allow your teacher and classmates to speak without interruption, when you participate in class discussions, and so on. However, students also compete with each other. Students who outperform their classmates can reap a variety of benefits, from increased social status to acceptance at top universities.

What Incentives Do We Have to Cooperate?

Humans are social beings. We live together in cooperative societies or work cooperatively in groups because such arrangements offer many benefits:

* **Performance of Tasks.** Cooperation allows us to perform tasks that we couldn't perform by ourselves—such as hunting large game, building a skyscraper, or putting on a play.
* **Access to Information or Resources.** Cooperation can give us access to information or resources we would not have access to otherwise. For example, two students could benefit from cooperating on a school project for which one has a collection of research materials and the other has a sophisticated computer graphics program.
* **Safety in Numbers.** This incentive is important not just for physical security but in battling any "enemy." For example, two political parties may cooperate with each other to defeat a third party.
* **Division of Labor.** Instead of everyone doing each part of a task, each person can focus on what he or she does well and then share the results.

What Incentives Do We Have to Be Competitive?

Despite these strong incentives to cooperate, in many situations we have more to gain by competing with and succeeding over others:

* **More or Better Resources.** Through successful competition, we may be able to win more or better resources, such as money or choice of mates.
* **Status.** Successful competition, either by itself or because of its rewards, can earn us a higher status in our group. For example, a class valedictorian and a high school football star both earn their positions by out-competing others.
* **Power or Authority.** By competing with others, an individual may achieve power or authority and the ability to assume a leadership position.
* **Individual Achievement.** We may compete to satisfy our need for individual achievement.

Social Dilemmas

If you look over the list of incentives for cooperation, you might notice that each is also a reason why cooperation is in an individual's best interest. But what if someone has more to gain by being selfish when everyone else cooperates? For example, if everyone used public transportation, air pollution would decrease. But if most people agree to use public transportation and you continue to drive, you reap the advantages of both decreased air pollution and the convenience of your own transportation. Do you act with **social responsibility,** for the good of the group, or do you act selfishly? The conflict between wanting to do what is best for the group and what is best for oneself is called a **social dilemma.**

The Prisoner's Dilemma

A classic social dilemma is the Prisoner's Dilemma. You and a partner are arrested for committing a crime. Being certain of your guilt but having no proof, authorities separate you for questioning and offer each a deal. The deal can have **four** possible outcomes:

1. If you admit some guilt but accuse *your partner* of the worst part of the crime and your partner remains silent, you will get a reduced sentence and your partner will serve the full sentence.
2. If your partner accuses *you* and *you* remain silent, he or she will get the reduced sentence and you will serve the full time.

3. If both of you remain silent, the authorities have no proof and both of you will go free.
4. If both of you accuse the other, you'll both serve the full sentence.

What do you do? The best outcome would occur if both of you remain silent, but can you take the chance that your partner will not tell on you if you remain silent? Unfortunately, your friend follows the same philosophy—you both tell on each other, and you both receive the full sentence.

Indeed, in most computer simulations of this type of dilemma, participants more often take the selfish approach. The issue of environmental pollution discussed in the text demonstrates the Prisoner's Dilemma at work in a broad social context.

Movements Toward Social Responsibility

Clearly, some problems, such as environmental pollution, can be solved only when individuals work together for the good of the larger group. Think of a three-legged race. Unless both participants win, neither wins.

People may be encouraged to work together for the common good if they:

* Understand that they share the same outcome with everyone else.

* Realize an individual benefit.
* Acknowledge that when many small individual contributions come together, they result in a significant outcome.

For example, we may collectively solve the pollution problem when we realize that pollution affects each of us, take advantage of individual benefits such as speedier car-pool lanes, and recognize the importance of our individual efforts.

Group Dynamics

Group members interact in ways that influence each other and the group itself. *Group dynamics* describes how groups behave—the factors that affect group decision making, how group roles function, and how different leadership styles affect the group.

Making Decisions

Whether we are members of a social club or a cabinet of presidential advisors, we often must make decisions as a group. To arrive at a group decision, members start out with individual decisions from which they must eventually reach a consensus.

Groups may find they arrive at a decision based on one of the principles shown below.

Several other factors can also influence the decision-making process.

Group Decisions
Majority Wins
The view with the most initial support is used as the group's decision.
Truth Wins
The final decision results from discussion or argument, based on the idea that the best decision will ultimately be chosen as more group members are convinced of its merit.
First-Shift Position Wins
The final decision goes in the direction of the first member to shift positions.

Group Polarization

Important decisions are often made by committee because common wisdom holds that group decisions should be less extreme than individual decisions. We assume that individuals start out with opposing views and eventually compromise on a "middle-of-the-road" solution.

According to extensive research by Eugene Burnstein, what happens in reality is often exactly the opposite. Researchers initially called this phenomenon the "risky shift," because it appeared that groups tended to move toward riskier decisions. However, further research indicated that groups tend to make the more *extreme* decision, whether riskier or more conservative, than any of the individuals would have made alone. This phenomenon is called **group polarization.** Although researchers cannot say why this happens, it has frightening implications for group decisions regarding issues such as declarations of war or jury verdicts.

Groupthink

Groupthink occurs when tightly knit groups place a higher valuation on consensus than on arriving at a good decision. Members may squelch dissenting opinions or ignore or suppress contradictory evidence and come to feel that there is only one course of action to consider.

In 1961 a troop of Cuban exiles, directed by the United States, attempted to invade Cuba and start an uprising. This military operation, called the Bay of Pigs invasion, failed disastrously, embarrassing the United States and intensifying U.S./Cuban hostilities. The decision to invade, made by President Kennedy and his military advisors, is considered to be a classic example of groupthink. Rather than considering all possible outcomes, the group convinced itself that the invasion could not fail.

Minority Influence

You might think that the majority viewpoint always wins out in group decision making. However, minority viewpoints can sometimes win approval, particularly if the minority member:

* Presents rational rather than emotional arguments.
* Maintains a consistent position.
* Shows confidence in the position.
* Has patience.
* Can win over at least one other member.

This is good news for the single voice in a group with opposing views. By following the guidelines above, the minority may turn the group around. Over time, minority influences can lead to major social changes, such as desegregation or voting rights for women.

Groups and Individual Performance

We've discussed how working cooperatively with others can allow a group of people to achieve results its members couldn't achieve alone. But do *individuals* work more effectively when they are in groups? Researchers have conducted a number of studies to find out.

Social Loafing. In one such study, subjects were asked to make noise by cheering and clapping, both alone and in small groups. Researchers found that as the group size grew, the effort expended and noise produced by each person decreased. When participation in a group makes us feel anonymous and we are not being evaluated individually, we may exert *less* effort. This phenomenon is called social loafing. We seem to reason that if we don't work very hard, somebody else will pick up the slack.

Social Facilitation. However, when we feel others may be evaluating our performance, we often exert *more* effort than we would if we were alone. In one experiment, observers watched joggers as they ran alone, then watched their performance as an attractive stranger walked toward them. The runners tended to speed up when they believed someone was observing them. Social facilitation refers to the effect—positive or negative—that the presence of others has on an individual's performance. Current research suggests that in the presence of others we often perform better than usual at tasks we have fully mastered but perform worse than usual at tasks we haven't yet mastered.

Group Roles

One way to help groups run smoothly is to assign different roles to different group members. Think about a professional sports team. One team member may guard part of the playing area, another may protect the goal, and still another may attack the opposing team's goal. In some groups, roles may be formally assigned; in others, members may simply acquire them over time.

Consider these benefits of group roles:

* Having distinct roles, including a group leader, establishes a structure or hierarchy for the group.
* Roles allow for a division of labor and help clarify each person's responsibilities and obligations.
* Assigning clear roles can cut down on social loafing, because each person has a specific task for which he or she is accountable.
* Group members may internalize their roles, thereby making them a part of their self-image.

Group Leadership

The success or failure of a group in attaining its goals may depend largely on the group's leader, who defines goals, plans activities, and directs group efforts.

Psychologists, historians, and other researchers have long tried to identify traits common to strong leaders. In 1991 S. A. Kirkpatrick and Edwin Locke identified some of the traits shared by successful business leaders:

* Drive.
* Honesty and integrity.
* Leadership motivation.
* Self-confidence.
* Cognitive ability.
* Expertise.
* Creativity.
* Flexibility.

Leadership Styles

Along with the leader's personal traits, his or her leadership style—how the leader works with the group—also affects the group's success in attaining its goals.

Task-oriented leaders tend to focus on the work of the group members, supervising them as they go. The task-oriented leadership style may be more effective in leading a group that is carrying out a specific job, such as building a clubhouse.

Person-oriented leaders tend to focus on giving group members emotional support and maintaining good interpersonal relationships within the group. The person-oriented leadership style may be appropriate to help a group reach a consensus decision, such as what style of band uniform to choose.

Current theories suggest that the best style of leadership varies according to the situation and that truly great leaders are flexible enough to switch leadership styles as circumstances demand.

RESEARCH

Prisoners and Guards

Psychologists Craig Haney, Curtis Banks, and Philip Zimbardo set out to explore the social processes at work in the prison system. They recruited a number of male college students with no history of emotional instability or antisocial tendencies. They randomly assigned half of the students to play the role of guards and half to play prisoners in a mock prison constructed in a campus basement.

The experiment was to last for two weeks. "Guards" wore uniforms, enforced prison rules, and provided prisoners with meals and a few recreational opportunities. They worked eight-hour shifts, between which they lived their ordinary lives. "Prisoners" wore smocks, were identified by numbers rather than names, and stayed in prison around the clock.

By just the second day, the roles began to control the people assigned them. Before the week was out, half of the "prisoners" had to be released early because they demonstrated extreme anxiety and depression. The "guards" had eliminated privileges and taken every opportunity to harass, humiliate, or punish the prisoners, freely staying beyond the end of their shifts. The experiment was stopped after only six days because the experimenters feared for the safety of the students.

The mock-prison experiment has much broader implications than showing why certain problems develop in a prison environment. It shows how easily we can internalize our social roles and how social roles can shape or even dictate our behavior.

Authority and Obedience

Obedience is the act of following orders given by someone in a position of authority. From early childhood, we are taught to respect and obey authority figures, such as parents, teachers, police officers, employers, coaches, church leaders, and others. Obedience to authority helps a society maintain order.

However, the Holocaust during World War II, the My Lai Massacre in the Vietnam War, and the mass suicide-murders at Jonestown, Guyana, in 1978, show the dark side of obedience. Each clearly demonstrates how blind obedience to authority can cause people to commit horrific acts of inhumanity.

Why Do We Obey Authority?

Studies suggest that most people have the capacity for blind obedience. (See Stanley Milgram's research described on the next page.) Here are some possible reasons:

* Most societies rely on hierarchies to provide social structure, organizational benefits, stability, peaceful relations, and group protection. Some researchers suggest we have an evolutionary tendency to accept such hierarchies.
* We are trained from birth to function within hierarchies, such as that of the family.

* Authority figures have the ability to punish or reward us.
* We have a desire to please authority figures.
* When we obey authority figures, we consider them—not ourselves—responsible for any consequences. We may say, "I was just following orders."
* The scope of the orders may start in a small way and escalate only gradually.

Personality Characteristics

It is easy to blame acts of brutality on a single "sick" individual who is not at all like us. However, the Holocaust could not have happened without the help of multitudes of ordinary people—law-abiding citizens and good neighbors.

The chilling results of Milgram's study suggest that most ordinary people will obey blindly—even if they are forced to act against their conscience, and even if they think they are harming someone. The traits most likely to lead to such obedience are not sadism or hatred but a tendency to behave submissively and uncritically to authority figures and a belief that one's life is controlled more by outside forces than by oneself.

CRITICAL THINKING

Was Milgram's Research Ethical?

Researchers often make the case that the benefit that comes from their discoveries about human behavior outweighs their questionable methods. Was Milgram's research ethical?

THE EXPERIMENT

In his classic study on obedience, Stanley Milgram recruited volunteers and told them he was looking at the effects of punishment on learning. Volunteers were instructed to deliver electric shocks to a learner strapped into a chair in another room. Each time the learner made a mistake, the volunteer was to increase the shock by 15 volts. The machine was marked to show that the shocks progressed from "slight shock," "medium shock," "very strong shock," "danger—severe shock," to "XXX."

The volunteers could hear the learners moan and cry out. When the volunteers complained about the cries, the experimenter said, "The experiment requires that you go on." The great majority of volunteers delivered "very strong" shocks, and more than half went up to the maximum—in spite of the cries and even after the learner stopped responding altogether.

The learners were not in fact receiving shocks, and after each experiment was over, the researcher explained the study to the volunteer. Critics object that the study was cruel, making subjects think they were harming—and perhaps killing—someone. Although they learned they had not hurt anyone, the volunteers were left with the realization that they were capable of doing harm.

Milgram insisted to his critics that his findings about human nature and obedience to authority were more important than the discomfort of the subjects. His supporters argue that his findings help explain such things as how the Nazis were able to get ordinary citizens to commit atrocities. What do you think?

THE PROCESS

❶ **Describe the experiment.** In your own words, summarize the experiment.

❷ **Provide evidence.** List the evidence from the case study that backs up the argument *in support* of Milgram's research.

❸ **Give opposing arguments.** From the case study and from your own experience, list the evidence that backs up the argument *against* Milgram's experiment.

❹ **Look for more information.** What else would you want to know before you decide? Make a list of your questions. Then research *Milgram* and *obedience* in an encyclopedia, on the Internet, or in the psychology section of the library.

❺ **Evaluate the information.** Make a chart with two columns:

Milgram's Obedience Studies	
Ethical	Not Ethical

Record the evidence and give each item a number from 1 to 5 to show its importance. Number 1 is most important.

❻ **Draw conclusions.** Write one paragraph explaining your view of the ethics of the experiment.

Helping Behavior

Helping others without expecting something in return is called **altruism.** Are people generally altruistic? Consider the following incidents that made the news:

* In 1982 an airplane crashed in Washington, D.C., plunging into the icy waters of the Potomac. As rescue crews threw lifelines to passengers in the water, one passenger repeatedly gave his lifeline to other passengers. They were pulled to safety, but the heroic passenger himself died.
* In 1964 a woman named Kitty Genovese was stabbed to death in New York City while 38 neighbors watched from their windows. Although the attack took almost half an hour, no one came out to help or even called the police.

Why Do We Help?

The Kitty Genovese case shocked the nation and triggered a number of studies about why people help or do not help others. Some of these studies suggest we are most likely to come to someone else's assistance when:

* The situation is clearly an emergency.
* The victim is similar to ourselves.
* We perceive that the victim did not bring the emergency on him- or herself.
* We know what to do or have some relevant expertise, such as knowledge of first aid.

But what causes us to help at all? Some studies suggest that our desire to help others may have selfish motivations and that we *do* receive something in return.

Emotions

According to some researchers, helping others helps us feel good about ourselves or prevents us from feeling guilty that we *didn't* help someone in need. A 1987 experiment supports this idea. In it, Robert Cialdini found that his subjects were less likely to help others if they were told they had been given a pill that would prevent their moods from changing.

Genetics

Some social psychologists believe that humans may be "programmed" to help others because we are social beings. Over time, this helpfulness can help us to survive by strengthening social bonds. Other researchers believe that we may be genetically programmed to help others *like ourselves* because in doing so, we may be helping more of our own genes pass to the next generation.

Why Don't We Help?

Media accounts of the day suggested that Kitty Genovese died because of the overall apathy and selfishness of American society. To explore this issue, researchers Bibb Latane and John Darley brought subjects into the laboratory supposedly for purposes of market research. Then, either alone or with others, the subjects witnessed a staged emergency—screams from another room, the sounds of medical emergencies, or the sudden appearance of smoke.

The researchers were surprised to find that most of the subjects, when they were alone, responded to the emergency. If they were among others, or thought that others were aware of the situation, they were much less likely to help. In fact, as the number of participants increased, fewer and fewer of them responded.

Psychologists suggest the following explanations for this phenomenon:

* Because many situations are ambiguous, we take our cues from others. For example, a fight between a man and a woman may be a mugging or a lovers' quarrel. If other witnesses don't respond, we don't view it as an emergency.
* When others are present, we worry about how they will judge our actions— or overreactions. We are inhibited because we don't want to look foolish.
* When alone, we feel a responsibility to act. When part of a group, we experience **diffusion of responsibility.** That is,

the same responsibility exists, but it is spread over a number of people, so each one feels less responsibility. The more people involved, the less responsibility each feels.

* We may assume that others are more knowledgeable or more capable of dealing with the situation than we are.

Sometimes people are afraid to ask for help for fear of appearing incompetent or weak. This is especially true in societies such as ours that value individual achievement. However, there are important reasons why you should ask for help if you need it, since people are often reluctant to offer help if a situation is ambiguous and they are not certain that someone is in distress. Others may not offer help because they fear their assistance will be seen as threatening or intimidating.

Aggression and Violence

In the wake of incidents such as the Columbine High School massacre, psychologists continue to debate the causes of **aggression**—behavior that is meant to harm someone. Why are people aggressive?

Frustration and Aggression

In the 1930s, a group of behaviorists developed the frustration-aggression hypothesis, identifying frustration as the cause of all aggression. Indeed, many aggressive incidents are directly triggered by frustration. Road rage is an example of aggression resulting from frustration—a fist fight erupts when one person steals another's parking space, cuts someone off, or otherwise interferes with another driver's progress. However, while psychologists agree that frustration often contributes to aggression, most no longer believe that frustration is the primary cause.

Generalized Arousal

Imagine that as you are on your way to school, a car careens around the corner and you have to run for safety. Then, just as you get to the library, another student takes the last computer terminal. Ordinarily you would shrug it off, but today you find yourself tensing.

You may not consciously connect the two incidents, but they may be connected just the same. Recent research suggests that strong physiological or emotional arousal may carry over from one situation to another. Even though the final incident is not intense, your strong pre-existing arousal could be the factor that tips the scales toward aggressive behavior.

Group Violence

What began as a peaceful political rally turns into a riot. The home team wins a championship, and fans respond by overturning cars and clashing with police. Why does a group setting sometimes cause people to behave more aggressively than they would otherwise?

* As we've previously discussed, groups often adopt a more extreme course of action than individuals.
* In a process called **deindividuation,** people in groups become less aware of themselves as individuals and less aware of their own values and the social norms they usually follow.
* Being in a group may impart a sense of anonymity. Without the threat of being judged individually, group members may lose their usual inhibitions.

Groups such as the Ku Klux Klan encourage deindividuation by wearing hoods—increasing the sense that members are part of a group, rather than a collection of individuals. Furthermore, wearing hoods assures anonymity. These factors may contribute to a loss of inhibition against aggressive behavior.

Environmental Influences

Today, debate rages over whether the constant bombardment of violent images on television and in movies contributes to aggression in our society. While long-term effects have yet to be proven or disproven, exposure to violent shows or movies does seem to raise levels of aggression in the short term.

In one study, moviegoers emerging from violent movies filled out questionnaires designed to measure aggressive tendencies. They scored higher on these tests than those waiting in line for the same movie. In another study, young children were shown films of adults playing with an inflated doll. The children who saw the adults attack the doll were much more likely to do the same when given the inflated doll to play with.

Some long-term studies suggest that people who watched a lot of television violence as children tend to show higher levels of aggression as adults. In addition, people with aggressive tendencies seem to prefer violent programming. This can lead to an endless cycle—people with aggressive tendencies watch more violent programming, which increases their aggressive tendencies, which leads to increased preference toward violent programming.

Researchers hypothesize that media violence contributes to aggressive tendencies because:

* Viewing such materials raises an individual's level of general arousal.
* People, especially children, tend to imitate what they see.
* Frequent exposure to media violence eventually desensitizes viewers.
* Aggressive people tend to seek out aggressive material, which causes them to become even more aggressive.
* Viewing aggressive material seems to weaken the viewer's inhibitions against violence.

These findings do not apply only to "shoot-'em-up" types of programs. Some studies indicate that watching aggressive sports events also increases aggressive tendencies.

The Freudian View of Aggression

Freud called aggression an inborn human trait. He believed that people are ruled by two instincts: *eros*, an instinct for pleasure and love, and *thanatos*, an instinct for self-destruction, sometimes called a *death wish*. He thought aggressive behavior was caused by the self-destructive instinct turning outward, toward others.

Freud also believed that aggressive energy builds up in people over time. This energy had to be released through **catharsis,** or individuals would erupt in a violent outburst. Catharsis could be achieved through playing or watching sports or through other intense experiences. However, current research suggests that these activities actually increase a person's aggressiveness.

The Evolutionary View of Aggression

Other scientists, such as Konrad Lorenz, also proposed that aggression is inborn. Unlike Freud, Lorenz looked for evolutionary connections, comparing human behavior with that of other animals. He suggested that aggressive tendencies helped humans survive and were therefore passed down to succeeding generations. For example, aggressive tendencies might prove helpful in hunting, in acquiring a mate, or in defending territory and resources.

However, opponents point out that if aggression were strictly an inborn human trait, all human societies should show it in about equal measure. Murder rates of different societies suggest that this is not the case. The murder rate in the United States is about eight times that of Norway, and some areas of New Guinea have a murder rate about 800 times higher than that of Norway.

Biological Explanations of Aggression

A number of biological factors, including the following, can also affect one's tendency to behave in an aggressive manner:

* Higher levels of testosterone, the male sex hormone, seem to be related to higher levels of aggression in men.
* Consuming alcohol seems to weaken inhibitions against aggressive impulses.
* Drugs such as amphetamines can cause individuals to misinterpret external cues and attack others they perceive as a threat.

* The hypothalamus controls rage and other emotions. Injuries or even allergies can affect its functioning.
* Chemical imbalances in the brain can keep a person from feeling empathy and other emotions that can inhibit aggression against others.

Learning and Cultural Explanations of Aggression

Most social psychologists today recognize learning and cultural training as important factors in aggression. For example, children may be rewarded for aggression when they acquire a toy they want by bullying another child. They may learn restraint when they are punished for aggressive behavior. Furthermore, children who grow up in abusive households are more likely themselves to adopt aggressive behaviors.

A culture's norms also play a role. For example, little boys may be told that they should "be tough" or "act like a man." Over time, we learn norms regarding:

* What people or groups of people we can act aggressively toward.
* What kinds of behavior by others deserve an aggressive response.
* When or under what circumstances aggression is appropriate.

Much of human behavior involves interactions with others, often in groups. Groups have spoken or unspoken rules, called norms, that tell group members how they should behave. Cooperation, competition, conformity, and obedience are aspects of group behavior.

Psychologists explore why people help or harm others. Current research suggests that such factors as biology, learning, cultural factors, genetics, and physiological state, as well as influences such as media violence, contribute to an individual's tendencies toward harming others.

Psychology — WORDS TO KNOW

aggression—behavior that is meant to harm another person or group of people. *p. 327*

altruism—helping others without expecting something in return. *p. 325*

catharsis—release of tension and anxiety associated with pent-up emotions. *p. 328*

conformity—act of adopting attitudes or behaviors that reflect the social norms of a group. *p. 315*

deindividuation—process through which people in groups become less aware of themselves as individuals. *p. 327*

diffusion of responsibility—responsibility that is spread over a number of people, such that each one feels less responsibility. *p. 326*

group—two or more individuals who interact with each other, share a common goal, have a relationship that is fairly stable over time, are interdependent, and recognize a relationship between themselves. *p. 313*

group polarization—tendency for a group's decision to become more extreme than those of the individuals in the group. *p. 319*

groupthink—tendency for tightly knit groups to adopt a unified opinion, ignoring dissent or contrary evidence. *p. 319*

individuation—act of emphasizing individuality. *p. 316*

norms—spoken or unspoken rules that tell us how others expect us to behave. *p. 313*

obedience—act of following orders given by someone in a position of authority. *p. 323*

peer pressure—pressure to conform to others like yourself. *p. 315*

social dilemma—conflict between wanting to do what is best for the group and what is best for oneself. *p. 317*

social responsibility—acting for the good of the group. *p. 317*

CHAPTER 20

Abnormal Psychology

In this chapter, you will learn about:

- **what abnormal psychology is and how it differs from normal psychology**
- **the major types of psychological disorders**
- **what we know about the causes of these disorders**

Everyone calls Susan a "neat freak." Her locker is always tidy, her clothes are always spotless, and she doesn't like art class because she doesn't like to get her hands dirty. Would you say her behavior is abnormal? Most people would not. But what if you found out that she washes her hands a hundred times a day? In this chapter, you will learn about some of the ways that psychologists distinguish normal from abnormal behavior.

When you hear the words "abnormal psychology," you may think of people who hear voices or have multiple personalities. Psychological disorders also include such varied problems as substance abuse, depression, attention-deficit hyperactivity disorder, and personality disorders.

Psychologists do not always agree on the causes of these disorders. Nature or nurture? Chemical imbalances? Social problems? Many disorders seem to be triggered by a combination of factors.

What Are Psychological Disorders?

As you probably know from everyday observations of family members, classmates, and strangers, people behave in a wide variety of ways. Some people may dress in a way you consider outlandish. Other people may "eat, drink, and sleep" sports. Is their behavior abnormal? Do they have a psychological disorder?

Identifying Abnormal Behavior

Something that is abnormal deviates from a standard, or norm. But what exactly is the "norm"? Few people agree on what is normal.

Therefore, psychologists analyze behavior according to specific criteria to help them decide whether an individual suffers from a psychological disorder. Rather than relying on personal notions of "odd" behavior, they look for the clues shown in the accompanying diagram.

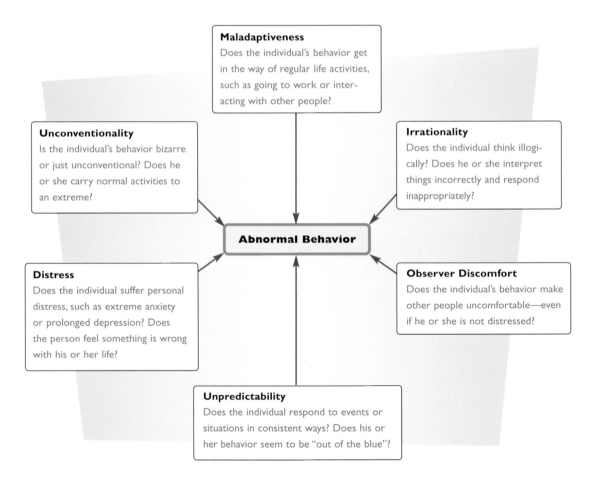

Maladaptiveness
Does the individual's behavior get in the way of regular life activities, such as going to work or interacting with other people?

Unconventionality
Is the individual's behavior bizarre or just unconventional? Does he or she carry normal activities to an extreme?

Irrationality
Does the individual think illogically? Does he or she interpret things incorrectly and respond inappropriately?

Abnormal Behavior

Distress
Does the individual suffer personal distress, such as extreme anxiety or prolonged depression? Does the person feel something is wrong with his or her life?

Observer Discomfort
Does the individual's behavior make other people uncomfortable—even if he or she is not distressed?

Unpredictability
Does the individual respond to events or situations in consistent ways? Does his or her behavior seem to be "out of the blue"?

Perspectives on Mental Illness

Unfortunately, the diagnosis of a psychological disorder sometimes carries with it a *stigma,* or social disgrace. In part, this is because the causes of many psychological disorders are still poorly understood. People who suffer from mental illness are sometimes considered weak by their peers.

Today, psychologists themselves often do not agree on what causes psychological disorders. The **etiology,** or cause, of a disorder is important because it may determine how the patient could best be treated. **Five** different perspectives on the causes of mental illness are described below.

❶ Biological Perspective

Many biological factors can affect mental health, including:

* Genetics.
* Chemical imbalances.
* Brain structure.
* Injuries to the brain.
* Certain infections.

Today, much research in this area focuses on identifying and treating chemical imbalances. Researchers continue to find new and effective drugs to help control depression, schizophrenia, and other psychological disorders.

❷ Psychodynamic Perspective

Psychologists who take a psychodynamic perspective look to an individual's unconscious—and his or her internal conflicts—for the cause of psychological disorders.

Through conversations, or "talk therapy," these psychologists help patients explore events and relationships over the course of their lives—particularly those of their early years—that may have shaped their attitudes toward others, toward themselves, and toward the world.

❸ Behavioral Perspective

Behavioral psychologists stress that life experiences condition us to respond to events or situations in a particular way. They believe that psychological disorders are the result of faulty learning. Therefore, when life experiences incorrectly reward some behaviors and punish others, children learn maladaptive ways of coping with life stresses—such as repeatedly washing one's hands to relieve anxiety.

Behavioral therapy to help individuals "unlearn" faulty learning is often used as a treatment for **phobias,** or persistent fears.

❹ Cognitive Perspective

Cognitive psychologists assert that psychological disorders arise from faulty thoughts. For example, if a person always thinks, "I'm not very interesting and nobody likes me," he or she becomes convinced that it is true. The person may misinterpret how people react to him or her and behave so defensively that people really do respond negatively. He or she may avoid interpersonal contact altogether or develop emotional disturbances such as depression.

Cognitive psychologists encourage patients to replace negative thoughts with others that are more helpful to them. Many popular self-help books are based on cognitive psychology—and the power of thinking positively.

⑤ Humanistic Perspective

Humanistic psychologists contend that each person has within himself or herself the potential for personal fulfillment. However, people do not strive for personal growth in a vacuum. Environmental forces act on the individual, too. Often people find their goals or desires in conflict with those of their families or of society at large.

Humanistic psychologists, then, assert that mental disorders arise because individuals adopt standards and values that conflict with their true inner feelings. Humanistic therapists work to help their patients identify and embrace their genuine goals and desires.

Combining Biological and Psychological Perspectives

Each of these perspectives adds to our understanding of psychological disorders, but none completely explains why some people develop a mental illness and others do not. Identical twins do not always develop the same disorder—nor do people who live through the same stressful events.

Most psychologists today believe that many psychological disorders are caused by an interaction of biological, environmental, and other factors, as shown in the diagram.

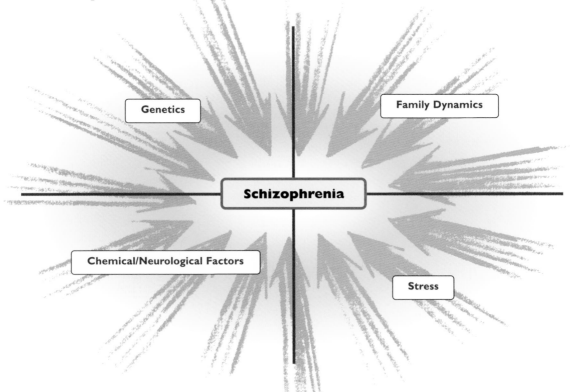

Genetics

Family Dynamics

Schizophrenia

Chemical/Neurological Factors

Stress

Autism and the Sally-Anne Test

Autistic children have difficulties interacting and communicating with people. Most researchers agree that autism is caused by some kind of brain damage. Researchers Baron-Cohen, Leslie, and Frith suggested that autistic people do not understand that people have thoughts and beliefs about the world, they do not develop a "theory of mind." They experimented with 3 groups of children: 20 autistic children, 14 Down's syndrome children, and 27 normal children. In the Sally-Anne test, they showed the children, individually, 2 dolls with those names. Sally had a basket, and Anne had a box. The experimenter had Sally take a marble, hide it in her basket, and leave the room. Then Anne "took" the marble out of Sally's basket and put it in her box. Children were asked where Sally will look for her marble. A child who understands that people have beliefs about the world would point to Anne's box. Eighty-five percent of the normal children and 86 percent of the Down's syndrome children gave this response, but only 20 percent of the autistic children did. In response to critics, the researchers repeated the experiment using real people instead of dolls. The theory that humans have a "theory of mind" which develops as a child matures unless there is brain damage is gaining acceptance.

Cultural Differences in Looking at Mental Illness

Although people in all cultures suffer from psychological disorders, not all disorders are found in all cultures. Nor do all cultures offer the same explanations. For example:

* The eating disorders *anorexia nervosa* and *bulimia nervosa* seem to occur only in Western societies.
* In Latin America, individuals might develop *susto*—unhappiness and sickness caused when the soul leaves the body after a frightening event.
* In the Middle East, people may laugh, shout, and bang their heads in a condition called *zar*. *Zar* is said to be caused by possession by spirits.
* Some Native American tribes recognize *ghost sickness*, in which bad dreams, hallucinations, dizziness, weakness, and other symptoms are caused by a preoccupation with death and dying.

Mental Illness in the Past

Through much of history, people blamed supernatural forces as the cause of bizarre behavior. Early treatment of mental illness included the use of amulets and incantations, even skull surgery to allow evil spirits to escape.

In ancient Greece and Rome, doctors began looking for the answers in heredity, biology, and psychology—prescribing baths, diets, exercise, bleeding, and relaxation.

During the Middle Ages, psychological disorders were often attributed to possession by the devil. In asylums, mental patients were "warehoused" and often mistreated.

In the early 1500s, Swiss physician Paracelsus attributed bizarre behavior to influence from the moon. (The word *lunatic* comes from *luna*, the Latin word for *moon*.)

From the eighteenth to twentieth centuries, asylums evolved from inhumane prisons to hospitals where the mentally ill can be treated and perhaps cured. The social stigma associated with these hospitals is still prevalent, however.

Classifying Mental Illness

Today, psychologists do not lump all forms of mental illness together into a single diagnosis of "insanity." For example, illnesses such as mental retardation and panic disorder have vastly different symptoms. Some disorders are present at birth, while others develop from medical conditions or environmental stress. Psychologists, therefore, assess mental health by considering **five** aspects:

1. Psychological disorders.
2. Personality disorders and mental retardation.
3. Medical conditions.
4. Social stress in the individual's environment.
5. An individual's overall level of functioning.

Most mental health workers today classify a mental illness by its symptoms, according to the *Diagnostic and Statistical Manual of Mental Disorders IV*-TR (2000), or *DSM-IV*. This classification system is defined by the American Psychiatric Association. The chart opposite shows how various forms of mental illness are classified in the *DSM-IV* and lists some examples.

DSM-IV Classifications	
Disorders usually first diagnosed in infancy, childhood, or adolescence	Mental retardation, autistic disorder, learning disorders, and attention-deficit hyperactivity disorder
Delirium, dementia, and amnesia and other cognitive disorders	Substance intoxication, dementia brought on by Alzheimer's disease, HIV, or head trauma
Mental disorders due to a general medical condition not elsewhere classified	Disorders that result directly from medical conditions
Substance-related disorders	Substance abuse and dependence, as well as mood, anxiety, and psychotic disorders caused by substance abuse
Schizophrenia and other psychotic disorders	Disorders causing individuals to lose contact with reality
Mood disorders	Major depressive disorder, dysthymia, and bipolar disorder
Anxiety disorders	Panic disorder, phobias, generalized anxiety disorder, and other disorders characterized by extreme anxiety
Somatoform disorders	Conversion disorder and hypochondriasis—where physical symptoms are present but have no underlying physical causes
Factitious disorders	Disorders in which individuals pretend to suffer from or intentionally produce psychological or physical symptoms
Sexual and gender identity disorders	Sexual dysfunction or gender identity disorders
Eating disorders	Anorexia nervosa and bulimia nervosa
Sleep disorders	Insomnia, hypersomnia, and sleep terror disorder
Impulse-controlled disorders not elsewhere classified	Kleptomania, pyromania, and pathological gambling
Adjustment disorders	Mood or behavior disorders triggered by a specific stressful event or situation
Personality disorders	Antisocial personality and other disorders that involve an individual's lifelong behavior patterns
Other conditions that may be a focus of clinical attention	Disorders in which psychological factors affect medical conditions, as well as problems related to abuse or neglect

Anxiety Disorders

Anxiety is a feeling of apprehension that danger or misfortune is looming, and that feeling is accompanied by physical symptoms, such as rapid heart rate, increased perspiration, nausea, or dizziness.

Anxiety disorders are among the most common psychological disorders, affecting about 10 to 15 percent of the U.S. population in any year.

Phobic Disorder

Do you have an irrational fear of spiders? Of heights? Of the dark? If so, you have a specific or simple phobia, which causes an inappropriate fear of an object or situation. Although most people have mild phobias, those with *phobic disorders* can be so overwhelmed by fear that it interferes with their lives. For example, a person with a phobia of dogs may walk blocks out of the way to avoid passing homes that have dogs.

A particularly disabling phobia is *agoraphobia,* or fear of public places. A person suffering from agoraphobia may be so terrified of going out into the world that he or she is virtually trapped at home. Agoraphobia affects about 3 to 6 percent of the population. It is often linked with panic disorder, another anxiety disorder.

You may know someone who has such severe "stage fright" that he or she can't give an oral report in class. This person has a *social phobia.* This differs from specific phobias because it revolves around an extreme anxiety over being observed by others.

Sidebar

A Few Phobias

Phobias can involve a fear of almost anything. Following are a few examples:

Acrophobia—fear of heights
Arachnophobia—fear of spiders
Aviophobia—fear of flying
Claustrophobia—fear of enclosed spaces
Hydrophobia—fear of water
Iatrophobia—fear of doctors
Mysophobia—fear of dirt
Ophidiophobia—fear of snakes
Thanatophobia—fear of death
Xenophobia—fear of strangers
Zoophobia—fear of animals

CAUSES: Today, phobias are thought to be learned responses to life experiences. A young child bitten by a dog may develop a fear of all dogs—even the smallest lap dog.

Generalized Anxiety Disorder

Unlike a person with phobic disorder, an individual with *generalized anxiety disorder* does not experience anxiety that is triggered by one particular object or event. Instead, he or she suffers from:

* An unfocused, persistent anxiety.
* Physiological symptoms of anxiety.

That person may worry about just a few areas of life or about everything from school exams to finances to relationships with family and friends.

Sufferers of this disorder may seek to reduce their anxiety by relying on alcohol or other anxiety-reducing drugs. In this way, they may develop substance-abuse problems that can be more detrimental than the anxiety disorder they hoped to alleviate.

CAUSES: Although this disorder seems to run in families, it is not clear whether heredity or family environment and learning plays the bigger role.

Panic Disorder

A person with *panic disorder* suffers from panic attacks—short but overwhelming bouts of anxiety that occur without warning. These panic attacks may include:

* Heart palpitations.
* Dizziness.
* Nausea.
* Fears of dying or going crazy.

These attacks typically have a quick onset and reach a peak in about 10 minutes. Although they may be short-lived, they are so frightening that more people seek help for this psychological problem than for any other. Because panic attacks are unexpected and may strike anytime, anywhere, many who experience them dread the thought of leaving home for fear of having an attack in public. Panic disorder is often accompanied by agoraphobia.

CAUSES: Sufferers of panic disorder may inherit a greater vulnerability to stress than others. They may also tend toward "catastrophic" thinking—seeing any physical symptoms as the beginning of another attack. Early childhood experiences may also play a part.

Post-Traumatic Stress Disorder

On April 19, 1995, terrorists bombed the Alfred P. Murrah Federal Building in Oklahoma City, killing 168 people and wounding 850 others. Many survivors of that blast now suffer from:

* Flashbacks.
* Nightmares.
* Emotional numbing.
* Depression.
* Feelings of survivor's guilt.

Post-traumatic stress disorder is a response to a harrowing experience, such as a natural disaster, military combat, or rape. People with this disorder may lose contact with reality and relive sights or sounds of the traumatic event, or they may avoid places and people that remind them of the event. Symptoms of this disorder may show up soon after the event, or they may first appear several years later.

CAUSES: Post-traumatic stress disorder is always a reaction to a harrowing or life-threatening experience. However, survivors of the exact same event may respond very differently; some may show few symptoms at all. This difference suggests that some people have a biological or psychological predisposition for the disorder.

Obsessive-Compulsive Disorder

Have you ever had an advertising jingle stuck in your head? Do you check your pocket for your keys several times before you leave home? Most people have mild obsessions and compulsions. **Obsessions** are recurring, unwanted thoughts, and **compulsions** are repetitive, ritualized behaviors.

Someone with obsessive-compulsive disorder suffers from:

* Obsessions and/or compulsions so extreme they disrupt everyday life.
* Anxiety.

Compulsions often take the form of counting or cleansing rituals. An individual with a cleansing compulsion may wash his or her hands a hundred times a day. Why can't he or she stop? While recognizing that endless hand-washing is unreasonable, the person lives in a state of constant anxiety that only compulsive behavior can relieve.

CAUSES: Current research suggests that obsessive-compulsive disorder may be caused by abnormal brain chemistry that causes sufferers to endlessly repeat the same activity. However, many psychologists support a psychological cause—that people develop obsessions and compulsions as maladaptive ways to relieve anxiety, guilt, or insecurity.

Somatoform Disorders

In many disorders, psychological symptoms arise from biological causes. In **somatoform disorders,** the opposite is true; physical symptoms arise from psychological causes. In other words, an individual suffers from physical symptoms even though he or she has nothing physically wrong.

Conversion Disorder

A person with *conversion disorder* may suddenly be unable to walk or to see. Although he or she is not faking these symptoms, there is no physical explanation. Symptoms may include:

* Paralysis.
* Blindness.
* Loss of feeling or sense of pain.
* Tingling sensations.
* Seizures.
* Loss of speech.
* Lack of concern.

Because these symptoms can mimic real physical disorders, doctors must be careful in diagnosing them. Sometimes the patient's symptoms are anatomically impossible—because they reflect not the mimicked illness itself but how the patient conceptualizes the illness. While some patients with this disorder exhibit a high degree of drama regarding their symptoms, many others show an extraordinary lack of concern about their sudden paralysis, blindness, or other symptoms.

CAUSES: In conversion disorder, the sufferer "converts" a psychological trauma into a physical one. For example, a soldier who witnesses horrific acts of torture may become unable to see. A traumatic event or situation usually triggers this disorder, but twin studies indicate that genetics are also involved.

Hypochondriasis

More common than conversion disorder is *hypochondriasis.* You might say that conversion disorder and hypochondriasis are opposites. In conversion disorder, a person develops a physical problem but doesn't seem to care. In hypochondriasis, the individual:

* Has no physical dysfunction.
* Is preoccupied with the state of his or her health.

Hypochondriacs tend to focus on normal variations in bodily functions as a sign of serious illness. They may, for example, misread a common headache as evidence of a brain tumor. They may go from doctor to doctor, looking for one who agrees with them. Although this disorder isn't usually too disruptive, the hypochondriac may become bedridden for the rest of his or her life.

CAUSES: Some researchers attribute hypochondria to the excessive attention a child received when sick. However, cognitive psychologists blame the disorder on an extreme fear of disease.

Dissociative Disorders

Sufferers of **dissociative disorders** escape from painful problems or situations by dissociating (cutting themselves off) from certain parts of themselves. The dissociation may happen suddenly or gradually, and it may be temporary or long-lasting.

Cultural contexts are especially important when considering dissociative disorders. In many cultures, dissociation from the self is an accepted and expected aspect of social or religious experiences and is not considered distressing.

However, the disorders described below can considerably disturb an individual's normal life functions and cause extreme distress as well.

Amnesia

Amnesia is a memory disturbance—the inability to recall certain events or even one's identity. Psychological stress can cause these kinds of amnesia:

* *Localized Amnesia.* An individual can't recall a traumatic event, such as a rape.
* *Selective Amnesia.* An individual can't remember certain details of a traumatic event.
* *Generalized Amnesia.* An individual can't recall the details of his or her entire life.
* *Continuous Amnesia.* An individual's memories stop at a certain event, and he or she can't recall anything that has happened since.

CAUSES: Medical problems can cause amnesia, but the types of amnesia discussed here are caused by traumatic events. Psychologists believe that an individual develops amnesia to repress painful memories.

Dissociative Fugue

People with *dissociative fugue* forget who they are and all details of their lives. Sufferers may wind up in an emergency room, unable to recall their identity, or, less commonly, they may actually move elsewhere and begin a new life with a new identity.

Occasionally an individual suffering from dissociative fugue keeps a new identity for years, but typically the condition doesn't last very long. When it ends, the individual may not recall what happened during that time period.

CAUSES: Psychologists believe fugue occurs as a result of serious, unresolved problems, such as dysfunctional marital relationships.

Dissociative Identity Disorder

Dissociative identity disorder is sometimes called "multiple personality disorder." In this debilitating disorder, an individual:

* Has two or more distinct identities or personalities that alternate control of his or her consciousness and behavior.
* Is unable to recall a quantity of personal information—and this "forgetfulness" cannot be attributed to black-outs, substance abuse, or other such causes.

A person who suffers from this disorder is not simply moody, nor merely acting differently in different social contexts. Different personalities actually control the sufferer at different times, and these personalities may include males and females, adults and children, timid and aggressive personalities, and so on. Some personalities may even seem to be at war with others. The primary personality, however, tends to be passive and depressed.

Each personality may go by a different name and have different memories and a different history. Because this information is not accessible to the other personalities, the individual seems to have "forgotten" it. Usually, at least some of the personalities are not aware of each other.

CAUSES: Dissociative identity disorder is thought to result from severe and chronic child abuse. To bear the brunt of abuse or protect himself or herself from it, a traumatized child creates another personality. The disorder is diagnosed much more frequently in women than in men. In addition, men with this disorder have an average of 8 personalities, while women sufferers have an average of 15. However, in extreme cases, the number may exceed 100.

Affective Disorders

Moods are part of the normal human experience. You probably feel happy when you do something fun with your friends. Maybe you feel "down" or "blue" when you do poorly on a test. An individual with an **affective disorder,** also called a mood disorder, experiences moods so extreme that they interfere with his or her emotional life and daily activities. These moods can be unrelated to the surrounding circumstances.

Dysthymic Disorder

Dysthymic disorder is a moderate depression—a feeling of "low spirits"—that lasts for a long time. During that time, the individual typically experiences:

* General unhappiness.
* Low self-esteem.
* Difficulty in concentrating.
* Little energy.
* Loss of interest in usual activities.

Although the symptoms are not as severe as those of major depression, discussed next, they continue for a longer period of time. In fact, the *DSM-IV* does not classify symptoms as dysthymic disorder until they last for at least two years. A person with dysthymic disorder may also experience bouts of major depression.

CAUSES: Dysthymic disorder seems to be caused by a combination of genetics and psychological stress.

Major Depression

Although major depression may not last as long as dysthymic disorder, its symptoms can be devastating. Someone with major depression may:

* Feel hopeless and worthless—as if there is no way out.
* Withdraw from all social interaction.
* Experience a pronounced change in eating or sleeping patterns.
* Lack energy to carry out even simple tasks.
* Lose interest in most activities.

As you might imagine, major depression can interfere with virtually every aspect of life—school, work, relationships with other people, and so on. It can also lead to substance abuse or, even more tragically, to suicide.

Major depression is not uncommon—some 10 to 25 percent of American women will experience it at some point in their lives, as will some 5 to 12 percent of American men. Unfortunately, depression often goes undiagnosed and untreated.

CAUSES: Major depression probably has both biological and psychological causes. In addition, a strong genetic component, hormone imbalances, abnormal levels of certain neurotransmitters, thyroid conditions, and other diseases or dietary deficiencies can also contribute to major depression. Some psychologists suggest that pessimistic thoughts or feelings that events are out of control help bring on the disorder. Stressful life experiences may trigger episodes in people who are genetically predisposed to depression. Depression is now often treated with anti-depressant drugs and/or cognitive therapy.

Bipolar Disorder

You may have heard this disorder called *manic-depression.* In **bipolar disorder,** the sufferer's mood alternates between two poles or extremes: depression and mania.

In the depressive state, the sufferer shows the symptoms of major depression. In the manic state, he or she may feel euphoric and extraordinarily energetic, talking without stopping and showing an exaggerated sense of greatness. He or she may go on spending binges or engage in other excessive or reckless behavior, needing little sleep.

While mania may occur without depressive episodes, it is more often part of bipolar disorder. Mania or depression that occurs by itself would be *unipolar*—going to only one extreme.

CAUSES: The causes of all mood disorders, including bipolar disorder, are thought to be similar to those of major depression.

Psychotic Disorders

Psychotic disorders are the most debilitating group of psychological disorders. Individuals who suffer from them lose contact with reality, which makes it difficult for them to carry on normal life activities.

During a psychotic episode, a sufferer may have **hallucinations,** in which he or she senses something that isn't there. Hallucinations may take any form, but auditory hallucinations, such as hearing voices, are the most common. Whatever form they take, they seem very real to the sufferer. He or she may also have **delusions,** unshakable beliefs that are obviously not true, such as believing that he or she is George Washington. In between these psychotic episodes, the sufferer may have coherent periods.

Schizophrenia

Schizophrenia may be the most disabling of all psychological disorders. Sufferers can often be out of touch with reality to the extent that they are unable to care for themselves. Because of this, most schizophrenics are hospitalized at some point in their lives, sometimes repeatedly. It is believed that a large number of schizophrenics make up part of the homeless population and do not care for themselves appropriately.

Schizophrenics make up about 1 percent of the world's population, and some 10 percent of schizophrenics eventually commit suicide.

Symptoms that have bizarre or exaggerated distortions are called *positive symptoms.* They include hallucinations, delusions, language anomalies, extreme agitation, and bizarre body postures. *Negative symptoms* are those that seem to be a diminished reflection of normal life, such as flat emotions or a general maladjustment.

Schizophrenics may have a great deal of trouble communicating, stringing together words by sound or association rather than meaning. Their thoughts may shift continuously from one thing to another.

There are several types of schizophrenia:

* *Disorganized Schizophrenia.* The most severe form of schizophrenia, this causes the sufferer's thought processes and language to be disturbed and incoherent. The sufferer might act in bizarre and obscene ways in public and his or her behavior may be described as "infantile."
* *Catatonic Schizophrenia.* This type involves disturbances of movement. People with catatonic schizophrenia may pace nervously at times or remain frozen in an odd position for hours. Sometimes, outside observers can "mold" them into a position, which they will then hold.
* *Paranoid Schizophrenia.* This involves having delusions of persecution. Individuals may think that family members are trying to kill them or that they are victims of a vast conspiracy. They may also have delusions that they are some famous or historically important figure.

* *Undifferentiated Schizophrenia.* This category describes patients whose symptoms are mixed and don't clearly fall into one of the other categories.

CAUSES: Schizophrenia seems to have a genetic component; close relatives of schizophrenics are more likely than others to develop the disorder. However, abnormal brain chemistry and physiology may be involved. Also, many sufferers come from an environment of severe family disturbances.

Sidebar

Schizophrenia Across Cultures

Although schizophrenia is found in cultures all around the world, people from different cultures tend to show different symptoms—suggesting that cultural factors influence the disorder. For example, Japanese schizophrenics tend to be rigid and withdrawn. Catatonic schizophrenia is far more common in developing countries than in the United States. Schizophrenics among African tribes are most likely to have disorganized schizophrenia.

Delusional Disorder

Delusional disorder, as its name implies, involves having strongly held beliefs that are not true. However, unlike the delusions of some schizophrenics, the delusions of individuals with this disorder are not bizarre. That is, they center around things that could actually happen, such as being continually spied on by the police, loved from afar, or deceived by a loved one. Sufferers generally do not have hallucinations; if they do, hallucinations are related to the theme of the delusion.

This disorder is uncommon, and its disruptive impact varies widely. Some sufferers are able to function relatively well in their jobs and social lives, while others cannot. For example, an individual who believes he or she is being stalked by assassins may severely limit outside activities for protection.

CAUSES: Little is known about the causes of this disorder. Some studies have suggested that relatives of schizophrenics are more likely than others to suffer from it, while other studies suggest there is no connection. Some psychologists believe that it is caused by childhood experiences.

Personality Disorders

Personality disorders are not like the other disorders discussed so far. Instead, **personality disorders** describe long-standing, maladaptive personality traits that are usually more disturbing to other people than to the individual. They may involve extreme self-centeredness or antisocial, highly dramatic, reclusive, dependent, or perfectionist behavior.

Antisocial Personality Disorder

When the *antisocial personality disorder* was identified in 1837, it was described as "moral insanity." The person with this disorder seems to have no conscience and is sometimes called a *psychopath* or *sociopath,* because he or she harms others and shows no remorse. People with antisocial personality disorders are often in trouble with the law.

Psychologists use **seven** telltale traits to identify the antisocial personality:

1. Lack of emotion.
2. Lack of conscience.
3. Ability to charm.
4. No strong motive for committing acts.
5. Inability to learn from experience.
6. Inability to retain relationships.
7. Indifference to punishment.

CAUSES: Although genetic and physiological factors may help bring on this disorder, family relationships and early learning experiences seem to play an important part—particularly when parents provide inconsistent discipline and values. Often there is a family history of alcoholism, abuse, or neglect.

Borderline Personality Disorder

Borderline personality disorder can be difficult to recognize because it shares traits with several other disorders. A primary characteristic, however, is interpersonal relationships that are intense and unstable. Mood shifts are also a common trait. The individual with borderline personality disorder is emotionally needy and may harm him- or herself or threaten suicide to manipulate people.

The *DSM-IV* classifies symptoms as borderline personality disorder if at least five of these behaviors are present:

* Intense fear of abandonment.
* Unstable and intense interpersonal relationships.
* Unstable self-image.
* Self-damaging emotional behavior.
* Self-damaging physical behavior, which may include suicide attempts.
* Fits of uncontrollable anger.
* Pronounced mood shifts.
* Dissociative symptoms.
* Chronic feelings of emptiness.

CAUSES: Borderline personality disorder seems to run in families. However, it is unclear whether children actually inherit this disorder or whether they learn from their parents unhealthy ways of interacting with others.

Sidebar

Substance Abuse

Not only is substance abuse itself a psychological disorder, it often results from or brings about other psychological disorders. For example, a person may abuse alcohol or another substance to numb feelings of depression.

Commonly abused substances include alcohol, depressants, stimulants, and hallucinogens. An individual is called dependent on a substance if he or she shows three of the following symptoms:

* Need for increased doses to produce the same effect.
* Withdrawal symptoms.
* Substance taken in greater amounts or for a longer period of time than intended.
* Failed attempts at controlling usage.
* Large amounts of time spent in obtaining the substance, using it, or recovering.
* Use interferes with social or other obligations.
* Continued use in spite of resulting physical or psychological problems.

Alcohol abuse contributes to about half of all suicides and murders and over half of all fatal automobile accidents in the United States.

Disorders of Childhood

Psychologists classify psychological disorders that appear in childhood separately from those that start in adulthood because of the emotional, cognitive, and developmental differences between children and adults. Abnormal behavior is sometimes difficult to assess in children because children develop at different rates.

Attention-Deficit Hyperactivity Disorder

Most children—and many adults—seem to have short attention spans. However, *attention-deficit hyperactivity disorder* (ADHD) is marked by these symptoms:

* Inattention.
* Physical hyperactivity.
* Impulsiveness.

Children with this disorder are easily distracted and hop from activity to activity. Because they are very active and don't have much self-control, they can be disruptive in classrooms. To be diagnosed with ADHD, their symptoms must be extreme enough to interfere with some aspects of life.

CAUSES: ADHD seems to have a genetic basis, but it may also be related to brain chemistry, the nervous system, or difficulties in pregnancy or delivery.

Autistic Disorder

The term *autism* is derived from the Greek word for *self*. **Autistic disorder** is a developmental disorder marked by severe communication and interpersonal difficulties and cognitive impairment. Even as infants, autistic individuals avoid interactions—such as eye contact or physical contact with other people, including their parents. Typical symptoms include:

* Avoidance of eye contact.
* Avoidance of physical contact.
* Preferring inanimate objects to people.
* Repetitious activities (arranging objects, rocking, or head banging).
* Becoming upset by changes in routine.
* Mental retardation.
* Language difficulties.

Autistic individuals may use only a few expressions or echo other people's words. Behavior modification may help autistic individuals function at a higher level, but few autistic children progress enough to live reasonably normal lives.

CAUSES: Autistic disorder was once thought to be caused by parenting styles that caused children to retreat into themselves, but current research shows it to be genetic. Other physiological factors, such as rubella during pregnancy, can also cause this disorder.

CRITICAL THINKING

Should the Insanity Defense Be Allowed?

In 1981 John Hinckley, Jr., shot President Reagan. Judged "not guilty by reason of insanity," he was sent to a mental hospital instead of prison. Much of the American public was outraged. A controversy arose: Should the insanity defense be abolished? What can you find out?

THE ISSUES

The term *insanity* was once a medical term for mental illness. Today it is a legal term. It describes a mental state in which a person can't tell right from wrong, can't comprehend that he or she is committing a crime, or can't control his or her behavior because of a mental disorder.

People who want to abolish this criminal defense cite the case of Dan White, who served only seven years for murdering two men. He was temporarily insane, he said, from the sugar in junk food—in what became known as the Twinkie defense. If the insanity defense is allowed, where do you draw the line? Psychotic disorders? Lack of conscience? Too much sugar? Furthermore, psychologists often cannot agree on a defendant's mental health; "experts" testify for both sides. Opponents argue that justice and public safety must come first.

People who believe in the insanity defense emphasize that it is used in less than 2 percent of all criminal cases—and is even less frequently successful. They stress that people who are mentally ill should not be held responsible for crimes they could not help committing. Some advocate that mentally ill criminals should be treated until they are no longer a threat to society—which may actually be longer than the prison term they would have received.

Today, different states have different policies regarding the insanity defense. Some states have banned it altogether. Do you think the defense should be allowed?

THE PROCESS

1. **Restate the issues.** In your own words, restate the disagreement.

2. **Provide evidence.** List evidence supporting the argument *for* the insanity defense.

3. **Give opposing arguments.** List evidence supporting the argument *against* the insanity defense.

4. **Look for more information.** Make a list of your questions. Research the use of the *insanity defense* on the Internet, in the psychology section of a library, or in the index of a psychology reference book.

5. **Evaluate the information.** Make a chart with two columns:

Banning the Insanity Defense	
For	Against

   Record the arguments in each column and rank each column of arguments in importance from 1 to 5, with 1 as the most important.

6. **Draw conclusions.** Write one paragraph supporting your answer to the question, "Should the insanity defense be allowed?" Be sure to explain your reasoning.

In diagnosing mental illness, psychologists and psychiatrists look for signs of abnormal behavior—of whether an individual's behavior is maladaptive, irrational, unpredictable, or bizarre, or if it causes distress to him- or herself or others.

Disorders are classified according to their symptoms. Some major categories of psychological disorders are anxiety disorders, somatoform disorders, dissociative disorders, affective or mood disorders, psychotic disorders, personality disorders, and disorders of childhood.

Biological issues—such as genetics or chemical imbalances—as well as psychological issues—such as internal conflicts, faulty thinking or learning, and thwarted ambitions—may trigger psychological disorders. Today, most psychologists assert that many psychological disorders are the result of a combination of biological and psychological factors.

Psychology

affective disorder—disorder in which an individual's moods are extreme enough to interfere with regular life activities. *p. 343*

amnesia—memory disturbance, such as the inability to recall certain events or even one's identity. *p. 341*

anxiety disorders—disorders in which the primary trait is a fear that danger or misfortune is looming; accompanied by physical symptoms such as rapid heart rate. *p. 338*

autistic disorder—developmental disorder marked by severe communication and interpersonal difficulties and cognitive impairment. *p. 348*

bipolar disorder—disorder in which one goes to the opposite extremes of mania and depression. *p. 344*

compulsions—repetitive, ritualized behaviors. *p. 340*

delusions—unshakable beliefs that are obviously not true. *p. 344*

dissociative disorders—disorders in which sufferers escape from a painful situation by disconnecting from certain parts of themselves, such as by developing amnesia or multiple personalities. *p. 341*

dysthymic disorder—moderate depression that lasts for at least two years. *p. 343*

etiology—origin or cause of a disorder. *p. 333*

hallucinations—experiences of sensations of something that isn't there, such as hearing voices or seeing visions. *p. 344*

more Psychology Words to Know

obsessions—recurring, unwanted thoughts. *p. 340*

personality disorders—disorders that involve long-standing maladaptive personality traits that are often more disturbing to others than to the individual. *p. 346*

phobias—irrational or inappropriate persistent fears. *p. 333*

psychotic disorders—disorders in which an individual loses contact with reality. *p. 344*

schizophrenia—psychotic disorder marked by confused thoughts, incoherent speech, delusions, hallucinations, flat or inappropriate emotions, paranoia, or disturbances of movement. *p. 344*

somatoform disorders—disorders in which physical symptoms arise from psychological causes. *p. 340*

CHAPTER 21

Therapies for Mental Health

In this chapter, you will learn about:

- how mental health problems are treated
- different types of mental health workers
- various approaches to psychotherapy

Imagine that all of your life, you've suffered from a fear of flying that has kept you from traveling with friends or from visiting places you've always wanted to see. Today's psychotherapists offer a number of alternatives to rid people of phobias, anxieties, or other limiting behaviors. It may be easier than you think.

Many different types of mental health professionals work in a variety of settings, from public health clinics to private practice and from hospitals to home visits. Therapists work with individuals, couples, families, and groups.

The treatments for phobias alone range from behavioral desensitization therapy that can extend over several months to a single visit with a Gestalt therapist. There may be as many as 250 different therapeutic approaches to psychological problems. Many of them are derived from or are combinations of the traditional psychological approaches described in this chapter.

What Is Therapy?

The National Institute of Mental Health estimates that 20 percent of adult Americans will, at some time, have a mental illness serious enough to require treatment. Others will have problems that limit their enjoyment of life. A wide range of treatments for psychological problems is available.

Mental Health Professionals

Type of Mental Health Professional	Typical Education/ Training	Typical Work
Psychiatrist	M.D., medical doctor with a psychiatry specialization; postgraduate training in abnormal behavior	Private or institutional practice; not only counsels people with serious mental disorders but also prescribes medication and administers biological therapy
Psychiatric Social Worker	M.A. in social work (two years of graduate-level courses in psychology plus practical training)	Private or institutional practice; counsels people with personal or family problems
Psychiatric Nurse	Nursing license with advanced training in psychology	Contact person between sessions with psychiatrist or counselor; may prescribe medication
Counseling Psychologist	M.A. or Ph.D. in counseling psychology	Private or institutional practice; counsels in a range of areas, such as developmental or family problems
Clinical Psychologist	Ph.D. in psychology	Works in hospitals and clinics; assists with treatment of and counsels people with psychological problems
Mental Health Counselor	M.A., counseling experience, and certification with the National Board for Certified Counselors	Services involve psychotherapy, human development, learning theory, group dynamics; helps individuals, couples, families; promotes healthy lifestyles
Advanced Registered Nurse Practitioner	M.R.N. (master's degree in psychiatric–mental health nursing)	Certified as clinical specialist; can prescribe medication; works with individuals, groups, and families

Psychotherapy treats psychological problems and disorders through an interaction between a client and a caring and highly trained mental health professional.

Biologically based therapy treats psychological problems and disorders through the use of drugs and other medical procedures.

Some therapies involve both the "talking" approach and the use of drugs.

The role of the patient or client in the treatment of mental health problems is extremely important. Many therapists aim to help clients understand their own abilities, concerns, goals, and relationships. Therapy encourages people to develop a sense of control or mastery over their feelings, thoughts, and behavior.

How Therapists Differ

Just as there are many different approaches to psychology, there are a wide variety of approaches to the treatment of psychological problems. A behavioral psychologist would lean toward conditioning methods of therapy, while one trained in psychoanalysis would look for solutions in the client's unconscious mind.

Today, the trend is toward an eclectic approach to psychoanalysis—using the treatment that seems best suited to an individual's particular problems. Psychologists use research to suggest which disorders respond best to various therapies.

Furthermore, a person seeking therapy may work with a number of different professionals, possibly including a psychiatrist, psychiatric nurse, psychologist, psychiatric social worker, and other mental health professionals.

Group vs. Individual Therapy

Mental health problems range from serious disorders, such as depression, schizophrenia, and bipolar disorder, to problems within a family, anxiety about a new job, or addiction to cigarettes. Likewise, therapy ranges from hospital treatment to a few visits to a local counselor. In either case, there are **two** main types of treatment.

1. **Individual Therapy.** Some people prefer to talk about their problems with a therapist in private. Individual therapy gives them more personal attention but may be more costly than group therapy.

2. **Group Therapy.** Advantages of group therapy include:
* The realization that one is not alone in having problems.
* The support of others who understand one's experience.
* The encouragement of seeing others change and grow stronger.
* The opportunity to change behaviors in a supportive environment.

Clients and therapists can work together to determine if group therapy is an appropriate method of counseling. There are a number of different types of group therapy:

* **Couples Therapy.** A therapist works with a couple to improve their relationship by learning new ways of expressing themselves and listening to one another.
* **Family Therapy.** This works on the premise that problems within a family arise as much from the interaction among individuals as from any one person. Family members learn to understand and communicate with one another in a nonthreatening environment.
* **Self-Help Groups.** These are composed of people who share a common problem, such as drug abuse, parental abuse, or compulsions such as gambling or shopping. Members of the group share experiences and solutions and support one another. One of the best known self-help groups is Alcoholics Anonymous.

Changing Attitudes Toward Mental Health

Mental disorders were once believed to be caused by some spiritual "intruder" that had entered the brain. Some ancient skulls show evidence of *trephining*—holes drilled in an attempt to let the intruder out. Religious rituals were often performed to exorcise or drive out these "demons."

As time went by, people with serious mental health problems, those considered a danger to themselves or others, were committed to asylums. In many of these institutions, patients were chained and neglected. Rarely were they offered any treatment. People with less debilitating problems were left alone to function in society. No help was available.

The modern approach to mental illness began in the nineteenth century, when the first patient case histories were written and the mentally ill were treated with more kindness. Although improved, mental institutions continued for many years as warehouses in which to store the mentally ill until they died.

Even modern care has its problems. The intention is to return as many individuals to society as possible through therapy and drug treatment. But as people are released, they lose the support of those who supervised their feeding, care, and medication. As a result, deinstitutionalization is generally believed to contribute directly to homelessness in the United States.

Psychoanalytic Therapy

The psychoanalytic approach to psychology began with Sigmund Freud's work with neurotic patients, and therapies based on this approach are still fairly common. Psychoanalytic and neo-Freudian psychodynamic therapies are useful when a person's reasoning and thinking processes are relatively intact and when the person is motivated to change. Freud developed a number of different techniques:

* *Dream Analysis.* Freud explored the content of dreams to reach their true, unconscious meaning.
* *Free Association.* In free association, Freud asked the client to relax and say whatever came to mind. He reasoned that unconscious material exerts pressure and would surface in a person's speech. Later, Jung asked patients to respond to a list of words designed to elicit various emotions or other content.
* *Interpretation.* After sufficient time in therapy had passed, Freud interpreted the conversations, dreams, and other content of analysis, seeking an underlying meaning and how it may affect feelings and behaviors.
* *Resistance.* Resistance occurs when a patient regularly avoids certain topics or disagrees with an interpretation. Freud felt that this was an important area to explore.
* *Transference.* Freud believed that if a patient began to see a therapist as a parent figure, this transference pointed to an underlying childhood conflict and could lead to further insight into the problem.

Psychodynamic Therapy

More recent neo-Freudian therapy does not place as great an emphasis on sexual drives or exploring the unconscious as Freud did. The many different psychodynamic approaches tend to take less time and be more flexible, depending on a client's specific problem. Here are some other differences between Freud and those who came later:

* Today's psychodynamic therapists prefer to sit face to face rather than have the client recline on a couch. This helps the client and therapist to develop a direct and personal interaction.
* Therapist and client agree in advance on the length of therapy—generally in terms of weeks rather than years. The client identifies specific goals that determine the end of therapy.
* Therapy explores current problems, values, and conflicts rather than early childhood experiences. However, childhood experiences may prove to be important.
* Therapy considers conscious conflicts, thoughts, and desires rather than the workings of the unconscious. The therapist offers interpretations to the patient, but if a patient disagrees, the therapist doesn't consider it resistance.
* Therapists still use transference. If, for example, a client transfers unconscious anger toward his or her father to the therapist, but the therapist reacts differently from the father, the client begins to understand that such anger may stem from unresolved feelings about the father.

Uses and Limitations of Psychoanalysis

Psychoanalysis and psychodynamics have proven most useful with fairly verbal clients who are able to utilize the insights they gain in therapy. These approaches are effective for patients with anxieties, mild depression, or difficulty with social relationships.

Psychoanalysis doesn't work for people with serious disorders such as schizophrenia because the client loses touch with reality. In addition, traditional psychoanalysis may take years of therapy and be prohibitively expensive.

Some suggest that a therapist's interpretation of a client's problems may not be as accurate as one would like because it may be colored by the therapist's own experiences.

As the cartoon indicates, therapists may use different approaches to the same problem.

▼

Behavioral Therapy

In contrast to psychodynamic therapy, traditional behaviorists focus on the behaviors themselves, with little regard for the workings of the mind. They argue that psychological problems are the result of unacceptable behaviors learned over the years. Although many behaviorists now acknowledge that a person's thoughts and feelings can be important, they still base many of their treatments on classical conditioning. Behavior modification and counterconditioning are two fundamental behavioral treatment methods.

Behavior modification is therapy that uses methods based on operant conditioning. (See Chapter 7.) It can be applied to just about any problem that can be objectively defined, provided that it is possible for the therapist to exert control over reinforcement.

EXAMPLE: In many schools, the "time out" technique is used for discipline problems. Rather than receiving the attention a disruptive student typically gets from teachers and fellow students, he or she is sent to an isolated area for a period of time. Behaviorists believe that removing the reward (attention) will discourage the student from such negative behavior in the future.

Often used to treat anxiety or fear, **counterconditioning** pairs the stimulus for an unwanted behavior with a new and more acceptable behavior. Behavioral therapists reason that one can't simultaneously experience opposing emotional states such as fear and pleasure.

EXAMPLE: In 1924, Mary Cover Jones eliminated a rabbit phobia in a young boy. Each time she placed a rabbit near the boy, she gave the boy a favorite food. Over time, the boy learned to associate the pleasurable experience of the food with the rabbit.

There are several approaches to counterconditioning.

Systematic Desensitization

Systematic desensitization is a therapy in which the therapist pairs relaxation techniques with gradual increases in anxiety. The therapist focuses on the behavior itself rather than the cause of the behavior. In many cases, people will feel better about themselves once they change their response, even if they never know why they had the fear in the first place.

EXAMPLE: A behavioral therapist might take a client with a fear of flying through the following **seven** steps:

Step 1: Teach client to relax.

Step 2: Ask client to think about flying.

Step 3: Have client relax.

Step 4: Continue steps 2 and 3 until client no longer becomes anxious when thinking about flying.

Step 5: Take client to airport.

Step 6: Have client relax.

Step 7: Repeat steps 5 and 6 until client no longer becomes anxious when at the airport.

The steps are continued gradually. The client sits in a plane, then sits in a plane with the engines running, then with the plane moving, and then, finally, as the plane takes off and flies.

Aversive Conditioning

In **aversive conditioning,** the therapist replaces a positive reinforcement for a behavior with an unpleasant consequence.

EXAMPLE: People suffering from alcoholism are sometimes given a medication that makes them ill when they drink. Therapists reason that if drinking results in a sufficiently negative experience, the behavior will cease. While this is effective about half of the time, it is unlikely to last unless other causes of the drinking are addressed.

Modeling

Because many people have efficient ways of dealing with anxieties, failures, or other negative stimuli, someone with less efficient behavior may learn how to change it through **modeling**—observing how the more efficient person (the model) behaves.

Flooding

With permission, the therapist brings the client in contact with his or her fears—either in the real world or by thinking about them—until the response is extinguished. This method, called **flooding,** works because the conditioned fear is not reinforced by anything dreadful happening.

Behavioral Therapy Approaches	
Operant Conditioning	**Aversive Conditioning**
Encourages a desirable behavior.	Extinguishes an undesirable behavior.
Rewards the new behavior with a positive reinforcement.	Replaces the positive reinforcement for the behavior with a punishment.

Cognitive-Behavioral Therapy

Many psychological problems around our relationships result from the way we interpret the world rather than the way it really is. Cognitive therapy attempts to make people aware of the negative thoughts that create negative feelings about oneself or others.

What does it mean when a friend chooses to do something with someone else rather than with you? We tend to assign meaning, not only to our own behaviors, but also to those of others. If some theorists are correct, we may not even have complete access to the meaning of our own behavior. To think that we can assign an accurate meaning to the actions of others borders on the ridiculous, as Cathy discovers in the cartoon below.

Thoughts, Feelings, and Behavior

Let's say that a friend has agreed to meet you at the mall. After waiting 30 minutes past the agreed-upon meeting time, what are you thinking? After reading each of these possible thoughts, figure out how you would feel and what action you might take.

* "He's never on time."
* "Maybe something more important came up."
* "What if she was in an accident?"
* "I'll have more time to shop."

Notice that each thought produces a different feeling, and each feeling produces a different action or behavior. If the thought about something "more important" triggered understanding that such things could occur, you would feel differently than if it triggered the feeling that you weren't very important. And each of those feelings would produce a different behavior if and when your friend did show up.

Cognitive behavioral therapy is about learning to use available information to make accurate and rational decisions. Although developing positive thinking habits is important for many who habitually think negative thoughts, positive thoughts might not be accurate or rational if, in our example, no one had heard from your friend in 24 hours.

Cognitive Restructuring

Developed by Aaron Beck, **cognitive restructuring** involves identifying and changing irrational statements that are part of one's automatic and ongoing "self-talk."

Beck believes that people who experience irrational self-talk engage in **four** behaviors:

1. As they perceive the world, they focus on ways in which it is a negative or harmful place and fail to attend to contrary information.
2. They overgeneralize, picking out only negative experiences in their lives to reach a conclusion that everything is negative.
3. They magnify unpleasant experiences totally out of proportion to their actual importance.
4. They think about life in absolute terms. "Everyone is out to get me." "I never do anything right."

Cognitive restructuring forces clients to challenge such self-talk. "You mean *no one* is kind or helpful?" "There's *not one person* who isn't out to get you?" "There's *never been anything* you've done right?" Because people answering such questions almost always are forced to acknowledge some good in their lives, they begin to recognize how biased their thinking has been. They are able to put more positive thoughts into action in their lives.

Rational-Emotive Therapy

Similar to cognitive restructuring, rational-emotive behavior therapy (REBT) goes further in identifying common irrational beliefs and in suggesting how thoughts influence emotions and behaviors. Albert Ellis's ABCD theory says that:

A. There is an event.

B. A person misinterprets the event.

C. B causes negative feelings and corresponding behaviors.

D. The person becomes capable of seeing the fallacy in B, and thus changing C.

Ellis claimed that some people tend to "awfulize" events in their lives—to see them in the worst possible way. He identified a number of irrational beliefs that he suggested were responsible for depression and anxieties. Here are a few of them:

* I must be loved or approved of by everyone.
* I must do everything correctly to be a worthwhile person.
* It is a catastrophe when things don't go my way.
* It is easier to avoid difficulties than to face them.
* There is a "right" and "perfect" solution for every problem.

The therapist using REBT often walks a fine line between maintaining rapport and positive regard for the client and confronting, sometimes bluntly, the error in the client's thinking. When respected therapists tell people that their thinking (belief) is "not rational," it sometimes makes them see the belief in a new way.

Uses of Cognitive-Behavioral Therapy

Cognitive-behavioral therapy has been shown to be effective for many different psychological disorders including depression, anxiety, and personality disorders such as dependence, hypochondria, histrionics, and multiple personality disorder. It is not, however, useful for clients who cannot maintain contact with reality.

Cognitive therapies tend to take much less time than psychoanalytic therapies. Some studies have shown that a single day of cognitive training can make a difference.

Humanistic Therapies

Similar to cognitive-behavioral therapy, humanistic therapy helps individuals develop self-awareness. Unlike psychoanalysis, humanists focus on:

* Awareness of present feelings rather than understanding the childhood experiences that influenced them.
* Conscious rather than unconscious thoughts.
* Accepting responsibility for one's emotions and actions rather than looking for the "meaning" of them.
* Promoting positive mental health rather than "fixing" negative mental health.

Cognitive-Behavioral Therapy and Depression

Holding negative views of the world, the self, and the future often leads to depression. One theory holds that people with depression do not use the "self-serving attribution bias" described in Chapter 18. Instead they relate their perceived failures to internal causes and their successes to external causes.

Adele Rabin and her colleagues pointed out this possibility to 235 depressed adults, indicating how such behavior might easily create depression. She then trained them to notice and change their habitually negative attributions. Rabin had the participants record the positive events of each day and write down the contributions that they made to the events. They also recorded negative events and listed external factors that contributed to those events. Compared to depressed people who did not do this, the depression of the participants decreased by almost half.

Person-Centered Therapy

Humanist Carl Rogers used a technique called **person-centered therapy**. Rather than interpreting their clients' experiences, person-centered therapists listen to what their clients say and encourage them to be true to themselves rather than acting as others wish. These therapists engage in **active listening**—repeating, restating, or asking for clarification of what a client has said.

Regardless of what a client says, the therapist must maintain what is called *unconditional positive regard.* As the therapist accepts clients for who and what they are, the clients begin to accept themselves and recognize that they have the responsibility to make whatever changes they feel are appropriate to achieving their potential.

Gestalt Therapy

Originally founded in the 1910s by Max Wertheimer and his associates, Gestalt therapy focused directly on perception and other cognitive processes. In the 1940s, Fritz and Laura Perls founded a branch of Gestalt therapy similar to, but more inclusive than, humanistic therapy. The word *Gestalt* refers to the scientific theory that the entire environment of which any event is a part must be included in understanding the event.

Phenomenology

Gestalt theory is based on the principle of **phenomenology**—the idea that what is subjectively felt in the present, as well as what is objectively known, are equally important. Gestalt therapists encourage people to become aware of their thoughts, feelings, and behaviors and to explore that awareness itself. These therapists help clients discover their own resources for dealing with present and future problems.

Gestalt therapists are trained:

* To put themselves as fully as possible into the client's experience.
* To express themselves to the client. As opposed to traditional humanistic therapy, the therapist is encouraged to describe his or her own perception of an experience. Thus, the therapist models a process that the client can copy and use.
* Not to manipulate or control the outcome of the interaction but instead to allow the client's words to guide the dialogue.
* To use the dialogue itself as the therapy—and not make it the subject of later interpretation.

Brain, Mind, Body Therapy

Gestalt therapy focuses on what is happening in the moment more than on the content of the dialogue. Clients can provide information to both themselves and the therapist in what they say, how they say it, and their body language during the dialogue. Gestalt therapists will question repetitive movements of body parts, tone of voice, or choice of verbs as clients describe their experiences. Because these behaviors are all part of the gestalt—the whole of the experience—they are presumed to have meaning.

Comparison of Therapies

Each type of therapy has its devotees and its critics. The effectiveness of any therapy depends on both the nature of the psychological problem and on the personal relationship between therapist and client. Ultimately, the success or failure of the therapy depends, in large measure, on that relationship.

Comparison of Therapies			
Type of Therapy	**Main Objective**	**Therapist/Client Relationship**	**Techniques**
Psychoanalytic/ Psychodynamic	To identify underlying unconscious meanings and their effects on feelings and behavior	Therapist remains neutral, eventually interpreting the meaning of what has occurred during the sessions for the client.	Dream analysis Free association Transference Resistance Interpretation
Behavioral	To extinguish unwanted behaviors or encourage desirable behaviors	Therapist manipulates stimulus/and or reinforcement.	Operant conditioning Aversive conditioning
Cognitive-behavioral	To help people become aware of the interaction of their thoughts, feelings, and behaviors	Therapist helps client to explore and analyze present experience.	Cognitive restructuring Rational-emotive behavior therapy
Humanistic	To help individuals explore their potential and promote mental health	The client is encouraged to talk about present experience with only minimal repetition and clarification from the therapist.	Person-centered therapy Active listening
Gestalt	To not only make clients aware of their cognitive processes, but to help them analyze that awareness	The client learns to use internal and external senses to increase self-responsibility and self-awareness.	Active listening Therapist/client dialogue and equal participation in change process

Biomedical Therapies

Various processes in the nervous system control our thoughts, feelings, and behaviors. In some cases, these biological processes develop problems, just as people can develop heart, lung, or liver problems. While some people are genetically predisposed to certain mental disorders, others can acquire them through accidents or environmental factors. Regardless of the cause, some psychological disorders benefit from biological, rather than psychological, treatment.

Types of Biomedical Interventions

Biomedical therapy may be recommended by a psychologist or other mental health professional but must be administered by a psychiatrist or medical doctor. The brain's functioning can be altered by:

* Changing its electrochemistry with drugs.
* Overloading the circuitry with electro-convulsive shock.
* Disconnecting the circuitry through surgery.

Psychopharmaceuticals, or drugs that have an effect on the operation of the central nervous system, are used for some psychological disorders.

Drug Therapies

Type of Drug	Prescribed for	Effect	Disadvantages
Antianxiety (Tranquilizers)	Reducing tension and anxiety	Depresses the central nervous system	Can become addictive; used without additional therapy, treats the symptoms without addressing the underlying causes
Antidepressant	Depression, eating disorders, panic disorder	Increases neurotransmitter production; increases activity level and decreases eating and sleeping problems	Dosage must be carefully monitored over time; studies show that cognitive therapy is as or more effective than drugs
Lithium	Bipolar disorder	Not completely understood, although it affects neurotransmitters	Occasional memory impairment, shakiness, or thirst
Antipsychotic	Schizophrenia	Blocks dopamine receptors in the brain, thus reducing awareness of irrelevant stimuli	Prolonged use can lead to balance and coordination problems; proper dosage is critical

CRITICAL THINKING

Is Society Becoming Too Reliant on Drugs?

Feeling stressed? Take a pill. Depressed? Take a pill. Want to quit smoking? Take a pill. People are increasingly bombarded with advertising for new drugs designed to "fix" problems. What are the alternatives? Is society relying too heavily on drugs for solving psychological problems?

THE ISSUES

As scientists learn more about the brain and the complex chemistries of thought and emotion, drug companies are designing more and more medications that influence the way people feel. At one time, people who wanted to feel less stressed, depressed, or fearful, or who wanted to rid themselves of unwanted habits, would seek the help of a qualified psychological professional. This professional might use any of the therapies mentioned in this chapter to assist the person. Today, advertising suggests that all anyone needs to do is "take a pill."

Opponents argue that we are far from understanding the complex chemical balance of the body and mind. If abusing illegal drugs disrupts a person's chemistry, is taking legal medications any safer? Many suggest that the first step in dealing with problems should be seeking the help of a psychologist. Few would suggest that serious mental disorders such as clinical depression shouldn't be treated with effective medications. But could people with less serious problems be making things worse in the long term? See what you can find out.

THE PROCESS

1. **Restate the issues.** In your own words, state the nature of the issue.

2. **Provide evidence.** From your own experience and from the information above, list the evidence *for* using medication to solve psychological problems.

3. **Give opposing arguments.** From your own experience and from the information above, list the evidence *against* reliance on medication to solve psychological problems.

4. **Look for more information.** What else would you like to know? Make a list of your questions. On the Internet, in the psychology section of the library, or in the index of psychology books, research *drug therapies for psychological problems.*

5. **Evaluate the information.** Make a chart with two columns:

Use of Drugs for Psychological Problems	
For	Against

   Record the arguments in each column and rank each item in importance from 1 to 5, with 1 as the most important.

6. **Draw conclusions.** Write one paragraph supporting your answer to the question "Is society relying too heavily on drugs to solve psychological problems?" Be sure to state reasons, not just opinions.

Electroconvulsive Therapy (ECT)

Unlike images that some people still have of "shock treatments" used in the 1930s, the passage of an electric current through the brain is done today under anesthesia. The patient has no memory of the treatment. ECT is an effective treatment for severely depressed patients who have not responded to drug therapy.

How ECT works is uncertain. It may calm certain centers in the brain or, like some drugs, affect the production or uptake of neurotransmitters.

Psychosurgery is the removal or destruction of parts of the brain. Psychosurgery is the most drastic and now least used of all biomedical techniques. In the 1940s and 1950s, thousands of severely disturbed patients underwent an operation called a **lobotomy** a severing of the connection between the site of emotions and the frontal lobes of the brain. The patients became lethargic and immature. Since the discovery of psychoactive drugs, psychosurgery is used only in extreme cases.

Does Therapy Work?

How effective is psychotherapy? In November 1995, *Consumer Reports* published an article concluding that:

* Patients benefited very substantially from psychotherapy.
* Long-term therapy was more effective than short-term therapy.
* Psychotherapy alone did not differ in effectiveness from medication plus psychotherapy.

* No specific approach to psychotherapy did better than any other for any disorder.
* Psychologists, psychiatrists, and social workers did not differ in their effectiveness.

A review of the study by the American Psychological Association pointed out that there are **two** different types of research on psychotherapy:

1. An *efficacy study* is done with carefully screened patients and in tightly controlled conditions over a fixed length of time. Regardless of the condition of the client at the end of the determined number of sessions, the therapy stops. At this time, the change in the client vs. clients in a control group is measured. This type of study is used to determine the effectiveness of a particular type of therapy for a particular type of mental disorder.

2. An *effectiveness study,* such as the *Consumer Reports* research, surveys people after they have received a variety of different types of psychotherapy. In the "real world," if one technique doesn't work, a therapist may try something else, or a client may seek another professional. Some treatments take a very short time and others extend beyond the time specified in the efficacy study.

The review pointed out that both types of studies contribute important, but different, information about therapy. Clearly, therapy is successful. However, the meaning of success varies depending on the type of study done.

1) Are you licensed to practice? ☑Yes ☐No
2) What approach to you recommend? _____
3) How long will it take? _____
4) How much will it cost? _____

The Ethics of Therapy

Because of the nature of the therapeutic relationship, the interests of the client must be protected. Ethical therapists:

* Must not use the relationship to gain social, sexual, monetary, or other personal advantage. This extends to interactions with the client and the maintenance of confidential client records.
* Must make the purposes and goals of the therapy clear to the client or his or her guardian. The client must be made aware of any potential risks.
* Must be aware of their own limitations and refer clients to someone else when necessary.
* Must intervene in the client's life only to the extent that the client wishes to make a change.

A few of the questions that therapists expect to answer when a client is looking for assistance with a psychological problem include:

* In what type of therapy(ies) are you trained? What degrees do you hold?
* Are you licensed in this state?
* What type of therapy do you feel would be effective for my problem?
* Approximately how long will it take?
* What would be the estimated cost of treatment?
* Do most insurance programs cover the type of therapy you do?

After a diagnosis, one may also ask:

* What mental disorder will be sent to my insurance company and placed in my file?
* Is this a temporary or a permanent diagnosis?
* Are there any other possible causes for my condition? Why did you rule them out?
* What does the diagnosis mean in terms of treatment and my future?

In general, the therapist must do everything possible to maintain the dignity of the client and the highest personal code of ethics.

A wide range of treatments is available for the 20 percent of adult Americans who have a mental illness serious enough to seek treatment. Attitudes toward mental health have changed from the past, when people with mental disorders were blamed for their conditions and treated poorly. Psychoanalytic therapy, behavioral therapy, cognitive-behavioral therapy, humanistic therapies, and biomedical therapies offer different approaches to meet the range of psychological disorders and client preferences. Professional mental health caregivers accept ethical standards for their interaction with patients.

Psychology

active listening—repeating, restating, or asking for clarification of what the client has said. *p. 363*

aversive conditioning—extinguishing an undesirable behavior by replacing the positive reinforcement for it with a punishment or unpleasant consequence. *p. 358*

behavior modification—changing a behavior by changing the response a person receives for that behavior. *p. 357*

biologically based therapy—treatment of psychological disorders through the use of drugs and other medical procedures. *p. 354*

cognitive restructuring—identifying and changing irrational statements that are part of one's automatic and ongoing "self-talk." *p. 360*

counterconditioning—pairing a stimulus for an unwanted behavior with a new and more acceptable behavior. *p. 358*

flooding—exposing a client to a harmless stimulus until the fear response to the stimulus is extinguished. *p. 359*

lobotomy—severing of the connections between emotional centers of the brain and higher thinking centers. *p. 367*

modeling—demonstrating how another person deals successfully with a situation. *p. 358*

person-centered therapy—approach in which the client talks and the therapist uses active listening. The client, not the therapist, interprets. *p. 363*

phenomenology—theory that subjective experience (feeling) is equally as important as objective knowledge. *p. 363*

psychosurgery—removing or disconnecting parts of the brain. *p. 367*

psychotherapy—treatment of psychological problems and disorders through an interaction between a client and a caring and highly trained mental health professional. *p. 354*

systematic desensitization—stepwise process for extinguishing a fear response. *p. 358*

References

CHAPTER 1

Adler, Leonore Loeb, and Uwe P. Gielen (Eds.). *Cross-Cultural Topics in Psychology.* Westport, Connecticut: Praeger, 1994.

Benjamin, Ludy T. (Ed.). *A History of Psychology: Original Sources and Contemporary Research.* New York: McGraw-Hill Book Co., 1988.

Damasio, Antonio R. *Descartes' Error: Emotion, Reason, and the Human Brain.* New York: Avon Books, 1994.

Federwisch, Anne. "Internet Addiction." *Healthweek/Nurseweek.* Aug. 8, 1997. http://www.nurseweek.com/features/97-8/iadct.html.

Hergenhahn, B. R. *An Introduction to the History of Psychology.* Belmont, California: Wadsworth Publishing Co.

Pinker, Steven. *How the Mind Works.* New York: W. W. Norton & Co., 1997.

CHAPTER 2

American Psychological Association Home Page. August 1999. http://www.apa.org/.

Evans and James. *An Invitation to Psychological Research.* Winston, New York: Holt, Rinehart, and Winston, 1985.

Ellis, Martha. "Nature vs. Nurture: The Invasion of the Mass Media" American *Psychological Association Psychology Teacher Network.* http://spsp.clarion.edu/topss/tptn7111.htm.

Kantowitz, Barry H., Henry L. Roediger III, and David G. Elmes. *Experimental Psychology: Understanding Psychological Research.* St. Paul, Minnesota: West Publishing Co., 1988.

People for the Ethical Treatment of Animals Home Page. Aug. 1999. http://www.peta-online.org/.

CHAPTER 3

Barmeier, J. *The Brain* (Lucent Overview Series). California: Lucent Books, 1996.

Bloom, Floyd E. "How New Approaches Contribute to an Understanding of the Nervous System: Where Do New Brain Medications Come From?" Paper presented at the annual meeting of the Society of Neuroscience, April 1999.

Byrnie, Faith Hickman. *101 Questions Your Brain Has Asked You About Itself But Couldn't Answer . . . Until Now.* Connecticut: The Millbrook Press, 1998.

Chudler, Eric H. *Neuroscience for Kids.* http://faculty.washington.edu/chudler/neurok.html.

Demasio, Antonio. "The Brain Behind the Mind." Paper presented at the annual meeting of the Society of Neuroscience, April, 1999.

Franklin, Jon. *Molecules of the Mind: The Brave New Science of Molecular Psychology.* New York: Atheneum, 1987.

Guyton, Arthur C. *Structure and Function of the Nervous System.* Maryland: W. B. Saunders, 1972.

Hall, Zach W. "New Approaches to Understanding the Nervous System." Paper presented at the annual meeting of the Society of Neuroscience, April 1999.

Heinemann, Stephen. "The Major Neurotransmitter Receptors." Paper presented at the annual meeting of the Society of Neuroscience, April 1999.

Llinás, Rodolfó R. "Understanding the Human Nervous System." Paper presented at the annual meeting of the Society of Neuroscience, April 1999.

"Nature, Nurture: Not Mutually Exclusive," *APA Monitor,* American Psychological Association. May 1997. www.apa.org/monitor/may97/twinstud.html.

Nemeroff, Charles B. "The Neuro-biology of Depression." *Scientific American* (June 1998).

On the Brain: Harvard Mahoney Neuroscience Institute Letter, Fall 1997/Winter 1998, Vol. 7, No. 1. http://www.med.harvard.edu/publications/On the Brain/Volume7/Number1/dialogues.html.

Ornstein, Robert, and David Sobel. *The Healing Brain.* New York: Simon and Schuster, 1987.

Restak, Richard M. *The Brain: The Last Frontier.* New York: Doubleday, 1979.

Snyder, Solomon H. "Molecule Messengers and Drugs in Psychiatry and Neurology." Paper presented at the annual meeting of the Society of Neuroscience, April 1999.

Tessier-Lavigne, Marc. "Genes and Neural Development: Generating and Regenerating the Nervous System." Paper presented at the annual meeting of the Society of Neuroscience, April 1999.

CHAPTER 4

Bloch, George. *Body & Self: Elements of Human Biology, Behavior, and Health.* William Kaufmann, Inc., 1985.

Hubel, David H. "The Visual Cortex of the Brain in Physiological Psychology," *Readings from Scientific American.* San Francisco: W. H. Freeman and Company, 1971.

"Pheromone Follies." *Discover* (September 1999).

Wertenbaker, Lael. *The Eye: Window to the World.* U.S. News Books.

CHAPTER 5

Crick, Francis. *The Astonishing Hypothesis: The Scientific Search for the Soul.* New York: Charles Scribner's Sons, 1994.

Gibson, J.J. *The Senses Considered as Perceptual Systems.* New York: Houghton-Mifflin, 1966.

Goldstein, E. Bruce. *Sensation and Perception,* 2nd edition. Belmont, California: Wadsworth Publishing Co., 1984.

Gregory, R.L. *The Intelligent Eye.* New York: McGraw-Hill Book Company, 1970.

Rhine, J. J., "Extrasensory Perception," *Journal of Abnormal and Social Psychology.* 1936.

Wertenbaker, Lael. *The Eye: Window to the World.* U.S. News Books.

CHAPTER 6

"Adolescent Sleep Needs and Patterns: Research Report and Resource Guide." *National Sleep Foundation Sleep and Teens Task Force.* http://www.sleepfoundation.org/publications/teensleep.html.

Brown, Thomas, and Patricia M. Wallace. *Physiological Psychology*. New York: Academic Press, 1980.

Damasio, Antonio. *The Feeling of What Happens: Body and Emotion in the Making of Consciousness*. New York: Harcourt Brace and Co., 1999.

Dennett, Daniel C. *Consciousness Explained*. Boston: Little Brown and Co., 1991.

Dement, W. C. *Some Watch While Some Must Sleep*. San Francisco: W. H. Freeman, 1974.

Pinker, Steven. *How the Mind Works*. New York: W. W. Norton and Co., 1997.

CHAPTER 7

An Introduction to Theories of Learning, 3rd edition. Englewood Cliffs, New Jersey: Prentice Hall, 1988.

Bower, Gordon H., and Ernest R. Hilgard. *Theories of Learning*, 5th edition. Englewood Cliffs, New Jersey: Prentice Hall, Inc., 1981.

Brooks, Michael Domjan (Ed.). *Domjan and Burkhard's The Principles of Learning and Behavior*, 3rd edition. Pacific Grove, California: Cole Publishing Co., 1993.

Cziko, Gary. *Without Miracles: Universal Selection Theory and the Second Darwinian Revolution*. Cambridge, Massachusetts: MIT Press, 1995.

Cole, Michael. *Cultural Psychology*. Cambridge, Massachusetts: Belknap Press, 1996.

Edelman, Gerald M. *Bright Air, Brilliant Fire: On the Matter of Mind*. New York: Basic Books, 1992.

Explorations in Learning & Instruction: The Theory into Practice Database. © 1994–2000. George Washington University. http://www.gwu.edu/~tip/.

Gazzaniga, Michael S. *Nature's Mind: The Biological Roots of Thinking, Emotions, Sexuality, Language, and Intelligence*. New York: Basic Books, 1992.

Lieberman, David A. *Learning: Behavior and Cognition*, 2nd edition. Pacific Grove, California: 1993.

CHAPTER 8

American Psychological Association Home Page. August 1999. http://www.apa.org/.

Pert, Candace B. *Molecules of Emotion*. New York: Scribner, 1997.

CHAPTER 9

Anderson, J. R., and G. H. Bower. *Human Associative Memory*. Washington, D.C.,: Winston & Sons, 1973.

Ask the Scientists: Susan Carey. PBS Scientific American Frontiers. http://www.pbs.org/saf/.

Cole, Michael. *Cultural Psychology: A Once and Future Discipline*. Cambridge, Massachusetts: Belknap Press, 1996.

Lakoff, George, and Mark Johnson. *Metaphors We Live By*. Chicago: University of Chicago Press, 1980.

Lakoff, George, and Mark Johnson. *Philosophy in the Flesh*. New York: Basic Books, 1999.

Pinker, Steven. *How the Mind Works*. New York: W. W. Norton & Co., 1997.

Pinker Steven,. *The Language Instinct: How the Mind Creates Language*. New York: William Morrow & Co., 1994.

Sternberg, Robert J., and Edward E. Smith. *The Psychology of Human Thought*. New York: Cambridge University Press, 1988.

CHAPTER 10

The Arc Home Page. http://TheArc.org/.

Bouchard, T.J., Jr. and McGue, M. "Genetic and Environmental Influences on Adult Personality: An Analysis of Adopted Twins Reared Apart." *Journal of Personality*, 58, 263–295.

Calvin, William H. "The Emergence of Intelligence." *Scientific American* (November 1998).

Council for Exceptional Children, VA; "Giftedness and the Gifted: What's It All About." *ERIC Clearinghouse on Handicapped and Gifted Children, ERIC Digest #E476*:

Eysenck, H. J. "Genetic and Environmental Contributions to Individual Differences: The Three Major Dimensions of Personality." *Journal of Personality* 58 (1990): 245–261.

Fincher, Jack. *Human Intelligence*. New York: G. P. Putnam's Son's, 1976.

Gardner, Howard. *Multiple Intelligences: The Theory in Practice*. New York: Basic Books, 1993.

Goleman, Daniel. *Emotional Intelligence: Why It Can Matter More Than IQ*. New York: Bantam Books, 1995.

Gottfedson, Linda S. "The General Intelligence Factor." *Scientific American* (November 1998).

Gould, Stephen Jay. *The Mismeasure of Man*. New York: W. W. Norton & Co., 1981.

Howard, Robert. *All About Intelligence: Human, Animal, and Artificial*. Australia: New South Wales University Press, 1991.

Hunt, Earl. "The Role of Intelligence in Modern Society." *American Scientist* (July/August 1995).

Jensen, Arthur R. *The g Factor: The Science of Mental Ability*. Westport, Connecticut: Praeger, 1998.

"Mainstream Science on Intelligence." *Wall Street Journal*, Dec. 13, 1994.

National Association for Gifted Children Home Page. http://www.nagc.org/Parentinfo/index.html.

Neisser, et al. "Intelligence: Knowns and Unknowns." *The American Psychologist*. (February 1996).

Paik, Han S. "One Intelligence or Many? Alternative Approaches to Cognitive Abilities." *Northwestern University, Evanston, Illinois*. http://www.galton.psych.nwu.edu/greatideas/papers/paik.html.

Plucker, Jonathan. "Intelligence Theory and Testing." *Indiana University, Bloomington, Indiana*. http://www.indiana.edu/~intell/map.html.

Steele, Kenneth. "Discordant Findings Raise Questions on Mozart Effect." *PsycPort* (August 25, 1999).

Sternberg, Robert (Editor). *Encyclopedia of Human Intelligence*. New York: Macmillan, 1995.

Sternberg, Robert. *The Triarchic Mind: A New Theory of Human Intelligence*. Penguin Books, 1988.

Yam, Philip. "Intelligence Considered." *Scientific American*. (November 1998).

CHAPTER 11

Berkliner, D. L., L. Monti-Block, C. Jennings-White, and V. Diaz-Sanchez. "The Functionality of the Human Vomeronasal Organ (VNO): Evidence for Steroid Receptors," *Journal of Steroid Biochemical Molecular Biology* 58, 259–265.

Damasio, Antonio R. *Descarte's Error: Emotion, Reason, and the Human Brain*. New York: Avon Books, 1994.

D'Andrade, Roy G. and Claudia Strauss (Eds.). *Human Motives and Cultural Models*. New York: Cambridge University Press, 1992.

Maslow, A. H. *Motivation and Personality* (Revised edition), New York: Harper and Row, 1970.

CHAPTER 12

American Academy of Child & Adolescent Psychiatry, 1997. "Understanding Violent Behavior in Children and Adolescents," http://www.aacap.org/publications/factsfam/behavior.htm

American Psychologcial Association, "Preventing Violence, The Importance of Early Intervention with Very Young Children," press release, Feb. 1999. http://www.apa.org/ppo/pi/violprev.html

Bernard, Bonnie, "Fostering Resilience in Children," *ERIC/EECE Newsletter*, Fall 1995. http://www.ericeece.org/pubs/nl/nlfa95.html

Caplan, Frank. *The First Twelve Months of Life*. New York: Perigee Books, 1993.

Caplan, Frank, and Theresa Caplan. *The Power of Play*. New York: Anchor Books, 1974.

Damon, William. *The Moral Child*. New York: Free Press, 1988.

Fraiberg, Selma H. *The Magic Years*. New York: Charles Scribner's Sons, 1959.

Fitzsimmons, Mary K. "Violence and Aggression in Children and Youth," *ERIC Clearinghouse on Disabilities and Gifted Education*, November 1998. http://eric.org/digests/.

Kagan, Jerome (Ed.). *The Gale Encyclopedia of Childhood and Adolescence*. Detroit: Gale Group, 1998.

Kohlberg, L. *The Philosophy of Moral Development*. New York: Harper and Row, 1981.

Lauter-Klatell, Nancy. *Readings in Child Development*. California: Mayfield Publishing, 1991.

National Clearinghouse on Child Abuse and Neglect Home Page. http://www.calib.com/nccanch/.

Schickendanz, Judith and David Schikendanz, Karen Hansen, and Peggy Forsyth. *Understanding Children*. California: Mayfield Publishing, 1993.

Seifert, Kelvin L., and Robert J. Hoffnung. *Child and Adolescent Development*. Boston: Houghton Mifflin, 1991.

Small, Melinda Y. *Cognitive Development*. Harcourt Brace Jovanovich Pub., 1990.

Spencer, Mary Ann. *Understanding Piaget*. New York: Harper and Row Pub., 1980.

Spock, Benjamin. *Raising Children in a Difficult Time*. New York: W. W. Norton & Co., 1974.

CHAPTER 13

Adams, Gerald R., Thomas Gullotta, and Raymond Montemayor (Eds.). *Adolescent Identity Formation*. Newbury Park: Sage Publications, 1992.

American Academy of Child and Adolescent Psychiatry Home Page. http://www.aacap.org/.

American Psychological Association Home Page. http://www.apa.org/.

Dacey, John S. *Adolescents Today*, 3rd edition. Glenview, Illinois: Scott, Foresman, and Co., 1986.

"Eating Disorders." http://www.mentalhealth.org/.

Feldman, S. Shirley, and Glen R. Elliott (Eds.). *At the Threshold: The Developing Adolescent*. Cambridge, Massachusetts: Harvard University Press, 1990.

Greenberg, Bradley S., Jane D. Brown, and Nancy Buerkel-Rothfuss. *Media, Sex, and the Adolescent*. Cresskill, New Jersey: Hampton Press, Inc., 1993.

Harris, S. M. "Racial Differences in Predictors of College Women's Body Image Attitudes." *Women's Health* 21, no. 4 (1994): 89–104.

Hauser, Stuart T. *Adolescents and Their Families*. New York: The Free Press, 1991.

Kagan, Jerome (Ed.). *The Gale Encyclopedia of Childhood and Adolescence*. Detroit: Gale, 1998.

KidsHealth Home Page. http://www.KidsHealth.org/.

Kohlberg, L. "The Adolescent as Philosopher: The Discovery of the Self in a Postconventional World." *Daedalus, 100, 1051–1086*.

LecFarling, Usha. "Doctor: Boys' Body Image at Risk, Too." *Seattle Times* (May 19, 1999).

Mulvey, Edward P., Michael W. Arthur, and N. Dickon Reppucci, "The Prevention of Juvenile Delinquency: A Review of the Research." *The Prevention Researcher* 4, no. 2 (1997).

National Institutes of Health. News release: "Response Statement on *JAMA* article (September 10, 1997) on the Adolescent Health Study."

Pajer, Kathleen A. "What Happens to 'Bad' Girls? A Review of the Adult Outcomes of Antisocial Adolescent Girls," *The American Journal of Psychiatry*, vol. 155 (7), July 1998.

Seifert, Kelvin L., and Robert J. Hoffnung. *Child and Adolescent Development*. Boston: Houghton Mifflin, 1991.

"The Teenage Years." *Mayo Clinic Family Health Book*. New York: William Morrow & Co., 1996.

The Transition to Adulthood, Pennsylvania State University; http://www.personal.psu.edu/faculty/n/x/nxd10/adolesc.htm

Walzer, Janet. "Weighty Issue." *Havard Medical Alumni Bulletin* (Summer 1997).

Wolman, C., Resnick, Harris, L. J., and Blum, R. W. *Journal of Adolescent Health* 15, no. 3: 199–204.

CHAPTER 14

Adler, Leonore Loeb and Uwe P. Gielen. *Cross Cultural Topics in Psychology*. Westport, Connecticut: Praeger Press, 1994.

Associated Press, "Walk on Berle, Caesar." *Missoulian*, Tuesday, October 26, 1999.

Birren, James E., R. Bruce Sloane, and Gene D. Cohen (Eds.). *Handbook of Mental Health and Aging*. San Diego, California: Academic Press, Inc., 1992.

1994 Information Please Almanac. Boston and New York: Boughton Mifflin Company, 1994.

CHAPTER 15

Berlyne, D. E. *Conflict, Arousal, and Curiosity*. New York: McGraw-Hill, 1960.

Cohen, Irving A., MD. *Addiction: The High-Low Trap*. Santa Fe, New Mexico, 1998.

Dreher, Henry. *The Immune Power Personality*. Dutton Signet, a division of Penguin Books USA, Inc., 1995.

Holmes, Thomas and Richard Rahe, "Social Readjustment Rating Scale." *Journal of Psychosomatic Research,* vol. II, 214, 1967.

Eysenck, M. *Attention and Arousal.* New York: Springer-Verlag, 1982.

Harris, Annette, "Stress!" *National Black MBA Association, Inc.* 1999. http://www.dcbma.org/forums/perspectives/stress.htm.

Hoffman, David L. "What Is Stress?" *Health World.* http://www.healthy.net/library/books/hoffman/nervousconditions/STRESS.htm

Hofstede, G. *Culture's Consequences: International Differences in Work-related Values.* Beverly Hills, California: Sage, 1980.

Mandler, G. *Mind and Body: The Psychology of Emotion and Stress.* New York: Norton, 1984.

Peterson, Karen S., "A Chuckle a Day Does Indeed Help Keep Ills at Bay," *USA Today Health.* http://www.bright.net/~jimsjems/usat12.html.

Selye, H. *Stress in Health and Disease.* Reading, Massachusetts: Butterworth, 1976.

Selye, H. "On the Benefits of Eustress." *Psychology Today,* 1978, 12, 60–64.

SUNY Potsdam Counseling Center. "Stress Management." http://www.potsdam.edu/.

Todd, Christine M. "Physical Stressors in Children," from *School-Age Connections, 2 (1).* Todd, C.M. (Ed.) Urbana-Champaign, IL: University of Illinois Cooperative Extension Service.

Whitman, Neal A. et. al., "Student Stress: Effects and Solutions." *ERIC Digest 85-1.* http://www.ed.gov/databases/ERIC_Digests/.

CHAPTER 16

Adler, Leonore Loeb, and Uwe P. Gielen, (Eds.). *Cross-cultural Topics in Psychology.* Westport, Connecticut: Praeger, 1994.

Heatherton, Todd F., and Joel L. Weinberger, (Eds.). *Can Personality Change*? Washington, D.C.: American Psychological Association, 1994.

Matthews, Gerald, and Ian J. Deary, *Personality Traits.* Cambridge, United Kingdom: Cambridge University Press, 1998.

Pervin, Lawrence A. (Ed.). *Handbook of Personality, Theory and Research.* New York: Guilford Press, 1990.

Romney, David M., and John M. Bynner, *The Structure of Personal Characteristics.* Westport, Connecticut: Praeger, 1992.

CHAPTER 17

Adler, Leonore Loeb, and Uwe P. Gielen, (Eds.). *Cross-cultural Topics in Psychology.* Westport, Connecticut: Praeger, 1994.

Beutler, Larry E., and Michael Berren, R. (Eds.). *Integrative Assessment of Adult Personality.* New York: Guilford Press, 1995.

Butcher, James N. (Ed.). *Clinical Personality Assessment: Practical Approaches.* New York: Oxford University Press, 1995.

Handler, Leonard, and Mark J. Hilsenroth, (Eds.). *Teaching and Learning Personality Assessment.* Mahwah, New Jersey: Lawrence Erlbaum Associates, Publishers, 1998.

Matthews, Gerald, and Ian J. Deary, *Personality Traits.* Cambridge, United Kingdom: Cambridge University Press, 1998.

Pervin, Lawrence A. (Ed.). *Handbook of Personality, Theory and Research.* New York: Guilford Press, 1990.

CHAPTER 18

Albrecht, Stan L., Bruce A. Chadwick, and Cardell K. Jacobson. *Social Psychology,* 2nd edition. Englewood Cliffs, New Jersey: Prentice-Hall, Inc., 1987.

Barone, David F., James E. Maddux, and C. R. Snyder. *Social Cognitive Psychology: History and Current Domains.* New York: Plenum Press, 1997.

Gazzaniga, Michael S. *Mind Matters: How the Mind and Brain Interact to Create Our Conscious Lives.* Boston: Houghton Mifflin Co., 1988.

Pervin, Lawrence A. (Ed.). *Handbook of Personality, Theory and Research.* New York: Guilford Press, 1990.

Rathaus, Spencer A. *Psychology: Principles in Practice.* Orlando: Holt, Rinehart, and Winston, 1998.

CHAPTER 19

"A Hero-Passenger Aids Others, Then Dies." *The Washington Post,* January 14, 1982.

Festinger, L. *A Theory of Cognitive Dissonance.* Stanford, California: Stanford University Press, 1957.

"The Prisoner's Dilemma Game," *The Economist* (US), Dec. 25, 1993.

Zimbardo, Philip G. *Psychology and Life* (13th ed.). New York: HarperCollins, 1992.

CHAPTER 20

American Psychiatric Association. *DSM-IV.* Washington, D.C. 1994.

American Psychiatric Association Home Page http://www.psych.org/.

Autism—PPD Resources Network http://www.autism-pdd.net/checklist.html.

Baron-Cohen, S., A. M. Leslie, and U. Frith. "Does the Autistic Child Have a 'Theory of Mind'?" *Cognition,* 21, 37–46.

Cornell Law School. http://www.law.cornell.edu/unabom/insanity.html

Costello, Timothy W., and Joseph T. *Abnormal Psychology.* Harper Perennial, 1992.

Sdorow, Lester. *Psychology.* Dubuque, Iowa: Wm. C. Brown Publishers, 1990.

CHAPTER 21

"Antidepressant Medications: Are They for You?" *Mayo Clinic Health Oasis Home Page.* June 1, 1999. http://www.mayohealth.org/mayo/.

Hauppage, Kanfer, Frederick H., Goldstein, Arnold P. *Helping People Change: A Textbook of Methods.* New York: Pergamon Press, 1986.

Pervin, Lawrence A. (Editor). *Handbook of Personality, Theory and Research.* New York: Guilford Press, 1990.

Credits

7 Wilhelm Wundt photo © Bettman/CORBIS **8**
William James photo © Bettman/CORBIS **8** Sigmund
Freud photo © Bettman/CORBIS **8** John B. Watson
photo © Underwood and Underwood/CORBIS **19**
Peanuts cartoon of July 16, 1975 PEANUTS reprinted
by permission of United Feature Syndicate, Inc. **27**
Jane Goodall photo © Kennan Ward/CORBIS **77** "The
Ames Room" © 1975, The Journal of Neurophysiology,
v. 38, p. 613-626. **81** "The Birth of Self-Consciousness"
© 2000 by Sidney Harris **99** "He Salivates" © 2000 by
Sidney Harris **102** B.F. Skinner photo ©
Bettman/CORBIS **104** "When you sit down" © 2000
by Sidney Harris **120** "To find out if you're someone
who could benefit from our…" © Randy Glasbergen
127 "Forgetfulness: The seven…" © 2000 by Sidney
Harris **136** "I've mapped out the concepts…" Printed
by permission of Gifted Psychology Press from "In
Search of Perspective" by Jean Watts. **178** Adaptation
of "Factors That Affect Hunger and Easting" from the
Brown & Benchmark *Introductory Psychology Bank* ©
1995. Reprinted by permission of McGraw-Hill, Inc.
237 "Let's try getting up every night at 2:00 AM to
feed the cat." © Randy Glasbergen **253** "The Social
Readjustment Rating Scale" © 1967, Journal of
Psychosomatic Research,v.II, p.214, 1967, Homes &
Rahe, with permission from Elsevier Science **270**
Adaptation of "The Four Temperaments" from "The
Causes and Cures of Neurosis," by H.J. Eysenck and
S. Rachman, © 1965. **274** "If I get the answer right,
does…" Printed by permission of Gifted Psychology
Press from "In Search of Perspective" by Jean Watts.
291 "Rorschach! What's to become of you?!" © 2000
by Sidney Harris **307** "Sell the IBM, but wait until…"
Printed by permission of Gifted Psychology Press
from "In Search of Perspective" by Jean Watts. **307**
DILBERT reprinted by permission of United Feature
Syndicate, Inc. **313** DILBERT reprinted by permission
of United Feature Syndicate, Inc. **337** Adaptation of
"DSM-IV Classifications" from *DSM-IV Sourcebook*
(1st edition) © 1994, reprinted by permission of
American Psychiatric Press.

Index

D

E

R

S